Partners Together in this Great Enterprise

The Role of Christian Zionism in the Foreign Policies of Britain and American in the 20th Century

David W. Schmidt PhD

Jerusalem, Israel

2011

Copyright © 2011 by David W. Schmidt

Partners Together in this Great Enterprise
The Role of Christian Zionism in the Foreign Policies
of Britain and America in the Twentieth Century
by David W. Schmidt

Printed in the United States of America

ISBN 9781597811316

All rights reserved solely by the author. The author guarantees all contents are original and do not infringe upon the legal rights of any other person or work. No part of this book may be reproduced in any form without the permission of the author. The views expressed in this book are not necessarily those of the publisher.

Unless otherwise indicated, Bible quotations are taken from the New American Standard Version. Copyright © 1977 by The Lockman Foundation.

www.xulonpress.com

Endorsements

It is well-known that evangelical Christian influence on political figures in Great Britain led in the 20th century to the creation of a Jewish State under Mandate status as well as to the United States promotion of the establishment of the State of Israel. What has been lacking in the study of these events is an investigation by an Evangelical researcher of the factors that resulted in the British abandoning their earlier commitment and the Americans acting upon it at the crucial moment in history. As the next crucial moment for Israel is upon us in the 21st century, an understanding of these causes and effects enables us to understand the present course the United States has pursued its foreign policy with the Jewish state and what may be the outcome for U.S.-Israeli relations in the days ahead. David Schmidt's important analysis is vital for both secular and church historians, political and social scientists, pastors, and all those interested in the connection between Christianity and Zionism at a time when these issues are at the forefront of theological controversy and geo-politics.
Randall Price, PhD, Executive Director, Center for Judaic Studies, Liberty University, Lynchburg, Virginia.

David Schmidt's work is important for understanding the Western world's relationship to the modern State of Israel.
William Schlegel, Associate Professor of Bible, The Master's College, Israel Bible Extension, Israel.

David Schmidt researched and proved that standing behind the British permission to build a National Home for the Jews in the Land of Israel were born-again Christians, who from childhood were taught to fear the Word of God and understand that God has a reason and a special purpose for the People of Israel in the Land of Israel. Many are the people who remember great events, but only a few know the souls who worked behind the scenes. This book grants the reader a rare and fascinating glimpse into the way in which God expresses His sovereignty, in order to manifest His perfect plan in all that relates to His Chosen People. This book should be mandatory teaching in every Bible School.

Meno Kalisher, Pastor,
Jerusalem Assembly House of Redemption, Jerusalem.

With thorough research and careful analysis, Schmidt proves that the powerful eschatological beliefs of a subset of evangelical Christian leaders provided a significant impetus for the creation of the modern state of Israel and continues to stimulate strong support for its existence in the 21st century in the face of concerted political and religious opposition.

Marvin Brubacher, Chancellor,
Heritage College & Seminary, Cambridge, Ontario

This enlightening book, comprehensive and thorough, portrays the significance of Christian Zionism in Britain prior to Israeli Statehood, and in America since Statehood.

Larry Rich, former Canadian Director,
Chosen People Ministries, Toronto.

"Partners Together in this Great Enterprise"
An Explanation of the Title of this Book

On July 20 1920, Arthur Balfour addressed the English Zionist Federation at Albert Hall in London to speak about the 1917 government declaration that bore his name. In his speech, he linked the fortunes of the British Empire to those of the Jewish people. Balfour not only referred to a political tie, but to a deeper spiritual bond. He dreamed of a day when the concept of a Jewish National Home in Palestine would become a living reality. He wanted British Christian Zionists to play a role in fulfilling that dream. The foundational concept of his speech was, "We are partners together in this great enterprise." Balfour told his Jewish audience, "If we fail you, you cannot succeed. If you fail us, you cannot succeed. But I feel assured that we shall not fail you and that you will not fail us; and if I am right, as I am sure I am, in this prophecy of hope and confidence, then surely we may look forward with a happy gaze to a future in which Palestine will indeed, in the fullest measure and degree of success, be made a home for the Jewish people."

The Jewish community in Palestine appreciated the support of British Christian Zionists. Jacob Meir, the Grand Rabbi of Jerusalem, wrote to Lord Curzon at the Foreign Office in London three months later, "From the first elected assembly of Palestine Jews, convened in Jerusalem, we feel certain that, under Great Britain's experienced guidance, the children of Israel will return to their boundaries and country will develop for benefit of all its inhabitants."

This book is based on the dissertation, "The Influence of Christian Zionism during the British Mandate of Palestine, 1917-1948," by David W. Schmidt, in partial fulfillment of a PhD Degree from the University of the Holy Land, Jerusalem, Israel, June 2009.

Acknowledgement

I wish to acknowledge here the contribution of my dear wife and lifelong best friend, Susan. Without her assistance and participation this book would not have been written. Just as the theme of this book is about a significant partnership in history, this book is the result of the abiding partnership that Susan and I share. Her constant encouragement, contributions and ideas were an essential part of the research and writing process. Besides this assistance, Susan contributed the contemporary pictures for this book.

David Schmidt, Jerusalem, May 2011

Overview

Following the fall of Jerusalem in 70 CE, culminating with the defeat of the Patriarchate in the 7th century, until the middle of the 20th century, the Jewish people were without a National Home of their own. During these centuries, they had a collective longing to return to the Land of Israel. Although it seemed the Jewish people were alone in their passion to return, some Christians shared this dream. This portion of the Christian community came to be known as Evangelical Christians, many of whom shared a belief in the eventual restoration of a Jewish Home.

For the past 1000 years, British culture was impacted and shaped by the Crusades, the Reformation and the printing of the Bible in English. A large segment of British society chose to follow a Christianity of personal faith apart from Rome. This faith included a belief in philosemitism and biblical prophecy. From the Puritans to the Victorian Evangelicals this community grew and eventually found political influence in both Britain and the United States. This Protestant branch of Christianity was unique in that it still saw the Jews as the Chosen People of God and believed the Jews should be restored to their land of Israel. This Christian Zionism would enjoy political influence in the 20th century in both Britain and later, in the United States.

The Balfour Declaration of 1917 was a unique gesture of support from the British Cabinet to World Jewry. Even though it was a political statement, it was given in a spirit of biblical belief and understanding, illustrating idealistic cooperation between British Evangelical Christians and Jews.

During the 31 years of British rule in Palestine, from 1917 to 1948, Evangelical Christianity gradually lost its influence in British society and politics. The ideals of Christian Zionism became a diminished value in Britain. By the 1940's the British were weary of the complexities of Palestine and turned the Mandate over to the United Nations. Parallel to this decline, between 1911 and 1955, Protestant Church attendance in Britain declined by 21 percent, during which time the population of Great Britain rose consistently.[1]

In 1948, the United States, influenced largely by Evangelicals, took on the mantle of Christian Zionism to become the first nation to recognize the new Jewish State. While the number of Evangelicals in Britain declined throughout the 20th century, the opposite was happening in America. The rates of Church adherence in the United States grew consistently from the founding of the country to the late 20th century. According to the research of Finke and Stark, only 17% of Americans attended Church in 1776. By 1980, approximately 62% of Americans attended Church with the majority of these Christians being conservative Protestants.[2]

During the second half of the 20th century, America remained the foremost advocate of Israel on the international stage. Accordingly, the research of Finke and Stark indicates that from 1952 to 1980, the percentage of Church adherents in America rose from 59% to 62%, with a significant percentage being Evangelicals inclined to support the ideal of Zionism.[3] Since the birth of the State of Israel in May 1948, the United States consistently used her veto in the United Nations Security Council to support Israel.

Perhaps this is linked to the fact that each one of the 112 Sessions of Congress in United States history has been predominately Protestant Christian. Even in the 112th Session (January 2011 to January 2013), 57% of the members of Congress and 55% of the Senators were Protestant Christians.[4]

In contrast to this history, American society appears to be changing in the early years of the 21th century. The prevalent culture in the United States may be drifting away from a Protestant Christian base. In the second decade of this new century, it remains unclear whether the United States will continue to be the international advocate of Israel, or will go the way of Britain and abandon previously made commitments to Zionism. Perhaps it would be timely, during these complex days, for America to consider the ancient promise in the Torah that God would bless those who choose to bless the descendants of Abraham (Genesis 12:3).

A hopeful sign for Israel occurred on May 24 2011, when Israeli Prime Minister Benjamin Netanyahu addressed a joint session of the Congress and Senate in Washington. Netanyahu must have been wondering if America was reconsidering her partnership with Zionism. He knew he was delivering his speech only five days after President Barak Obama declared his desire to see Israel return to pre-1967 borders. Netanyahu also knew that most of the members of the Congress and Senate might have a different opinion. Upon entering the chamber, the Israeli Prime Minister received a four-minute standing ovation. In his speech, Netanyahu appealed for the continued support of the American people for Israel. His message was well received, being interrupted by applause 56 times. President Obama was not in attendance.

At the end of his speech, Benjamin Netanyahu concluded by declaring, "Providence entrusted the United States to be the guardian of liberty. All people who cherish freedom owe a profound debt of gratitude to your great nation. Among the most grateful nations is my nation, the people of Israel, who have fought for their liberty and survival against impossible odds in ancient and modern times alike. I speak on behalf of the Jewish people and the Jewish State when I say to you, representatives of America, Thank you. (Applause). Thank you. Thank you for your unwavering support for Israel. Thank you for ensuring that the flame of freedom burns bright throughout the world. May God bless all of you, and may God forever bless the United States of America. (Cheers, extended applause). Thank you very much. Thank you. Thank you very much. Thank you." (Extended applause).

Table of Contents

Page   ix   Overview

Page   xv   Research Process

Page   xix   Introduction

Page   35   Chapter One: The Role of Christian Zionism behind the Balfour Declaration in 1917

Page   80   Chapter Two: The Place of Christian Zionism in the Establishment of the Mandate, 1918-1928

Page   134   Chapter Three: The Challenges of the Mandate and the Decline of British Christian Zionism, 1929-1939

Page   193   Chapter Four: Christian Zionism Waits through the War Years, 1940-1945

Page   214   Chapter Five: The British Abandon and America Assumes the Mantle of Christian Zionism, 1945-1947

Page   285   Chapter Six: The End of the Mandate and the Significance of Christian Zionism in the American Recognition of Israel in 1948

Partners Together in this Great Enterprise

Page 318   Chapter Seven: Various Christian Denominations and their Views on Zionism

Page 338   Chapter Eight: British Closure and American Christian Zionism Following Israeli Independence, 1949-21st Century

Page 357   Conclusion

Page 373   Notes

Page 433   Appendixes

Page 441   Bibliography

Research Process

Besides checking relevant published material related to this theme, the author interviewed individuals who provided information as primary and secondary sources. In addition, the following were accessed,

- British Government Cabinet Minutes, various years
- The McMahon Letters, 1915-1916
- Palestine Royal Commission Report 1937 (Peel Commission Report)
- House of Commons, Parliamentary Debates, various debates from the 1930's and 1940's
- House of Lords, Parliamentary Debates, various debates from 1920-1939
- House of Representatives, United States of America, House Resolutions 418 and 419
- United Nations, Report to the General Assembly by the United Nations Special Committee on Palestine, Geneva, Switzerland, August 31 1947

From British Archives, unpublished material from the significant personalities of the time period. Among these were the members of the Cabinet in 1917 who scripted and approved the Balfour Declaration, all seven High Commissioners, major British political figures during the Mandate, as well as major American politicians of the period. Archives accessed were:

- The Middle East Center Archives, St. Anthony's College, Oxford
- The Jerusalem and East Mission Archive, Oxford
- Rhodes House Library, Oxford
- The House of Lords Archive, London
- The Special Collections and Archives, Keele University Library
- The Churchill Archives, Cambridge
- The National Archives, London

From Archives in Israel, personal papers and correspondence from the High Commissioners, British political leaders, Jewish and Arab leaders of the period and American political leaders. Archives accessed in Jerusalem were,
- The Ben Zvi Memorial Archive
- The Central Archives for the History of the Jewish People
- The Central Zionist Archives
- The Christ Church Heritage Centre
- The Institute of Contemporary Jewry Oral History Division Archives
- The Israel State Archives
- The Jerusalem Post Archives
- The Jerusalem Municipality City Archives
- The Menachem Begin Archive
- The Yad VaShem Archive

Other locations in Israel accessed,
- The Chaim Weizmann Archives, Rehovot
- The David Ben Gurion Archives, Sde Boker, Negev
- The David Ben Gurion House, Tel-Aviv
- British Detention Camp Atlit Museum, Atlit

Further sites in Israel from the Mandate that proved helpful in understanding the period were,
- Government House in West Jerusalem, now the UN headquarters for the region

- St. Andrews Church in West Jerusalem and St. Georges Church in East Jerusalem
- King David Hotel, West Jerusalem
- The American Colony Hotel, and The Spafford Children's Hospital, East Jerusalem
- British Central Prison, Jerusalem, now a museum
- British Mandate Courthouses, Jerusalem, now Israeli Courthouses
- Various British and Anzac battle sites, Gaza and Negev
- Various British and Anzac War Cemeteries, Negev and Jerusalem
- Various British police stations and fortresses, Jerusalem and Latrun
- Various sites of the 1937 Peel Commission, Jerusalem
- Augusta Victoria Hospital, Mount of Olives, East Jerusalem, first home of the High Commissioner

Introduction

This book examines the influence of Christian Zionism on the British government's dealings with Palestine from 1917 to 1948, and follows the gradual passing of this influence to the government of the United States. A link will be established between the conversely subsiding British Christian Zionistic ideal in the later years of their Mandate of Palestine and the corresponding growth of Christian support for Zionism in the United States during those years. By examining British and American policies toward Zionism and Israel during this time period, it is possible to see a sharp diversion from what might be considered rational foreign policy. The political influence of Christian Zionism during this period has rarely been fully addressed and deserves attention.

Although it will be acknowledged that a number of material motivations influenced British and American policy decisions in Palestine during this period, this book will focus on only one idealistic impulse, that of Christian Zionism. The material motivations for Christian Zionism in Britain and the United States during this period are already well documented and can be summarized as follows: imperial expansion of the British Empire, desire for expanded economic trade, the winning of worldwide Jewish favour, geopolitical Cold War posturing and securing Jewish votes at home.

It is recognized that the history of the British Mandate in Palestine has already been well documented and is not the focus of this book. It is also recognized that the various material and idealistic motivations for the British to be in Palestine have previously been presented by a variety of scholars. A study of these motivations is not the purpose of this book. It is further recognized that the reasons for American support of Israel have been previously researched and are not the focus of this book. For further study on these topics, please refer to previously published works.[1]

The purpose of this book is to examine the relevant issues from a new perspective to discern the significance of the Christian Zionist religious motivations of the British and Americans political leaders during the years of the British Mandate in Palestine and through the rest of the 20th century.

Defining Terms

Christian Zionism is a religious belief among some gentiles of the Christian faith that the return of the Jews to the Holy Land and the restoration of a physical Israel is in accordance with biblical prophecy.[2] Furthermore, Christian Zionism is motivated by a biblically based religious conviction that the Jewish people are still God's Chosen people and are entitled to possess the land of Israel for all time. This belief is based on a specific interpretation of Scripture.[3] Christian Zionists worked for the Restoration prior to Israeli independence and continued to support Israel after her establishment in 1948. In his study on the subject, Paul Merkley observed that to Christian Zionists, the reality of the new State of Israel constituted proof of the faithfulness of Scripture.[4]

Christian Zionism is not just a political longing for a return of the Jewish people to live in Palestine. It is a biblically inspired hope for a newly restored autonomous Israel. Christian Zionists believed the Old Testament prophecies of the restoration of Israel required a legitimate descendant of the Kings of Israel to occupy the Davidic throne.[5] According to Kelvin Crombie, historian at Christ Church in Jerusalem, the 17th century Puritans of Britain believed that the promises of the Hebrew prophets for the restoration of Israel could only be fulfilled if the Jewish people once again lived in their own land.[6] Herbert Samuel, a Jew and the first High Commissioner of Palestine, understood the Christian Zionist dream of a restored political Israel. He wrote in 1945, that he believed the motivation for Christian Zionism was "a genuine sympathy with the aspirations of Jews for a restoration in Palestine."[7]

Christian Zionism is not merely stirrings of admiration or sympathy for the Jewish people or a sentimental belief that they deserve a home of their own. Rather it is an intentional and logical response to a specific Christian belief system. Christian Zionism is more than a positive attitude toward Jews and Israel. It is not simply a support for Israel based on feelings of guilt for anti-Semitism, or sympathy because of the Diaspora and Holocaust. It is also not a political position based on Cold War posturing, or anti-Arab sentiments.

Despite the possibility that idealistic motivations may have played a role in British and American policy decisions during the Mandate, these motivations, however admirable, are not to be confused with the religiously inspired impulses of Christian Zionism. Following WW2, most nations of the world saw a need to treat the surviving Jews with justice. According to Merkley, in 1947, the need for justice "was based both on the 2000 year Diaspora and the recent Holocaust. The physical requirements of hundreds of thousands of Holocaust survivors added to the urgency of the cause."[8]

In contrast to Christian Zionism, Replacement Theology is also a Christian view based on specific interpretations of Scripture. This view teaches that it was God's plan that the Jews should be scattered and suffer according to the prophecies of certain Old Testament prophets and Jesus himself.[9] Merkley identified the essence of Replacement Theology by explaining,

> The Church was ready with the explanation that this state of affairs had been predicted by Jesus of Nazareth. The scattering of the Jewish people was God's judgment of their rejection of their Messiah, and proof of Christianity's claims to succession to the promises made to Abraham in the book of Genesis.[10]

It will be shown that the Roman Catholic Church and the majority of mainline liberal Protestant Church denominations have historically held to the doctrine of Replacement Theology. A critical factor in determining a Church's view of Israel is how they interpret prophetic Scripture. A more allegorical approach to eschatological hermeneutics will tend to result in a Replacement Theology position, in that the "Church" has replaced "Israel" in the divine plan of end times. If however, a more direct understanding of prophetic Scripture is taken, the reader will conclude that Israel and the Church are separate entities and that Israel is still a valid nation in God's future prophetic plan.[11]

Five Commonly Accepted Views More Closely Examined

By subjecting five commonly accepted views to closer examination, this book focuses on new research and insights that highlight the political complexities of the religious impulses of the British and American governments toward Zionism during the 20th Century.

First, the state of research to date has suggested that Christian Zionism in Britain played an important, but small role, in the British interest in the Holy Land. This thinking is supported in the writings of Arthur Koestler (*Promise and Fulfillment, Palestine 1917-1949*), Isaiah Friedman (*The Question of Palestine, 1914-1918*), Cecil Roth (*Remember the Days*) and Mayir Verete (*From Palmerston to Balfour*).

This book, however, will show that Christian Zionism was a significant motive behind British interest in the Holy Land at the beginning of the 20th century. While scholars such as Barbara Tuchman, Norman Rose and Yaakov Ariel have generally held to this position, this book goes beyond their views to make further claims. The unique Protestant Christianity of Britain encouraged a commitment to the study of the Bible and the recognition of the Jews as the divinely Chosen People. The role of Protestant Nonconformists in British politics will be seen to be significant in British culture by the beginning of the 20th century. Even though Evangelicals formed a demographic minority in modern Britain, they influenced politics out of proportion to their numbers.

Second, the state of research to date has suggested that the Balfour Declaration was primarily motivated by imperialistic ambition. It has been suggested that although religious motivations were present, they but played a small secondary role. Academics who have held this view are Leonard Stein (*The Balfour Declaration*), Mayir Verete, Isaiah Friedman and Ronald Saunders.

This book, however, will show that Christian Zionism was a major incentive motivating the British Cabinet to issue the Balfour Declaration in 1917. At that time, British Christian Zionists were more committed than many British Jews to a Jewish homeland. This religious motivation represented a deeper, more powerful force within the thinking of some of Christian these men than any political issue. While it should be recognized that various factors were strong considerations of the government for issuing the Balfour Declaration, it will be shown that Christian Zionism was a significant reason.

Third, the state of research to date has suggested that Britain quit Palestine because she found herself in an unmanageable position politically and militarily and thus gave up the Mandate. Some key proponents of this thinking are Martin Kolinsky (*Britain's War in the Middle East, Strategy and Diplomacy, 1936-42*), William Roger Louis (*The End of the Palestine Mandate*), Naomi Shepherd (*Plowing Sand-British Rule in Palestine 1917-1948*), and Michael J. Cohen's (*Why Britain Left: The End of the Mandate*).

This book, however, will demonstrate that a decline in the influence of Christian Zionism in Britain was a primary reason for the British departure from Palestine. The gradual reduction of numbers and influence of British Evangelicals was linked to a decline in political support for Zionism. With this change, both the British people and the British government lost heart for the "enterprise" (as Arthur Balfour called it) of restoring a National Home for the Jewish people in Palestine. Steven Koss's, (*Nonconformity in Modern British Politics*) was helpful in this area.

Fourth, the state of research to date has suggested that American recognition of Israel in May 1948 was largely the result of a blend of domestic policy of appealing to Jewish American votes, humanitarianism, and geo-political Cold War posturing. (See Michael J. Cohen, *Truman and Israel* and Stanley Taylor, in Michael T. Benson, *Harry S. Truman and the Founding of Israel*).

This book, however, will show that Christian Zionism was a significant factor behind American recognition of the new State of Israel in 1948, which came about largely because of the same philosemitic impulses that motivated Lloyd George and Balfour to publish the Balfour Declaration in 1917. The unique role of Harry Truman will be studied, particularly his Baptist convictions and personal support for Israel against the advice of his State Department. As Evangelical Christianity grew and prospered in the United States in the early 20th century, so did the hope of a restored Israel.

According to the research of Finke and Stark, from 1860 to 1926, the percentage of Church adherents in America grew from 37% to 56%.[12] The works of Robert T. Handy (*The Holy Land in American Protestant Life 1800-1948*) and Lawrence Davidson (*America's Palestine*) were helpful in this area.

Fifth, the state of research to date has suggested that continued American political support for Israel after independence in 1948 was due primarily to pressure from the Jewish lobby in Washington and to Cold War necessities. (See, Michael T. Benson, *Harry S. Truman and the Founding of Israel*).

This book, however, will show that Christian Zionism was an important influence in the consistent continuation of American support for Israel during the second half of the 20th century as Gentile American Zionists maintained an influence in American foreign policy toward Israel long after initial recognition in 1948. Even into the 21st century, Christian Zionism remained a relevant factor in the United States, motivated to a large degree by American Christian Evangelicalism.

Ancient Origins of Zionism

The claim of a Chosen People promised to a special land first emerges from the Jewish *Old Testament*, or TNK account. Palestine was known as "Canaan," inhabited by a mixture of various local tribes, changing over the centuries. The patriarch Abraham, in the biblical account, traveled to Canaan from Ur (modern Iraq) in approximately 2000 BCE. His son Isaac and grandson Jacob remained in the land of Canaan. All three generations believed God had divinely given the land to their descendants forever.

According to the Torah account of Genesis chapter 12, God gave the land to the descendants of Abraham, and to Abraham's descendants Isaac and Jacob. In Genesis chapter 26, the Torah account reaffirmed eternal ownership of Canaan to the descendants of Isaac. In Genesis chapter 28, the divine promise of the land was renewed to Abraham's grandson Jacob.[13] These three ancient Hebrew patriarchs all lived for a time in Canaan. This biblical account is generally accepted as authoritative to a large segment of Jewish and Evangelical Christian communities.

According to the Genesis account, Jacob and his family later moved to Egypt to escape a famine in Canaan. These descendants of Abraham came to be known as "Hebrews."[14] In the Torah account of Exodus, the Hebrews became slaves in Egypt. After approximately four hundred years of slavery, the Hebrews left Egypt under the leadership of Moses. They crossed the Sinai desert in anticipation of reentering Canaan. In the biblical account of Joshua, the Hebrews entered Canaan through Jericho and conquered the land. At this time, the Hebrew people were referred to as the "Israelites." The land they moved to became known as the land of Israel, or "Eretz Israel" in Hebrew. Later, during the reign of David, their capital city was Jerusalem, also known as "Zion."[15]

According to the biblical account, the ancient Israelites reached their zenith of political power approximately 1000 BCE, during the reigns of David and Solomon. After this, the land was divided into two kingdoms, Israel and Judah. Israel was conquered by the Assyrians in 722 BCE, followed by the Babylonian conquest of Judah in 586 BCE. During this later conquest, the Jerusalem Temple was destroyed and the majority of the Jewish people were forced into Babylonian exile.

After approximately 70 years in Babylon, many of the Jewish exiles returned to Israel where they established various semi-autonomous Jewish regimes, and finally one independent Jewish government.[16] From those ancient days until the 20th century, the land of Israel was conquered and occupied by a wide succession of regional and world powers. The people of Israel gradually became known as *Jews*,[17] and were scattered throughout the world. The Jewish people never completely gave up the belief that the land of Israel was theirs by divine right. They believed, according to the promises of the Torah and the Jewish prophets, that someday they would return to their land and the throne of David would be restored.

In the second century CE, the Roman Emperor Hadrian imposed the name *Palaestina*, or "Palestine" on the land of Israel after the second Jewish rebellion in 135. Hadrian took the name from the ancient Philistines who had once lived in the land and were the enemies of the Jews. Hadrian destroyed the city of Jerusalem and devastated most of the land. In English, the name Palestine is still used by some to refer to the land the Jews called Israel.

Subsequent to the decline and fall of Rome, the Eastern Roman Empire provided a long succession of Patriarchs to oversee Palestine. In 638, Caliph Omar Ibn al-Khattab conquered Jerusalem in the name of Islam. Omar had been a close friend of Mohammad, who had died only six years earlier. Steven Runciman wrote one of the finest and most comprehensive accounts of the Crusades from a British perspective in the 1950's. In his study, Runciman described the last Patriarch Sophronius showing the triumphant Caliph the holy sites of Jerusalem. "Watching him stand there, the Patriarch remembered the words of Christ and murmured through his tears, 'Behold the abomination of desolation, spoken of by Daniel the prophet.'"[18]

During much of the Muslim rule, the land of Israel remained under-populated and economically devastated. The arrival of the Crusaders in 1099 brought a Roman Catholic regime to the land that lasted for 191 years before various foreign Muslim regimes returned to occupy the land. The Turks seized Palestine in 1517, and for the next 400 years, the land was a desolate Ottoman outpost. During these years, there was no autonomous local government and most of the tax revenues were sent to Istanbul. The Ottomans established the land as a province of Syria, ruled from Damascus. With the exception of the Crusader rule, the land had been under Muslim control for nearly 1300 years, until the arrival of the British in 1917.

The Memory of the Crusades in Britain

Christianity was established early in Britain when Roman Christians arrived in the 2nd century CE. From these early days, British attitudes regarding the land of Israel and the Jewish people have traditionally been strongly held. These attitudes can be first clearly identified through the effect of the Crusades on the British mindset.[19] Crusaders from Britain fought and died in the Holy Land for nearly two centuries. This experience left a deep impression upon the national psyche of the people. Barbara Tuchman noted, "It may be that the Bible would never have been able in a later time to take such deep root in the English body had not English blood been shed in the land of the Bible over so many years."[20]

In his study of the Crusades, Runciman attempted to define the motivations for the Crusades. He explained that the Church of the Holy Sepulcher was the holiest sanctuary in Christendom and that it was now under Muslim control.[21] The importance of Christian pilgrimages to Jerusalem was also a factor, necessitating Catholic supervision of these journeys. Runciman noted that European Christians expected to be able to travel safely to the Holy Land. "That life in Palestine should be orderly enough for the defenseless traveler to move and work in safety, and secondly that the way should be kept open and cheap."[22]

As for the official motivation for the Crusades, Runciman referred to a speech by Pope Urban II delivered on August 5 1095. Four contemporary chroniclers reported the Pope's words, but all wrote years later. There are some differences in their accounts, but they agree on some similar ideas. The Pope stressed the special holiness of Jerusalem, and described the sufferings of the pilgrims that journeyed there. The Muslims were advancing into Christian lands and Eastern Christendom was appealing for help. The people should fight a righteous war, doing the work of God and God would lead them. At the end of the speech, the people cried out, "Deus le Volt!" "God wills it!" Reportedly, hundreds of listeners fell to their knees begging permission to join the expedition.[23]

Tuchman speculated that the 1917 British invasion of Palestine was somehow redemption for Crusader failures.

> And so General Allenby entered Jerusalem in 1918, succeeding where Richard the Lion-Hearted had failed. But for that victory, the restoration of Israel might not yet be an accomplished fact. Nor would Allenby have succeeded if Richard had not tried, that is to say, if Christianity had not

originally supplied the basis for the attachment to the Holy Land.[24]

Even English royalty referred to this final Crusade concept on at least one occasion. During World War 1, Colonel Richard Meinertzhagen, intelligence officer for General Allenby, met with King George V for regular briefings on Palestine. During one of their sessions, the King suggested that the conquest of Palestine was a completion of the Crusades. Meinertzhagen's biographer, Peter Capstick wrote, "At one such briefing the King spoke of the 'Final Crusade' concerning Palestine."[25]

After the Crusades were finished, the British people viewed the Holy Land as part of their own Christian heritage. Even centuries after the last Crusades, many in Britain saw the land of Israel as a place to be re-connected back to Christendom. Palestine was the land of the Bible, wrongfully under the control of the Muslims. The British had a strong inclination to see their nation as the world leader in morality, justice, and biblical values. Speaking of the Crusades, Silas Perry, an influential British Christian Zionist during the 1930's and 1940's, wrote,

In surveying the stirring panorama of recent events in the Middle East generally, events which recall the glories and tragedies of the past, what is the particular significance of Palestine to so very many people in various lands? Although a little strip of a country, it holds associations which grip the soul of men. Such holy soil, such an atmosphere of high ideals, would form the most appropriate setting for the rebirth of hope in mankind. And, as a helpful step toward the fulfillment of this hope, it has fallen to the lot of Britain, another small country but one which, nevertheless, is the invincible stronghold of justice and freedom, to set an example that will serve as a guiding star to humanity.[26]

The Contribution of the English Bible to British Christian Zionism

The British people derived their knowledge of the land of Israel primarily from the Bible. The importance of the English Bible in the British mindset cannot be overestimated. It was the foundation of law and social attitudes. It has been the best-selling book and the most influential piece of literature in British society. Tuchman wrote, "Without the background of the English Bible it is doubtful that the Balfour Declaration would ever have been issued in the name of the British government or the Mandate for Palestine undertaken."[27] In 1875, Dr. William Thomson, Archbishop of York, spoke to a gathering of the Palestine Exploration Fund. He explained what the Bible and Palestine meant to him. "Our reason for turning to Palestine is that Palestine is our country. I have used that expression before and I refuse to adopt any other." He went on to say that Palestine had given him the "laws by which I live" and the "best knowledge I possess."[28]

Early in the 16th century, copies of the Bible became available to the common people of Britain, influencing how the entire nation thought and acted. According to Tuchman,

In the year 1538 Henry VIII issued a proclamation ordering "one book of the whole Bible" to be placed in every Church in England. With the translation of the Bible into English and its adoption for an autonomous English Church, the history, traditions, and moral law of the Hebrew nation became part of English culture; became for a period of three centuries the most powerful single influence on that culture.[29]

There was a passion in Britain for the Bible, and the people thought it natural to perceive a strong link between the Bible and the Land of the Bible. Perry noted,

> The very mention of the word "Palestine" recalls to us the Holy Land, or the Promised Land, or the Land of the Israelites. For many centuries, as we all know, it was "the" Home of the Jews. Out of this people, sometimes called the people of the Book, sprang law-givers, reformers and spiritual thinkers of imperishable memory.[30]

In certain respects, the people of Britain developed a greater attachment to the Old Testament than to the New Testament. Many felt a stronger attraction to the heroes of Jewish history than to the saints of the New Testament gospels. In a strange twist of history, one small island country chose to establish her identity based on the historical accounts of a tiny Semitic nation that had lived in a far off land thousands of years before. Centuries of Church decorating in Britain attest to this mentality. Tuchman observed,

> Among the "Nine Worthies" of history, "three paynim (sic), three Jews and three Christian men" whose figures so often appear carved over Church doors or embroidered in tapestry, the three Jews were represented by Joshua (not Moses), David, and Judas Maccabaeus...Here is the curious fact of the family history of one nation becoming the national epic of another. After the publication of the King James Version in 1611, the adoption was complete. The Bible was as much England's own as Good Queen Bess or Queen Victoria.[31]

Arthur Balfour was given the privilege of delivering the opening address of Hebrew University in Jerusalem on April 1 1925. He used the occasion to express his belief about the importance of the English Bible to the culture of his country. "All of the English-speaking people have been brought up on a translation into English of the Hebrew Scripture, and that translation is one of the great literary treasures of all who speak the English tongue."[32]

The Setting: Christian Zionism at the Beginning of the 20th Century

Christian Zionism originated in Europe during the Protestant Reformation of the 16th century. According to Ronald Stockton in his work "Christian Zionism: Prophecy and Public Opinion," it was generally acknowledged that modern Jewish Zionism originated in the Jewish communities of Europe in the late 19th century. Stockton, however, pointed out that "Christian Zionism predates these events by 300 years." He believed modern Zionism began in the 16th century when western European Protestants began to challenge Roman Catholic authority. Prior to that, Christian perspectives on Israel, Jews and biblical prophecy followed the Replacement Theology teachings of St. Augustine and the Roman Church. These teachings held that the Church of Rome represented the Kingdom of God on earth and that Jews were an unrepentant remnant.[33]

One of the main Christian groups who rejected Replacement Theology was the dissenting Protestants of Britain, particularly the Puritans. Instead, the Puritans and their spiritual descendants, the Victorian Evangelicals adopted a Premillennialism view of eschatology which was the belief that Jesus will return to earth to establish the Millennial Kingdom."[34] This was the view adopted by most Evangelicals in Britain and America.

Furthermore, some Christian Zionists believe that the return of the Jews to Israel is a prerequisite for the Second Coming of Jesus. The idea that Christians should actively support a Jewish return to the Land of Israel, as a means of fulfilling biblical prophecy, has been common in Protestant circles since the Reformation. The term Christian Zionism was popularized in the mid-20th century. Prior to that time, the common term used was Restorationism.

Yaakov Ariel, in his work on the subject, observed that the concept of Dispensationalism was also a necessary component of Premillennialism. Dispensationalism was the doctrine that divides human history into ages, or dispensations"[35] This teaching included the expectation that the next and final stage of God's plan for the world would be a restored Jewish Messianic Kingdom. Ariel noted that Dispensationalism was shaped in Britain during the 1820's to 1830's, and in America during the 1860's and 1870's.[36] This development took place primarily in four Evangelical denominations: Presbyterian, Methodist, Congregational and Baptist.[37] According to Ariel, most British and American Evangelicals accepted Premillennialism by the late Victorian period. "Since the late 19th century, most American Premillennialists have been Dispensationalists which has been the most influential eschatological school in the country."[38]

This eschatological doctrinal development was significant in that the growing Evangelical Churches of the late Victorian period now had a unified eschatology which gave them a common expectation for a restored Israel. According to this teaching, a Jewish Messiah (Jesus) would soon return to establish his Millennial Kingdom. It therefore made sense to honour the Jewish people and facilitate their Zionist endeavours.

Perhaps not understanding the eschatological doctrinal position of the Catholic Church, Theodore Herzl sought the support of Pope Pius X for a Jewish State. Arriving at the Vatican in January 1904, Herzl first met with Vatican Secretary of State Cardinal Merry del Val. The Cardinal told Herzl, "As long as the Jews deny the Divinity of Christ we certainly cannot side with them...how can we agree to their retaining possession of the Holy Land?"[39] Herzl eventually had an audience with the Pope and requested Catholic support for the Zionist Movement. The Pope responded,

> We are unable to favour this movement. We cannot prevent the Jews from going to Jerusalem, but we could never sanction it. The ground of Jerusalem if it were not always sacred, has been sanctified by the life of Jesus Christ. As the Head of the Church, I cannot answer you otherwise. The Jews have not recognized our Lord; therefore we cannot recognize the Jewish people.[40]

Following the Reformation, now separated from the Roman Church, the Anglican Church defined itself into two camps. One was the High Anglican Church, which continued to follow a Roman liturgy style, and the other was the Puritan inspired Evangelical Low Anglican Church, functioning with a high regard for Bible teaching and a minimum of liturgy. Various Evangelical Churches later branched out of the Low Anglican Church: Presbyterians, Baptists, Congregationalists, Quakers and Methodists. These denominations carried on the Puritan convictions of personal faith, congregational Church government and the importance of biblical teaching. These Puritans inspired communities viewed the Jewish people as still the Chosen People of God, still the heirs of the promises of God as recorded by the Jewish prophets of the Old Testament.[41]

For nearly 200 years, Britain sent colonists to America to populate the New World. A large proportion of those who made the journey were dissenting Puritans seeking a place to live out their faith in a freer environment. However, unlike Britain where Nonconformist Protestants remained a minority, in most of the America colonies they comprised the majority. As their numbers grew, their influence in society also increased.

The Issue of Christian Zionist Motivation

The question should be asked what Christian Zionists might have hoped to gain by assisting the Jews in their Zionist dream of creating a restored Israel. What possible motives did they have for their commitment to Zionism? Regarding the issue of converting Jews to Christianity, Yaakov Ariel noted that by the 1880's in America, there was influential Christian missionary activity among the Jews.[42] While this was alarming to some Jews, there was not necessarily a link between Christian Zionism and missionary enterprise toward Jews. Men such as Lloyd George, Balfour, Smuts, Churchill, and Truman were Christian Zionists but did not concern themselves with the issue of Jews converting to Christianity. Besides this, the essence of Christianity was to spread the message of the gospel throughout the world, without any specific community being targeted or excluded.

Another possible motive could be a Christian end-times preparation. This was the idea that Christian Zionists believed a restored Israel would bring about the end of the world and the destruction of the Jewish people. According to Ariel, "A restored Israel would prepare the ground for the great events that would take place after the rapture."[43] This claim represents a misunderstanding of Evangelical eschatology. Premillennial Dispensationalism does not believe that Jews will convert to Christianity in the end times, but rather that the Kingdom of Israel will be restored.

The real motive for Christian Zionism in 1917 can be best understood as a spiritual impulse linked to political expediency. In principle, helping the Jews return to their "Promised Land" could accomplish several benefits. Such an action would fulfill the religious ideals of Christian Zionists. It would also create a rush of philosemitic goodwill feeling across Britain that Christians had accomplished something significant for the Jews.[44] In addition, it might also win the favour of the Jews of the world, turning an impoverished, desolate land into a productive, contributing region.

Herbert Samuel noted that the goodwill of "a whole race may not be without its value."[45]

Politics alone cannot fully explain the motives of the men involved in making policy decisions regarding Palestine. The influence of personal Christian Zionist religious beliefs must also be considered factors. Until now, the importance of the political influence of Christian Zionism has not been fully appreciated. Politics alone cannot fully explain the interest the British had in Palestine in the early 20th century. The view that political pragmatism was the motivation of the British to enter Palestine fails to appreciate the significant influence that Christian Zionist idealism once had in Britain, and later had in the United States.

Chapter One

The Role of Christian Zionism behind the Balfour Declaration in 1917

Introduction

This chapter will demonstrate that the influence of Christian Zionism was one of the most important factors motivating the British to issue the Balfour Declaration in 1917. While it will be acknowledged that a variety of factors influenced the Cabinet, it will be argued that the commitment of leading Cabinet members to the Zionist cause was one of the weightiest among several motivations.

In order to understand the reasons the Cabinet had for issuing the Balfour Declaration, the various motivation theories be surveyed. The significance of the religious backgrounds of the Cabinet Ministers will then be studied to establish how their personal belief systems influenced their actions. In order to contextualize this unique political decision, the issues of Jewish anti-Zionism and a largely non-English Cabinet will also be examined.

The Significance of the Balfour Declaration

On November 2 1917, the British Cabinet issued a statement which has come to be known as the "Balfour Declaration." In the Declaration, the Cabinet stated its sympathy with Jewish Zionist aspirations for the establishment of a National Home in Palestine for the Jewish people. The Balfour Declaration was significant for several reasons. It became the foundational British policy statement for political change in Palestine, initiating steps which led to the British Mandate. It also led indirectly to the creation of the State of Israel in 1948. The Balfour Declaration read,

Foreign Office

November 2, 1917

Dear Lord Rothschild,

I have much pleasure in conveying to you, on behalf of His Majesty's government, the following declaration of sympathy with the Jewish Zionist aspirations which has been submitted to, and approved by, the Cabinet.

His Majesty's government view with favour the establishment in Palestine of a national home for the Jewish people, and will use their best endeavours to facilitate the achievement of this object, it being clearly understood that nothing shall be done which may prejudice the civil and religious rights of existing non-Jewish communities in Palestine, or the rights and political status enjoyed by Jews in any other country.

I should be grateful if you would bring this declaration to the knowledge of the Zionist Federation.

(was signed)

Arthur James Balfour

The Question of Motivation

What motivated the Cabinet to publish the Balfour Declaration? It is very difficult to find a parallel situation in the history of international relations where a world power offered such significant unilateral political assistance to a tiny dispersed global community. Ten years later, in 1927, Arthur Balfour commented on how extraordinary the Balfour Declaration was. "The experiment was admittedly a bold one, dealing with a unique situation in a manner wholly without precedent in history."[1]

When the Declaration was issued, the Cabinet gave no explanations, no reasons and no conditions. The matter was not debated or voted on in either the House of Commons or the House of Lords. The decision was made exclusively by the members of the Cabinet. Because of how problematic the Mandate turned out for the British during the next 31 years, historians have since speculated about what the motivating factors behind the government's decision to take such action. While it will be recognized that there were various political factors that motivated the Cabinet to publish the Balfour Declaration, it will be argued that the foremost motivation was a Christian Zionist spiritual impulse to facilitate the restoration of Israel in Palestine for the lasting good of the Jewish people.

The Historical Context of the Balfour Declaration

David Lloyd George became Prime Minister unexpectedly in December 1916.[2] During his tenure as Prime Minister, Herbert Asquith and most of his Cabinet did not express an interest in Zionism. In January 1915, when Cabinet Member and Home Secretary Herbert Samuel, a Jew, presented the Cabinet with his report on "The Future of Palestine," Prime Minister Asquith found it distasteful. Samuel, he noted, proposed, "The British annexation of Palestine, a country the size of Wales, much of it barren mountain and part of it waterless."[3] However, Lloyd George had previously shown an interest in Zionism in Cabinet meetings. Asquith noted, "Curiously enough, the only other partisan of this proposal is Lloyd George."[4] At this time, Weizmann sought out Lord Bertie, the British Ambassador in Paris, whose reaction was negative. Weizmann recalled, "Lord Bertie, who was a Catholic, considered the whole thing 'an absurd scheme' and trembled as to 'what the Pope would say.'"[5]

Even at this high level of national politics, religious prejudice influenced opinions. Lloyd George did not view Asquith with respect, privately revealing his displeasure that Asquith left the Nonconformist Congregational Church to become an Anglican. In her diary, A. J. Sylvester, Lloyd George's secretary, recorded Lloyd George saying, "The worst thing Asquith had ever done had been to join the Church of England. He had been the son of a Nonconformist Minister. He had not joined because of principle but, L.G. could only suspect, because of society."[6]

It was understandable that Asquith's shift to the Anglican Church would have been odious to Lloyd George. Like Asquith, Lloyd George was raised in the home of a Nonconformist Minister. The basic tenant of the Nonconformist movement was to be free from the authority of the Anglican Church. In Wales at this time, the great majority of the people rejected the established Church of England, regarding it as an imposed foreign organization.[7] Early in life, Lloyd George adopted the religious rebellion of the Nonconformist movement. As a boy, he would not participate in the mandatory Anglican catechism class. Frank Dilnot, one of Lloyd George's biographers, explains, "David refused to recite Church catechism...It was the first outbreak of his desire for revolt against the powers that be...and the satisfaction of that instinct for audacious action which has marked him ever since."[8]

Just before the Great War began, Lloyd George witnessed one of the victories for which he had hoped. The Anglican Church in Wales was disestablishment, to the delight of the majority of the Welsh population.[9] Lloyd George suspected Asquith joined the Anglican Church in order to improve his place in society. Such a move would also be accompanied by a change in religious doctrine for Asquith. The Nonconformist Churches taught Zionism while the Anglican Church usually did not. Asquith maintained his coldness to Zionism throughout the rest of his life. In 1924, while traveling to Palestine, he wrote of his indifference, "The talk of making Palestine into a Jewish National Home seems to me as fantastic as it always has done."[10]

Upon becoming Prime Minister, Lloyd George immediately created a small inner Cabinet of five men. This Cabinet included Lord Curzon as Lord President of the Council and Leader of the House of Lords; Andrew Bonar Law as the Chancellor of the Exchequer and Leader of the House of Commons and Lord Milner as Minister without Portfolio. The fifth member, Arthur Henderson, was the unofficial representative of the Labour Party.

In the following months, other men were invited to join the Cabinet and participated in the debate on Palestine. Arthur Balfour was Foreign Minister, Jan Christian Smuts represented South Africa, George Barnes was from the Labour Party, Lord Milner was a Minister without Portfolio and Edwin Montagu was the Secretary of State for India. Although aides and advisors were involved, the Cabinet debated and approved the Balfour Declaration. They represented a wide spectrum of social backgrounds and all the contemporary political Parties.

Unlike the Asquith government, the Cabinet of Lloyd George took an interest in Zionism. The concept of facilitation a Jewish National Home in Palestine was moved to a high place on its agenda. Lloyd George and Balfour began to make plans to issue a pro-Zionist statement and to invade Palestine. Arthur Koestler, in his work "Promise and Fulfillment," commented on the uniqueness of the Cabinet's action. "The whole thing was unorthodox, unpolitic, freakish. For one glorious moment, the British Cabinet assumed the role of Messianic providence. Politics was lifted from the trivial to the romantic plane."[11]

One of the first war policy decisions Lloyd George implemented in early 1917 was to turn his attention to the Eastern Front. The fighting in Western Europe had been costly and inconclusive. Lloyd George believed more could be accomplished by engaging the Turks in the east. An essential part of this change in strategy would be support for Zionism and a plan to invade Palestine.

The Five Main Theories for the Motivation behind the Balfour Declaration

There are five main theories that attempt to explain the motivation behind the Balfour Declaration. The first is the theory of winning Jewish favour in order to benefit British war aims. The second is the theory of remorse; that British Christians wished to redeem themselves for past offenses to the Jews. The third is the gratitude theory; that the Cabinet was paying Chaim Weizmann back for wartime scientific contributions. The fourth is the theory that the Cabinet desired to occupy Palestine in order to expand the Empire. The fifth is the theory of Christian Zionist motivation. It will be shown that although all these theories have some measure of validity, it was Christian Zionism that was the most significant single factor motivating the publication of the Balfour Declaration.

The Winning of Jewish Favour Theory

The first explanation for the motivation behind the Balfour Declaration supposes that the Declaration would stimulate the world Jewish community to support Britain both politically and economically. After the Great War, historians have credited Weizmann and other Jewish Zionists with persuading the Cabinet to publish the Declaration.[12] Leonard Stein's work "The Balfour Declaration" was an early study of the topic. Stein's theory was that the motivations of the Cabinet had to do with a combination of political factors. One was the Russian Revolution and British fears that Russia would drop out of the war. It was supposed that the Jews of Russian would somehow keep Russia fighting if they believed that they were also fighting for a National Home in Palestine.

While testifying to the Peel Commission of 1937, Lloyd George seemed to affirm this theory. He gave testimony of the serious military situation of the Allies in 1917. The Romanians were defeated, the Russians were demoralized, the French were unable to take the offensive, the Americans were not yet in the trenches and German submarines had sunk millions of tons of British shipping. Lloyd George testified,

> In this critical situation, it was believed that Jewish sympathy or the reverse would make a substantive difference one way or the other to the Allied cause. In particular, Jewish sympathy would confirm the support of the American Jewry, and would make it more difficult for Germany to reduce her

military commitments and improve her economic position on the Eastern Front.[13]

Lloyd George claimed the Jews promised, "...to do their best to rally Jewish sentiment and support throughout the world to the Allied cause. They kept their word."[14]

Despite his claims, Lloyd George's 1937 testimony lacked documented support and sound reasoning. He leaves one wondering whom these Jews were who promised to "rally Jewish sentiment," and how they fulfilled this promise. Considering the weighty personalities and political power of the men of the Cabinet in 1917, it is difficult to conceive that Weizmann or anyone else could have convinced the Cabinet to support Zionism against their will. These were men accustomed to making decisions of the highest order. They knew their political decisions had to be for the good of the nation, and to be perceived to be for the good of the nation. More than this, their decisions had to be defendable. It is unlikely they would have collectively allowed themselves to be persuaded against their better judgment by influences outside of government circles.

Certainly, the Cabinet was interested to some extent in winning Jewish favour. In addition, there was concern that Germany might precede them in making a Zionist statement and thereby possibly win the favour of millions of European Jews. During the Cabinet debates on the Declaration, Balfour himself expressed that action needed to be taken because Germany might also be considering issuing a statement in favour of Zionism.[15] On another occasion in Cabinet, Balfour pointed out the need to rally Jewish influence to counteract German propaganda in Russia.[16]

In his 1939 memoirs, Lloyd George acknowledged this fear. "The German government were making great efforts to capture the sympathy of the Zionist movement."[17] Leonard Stein noted that the Foreign Office, in the autumn of 1917, was firmly under the impression that the Germans were courting the Zionists. It was expected that they might at any moment identify with the Zionist cause, thus providing themselves with a useful instrument of political warfare.[18]

A further international factor had to do with the United States. America declared war on Germany in April 1917, but was slow to mobilize. The British feared America would not enter the war soon enough to make a difference. The theory followed that American Jewry would be encouraged by the Balfour Declaration. They would then exert political influence to motivate America into joining the fighting sooner. In his 1936 memoirs, Lloyd George wrote that through the Declaration, the Cabinet hoped to secure for the Allies both the sympathy of the Jews of Russia, who "wielded considerable influence in Bolshevik circles" and "the aid of Jewish financial interests in the United States."[19] Stein qualifies the notion that the government would behave in such a manner.

Though the Declaration had a strictly practical purpose related to the war situation at the time, it is not to be accounted for merely as an eleventh-hour device for dealing with a problem of political warfare. Behind it lay the long story already told in full-the links forged between Great Britain and the Zionists by their early pre-war contacts, the instinctive sympathy with Zionist aspirations shown by leading British statesmen.[20]

One of the most outspoken members of the Cabinet, Jan Smuts, seemed to back this point but with a qualification. Speaking in London in 1949, Smuts told his audience that a powerful argument in favour of the Declaration had been that "it would rally Jewry on a worldwide scale to the Allied cause." However, he added, "Moral and religious motives reinforced the political considerations."[21]

Blanche Dugdale, niece and Balfour's official biographer, challenged the notion of the creation of the Declaration out of a desire to win the favour of world Jewry. She pointed out that, at the time, American Jewry was generally opposed to Zionism. "As late as January 1918, our Ambassador in Washington reported on the authority of Mr. Justice Brandeis himself, that the Zionists 'were violently opposed by the great capitalists, and by the Socialists, for different reasons.'"[22]

Isaiah Friedman, in his work "The Question of Palestine," explained that the British believed Jewish influence in the American press to be substantial. It was expected that this influence could be potentially beneficial to the cause of the British war effort to enlist the backing of American Jewry. Although some American Jewish leaders were not necessarily accepting Zionist ideals, they might be eager to assist colonization in Palestine. One of the problems with this theory was that a large proportion of American Jews were indifferent as to which great power would hold sovereignty over Palestine. According to Friedman,

A wide section of American Jewry favoured the development of an autonomous Jewish settlement in Palestine under Ottoman sovereignty...The Balfour Declaration was meant to convert them (American Jewry) to the idea of a British, alternatively an American trusteeship, and obtain President Wilson's endorsement.[23]

Friedman credits Mark Sykes[24] and certain Jewish Zionist leaders in Britain for initiating events that ultimately led to the Declaration. Friedman believed that Mark Sykes met with Zionist leaders and started a chain of events leading up to the Balfour Declaration."[25] This theory relies too much on supposition. The men of the Cabinet were not obligated to make decisions based on such outside pressures. The influence of Mark Sykes and Rabbi Gaster was significant, but not decisive.

It was the opinion of Mayir Verete, who extensively examined the background of the Balfour Declaration, that Weizmann and other Jewish Zionists played no role in influencing events. Verete wrote, "It seems to me that, in so far as the Declaration is considered, it is of no significance how many times Weizmann or Sokolow visited the Foreign Office."[26] Rather, Verete placed significance upon the Zionist sympathies of the men in the Cabinet. He refers to the sustained declared support of some of the Cabinet members in the years following the Great War.

> One must, however, admit that it was nice and convenient and agreeable that Balfour, Lloyd George, Smuts, as well as some important personages in the highest reaches in general, were sympathetic to the Zionist cause. This attitude was of considerable importance mainly after the Declaration.[27]

Regarding the political importance of Weizmann during the war years, Stein evaluates that Weizmann "was an important, but not a dominating figure...When war broke out, he had no such pre-eminence as to make it seem natural to turn to him for leadership."[28]

The theory of attempting to win the favour of the Jews of the worldview can be evaluated as overly simplistic and not sufficiently documented. Importantly, it does not present a case consistent with the testimony of Arthur Balfour. At a private gathering a few weeks after the Declaration, Balfour was asked whether it represented a bid for Jewish support in the war. He at once replied, "Certainly not."[29]

The Remorse Theory

The second theory for the motivation behind the Balfour Declaration is the remorse theory, which argues that the Cabinet, out of a sense of Christian guilt, issued the Balfour Declaration. This theory suggests that out of a desire to make things right again for the Jews because of centuries of Christian persecution of Jews, the men of the Cabinet issued the Declaration.

Leonard Stein addressed this theory. "Balfour had spoken against the persecution of the Jews saying, 'The treatment of the race has been a disgrace to Christendom,' and saw the establishment of a Jewish state as an historic act of amends."[30] However, even if Balfour did recognize the historic mistreatment of the Jews, he did not link it to his personal motivation behind the Declaration which bore his name. As a Nonconformist Evangelical Christian, Balfour would not have associated himself or his denomination with the historic anti-Semitism of Christendom, particularly of the Catholic Church. Churchill wrote for the *Strand* magazine at the time of Balfour's death, "His aversion from the Roman Catholic faith was dour and inveterate."[31] There is no record of the other members of the Cabinet citing remorse as a motivation for the Balfour Declaration.

The Gratitude Theory

The third proposed explanation for the motivation behind the Balfour Declaration is the gratitude theory. This theory proposes that the Balfour Declaration was a British government repayment for the scientific assistance of Chaim Weizmann during the Great War.

The background context for this theory is linked to the fact that, throughout the war, Jewish chemist Chaim Weizmann conducted scientific research in England. Most importantly, he invented a new chemical procedure for producing acetone, a critical ingredient in the manufacturing of explosives. This discovery greatly aided the British at a crucial time. Lloyd George referred to this in his memoirs in 1936. By this time, conventional thinking in Britain was that the Mandate was a costly tragedy. It is possible that Lloyd George played into this thinking, trying to convince the British public (and perhaps himself) that the government owed Chaim Weizmann a great debt.[32] He utilized a prevalent idea of the day that the influence of Jews could determine the outcome of wars and topple regimes. He explained that Britain simply had to "make a contract with Jewry."[33]

According to Lloyd George's 1936 memoirs, he and Chaim Weizmann had had a private conversation in 1916 in which Lloyd George asked Weizmann what honour Weizmann would like to receive for his research work. Weizmann responded that he wished no honour for himself, but for his people he would like to see a British government statement of support for Zionist ideals. Lloyd George concluded his recollection by stating,

He then explained his aspirations as to the repatriation of the Jews to the sacred land they had made famous. That was the fount and origin of the famous declaration about the National Home for Jews in Palestine. As soon as I became Prime Minister, I talked the whole matter over with Mr. Balfour who was then Foreign Secretary.[34]

However touching the account of this dialogue may be, it is difficult to take seriously. Weizmann refused to collaborate the story. No other Cabinet member from 1917 recalled such a decision. The Cabinet minutes do not contain any discussion on the subject. David Fromkin, in his work, "A Peace to End all Peace," commented with skepticism, "Years after the war, Lloyd George, in writing his memoirs invented the story that he had given the Balfour Declaration in gratitude for Weizmann's invention. Weizmann's important invention was real, but Lloyd George's story was a work of fiction."[35] It should be noted that Weizmann's scientific contribution to the British during the Second World War was again significant, but came with no hint of a British government reward.

It is important that Arthur Balfour denied this reason as a motivation for issuing the Balfour Declaration. Asked bluntly by Richard Meinertzhagen whether the Declaration bearing his name was a reward for wartime services, Balfour replied emphatically that both he and the Prime Minister had been influenced "by the desire to give the Jews their rightful place in the world; a great nation without a home is not right."[36] Meinertzhagen was politically active in Palestine since the 1917 invasion and had a high level of credibility.[37] Lloyd George's claim will be looked at more deeply in this chapter when the personal motivations of the various men of the Cabinet are examined in further detail.

The Expansion of the Empire Theory
The fourth explanation for the motivation behind the Balfour Declaration is that it would serve British imperial interests. This is the most generally accepted explanation for the motivation behind the Declaration. Several scholars who have addressed this issue have concluded that it was the needs of the war that were responsible for the publishing of the Balfour Declaration. Mark Levene, in his article "Edge of Darkness," pointed out that, "Notably Mayir Verete, Isaiah Friedman and Ronald Saunders have stressed the primacy of wartime political considerations."[38] Jehuda Reinharz observed, "There is little doubt in the minds of all the historians who have occupied themselves with the origins of the Balfour Declaration that it was meant, first and foremost, to serve British aims and interests."[39] In later decades, Jewish opponents to the British Mandate believed the motivation for the Balfour Declaration was exclusively to expand the Empire. Their opinions helped to popularize this view.[40]

Verete concluded that the Cabinet was primarily motivated by thoughts of Empire in the hope that they would win Palestine from the Turks through the fortunes of war. Verete lists these benefits in a convincing manner, explaining that the British government wanted possession Palestine for a variety of security reasons.

> We therefore can hardly wonder that Grey and Kitchener-as well as Cecil, Crewe, Curzon, Lloyd George...wanted the country, or at least, a considered part of it: for a defense

in-depth of the Suez Canal and Egypt, for serving the "strategic necessity of an overland communication between the Mediterranean and Mesopotamia," for a naval base in Haifa, to command the Gulf of Aqaba and northern Arabia... for having-as Sykes explained –"a belt of English-controlled territory between the Sharif of Mecca and the French (in Syria).[41]

This view makes some sense in that the Balfour Declaration would later give Britain diplomatic legitimacy for maintaining a governing presence in Palestine after the war was over. Control of Palestine would link British strategic control across the Middle East. The potential benefits to the Empire would be manifold. There would be greater security for the Suez Canal and an overland rail route to India could be considered. The material needs of the far-flung Army and Navy could be better served, and the economic ties to India would be more secure.

John Marlowe, in his work, "Arab Nationalism and British Imperialism, A Study in Power Politics," believed the British had primarily political motives for their Middle East policy. He believed the British wanted the power to maintain military bases, ports and airfields, plus the ability to move military and commercial supplies freely. "In 1936, as in 1916, Great Britain's interest in what was coming to be known as the Middle East was primarily strategic."[42]

Friedman examined all the factors that might have motivated the Declaration. He recognized the religious sympathies of Balfour and Lloyd George, but concluded this was a secondary factor in the overall picture. Friedman's view is that although a combination of factors worked together to produce the Balfour Declaration, it was a desire for national security that was the main motivation. A British presence in Palestine through a Jewish National Home would certainly contribute to greater international British security. Friedman believed the various motivations were somewhat influenced by timing. He pointed out that once the Declaration was published, the Zionists of Britain enthusiastically backed the idea of a British Palestine.

As the official records show, sentiment does not determine state policy. The Declaration would hardly have been made unless it had been the considered judgment of the Foreign Office and the War Cabinet that it was clearly in the British interest to do so. There was a combination of motives rather than one which led to the final decision, but what dominated was the desire for security...In England the Zionists were in a state of near euphoria. They embarked on a massive campaign to popularize the idea of a British Palestine and gave maximum publicity to the Declaration.[43]

In his final address to the Cabinet regarding the Declaration, Balfour acknowledged that although there would not be immediate Jewish autonomy in Palestine, his wording seems to allow for eventual Jewish independence. "It did not necessarily involve the early establishment of an independent Jewish State, which was a matter for gradual development in accordance with the ordinary laws of political evolution."[44] Had Balfour's motives been to expand the Empire, it is unlikely he would have given such allowances.

Verete likewise recognized these various motives in the minds of the British politicians. In his article, "The Balfour Declaration and its Makers," he credited the Cabinet with taking the initiative in writing the Balfour Declaration. He also believed Weizmann and Sokolow understood the British probably intended to keep Palestine for their own.

> They placed their faith in Balfour and Lloyd George and in the group of Englishman with whom they worked, and perhaps also in the British generally; and they relied on the Declaration as a pronouncement in the nature of a gentleman's agreement: in exchange for that measure of promise by the government to help them establish a National Home, they would do whatever they could to ensure that Britain alone would be the ruler of Palestine.[45]

An interesting aspect of Verete's theory is the claim that the Balfour Declaration was part of a British ploy to escape certain obligations of the Sykes-Picot agreement. The British had occupied Egypt since 1882, and now they were interested in securing

Palestine. Since France was also claiming Palestine, Verete believed that Britain also wanted it as a connecting land link to the Persian Gulf and for meeting any possible attack from Russia in the north.[46] According to Verete, "The occupation coupled with support of the Zionist cause was the neatest, most convenient and becoming way of making France abandon her share in Palestine."[47] Mark Sykes guided the British government in 1915-1916 to an agreement with France as to how the Middle East would be divided between them should the Ottoman Empire be conquered. The document became known as the Sykes-Picot agreement.[48]

Therefore, according to Verete, Sykes turned to the Zionists, finding Weizmann and Sokolow. The relationship began when Sykes and the Prime Minister thought it right to initiate talks.[49] Verete believed that Mark Sykes and Lloyd George, both patriots and imperialists, schemed to secure Palestine for Britain. This theory suggests that these two men conspired together to use both imperial and Zionist ambitions to achieve their aim. Verete summarized, "Lloyd George wanted Britain to gain some material benefit while assisting God's purpose." Verete believed the Cabinet then decided to find a way to seize Palestine and used the Zionists to cover for their political motives. "The British wanted Palestine-and very much so-for their own interests, and that it was not the Zionists who drew them to the country."[50]

Verete built his case by noting that the Jewish Zionists of Britain did little to initiate events. "Nor were the Zionists the first to bring the question of Palestine and her future before the British government during the war; neither was it the Zionists who initiated the negotiations with the government, but the government that opened up negotiations with them."[51] Verete pointed out that the Sykes-Picot agreement was decided without the Zionist leaders, and without any mention of Zionists or Jews.[52]

Illustrating the passivity of the Jewish Zionists, Verete pointed out that during the first 28 months of the war, Weizmann had no contact, on the whole, with those engaged in formulating foreign policy, nor did the Zionists submit a single memorandum to the Foreign Office.[53] Verete concluded, "It was not the Zionist leaders who taught the English how much they needed Palestine and not they who pulled them into the country."⁵⁴ However cold Verete's assessment is of Zionist efforts, one is left to wonder how the Jewish Zionists ever thought their plans would work without the British conquering Palestine. Verete concluded that the origin of the Balfour Declaration was all political.

> For the purpose of a government's Zionist policy in itself, it was not very important what the Zionists did, nor was there any need for Weizmann or Sokolow in particular; just as the Zionism of Balfour, Lloyd George, Milner and Smuts or of the War Cabinet which approved of the Declaration, was of no great consequence either.⁵⁵

According to Verete, "Britain was seduced. She was ready to be seduced by any Zionist of stature."⁵⁶ To an extent, this could be true. The Balfour Declaration and subsequent conquest of Palestine was a political win for both politics and religion. Skilled politicians have long been adept at mixing their purposes and masking their motives. However, Verete fails to give appropriate credit to the influence of Zionist ideals.

It was clear that both the Jewish Zionists and the Cabinet believed some great political power needed to claim sovereignty over Palestine, at least on a temporary basis. It should be noted that the concept of an independent Jewish State was not discussed at any level in 1917. It was with this understanding that men like Weizmann and Sokolow continued their long cooperation with the British. The reality was that their position was so weak politically that they had no choice. In 1917, the concept of the restoration of Israel was so hypothetical, and the position of the Jewish Zionist leaders so weak, that they were willing to link their fortunes to the apparent goodwill of the British.

Blanche Dugdale, Balfour's niece, believed the authors of the Balfour Declaration knew they were only beginning the process of the restoration of Israel. They did not know how Zionism would be fulfilled, but they wanted to initiate the process. Dugdale wrote later that a renewed Israel would not be possible unless "Eretz Israel be allowed to develop naturally, as was intended when the Balfour Declaration was signed."[57]

While it is apparent the British Empire would stand to benefit from expanding its territory into Palestine, this was not a motivation that can alone explain why the Cabinet acted as they did. During the months of deliberations, and even to final day of debate (October 31 1917), the British did not yet physically control any territory in Palestine. While the Empire expansion theory explains something of the Cabinets motives, it should remain a secondary motive compared to the Zionists ideals held by most Cabinet members.

The Christian Zionist Theory

The fifth theory for the motivation behind the Balfour Declaration was Christian Zionism. Although other political motives played a part behind the issuing of the Balfour Declaration, the religious consideration of Zionism was the primary single motivating factor. This spiritual motive was a deeper, more powerful force within some of these men than any of the other political issues.

Eitan Bar Yosef, in his work "Christian Zionism and Victorian Culture," asked how the idea of restoring the Jews to Palestine shifted from a notion of religious biblical prophecy in the 19th century to the sphere of practical politics in 1917.[58] This is an important question. The answer lies in the fact that in 1917 the Christian Zionists in the Cabinet had the opportunity to act on their beliefs. Political power was in their hands, and they made a decision to act.

Bar Yosef had difficulty understanding how 20th century Christian Zionism represented the same belief system as 19th century British philosemitism. "The idea of Jewish restoration was inviting, both ethically and aesthetically; it presented the end of the Wandering Jew's saga and provided a sense of closure; but it was not what Victorian Christian Zionism was really about."[59] Bar Yosef missed the fact that Evangelical Christian doctrine had not changed, but rather had remained constant. The difference now was the ability of the Cabinet to act. While the Victorian Evangelicals could only dream of restoring Israel, the Evangelicals in the Cabinet in 1917 knew they had the political authority and military power to carry out their beliefs.

Most of the men in the British Cabinet of 1917 were raised in that segment of British Protestant Christianity known as Evangelicalism. They were familiar with the Old Testament Scriptures and they were aware of biblical prophecy concerning the Jewish people. As a Jew, Samuel was aware of these Evangelical aspirations for Zionism when he wrote to the Cabinet in 1915, "Widespread and deep-rooted in the Protestant world is a sympathy with the idea of restoring the Hebrew people to the land which was to be their inheritance, an intense interest in the fulfillment of the prophecies which have foretold it."[60]

Much has been made of the early Zionist influence of C.P. Scott, the editor of the daily newspaper, the *Manchester Guardian.* Not a particularly religious man, Scott was an open-minded liberal who favoured the nationalistic ideals of Zionism. He introduced Chaim Weizmann to Lloyd George, Balfour and Samuel. The question of when Balfour and Lloyd George first adopted Zionism is crucial. It has long been assumed in some Jewish circles that Weizmann persuaded Balfour and Lloyd George to become Zionists.[61] However, a closer examination of the lives of these politicians will reveal that they were committed Zionists long before they met Weizmann. The role of Scott and Weizmann behind the Balfour Declaration was convenient, but not essential. Leonard Stein believed that Scott's personal exertions behind the scenes made Weizmann seem important. It was Scott who first brought Weizmann to the notice of Lloyd George. Then in 1917, "With his long standing association with the new Prime Minister, Weizmann was in a particularly advantageous position for advocating the Zionist cause in the highest quarters."[62]

Although the British politicians who wrote the Balfour Declaration differed widely in their class backgrounds and upbringing, they shared many of the same spiritual beliefs. Herbert Samuel wrote in 1945 that the motivation for the Balfour Declaration was "a genuine sympathy with the aspirations of Jews for a restoration in Palestine."[63]

The Motivations of the Men of the Cabinet

The backgrounds and motivations of the men of the Cabinet will be examined in the following way. These ten men will be divided into three categories. First, those whose motives are the most unambiguous will be examined; Alfred Milner, George Curzon, Jan Smuts, Edwin Montagu and Arthur Balfour. Second, those whose motives are somewhat unclear will be reviewed: Arthur Henderson, George Barnes, Edward Carson and Andrew Bonar Law. Third, the Prime Minister, David Lloyd George will be studied in a category of his own, a complex man with manifold motivations.

The Secular Support of Lord Milner

Lord Milner was a career politician with no strong religious views. He was committed to the expansion of the Empire and backed the Balfour Declaration. Milner made it clear he believed a Jewish National Home in the Empire would be of economic and military benefit to Britain. Milner supported the Balfour Declaration, and seemed to support Zionism as early as the days of Theodore Herzl. In his work, "The Vision was There," Franz Kobler noted that Lord Milner was, "an ardent pro-Zionist during Herzl's lifetime."[64]

Lord Milner possessed an influential personality. Fellow Cabinet member Edward Carson stated, "Of course Milner and Curzon were the only two, besides Lloyd George himself, who counted, and of these Milner was by far the more useful and influential."[65] Stein commented, "It was fortunate for the Zionists that this was so, for...Milner was among their firmest supporters."[66] Although no statement of personal faith from Lord Milner is documented, Milner's biographer, Vladimir Halperin, claimed Milner supported Zionism early. "As far back as 1915, Milner had realized the need for a Jewish National Home and had never ceased to be warmly in favour of its creation."[67]

Within the Cabinet, Alfred Milner stands in a category by himself. He was apparently non-religious, yet he backed a declaration that had religious undertones. The explanation could simply be that Milner supported the British Empire, and he viewed the Balfour Declaration as being good for the Empire. Speaking before the House of Lords in 1923, Milner said, "I was party to the Balfour Declaration. Personally I believe the policy to be a good one, and that steadily persisted in, it will lead to good results."[68] However, Milner did have some of the same concerns as Curzon, that the religious rights of the various inhabitants would be respected. They had both worked in the East, with Milner being a recognized expert on Egypt. Milner spoke of this in 1923 when he addressed the House of Lords. It seems he believed Palestine needed a foreign power to keep the peace.

> You cannot have either an Arab government in Palestine or a Jewish government in Palestine, but you must have in that country some neutral Power which will keep the balance between the different races...To hold the balance even between these various interests...some Mandatory Power will always be required.[69]

Milner was an experienced and capable administrator. He considered himself an authority on the Middle East. In his biography of Milner, Halperin claimed that Milner preached, "The new doctrine of Liberal imperialism which was based on a belief that amounted to religion in the mission of the British Empire throughout the whole world."[70] Perhaps Milner was an ideological Zionist, but it seems more likely that he was looking for another way to expand the Empire. A Jewish National Home would serve that purpose.

The Thoughtful Opposition of George Curzon
George Curzon, the eldest son of an Evangelical Anglican Minister, raised objections to the Balfour Declaration from the beginning. Curzon's warnings were understandable. As the former Viceroy of India, and the only man in the Cabinet to have visited Palestine, he understood the religious and political complexities of the East. Curzon warned of offending the Muslims and of the inhospitable terrain of Palestine. He told the Cabinet that the idea of creating a National Home for the Jews in Palestine was a policy "very widely removed from the romantic and idealistic aspirations of many of the Zionists leaders." He further argued that Palestine could only ever provide a home for a small section of the Jewish people.[71]

There is no evidence of Curzon being ideologically opposed to Zionism. He was doubtful that a Jewish National Home in Palestine could be a reality. From his experience in India, he knew the potential problems of religious conflicts. In the October 4 Cabinet meeting, he talked about his visit to Palestine. "Palestine was for the most part "barren and desolate...a less propitious seat for the future Jewish race could not be imagined."[72] Although there was wisdom in his council, it was fortunate for the cause of Zionism that his advice was not taken. The troubled British rule in Palestine during the next 31 years showed the validity of his warnings. Finally, on the last day of the debate, as a display of unity with the Cabinet, he grudgingly gave his approval.

Whatever Curzon believed personally about Zionism and the Jewish people, he was realistic when it came to the complexities and pitfalls of Middle East foreign policy. He did not see Palestine with the biblical idealism of Lloyd George, Balfour and Smuts, but rather he foresaw the inevitable clash of Zionism and the Arab population of Palestine. Curzon's biographer, David Gilmour, observed that Curzon, "...predicted accurately as it happened, that Zionism could not be established without the removal of many of the native Arabs."[73] Tuchman observed that Curzon "opposed the Balfour Declaration...not because he sympathized with the anti-Zionist position, but because the Declaration committed Britain to an uncomfortable responsibility."[74]

In October, Curzon submitted a memorandum to the Cabinet in opposition to a declaration of sympathy with Zionism. He asked the Cabinet to beware they were not encouraging hopes that could not be realized. Curzon pointed out that Palestine was a poor country devoid of natural resources. "That a country which cannot within any approximate period contain anything but a small population, which has already an indigenous population of its own of a different race."[75] Curzon was one of the wealthiest men in the Cabinet, having affluent Jewish friends. Perhaps he doubted that the Jewish people he knew would be interested in emigration to Palestine to undergo the great physical hardships required for the rebuilding of the land. Curzon articulated his case well, but he did not have his way. Gilmour wrote, "The debate over the Balfour Declaration was one of a series between 1905 and 1923 in which Curzon won the argument and Balfour won the battle."[76]

There lies here the possibility that since the other Cabinet members had never seen the terrain of Palestine, their interest in Zionism perhaps was prone to be overly influenced by religious values and images. Curzon was unimpressed by romantic notions of a Jewish restoration in Palestine. He knew the actual resettling of the land would be very difficult or even impossible. Within the Cabinet, Stein termed Curzon "The most knowledgeable on Middle East affairs."[77]

Throughout the Cabinet debates, Curzon opposed the Balfour Declaration. His manner was sometimes harsh, but he declared his reasons for opposing. He believed that a Declaration in favour of Zionism would place upon Britain a commitment that she would not be able to keep.[78] He asked the Cabinet how it was proposed to get rid of the existing majority of Muslim inhabitants and introduce Jews in their place.[79] In the end, however, Curzon felt pressured into agreeing with the Declaration. Years later, speaking of his struggle with Balfour, Curzon complained, "I fought him strenuously, but vainly in his unfortunate insistence upon the Jewish National Home in Palestine, in which, ignorant of the facts and regardless of the future, he forced his pledge upon the Cabinet in order to placate the Jews and bring them in on our side in the war."[80]

There could also have been another factor to Curzon's opposition. On a personal level, he carried a bitter animosity to Balfour. It is hard not to wonder if at least a part of Curzon's lack of co-operation was personal. Years before, when Balfour was Prime Minister and Curzon was Viceroy of India, a political dispute divided the two men. Curzon resigned and seemed never to forgive Balfour.[81] Leonard Mosley, another biographer of Curzon, observed, "Curzon hated Balfour...He had never forgiven Balfour for his abandonment of him in India."[82] He once said of the character of Balfour,

The truth is that Balfour, with all his scintillating intellectual exterior, has no depth of feeling, no profound convictions, and strange to say, no real affection. When the emergencies came, he would drop, desert, or sacrifice any one of us without a pang, as he did me in India.[83]

Could it be that Curzon withheld his approval of the Declaration until the end in order to harass the man whom he despised? In her biography of Jan Smuts, Sarah Millin speculates, "There was no love between them, as they faced each other, Curzon smoldering, hostile, Balfour coolly contemptuous across the Cabinet Room table at 10 Downing Street in 1917."[84]

Despite this personal issue, Curzon was still a professional politician. Following the decisive Cabinet meeting on October 31, Curzon gave his approval. Speaking immediately after Balfour, Curzon admitted the force of arguments were in favour of the Declaration and believed the majority of Jews held Zionist opinions.[85] He did not share Montagu's views but could not embrace Balfour's optimism about Zionism. He was afraid the British were raising "false expectations which could never be realized." He conceded that some expression of sympathy would be a "valuable adjunct" to British propaganda.[86]

The Reformed Zionism of Jan Christian Smuts

A third member of the Cabinet who supported the Balfour Declaration because of biblical idealism was Jan Smuts. As a former Boer general, it was not of great importance for Smuts to see Palestine included as part of the British Empire. At the time of the Declaration, he made a statement about his personal hopes for what the Jewish people would be able to do in Palestine. Smuts hoped to see "In generations to come, a great Jewish State rising there once more."[87] Smuts defended the decision of the Balfour Declaration all of his life. Stein claimed, "In the post-War years no statesman of comparable stature fought more strongly than Smuts for the honoring of the Declaration, or proclaimed more emphatically his belief in its wisdom and justice."[88]

Jan Smuts was raised in the Protestant Reformed Church in South Africa. This was a Christian denomination stemming back to the Reformation that identified strongly with the value of Bible teaching. With historic roots back to Holland, the Reformed Church emphasizes a born again faith and an aversion to Roman influences. Strong Old Testament teaching resulted in an identity with the Jewish people.[89] Smuts received Bible teaching in his Church and at home despite the fact that he did not attend school until the age of 12.[90] Smuts commented about his religious training to a Jewish audience in 1919.

> I need not remind you, that the white people of South Africa, and especially the older Dutch population, have been brought up almost entirely on the Jewish tradition. The Old Testament, the most wonderful literature ever thought out by the brain of man, the Old Testament has been the very marrow of Dutch culture here in South Africa. I am sure that there are thousands, tens of thousands, of Dutch people in this country who know the Old Testament better than many Jews themselves.[91]

Jan Smuts was the only member of the 1917 Cabinet to live to see the State of Israel proclaimed in 1948. At that time, as the Prime Minister of South Africa, he pushed for his country to recognize the State of Israel immediately.[92] He hoped South Africa would be the first nation to recognize Israel. (The United States had that distinction). Smuts believed he had the backing of his nation, declaring, "In South Africa, all Jews are Zionists, and the Christians are pro-Zionists."[93]

Even before the Balfour Declaration, Smuts showed favour to the Jewish community of South Africa. Before departing South Africa in 1917 to join the Cabinet in London, an article about Smuts appeared in the Johannesburg *Zionist Record*. The article referred to an Education Act favourable to the Jewish community that Smuts had been advocating. It read in part, "In his Transvaal Education Act...he (Smuts) laid down conditions that must be considered distinctly favourable to the Jewish community...It is known that in politics he favours those Jewish influences which are exercised for the country's good."[94]

Chaim Weizmann also received similar pro-Zionist assurances from Smuts. In 1917, Weizmann wrote in his diary, "I had another talk with Smuts...and obtained from him the expected reiteration of his loyalty."[95] All his life, Smuts supported any effort relating to the Jewish people and Zionism. Speaking to a South African Jewish group in 1919, Smuts declared,

Your people, your little people, has had a mission, a civilizing mission, in the world second, perhaps to none among the nations of the earth...and I do not see why they should not once more play a great part in the history of the world.[96]

The personal Bible background of the Protestant reformed faith of Jan Smuts motivated him to back the Balfour Declaration in 1917. Outliving all of the other authors of the Balfour Declaration, Smuts consistently used biblical arguments for his support for Zionism for the rest of his life.

The Jewish Anti-Zionism of Edwin Montagu

One of the most ironic aspects of the Balfour Declaration was the reaction of Edwin Montagu. As the only Jew in the Cabinet, he was the only Cabinet member to oppose the Declaration in the final vote. He opposed Zionism in general and the Balfour Declaration in particular. In Cabinet, he had earlier objected to the formation of a Jewish Regiment since it would "force a nationality upon people who had nothing in common."[97] He was uncompromising in his opposition to the Zionist movement. Montagu declared, "I would willingly disenfranchise every Zionist. I would be almost tempted to proscribe the Zionist Organization as illegal and against the national interest."[98]

The broader picture was that Edwin Montagu's views were common among many well-established British Jews. They believed a Jewish National Home in Palestine would become an international Jewish ghetto, the repository of all the expelled Jews of the world. Friedman commented on the differences of opinion between the Jewish politicians Samuel and Montagu concerning Zionism, "At stake was the question whether recognition of Jews as a nation would impair their civic status in their countries of domicile."[99]

Jewish anti-Zionism was strong in Britain even before the time of the Balfour Declaration. In 1909, in opposition to the concept of a Jewish National Home, 25 Jewish students at Oxford and Cambridge Universities staged a protest against what they called "Zionist activities."[100] In May 1917, the Conjoint Committee of

British Jewry published an anti-Zionist open letter in the London *Times*. Part of the letter read,

> The Conjoint Foreign Committee of the Board of Deputies of British Jews and the Anglo-Jewish Association deem it necessary to place on record the views they hold on this important matter...The Committee strongly and earnestly protests the idea that a political centre and an always available homeland in Palestine are necessary...Emancipated Jews in this country regard themselves primarily as a religious community...the establishment of a Jewish nationality in Palestine founded on this theory of Jewish homelessness, must have the effect throughout the world of stamping the Jews as strangers in their native lands, and of undermining their hard-won position as citizens and nationals of those lands. [101]

In his work, "English Zionists and British Jews," Stuart Cohen observed that Jews at this time who were against Zionism sometimes referred to it as "Political Zionism," as opposed to the idea of Jewishness being a religion.[102] Cohen gave credit to Weizmann's determined leadership in eventually overcoming much of this Jewish anti-Zionist sentiment. Cohen wrote, "Weizmann's leadership was ambitious and purposeful...The Zionists were by and large an overtly ambitious group of men. However glaring their faults, they must be credited with having seized the communal initiative."[103] In the month following the Balfour Declaration, the London Bureau of the World Zionist Organization celebrated the Balfour Declaration, issuing what they called the "Zionist Manifesto." Part of the Manifesto read, "To the Jewish People: The second of November, 1917 is an important milestone on the road to our national future."[104]

Despite the leadership and success of men like Weizmann, Jewish opposition to Zionism did not fade easily. Even three years after the Declaration, Israel Zangwill, writing in the *Jewish Chronicle* in 1920, complained of the "Mirage of the Jewish State." He wrote that the Jews "blew the Shofar in Jerusalem as if the Messiah had come, but not really restoring Israel." Zangwill recognized that Balfour "honestly meant to restore Palestine to the Jews," and recognized that Lloyd George and Balfour were "motivated like Cromwell in 1656 when he readmitted the Jews back into Britain."[105]

In anticipation of leaving for India, Edwin Montagu challenged the Cabinet with a dilemma. According to Lloyd George, Montagu asked the Cabinet, "...how would he negotiate with the people of India on behalf of His Majesty's government if the world had just been told that His Majesty's government regarded his National Home as being in Turkish territory?"[106]

In mid October 1917, Edwin Montagu departed to fulfill his obligations as Secretary for India. Before leaving, he protested the Declaration one more time. "The Jews are not a nation. A National Home would turn them into aliens and expose them to expulsion, while Palestine would become the 'world's ghetto.'"[107] He then circulated a memorandum with a statement from Rabbi Adler, written in 1878, as the most authentic religious definition of Jewish identity.[108] Montagu was sincere in his concerns and passionate in his delivery, but he failed to sway the Cabinet.

According to Weizmann, Montagu was a representative for a Jewish anti-Zionist cause whose efforts were "...responsible for the compromise formula which the Cabinet submitted to us a few days later." Weizmann claimed Montagu pressured the Cabinet to modify the phrase, "Palestine should be reconstituted as the National Home of the Jewish people" into the diluted final form, "the establishment in Palestine of a National Home for the Jewish people."[109] The Peel Commission of 1937 also arrived at the conclusion that the wording of the Balfour Declaration was a compromise between the Cabinet Ministers.

> We have been permitted to examine the records which bear upon the question and it is clear to us that the words "the establishment in Palestine of a National Home" were the outcome of a compromise between those Ministers who contemplated the ultimate establishment of a Jewish State and those who did not.[110]

Weizmann called Montagu, "One of our bitterest opponents," complaining, "The rich and powerful Jews were for the most part against us."[111] At the time of the Declaration, the Jewish opposition to Zionism perplexed some British Evangelical Christians. Leo Amery, a Christian Zionist, believed a National Home for the Jews would serve the interests of Jews in England. He wrote to Edward Carson, "I do not think myself that the position of the English Jew would be prejudiced by Zionism-on the contrary, once there is a National Home for the Jewish persecuted minority, the English Jews will not have anything to trouble about."[112] In the end, Edwin Montagu left for India with his views clearly articulated for the Cabinet's consideration. The Cabinet then proceeded to approve the Balfour Declaration in spite of his protests.

The Christian Conviction of Arthur Balfour

Arthur Balfour was also raised from his youth with a knowledge of the Bible. His mother, an Evangelical Presbyterian played a key role in imparting this teaching to him. She prayed regularly for her children to follow the faith, even writing a personal prayer for her children. "Give me grace to trust my children-with peace that passeth all understanding-to Thy love and care...and especially that I may guide with the love and wisdom which are from above the religious education of my children."[113]

As a young boy, Balfour did not attend school, but rather was tutored at home by the family Pastor. Balfour's niece, Blanch Dugdale, commented, "Long before he ever heard of Zionism, Balfour, steeped in the Bible from childhood, had felt a particular interest in the 'people of the Book'...it was a lifelong interest that originated in the Old Testament training of his mother and in his Scottish upbringing."[114] Blanche Dugdale is a credible commentator on Balfour, being his niece and his official biographer. Regarding Balfour's interest in the Jewish people, she wrote, "He always talked eagerly on this and I remembered in childhood imbibing from him the idea that Christian religion and civilization owes to Judaism an immeasurable debt, shamefully ill repaid."[115]

Arthur Balfour was perhaps the most committed Christian in the Cabinet. Even as a busy politician, he made the time to speak on Christian themes and write books on theology. In 1895, he wrote a theology book entitled "The Foundations of Belief," which was partly a compilation of theology lectures he had delivered at Cambridge University in 1893. This publication followed a similar book Balfour published in 1893 entitled "A Defense of Philosophical Doubt."

Balfour's interest in the restoration of Israel went beyond political necessity. In April 1915, he unilaterally declared his support for Zionist aspirations when he traveled to America in his capacity as Foreign Minister. It was during this visit that he simply declared to Supreme Court Judge Louis Brandeis, "I am a Zionist."[116] Balfour was comfortable relating his support of Zionism to his biblical beliefs, stating only a few months after the Declaration was published, "Both the Prime Minister and myself have been influenced by a desire to give the Jews their rightful place in the world; a great nation without a home is not right."[117] One of Balfour's biographers, Max Egremont, observed,

> For Balfour, diplomatic opportunism and personal idealism came together in the declaration. In Weizmann, he met an inspirational articulator of a message which took him back to the stern Old Testament tenants of his mother's Low Church faith and the Presbyterianism of the Scottish Lowlands.[118]

Balfour's sympathy for Zionism is well documented in the years following the Great War. In 1920, he spoke to the English Zionist Federation at Royal Albert Hall. Balfour told the crowd, "For long I have been a convinced Zionist."[119] In a private conversation recorded by Blanche Dugdale in 1926, Balfour told his niece, "As you know, I have always been a Zionist, long before the War."[120] Beyond this, Balfour believed the case for a Jewish restoration in Palestine more significant than the Arab claims to the land. In 1917, Balfour wrote to Lloyd George, "Zionism is more important than the desires and prejudices of the 700,000 Arab who now inhabit it."[121]

After the Great War, Balfour did not abandon his interest in Zionism. Rather, he valued for the rest of his life what he had done for the Jewish people. His accomplishments in life were manifold.

He served as Prime Minister, received honourary doctorates, authored books and addressed foreign governments. Yet, despite all this, the accomplishment he valued most in his life was the Balfour Declaration. When he was near death in 1930, Balfour stated to his family that he viewed his work for the return of the Jews to Palestine as, "possibly the most worthwhile thing he had ever set his hand to do."[122]

Despite the high opinion Dugdale ascribes to Balfour's Zionism, she wanted to make it clear he was not alone in his views. She believed the sentiments of the Declaration enjoyed wide support within the Cabinet. "It is very important not to overestimate the influence Balfour had on the Balfour Declaration. It was the result of a decision after very careful consideration by the whole British Cabinet, for which the whole British Cabinet shared responsibility."[123]

While it is true that the whole Cabinet shared the responsibility for the Declaration, the cool, intelligent thoughtfulness of Balfour gave it the credibility that it needed. Like his friend Lloyd George, Balfour desired to see the Declaration issued. He had a quiet respectful nature, and was not inclined to push his views on others. There is no evidence that he tried to convince any of the other Cabinet men of the merits of Zionism. Friedman commented on the character of Balfour,

Balfour was a convinced Zionist, and required no further education on its merits. However, whatever his personal inclination, it does not seem that he ever attempted to impose his views on his subordinates when they differed markedly from his own.[124]

As the Foreign Minister and a former Conservative Prime Minister, Balfour was the oldest and one of the most influential members of the Cabinet. He was probably appointed by Lloyd George to add weight and credibility to the Coalition government. Doreen Ingrams added, "By 1916, Balfour had become an intellectual ornament to virtually any possible government."[125] Nevertheless, Balfour had strong biblical motives for advocating a public statement on Zionism. Tuchman commented,

> In Balfour the motive was biblical rather than imperial... Though he was the reverse of Shaftesbury, not ardent but

a skeptic, not a religious enthusiast but a philosophical pessimist, he was nevertheless strongly infused, like the Evangelicals and the Puritans, with the Hebraism of the Bible.[126]

Even in his death, Balfour's values were shown. He ordered for his tombstone the lofty spiritual claim of the apostle Paul, "I have fought a good fight, I have finished my course."[127] The lasting effect that Balfour's beliefs had on his family can be noted. Arthur Lytton, 3rd Earl of Balfour, (Arthur Balfour's nephew), supported Youth Aliyah.[128] In 1939, Lytton offered Whittingehame, the Balfour family estate, as a training school for Jewish refugee children from Germany. In addition, Balfour's niece Blanche Dugdale volunteered for many years in the political department of the Jewish Agency in London.[129] Dugdale explained her dedication. "Zionism is a very deep thing. But if I have to sum it up briefly, I would say that the ideal of Zionism is to restore self respect to the Jewish people, and thus to bring back the Jewish nation into the respect of the other peoples of the world."[130]

The case for Balfour's commitment to the Bible and a return of the Jews to Palestine is strong. He believed in, and was dedicated to both. He was a man of high birth and wealth who felt no need to promote himself or impress others. It seems clear that Balfour put his influence behind the Balfour Declaration largely because of his personal beliefs. Tuchman claimed, "Mr. Balfour left no memoirs and made no claims, but it was not an accident of office that the Declaration bears his name."[131]

The Labour Participation of Henderson and Barnes

Arthur Henderson was a prominent member of the Labour Party. After being converted at age 16 to a personal Christian faith by the evangelist Gipsy Smith[132], Henderson later became a lay preacher, having his own Methodist Church at Barnard Castle.[133] John Grigg, in his biography of Lloyd George, commented that Henderson was a Methodist, "grounded in Wesleyan lay preaching."[134] Henderson and another Scot, Keir Hardie, were two of the leading Labour Party leaders in Britain during the Great War. Both men identified personally with Evangelicalism. According to Colin Ford in his work "A Hundred Years Ago: Britain in the 1800's," Keir Hardie relinquished his atheism in 1879 and joined the Evangelical Union, at the same time that Arthur Henderson was converted.[135]

In Henry Pelling's work about the history of the British Labour Party, he claimed that one of the traditional values of the Labour Party was the "support of religious Nonconformity."[136] Even though he left the Cabinet before the Balfour Declaration was published, Henderson supported the ideal of Zionism.[137] In August 1917, Arthur Henderson resigned from the Cabinet and turned his seat over to his colleague George Barnes as the Labour Party representative in the Coalition government. In August 1917, both Barnes and Henderson contributed to an official Labour Party memorandum which strongly endorsed Zionism. It stated in part,

The British Labour Movement demands for all Jews in all countries the same elementary rights of tolerance, freedom of residence and trade, and equal citizenship that ought to be extended to all inhabitants of every nation. It further expresses the opinion that Palestine should be set free from the harsh and oppressive government of the Turk, in order that this country may form a free State under international guarantee, to which such of the Jewish people as desire to do so may return and may work out their own salvation, free from interference by those of alien race or religion.[138]

Although the international influence of the British Labour Party was still small at this point in history, this memorandum is a remarkable document. Declarations of approval from Barnes and Henderson for Zionism are scarce, but their high level of participation in this memorandum makes a strong statement. The wording of the memorandum was so positive to Zionism that it caught the attention of Chaim Weizmann. Reinharz noted, "According to Simon Marks, who saw Weizmann daily in the bureau, Weizmann felt frustrated that his own diplomacy had failed to win a similar declaration from the government."[139] It is true that wording of this Labour Party statement is in some ways stronger than the Balfour Declaration itself, calling for a "Free State...to which...the Jewish people may return."[140]

Regarding George Barne's views on Zionism, there is additional evidence to be found in a personal letter from Weizmann to Judge Brandeis in October 1917 claiming Barnes as one of the men who "advocated our cause very strongly."[141] In his autobiography, published in 1923, Barnes stated that he intended to give the Jews "only a right of asylum and citizenship in the country which to them had a peculiar interest as a cradle of their race."[142]

Every indication is that George Barnes offered his support for the Balfour Declaration from the beginning of the matter. It should be considered that both Henderson and Barnes were working class men propelled into the Cabinet because of the war. They were in the government as representatives of the Labour Party so that the working people of Britain would have a voice in the wartime Coalition government. It seems that neither Henderson nor Barnes knew a great deal about foreign policy. Most of the other men around the table were educated and had achieved status in society. It was therefore appropriate that in light of their social status and backgrounds, that these two Labour Party representatives in the Cabinet would play the role of quiet approving partners to the Declaration.

The Supportive Role of Edward Carson

Edward Carson was an Irish lawyer who grew up in an observant Presbyterian Ulster family. In his adult life, he was a Protestant religious symbol, famous for his successful role in the 1895 prosecution of Oscar Wilde for homosexuality. During the Cabinet debates of 1917, Carson put his support behind the Declaration. Perhaps this may have had something to do with the personal relationship of trust between Carson and Balfour. In his official biography of Carson, Edward Marjoribanks claimed a close trusting relationship between Balfour and Carson.[143]

As a Protestant Christian political leader, Edward Carson was also seen as a spiritual leader to the Protestants of Ulster. Part of Carson's work for Ulster was in keeping it free from the influence of the Catholics to the south. As a lawyer, Carson was ruthless in the pursuit of justice. Perhaps his zeal was influenced by his personal religious righteousness. As a young man growing up in

Belfast, Harold Arkell joined thousands of others at the funeral of Edward Carson in 1935. Sixty years later, Arkell recalled how Ulster Protestants upheld Carson as a spiritual example of a godly Christian man.[144] There is no evidence of Carson speaking against the Balfour Declaration. However, he was known to be capable of expressing a contrary opinion if he chose to. In his memoirs, Lloyd George commented about the difficulties working with Carson,

> Even as a member of the Cabinet he had the fatal defect ingrained by centuries of habit in all men of his race-he was naturally opposed to every government. Whether in or out of office, he was always "agin (sic) the government for the time being."[145]

Since Carson had been First Lord of the Admiralty from December 1916 to July 1917, it is likely that he would have been aware of Weizmann's contribution to the war. Nevertheless, Carson remained silent on the matter. Stein was able to find only a shred of evidence regarding his view of Zionism, "Nothing is known about his views on Zionism, except that, in response to the British Palestine Committee's appeal for support in the winter of 1916, he had...expressed 'general sympathy.'"[146]

Perhaps the question of Carson's silence may have a simple answer. He was in the Cabinet to represent Ulster. He was a tight-lipped criminal lawyer who rarely spoke unless he had to. He once declared, "It is only for Ireland that I'm in politics."[147] It seems clear from Carson's character that if he had been opposed to the Balfour Declaration for any reason, he would have said so. Carson was known for opposing Lloyd George on other matters. It is more than interesting that he remained silent about the Balfour Declaration. In the case of Carson, silence probably meant consent.

The Quiet Backing of Bonar Law

Other members of the 1917 Cabinet are less well known, but still their support was essential. Andrew Bonar Law was raised in the home of a Presbyterian Minister in New Brunswick, Canada. After moving to Britain, he became a politician and briefly served as

Prime Minister. Bonar Law was a man who tended to say little and write even less. Even though he was the son of a Minister, nothing is documented about what he had to say about his personal faith. Bonar Law was long involved in the Ulster Protestant movement against Catholicism, but this was largely a political issue.

It seems it was his nature not to express his religious feelings. His personality has been summarized as "A somber, middle-class, teetotal, Scotch-Canadian businessman."[148] Bonar Law was a man who did not seek the political spotlight. In December 1916, when asked by the King to form a government, Bonar Law recommended instead David Lloyd George, who assumed office the next day.[149]

Little has been found as to Bonar Laws views on Zionism. Leonard Stein admits, "Bonar Law's views on the Zionist question are unknown."[150] Bonar Law's son, Lord Coleraine, told Stein that he was unable to find any evidence as to his father's attitude toward the Balfour Declaration. In addition, Robert Blake, Bonar Law's biographer admitted that his search "elicited no information on the subject."[151] Only two main issues occupy Bonar Law's diary in the fall of 1917. One was the "trouble" over letting Churchill into the government, and the other was the trench fighting on the Western Front.[152]

Despite the lack of information, it is still possible to determine something of the position and role of Bonar Law regarding the Balfour Declaration. After meeting with Chaim Weizmann in 1917, newspaper editor C. P. Scott wrote in his journal, "Weizmann hopeful as to government declaration of Zionist policy in relation to Palestine. Bonar Law the difficulty-not hostile but pleading for delay."[153] This would be consistent with Blake's opinion of Bonar Law's character, that he had "instinctive skepticism and caution."[154] On December 14 1917, when Lord Rothschild and other Jewish Zionists met the Cabinet to thank them for the Balfour Declaration, Bonar Law received the Jewish committee. However, according to Stein, "His polite acknowledgment tells us nothing about his personal opinions on the subject."[155]

There is no evidence that Bonar Law participated in the debate surrounding the Declaration. He was hardly a passive man void of opinions, but rather he was a wise and careful administrator.

Bonar Law probably regarded the debate as a diversion from more important issues, but went along with the rest of the Cabinet. His biographer writes regarding the nature of Bonar Law compared to his peers, "Bonar Law was a far 'safer' man from a Party point of view than any of them."[156] In 1922, he became Prime Minister, but fell ill and died in 1923 without leaving any memoirs behind.

The Manifold Motivations of David Lloyd George

Martin Gilbert believed David Lloyd George was the main figure behind the Balfour Declaration.[157] There is good reason to say this. Lloyd George's origins differed from most Victorian politicians. His father died when he was only three, and his mother then gave him up to an uncle who served as a lay Pastor. Lloyd George was thus raised with simple Bible teaching imparted to him by his uncle Richard Lloyd, a Welsh Baptist Pastor with a strong Puritan influence. A family member observed, "Richard Lloyd, the master shoemaker, had inherited from his father David the position of unpaid Pastor and preacher in the Campbellite sect of the Baptists known as the Disciples of Christ."[158]

In the late Victorian period, most of the people of Wales were followers of the Nonconformist tradition. The simple rote-memory teaching of Bible content to small children was one of the highest values of society. This was true in the case of young Lloyd George. Chaim Weizmann observed about Welsh society, "Welsh children learned long chapters of the Bible by heart and usually knew the geography of Palestine before they knew their own."[159] Weizmann recalled the Bible knowledge of the Prime Minister, noting that Lloyd George confessed the place names in Palestine were "more familiar to me than those of the Western Front."[160] A descendant of Lloyd George commented on his uniqueness.

> Lloyd George was not, like Asquith or the other members of the Cabinet, educated at a public school on Greek and Latin classics; he was brought up on the Bible...Unlike his colleagues, he was aware that there were age-old tendencies in British Evangelical and Nonconformist thought that

favoured the return of the Jews to Zion, and a line of Christian Zionists which stretched back to the Puritans.[161]

Lloyd George's interest in Zionism predated his meetings with Chaim Weizmann. Early in his political career, the Jewish community took note of him as a rising politician who supported Zionism. In 1905, when he entered the newly formed Liberal Cabinet, the *Jewish Chronicle* reported, "As becomes the doughty Welsh Nationalist, Mr. George is an ardent believer in the Zionist Movement."[162] Verete commented about the personal Zionism of Lloyd George,

Lloyd George had genuine sympathy for the Zionist cause. He wished the Jews to return to their Palestine. He came from those fundamental Protestants who not only regarded themselves as the true Christians and felt hostile to the Catholics, but held to the belief that the return of Israel was "nigh at hand" and that England was destined to help them.[163]

Of all the men in the Cabinet, Lloyd George probably possessed the best knowledge of the Scriptures. Lloyd George backed the Balfour Declaration from the beginning. For him it was the fulfillment of a long-held dream. More than anyone else, he pushed and fought for such a statement. His idealism and passion were essential in order to see the Balfour Declaration issued. Friedman believed his role behind the Balfour Declaration was more significant than that of Balfour. "The lead in shaping Middle East policy was given by Lloyd George, and his responsibility for the Declaration was greater."[164]

Looking back over the decades since the Great War, it is still somewhat difficult to understand why it was important to Lloyd George to conquer Palestine and help the Jewish people re-establish their ancient nation. Fromkin believed that even some of Lloyd George's contemporaries underestimated the strength of his convictions. Fromkin observed, "He wanted to encourage the development of a Jewish homeland in Palestine. His colleagues failed to understand how strongly he held these views."[165] In a speech to the Jewish Historical Society of England in 1925, Lloyd George told the audience that the Hebrew history of the Bible was the basis of Welsh education.

> On five days a week in the day school, and on Sunday in our Sunday schools, we were thoroughly versed in the history of the Hebrews. We used to recite great passages from the prophets and the Psalms. We were thoroughly imbued with the history of your race in the days of its greatest glory, when it founded that great literature which will echo to the very last days of this old world, influencing, moulding, fashioning human character, inspiring and sustaining human motive, for not only Jews, but Gentiles as well.[166]

Twenty years after the Cabinet decision of 1917, Lloyd George continued to defend his Zionism. He told the 1937 Peel Commission that the stopping of Jewish immigration to Palestine would be a "fraud." He took the same firm stand against the White Paper of 1939.[167]

However, as already noted, confusion arose when Lloyd George published his memoirs in 1936 where he claimed that the Balfour Declaration had been a reward to Chaim Weizmann on behalf of the Jewish people. Lloyd George was the only Cabinet member to make such a claim. If it were true, it would certainly have been a key issue in the Cabinet debates of 1917 and Balfour would have had something to say about this "reward." As well, the other Cabinet members would surely have commented on this matter and Weizmann would certainly have mentioned it.

This revelation by Lloyd George in 1936 of a Jewish reward was never substantiated or documented by anyone else. However, it is important to note that this was not the first time Lloyd George made this claim. He verbalized the story in 1925 in his speech to the Jewish Historical Society of England.

> I felt a deep gratitude, and so did all the Allies, to the brilliant scientific genius of Dr. Weizmann. When we talked with him and asked him, "What can we do for you in the way of any honour?" he replied, "All I care for is an opportunity to do something for my people."...So the case was put before us, and when the War Cabinet began to consider the case for the Declaration, it was quite unanimously in favour.[168]

It seems that Lloyd George's claim in 1925 escaped wide public notice, partly because he was speaking to a sympathetic Jewish group and partly because the speech was not widely published. However, the question still remains as to why would Lloyd George make such an unsubstantiated claim. To answer this question, it is necessary to note something of the man's character. Despite his Bible-based upbringing, it was apparent he did not consistently implement the moral values he was taught. The life of Lloyd George does not match the moral code of the Welch chapel. To illustrate, he was known to be long unfaithful to his wife, having a mistress throughout his political career.

Besides this, Lloyd George was not known for being a fully honest man. His inclination to misrepresent the truth manifested itself several times in his public life. One example of this was a stock market scandal in 1913 that nearly ended his political career and severely damaged his reputation for integrity.[169] Another example occurred in the spring of 1918 when Lloyd George was caught misrepresenting troop strengths in the House of Commons.[170] Even though he was a man of high ideals, it was consistent with his character to offend the truth if it served his immediate needs.

Furthermore, such a claim reflects the complex character of the man himself. Lloyd George became known in his later years as a man who could survive scandal, but could not really be trusted. As he grew older, he became looser with his opinions. Once, at a dinner party with Winston Churchill and others in 1936, he stated, "Success in politics depends upon whether you can control your conscience."[171]

Regarding Lloyd George's memoir statements, Koestler wrote, "If one reads Lloyd George's evidence carefully, one is led to suspect that he deliberately overstates the opportunistic motivations of the Balfour Declaration-as if trying to cover up the romantic impulses behind it."[172] Tuchman commented on this matter in the only personal footnote of her book "Bible and Sword."

> Lloyd George's afterthoughts on the motivation of the War Cabinet in issuing the Balfour Declaration have bewitched and bewildered all subsequent accounts of this episode.

Unquestionably, he doctored the picture. Why he did so is a matter of opinion. My own feeling is that he knew that his own motivation, as well as Balfour's, was in large part a sentimental (that is, a biblical) one, but he could not admit it.[173]

It may be the case that, late in life, Lloyd George was embarrassed by his earlier biblical faith. Perhaps he wanted to persuade people that he had more rational motives for his actions in 1917. To add to this, by the 1930's, the Mandate was going badly for Britain. Perhaps Lloyd George wanted to assure the British people that they had entered Palestine in 1917 with the wisest of intentions. Tuchman speculated that when Lloyd George wrote his memoirs he could not admit that he used his Old Testament nostalgia as a motive for plunging Britain into such a "painful, expensive, and seemingly insoluble problem as the Mandate of Palestine."[174]

Despite this new revelation late in life, it is still clear that Lloyd George entered into his 1917 commitment to the Balfour Declaration with a mix of motives, but was primarily motivated by a Christian commitment to the restoration of Israel.

The Uniqueness of a Non-English Cabinet

A paradox accompanied Lloyd George's Cabinet of 1917. Even though these men led the government of Great Britain, only Curzon and Montagu were English. The other eight were born and raised outside of England. Lloyd George was from Wales. Balfour, Henderson and Barnes were from Scotland. Carson was from Northern Ireland. Bonar Law was from Canada. Milner was from Germany and Smuts was from South Africa. This outside factor contributed to the dissenting mentality of the men, for it was in the outlying regions of Wales, Scotland, and Northern Ireland that the influence of Nonconformity was the strongest.

Furthermore, even though the Established Church of England was, and remains, the Anglican Church, none of the members of the Cabinet in 1917 were High Anglicans. Lloyd George was a Baptist. Balfour, Bonar Law and Carson were Presbyterians. Henderson was a Methodist. Curzon was a low Anglican and Smuts was Christian Reform. Although Barnes did not have a strong personal religious affiliation, he was the head of the Labour Party at a time when Nonconformity was promoted as one of the Party's values. Milner was apparently nonaffiliated and Montagu was Jewish. The Cabinet was therefore free from the influence of high Anglican doctrine which tended to Replacement Theology and opposition to Zionism.

The Final Decision of the Cabinet

The Cabinet discussion of the declaration intensified in October. On October 4, the Cabinet decided to consult President Wilson and also some Anglo-Jewish leaders who held opposing views.[175] It was at this time that the Cabinet became concerned that Germany might also be considering issuing a statement in favour of Zionism.[176] Finally, on October 17, the Cabinet decided there was no need for further delay.[177] Balfour himself added another reason for action. He pointed out the need to rally Jewish influence to counteract German propaganda in Russia.[178]

The Cabinet meeting of October 31 was decisive. Arthur Balfour opened the meeting by summarizing the intense debate on the matter. A final draft of the text was presented. According to Balfour's biographer Blanche Dugdale, "Balfour made it quite clear that he wanted to issue a statement endorsing Zionist aims."[179] The Cabinet minutes of Balfour's full statement are worthy of note,

> The Secretary of State for Foreign Affairs stated that he gathered that everyone was now agreed that, from a purely diplomatic and political point of view, it was desirable that some declaration favourable to the aspirations of the Jewish nationalists should now be made. The vast majority of the Jews in Russia and America, as indeed, all over the world, now appeared to be favourable to Zionism. He gathered that the main arguments still put forward against Zionism were twofold: (a) That Palestine was inadequate to form a home for either the Jewish or any other people. (b) The difficulty felt with regard to the future position of Jews in Western countries. With regard to the first, he understood that there were considerable differences of opinion among experts regarding the possibility of the settlement of any large

population in Palestine, but he was informed that, if Palestine were scientifically developed, a very much larger population could be sustained than had existed during the period of Turkish misrule. As to the meaning of the words "National Home," to which the Zionists attached so much importance, he understood it to mean some form of British, American or other protectorate, under which full facilities would be given to the Jews to work out their own salvation and to build up, by means of education, agriculture and industry, a real centre of national life and culture and focus of national life. It did not necessarily involve the early establishment of an independent Jewish State, which was a matter for gradual development in accordance with the ordinary laws of political evolution. With regard to the second point, he felt that, so far from Zionism hindering the process of assimilation in Western countries, the truer parallel was to be found in the position of an Englishman who leaves his country to establish a permanent home in the United States, whereas, in the present position of Jewry, the assimilation was often felt to be incomplete, and any danger of a double alliance or non national outlook would be eliminated.[180]

When the Cabinet finally made the decision, the matter was settled by the simple fact that the majority wanted it.[181] To summarize, three men were most enthusiastic in their support for the Declaration, five others gave their approval, and one opposed it. Lloyd George, Balfour and Smuts were the ones strongly behind the Declaration. These three defended the Declaration for the rest of their lives. As late as 1929, Arthur Balfour, Lloyd George and Jan Smuts together sent an open letter to the London *Times* declaring their ongoing support for Zionism.[182]

The other members of the Cabinet who gave their approval were Bonar Law, Carson, Barnes, Milner and Curzon.[183] The first three were in favour of the Declaration, but had little to say about the matter. Their religious backgrounds could have made them, if not sympathetic to the Zionist camp, at least not opposed to it in principle. Milner greatly favoured the Declaration, but being apparently non-religious, he made it clear that he did so because he believed the Declaration would be good for the Empire.[184]

Verete's comments on these Cabinet discussions are noteworthy. He believed the intentions of the Cabinet to be exclusively political, claiming that the Cabinet's last discussion of October 31 conveyed the impression of mere formality.[185]

> Nothing was said at the meetings about the justice of the Zionist cause as such, or the rights of the Jews, as that of any other nation, to have a National Home of their own. There was of course, no mention of the intention to diddle France out of Palestine. Of such matters, the English are not in the habit of speaking openly, especially in public.[186]

Although Verete is correct regarding the issue of France, he missed the idealistic tone of Balfour's comments.

Conclusion

Political explanations alone fail to explain the motivation behind the Balfour Declaration. They do not sufficiently account for the influence of certain religious beliefs maintained by a number of the Cabinet members at this time. It is apparent there were a number of factors that motivated the Cabinet of 1917 to issue the Balfour Declaration. Having examined these factors, and the men who made the decision, it is evident that the various political factors were less strong individually than the motive of sympathy for Zionism.

The Balfour Declaration was not a sudden random act of a desperate government. It was a carefully considered statement that reflected the personal faith of several of the Cabinet members who commissioned it. A practical political consideration was that the Declaration was decided on October 31, the same day Allenby launched his attack on Beer Sheva, opening the way into Palestine. The question can be asked whether the political motives alone would have sufficed to bring about the Declaration. Being hypothetical, the question cannot be answered definitively, but a negative response would seem appropriate. In any case, the evidence indicates a strong religious motivation within the Cabinet.

Barbara Tuchman, in a humorous way, attempted to explain the complexities of analyzing the roles of the various men. She acknowledges the difficulties of arriving at a definitive conclusion as to where the credit should go.

> According to whose memoirs one reads, one can come away with the impression that Lloyd George was finally responsible; or, no, that Sir Herbert Samuel really persuaded the Cabinet; or, wait a moment, that of course Dr. Weizmann pulled all the wires behind the scenes.[187]

Although a mix of reasons motivated the Balfour Declaration, the Cabinet took advantage of the political circumstances they found themselves in to publish a declaration that reflected the personal religious convictions of several leading members. They realized that they were in a position of power to shape world history. Charles Townshend, in his article, "Going to the Wall," acknowledged the challenge the British had set out for themselves. "In Palestine, the British set out to create something unique in the modern international system."[188]

Although religious belief was a significant motivation behind the Balfour Declaration, career politicians like Balfour and Lloyd George could not openly make decisions for the Empire based on their personal sentiments alone. The decisions they made had to make political sense both to themselves, and to the public. Blanche Dugdale commented, "The Balfour Declaration was the first constructive step toward a solution of the Jewish problem on a national basis, but it was not made under the pressure of pity or without proper consideration.[189]

The political influence that existed between British Evangelicals and Jewish Zionists lasted for a brief moment in history. Both groups had agreed on a common goal; the restoration of the Jews to Palestine. Ten years after the Declaration, in November 1927, Balfour made a speech to the Anglo-Palestine Club at the Hotel Cecil in London. He spoke about the efforts of the Jewish settlers in Palestine, and gave the Balfour Declaration a high place not only in Jewish history, but also in world history.

If those efforts meet with all the degree of success which the Zionists hope for, 1917 will indeed be a date, a blessed date, not merely in the history of Palestine, not merely in the history of Jewry, but, as I think and believe most firmly, in the history of the world itself.[190]

The Balfour Declaration was a unique, positive gesture from the British Cabinet to World Jewry. Even though it was a political statement, it was given in a spirit of biblical belief. It illustrated co-operation between Evangelicals and Jews. The Balfour Declaration could not have been completely a Jewish enterprise because the Jewish community lacked the necessary unity, military power, and world support. It could not be completely a Gentile enterprise, because one group of people could not impose a selected destiny upon another people. Truly, it had to be a partnership, as Balfour said, "We are partners in this great enterprise."[191]

In the minds of writers of the Balfour Declaration, there were political factors motivating them, but for many of them, it was either partially or primarily a religious decision. The complexities of the political situation at hand gave this unique group of men the opportunity to carry out what they perceived to be a great historic accomplishment. Of the ten men in the Cabinet in November 1917, seven were Evangelicals.[192] Three were raised in the homes of Evangelical Ministers[193] and one was an ordained Methodist Minister.[194] No High Anglicans sat in Cabinet, and the only vote against the Balfour Declaration was made by Edwin Montague, a Jew. These men were in the position to do something unprecedented to help the Jewish people, a people that according to their biblically conditioned views constituted God's Chosen People.

Having established the role of Christian Zionism in the publishing of the Balfour Declaration, this book will now proceed to determine the role of Christian Zionism in the establishment of the British Mandate in Palestine.

Chapter Two

The Place of Christian Zionism in the Establishment of the Mandate 1918-1928

Introduction

This chapter will demonstrate that following the Balfour Declaration and the British conquest of Palestine in 1917, Christian Zionists in Britain attempted to influence events in Palestine according to their religious ideology. This chapter will survey the years 1918 to 1928, the time period in which the Mandate was established, until the beginning of the Arab riots in late 1928.

So strong was their commitment to Zionism that Gentile Evangelicals took more interest in assisting the Jews than in assisting the indigenous Christian communities of the Middle East. Following the ratification of the Balfour Declaration by the League of Nations in 1922, these Christian Zionists continued to press for the restoration of Israel. The lofty hope of a "National Home for the Jewish people" would prove difficult to define, and even more difficult to implement. Through the 1920's, with their political influence diminishing, British Christian Zionists looked to various Palestine High Commissioners and low level politicians such as Josiah Wedgewood to support their cause. During the decade, new stirrings of American Christian Zionism were beginning, which would eventually prove to be more influential than their British counterparts were.

Following the conquest, Palestine needed to be governed. Soon British bureaucrats, military men and clergy were settling into their new life in Palestine. Many sent for their families to join them. Some Christian Zionists such as Wyndham Deedes, because of their love for the land of the Bible, requested political postings in Palestine. In Jerusalem especially, the British established their own society. It was fashionable for bureaucrats and officers to move their families into the stately stone homes of the German Colony in west Jerusalem.[1]

As British civilians arrived in Palestine to engage in various enterprises, some brought with them a high level of enthusiasm. Many were raised on Bible teaching in Britain and were thrilled to live in the land where the Bible was written. Susanna Emery, a recently arrived English schoolteacher, wrote to her mother about Jerusalem, "My dear mother, I have been exploring the town with great energy. It is simply wonderful-colours run riot everywhere-it is like a vast kaleidoscope of fairyland and everywhere else jumbled together...These streets are wonderful to watch, like everything else."[2]

The Workings of the British Government

It would be helpful at this point to review the authority structure of the British government during their years in Palestine. The decision to publish the Balfour Declaration was unique in that it was a decision made exclusively by the Cabinet. Following Allenby's military conquest, Palestine was governed by a military administration. After the Mandate was ratified by the League of Nations in 1922, Palestine was governed by a High Commissioner who reported to the Colonial Secretary at the Colonial Office in London.[3] The Colonial Secretary in London and the High Commissioner in Jerusalem were usually the most significant political authorities during the Mandate years.[4]

Throughout the years of British rule in Palestine, it was difficult for the government to establish a consistent policy. If measured from 1917 to 1948, there were 19 Colonial Secretaries over the 31 years of British rule. This represented a change of Minister every year and a half. It is therefore easy to understand how Colonial Office policy could become muddled over the decades.[5] The High Commissioners tended to stay at their post for longer periods, serving for an average of about three and a half years each. Parallel to the changes in Colonial Secretaries was an almost equally constant changeover in the Foreign Office. There were 12 Foreign Ministers during the 31 years of British rule in Palestine, with each Minister staying in office for an average of two and a half years. Ernest Bevin, the last Foreign Minister during the Mandate, served the longest at nearly three years.[6]

In each of the larger departments, such as the Colonial Office and the Foreign Office, a senior civil servant was selected to serve as the Permanent Secretary. This was the Chief Administrative Officer, subject to the direction of the Minister. Although the Permanent Secretary held an important civil servant position, he did not make, or influence policy. Some of the more prominent Permanent Secretaries for the Colonial Office during the early years of the British administration in Palestine were Sir George Fiddes (1916-1921), Sir James Masterton-Smith (1921-1925) and Sir Samuel Wilson (1925-1933).

Besides the Permanent Secretary, the Parliament Under-Secretary also assisted the Minister. The first Parliament Under-Secretaries during British rule in Palestine were Leo Amery (1919-1921), Edward Wood (1921-1922), William Ormsby-Gore (1922-1924), Lord Arnold (1924), William Ormsby Gore (1924-1929), William Lunn (1929 and Drummond Shiels (1929-1931). These men were also without official influence, and carried out the directives of the Minister. However, when men such as Amery and Ormsby-Gore later became Colonial Secretaries, they worked on behalf of the Zionist cause from within the Colonial Office.[7]

The question could be asked if the long-term policies of the government were ever changed or abandoned. This was not really the case, since the British government policy toward Palestine was never clearly or fully stated. Rather than changing policy, subsequent British governments simply altered their definition of what the National Home should look like. This happened twice in significant ways. The first time was in 1922 with the so-called Churchill White Paper and the second time was in 1939 with the MacDonald White Paper.

The Lost Issue of Christians Helping Christians

Upon the conquest of Palestine, it might have seemed natural for the British to offer political assistance to the various Christian communities of the Middle East, but this was not the case. Why was it that the British did not identify with these other Christians? In a matter of months, millions of Arab and Armenian Christians had been delivered from Turkish Muslim rule. Yet, this political reality was not an important issue in Britain. The truth was that assisting the indigenous Christian communities of the region was not a priority of the British government or the British people. Religiously and politically, the British identified more with returning Jews to Palestine than they did with assisting the indigenous Arab and Armenian Christians.

This plight of the Armenian people at this time was particularly serious. During the Great War, this community suffered greatly at the hands of the Turks. Even though the Armenians petitioned the League of Nations for a National Home of their own, the nations of the world took little interest.[8] In 1921, Winston Churchill informed the Prime Minister and the Cabinet of the terrible plight of the Christian Armenians in the Middle East, telling the Cabinet of still "14,000 Armenian refugees for whose maintenance no provision is made."[9] No political action was taken.

The explanation for this behaviour lies in the fact that both Britain and America were predominantly Protestant countries. Most western Protestants, particularly Evangelicals, simply did not see the Armenian and various Arab Christian communities as being truly "Christian." This judgment broadly applied to the Latin Church, as well as the eastern Churches: Greek Orthodox, Coptic, Armenian, Syrian Orthodox, etc. Even the Holy Sites of the traditional Churches offered little interest to British Protestants. Western Evangelical Christians tended to hold to a faith based on personal reality, putting little significance in Holy Sites, liturgy or relics.[10]

To the British, the local Roman Catholic and Eastern Christian communities were of little political or spiritual relevance. At this time, some European Catholic countries took note of this and pressed Britain to be more protective of the traditional Christian Holy Places.[11] In 1922, Arthur Balfour reported to the Cabinet that several foreign Catholic governments were petitioning the Foreign Office to be assured of the protection of the Holy Places; something the British government had not made a high priority.[12]

Following the British conquest of Palestine, the Catholic Church had other interests than merely protecting the Holy Sites. Catholic theology necessitated that they be opposed to a restoration of Israel. This doctrine was in sharp contrast to Evangelical teaching which viewed Zionism favorably. In 1922, Balfour wrote to Maurice Hankey, Secretary to the Cabinet, of the objections raised by the Vatican, which influenced a delay in having the Mandate formally approved by the League of Nations. Balfour reported that the Catholic countries of France, Poland, Spain. Italy and Brazil were reluctant to cooperate because of the Vatican. "The Vatican would seem to have redoubled its efforts to stir up opposition to the draft Mandate as it stands at present."[13]

Not seeing the Arab Christians as truly Christian, western Protestants sent their own missionaries to win these Christian Arabs to a more Evangelical Christian faith. The Foreign Office kept record of their activities and facilitated the missionaries if possible. According to the records of the period, many British Protestant missionaries were linked together in their work with Americans missionaries. This makes sense in that they were doctrinally compatible. These missionaries sought converts equally from the Muslim, Jewish, Armenian and Arab Christian communities.[14] The Foreign Office especially took notice of the persecution of new Christian converts.[15]

Two Different Christian Views of Zionism

After the British conquest of Palestine, some of the western Christians in Palestine were alarmed at the new energy of Zionism. This concern was evidenced in the leadership of St. George's Anglican Church in East Jerusalem which was a high Anglican Church mainly serving the Christian Arab community. Established in 1839, it was the local home base for what the Anglican Church called the "Jerusalem and Eastern Mission." Shortly after the British conquest, Zionism was the main theme of the Jerusalem and Eastern Mission annual meeting. Holding to Replacement Theology, the gathering was hostile to Zionism. According to Inger Okkenhaug, who was in attendance, "At the annual meeting in 1919, Bishop MacInnes defined the greatest problem for the Jerusalem bishopric as Zionism." According to MacInnes, who was Bishop of St. George's Cathedral for the first years of British rule in Jerusalem, secular Jews were returning to Palestine for nationalistic reasons, not under the guidance of the Holy Spirit. Combined with this was a fear of the reaction of the Arab population to the arrival of Jews.[16]

In contrast to the views of St. George's, the low Anglican "Christ Church" at Jaffa Gate was supportive of the idea of a restored Israel. They viewed the Balfour Declaration as a prelude to the restoration of Israel and the return of the Jews.[17] Shortly before the arrival of the Allenby, the Anglican Bishop of Jerusalem, G.F. Popham Blyth of St. George's Church made a break with the more Zionistic ministry of Christ Church. Bishop Blyth made it clear he was opposed to the proselytizing of the Jews and the support of Jews returning to Palestine.[18] At this time in Jerusalem, St. George's had greater influence and resources than the smaller Christ Church.

Since a high percentage of the British bureaucrats and officers in Palestine were raised as high Anglicans, many were predisposed to be antagonistic to Zionism. According to Bernard Wasserstein, after 1918, "There were a few who supported Zionism out of an Evangelical Protestant conviction, but the general tenor of Christian teaching about Jews in this period was a different sort...the general political and social mentality predisposed the British officials to dislike Jews."[19]

The reality was that the various British military personnel and civil administrators held to both views. Some of Allenby's officers appreciated the sentiments of the Balfour Declaration and openly said so. Richard Meinertzhagen, one of Allenby's intelligence officers during the campaign, wrote to Prime Minister Lloyd George expressing his approval for government policy, "We are very wise in allowing the Jews to establish their National Home in Palestine."[20] Meinertzhagen came from a family of active Zionists whose behaviour was not always conventional. His great grandmother, Mary Seddon, bought a white donkey in 1823 and headed from her home in England to Palestine. Her husband caught up with her in

Calais, brought her back to England where she was committed to a lunatic asylum.[21]

Although some British administrators in Palestine consistently held their views regarding Zionism, others changed their opinions. In November 1919, General Louis Jan Bols arrived in Palestine to serve as the new Chief Administrative Officer. At first an aggressive Zionist, he initially requested funds to purchase land for Jews and promote Zionism. Within five months of his arrival, Bols changed his position and demanded the end of the Zionist Commission. He believed the Jews were being too demanding.[22] On the other hand, Ronald Storrs, son of an Evangelical Minister, and destined to be Governor of Jerusalem, never wavered from his commitment to Zionism.

The Balfour Declaration promised protection of the civil and religious rights of the non-Jewish communities in Palestine. That particular clause was now beginning to emerge as a challenge to the British. Balfour was optimistic a political solution could be found in Palestine. He desired to see the establishment of a Jewish political presence in Palestine without the displacement of the local Arabs. He believed all this to be possible along with the ultimate success of Zionism. In 1919 he wrote, "The historic claim of the Jews would predominate, provided that a home can be given them without either dispossessing or oppressing the present inhabitants."[23] However, it did not take long for the pressure to begin. Six months after the Balfour Declaration was published, Lloyd George and the Foreign Office received a letter from the Zionist Commission stating that the Commission was impatient for action, fearing the British may go back on their word.[24]

Zionist Influence at the Paris Peace Talks

The Paris Peace Talks began in January 1919. In the beginning, the delegates met at the palace of Versailles outside Paris. The four leading Allied countries were Britain, France, Italy and the United States. At first, the spirit of the Conference was largely linked to the Fourteen Points proposed by President Woodrow Wilson of the United States. Wilson believed achieving a successful peace was as important as winning the war. His declaration that all nations had a right to "self determination" was exhilarating for some but frightening for others. Many small, disfranchised communities in the world took note of these words. Among these indigenous groups were the Chinese, Kurds, Armenians, Poles, Serbs and Croats. Considering this, it was remarkable the Jews received so much attention.[25] The answer can be realized in the underlying commitment to Zionism among many of the delegates.

Prime Minister Lloyd George led the British delegation throughout the three years of the Peace Talks, attending 33 conferences related to the Versailles settlement. During these years, he enjoyed popularity in Britain as "the man who won the war." Lloyd George had personally backed the Balfour Declaration in 1917 and continued to endorse it. However, he knew he was also entrusted by the British nation to bring home a suitable peace treaty and a new world order.

President Woodrow Wilson led the American delegation at the Versailles Conference. Wilson's upbringing was similar to that of Lloyd George in that he was also raised in the home of an Evangelical Minister. In Wilson's case, his father was ordained by the Presbyterian Church. Before entering politics, Wilson served as the President of Princeton University at a time when Princeton Seminary was one of the most influential Evangelical Seminaries in the United States. Prior to the Versailles Talks, Wilson had expressed to Rabbi Stephen Wise how pleased he was to "be able to help restore the Holy Land to its people."[26]

Wilson's good friend Louis Brandeis may also have influenced Wilson at this time. Brandeis was Jewish and an important supporter of the American Zionist movement. In 1916, Wilson appointed him to the Supreme Court, the first Jew nominated for this position. Both Lloyd George and Wilson came to the Versailles Conference with an instinctive religious affection for the Jewish people and a commitment to Zionism. According to Melvin Urofsky, in his work, "American Zionism from Herzl to the Holocaust," Wilson showed "overt sympathy for Zionist aspirations" at the Versailles Talks, but was hindered in that neither Edward House, Wilsons's closest advisor, nor Secretary of State Robert Lansing, wanted to entangle Zionist interests in American foreign policy.[27]

Urofsky observed, "No matter how friendly Wilson might be to Zionist hopes, a President of the United States had to take into account all considerations. At no time could Wilson be asked to give undue precedence to the dreams of Jewish nationalism."[28] Urofsky concluded, "While Wilson personally aided the cause, he failed to create a permanent policy that would sustain the Zionists."[29] At this time, the United States was clearly not ready to assume a major role in world politics, especially in the Middle East.

Prime Minister Georges Clemenceau led the French delegation at the Conferences. He was the oldest of the Allied leaders and had a reputation of being a long-time radical left wing politician. In his own way, Clemenceau also displayed philosemitism and sympathy for the Jewish people. However, his philosemitism was not derived from the same source as the Zionism of Evangelical Christianity. Rather it was based on the French republican notion of egalitarianism. Years before, he was instrumental in reversing the guilty verdict against Captain Alfred Dreyfus.[30]

As a Catholic, Clemenceau still viewed the Jews as responsible for the death of Christ. In 1919, at the Paris Peace Conference, he did not share the Zionist views of the British and Americans. At the Conference, Weizmann told Meinertzhagen of a conversation he had had with Clemenceau, recalling, "The Frenchman was sympathetic to the whole Jewish National Home concept, but told me that Christians could never forgive the Jews for crucifying Christ."[31] Despite any personal sympathy Clemenceau might have had for Jews, his Catholic thinking make it impossible for him to match the Zionist views of his Evangelical colleagues from Britain and America.

The Mandate Concept for Palestine

Mandates were a new idea to emerge from the Versailles Talks. The concept was that the strong western nations would occupy and protect the weak developing nations and ultimately reward them with political autonomy. The mandate concept reflected a new world order following the Great War. It was something less than colonization but more than mere occupation.[32] According to Margaret MacMillan in her work, "Paris 1919," the word "Mandate" was intended to be a benign term that denoted something more legitimate that unilateral land grabbing.³³ Although preparations for independence were discussed, in reality, Palestine, like other Mandate territories, was not groomed for independence. Eventually it was decided which countries would hold Mandates in the Middle East. France would have Syria and Lebanon, while Britain would have Palestine and Transjordan.

The idea of the United States assuming responsibility for some of the Mandates was discussed. However, there were a number of problems. First, the United States had not declared war on the Ottoman Empire. Second, she was inexperienced as a colonial power. Third, American missionaries in the Ottoman regions had been advocates of the Armenian community, thus alienating themselves from the Turks. In summary, the Americans, at this time, simply did not possess the qualifications to carry out such a responsibility.

The official Treaty of Versailles was signed on June 28 1919, exactly five years to the day after the Great War began. Although this officially ended the war, much discussion remained. Final decisions about Mandates were left for later.³⁴ The League of Nations would not officially approve the British Mandate for Palestine and Trans-Jordan until 1922. Until then, the Balfour Declaration was only a statement of British policy.

George Curzon became Foreign Secretary in the autumn of 1919. Never a Zionist, he was determined to dilute the draft Mandate to give his position more authority and Weizmann's less.³⁵ Curzon claimed as his reason, "I can see Weizmann coming to me every other day and saying that he has a *right* to do this, that or the other in Palestine! I won't have it!"³⁶ In March 1920, when Curzon read a new draft Mandate from the Zionist Organization, he wrote his response. "The Zionists are after a Jewish State with the Arabs as hewers of wood and drawers of water...I want the Arabs to have a chance and I don't want a Hebrew State."³⁷ In the end, according to John McTague in his article "Zionist-British Negotiations over the Draft Mandate for Palestine, 1920," McTague argued that Curzon succeeded in "watering down" the 1919 draft, which would have given the Zionist Organization more concrete guarantees for freedom of action.³⁸

The Arab Response to Zionism

At the highest diplomatic levels during these years, relations between the Zionists and the Arabs seemed cordial. At the Versailles talks, Chaim Weizmann and Emir Feisal, the son of the Sherif of Mecca and ally of the British, signed a special goodwill agreement regarding Palestine. The agreement stated that Jewish immigration would be encouraged. There appeared to be an understanding that Feisal would receive a Kingdom for himself.[39] It seems that, at the time of the Versailles Conference, the Arabs had an idea they would be given independence over a vast Arab Kingdom stretching from Iraq to Yemen.

With this understanding in mind, Prince Feisal seemed supportive of the Jews establishing themselves in Palestine. In December 1919, he sent a letter to Herbert Samuel expressing his commitment to their "common cause."[40]

Peace Conference
Secretary of the Hedjaz Delegation
Paris, 10 Dec 1919

Dear Mr. Samuel,

I was very pleased to learn that you have used the occasion of the second anniversary commemorations of the Balfour declarations to dissolve the misunderstanding created by the publication of my interview in the Jewish Chronicle Review of last month.

I have a firm conviction that the mutual confidence established between us, and the perfect corresponding of our points of view which has created an understanding between Dr. Weisman and I, will stop similar misunderstandings and will maintain between us the necessary harmony for the success of our common cause.

Please be sure, dear Sir, of my utmost consideration.

Feisal

Feisal was not the only Arab leader to acknowledge the claims of the Jews. Even his brother Abdullah gave grudging recognition of the need for a place for the Jews in Palestine. However, Abdullah was not quick to relinquish his understanding of promises made by Sir Henry McMahon. In his memoirs, Abdullah wrote, "The language used by the British representative was vague enough to give the Arabs a case for their contention that Palestine did fall within the area where the Arabs had been promised independence."[41] During the Versailles Conference, Abdullah commented on the Balfour Declaration, approving of the Jews being given a home of their own, "...gave a third party, the Jews of Zionist leanings, an interest in Palestine."[42]

Christian Preference for the Zionist Cause

By the end of the Peace Talks, the opportunity for national self-determination was not granted to all nations seeking it. Armenian delegates also made their appeal for protection and independence at the Versailles Conference. They explained how they had been liberated from the Turks and now needed western Christian sponsorship.[43] Although they were an ancient community, the first nation to embrace Christianity, they received sympathy but no real assistance. Clearly the British and American delegates identified more with Jews and Zionism that with the Christian Armenian community.

When the Zionist Mission appeared before the Supreme Council of the Versailles Peace Talks, many Jewish delegates addressed the Council. Weizmann spoke first, followed by the Polish writer Nahum Sokolow. The Russian Jew Menachem Ussishkin spoke in Hebrew. They all emphasized the history of Jewish suffering.[44] When Chaim Weizmann was asked what he thought the term "National Home" meant, he replied that the country "would ultimately become as Jewish as England is English."[45]

Colonel Richard Meinertzhagen was in Palestine during the Versailles Peace Talks. His influence was growing as he was one of the first to predict the seriousness of the coming struggle between the Jews and Arabs in Palestine. While still serving with Allenby after the conquest of Palestine, he wrote in his diary that he believed Zionism was destined to be a world force that would "outlive its lawless cousin-Bolshevism."[46] Meinertzhagen was bold and opinionated. Even in his day, his comments were not always politically acceptable. In a memorandum to Lloyd George in 1919, he told the Prime Minister that the Peace Conference had laid two eggs: Jewish Nationalism and Arab Nationalism. He wrote that the two would grow up, "the Jew virile, brave, determined and intelligent. The Arab decadent, stupid, dishonest and producing little beyond eccentrics."[47]

British Evangelicals Begin to Lose Influence

Following the Great War, Britain began to undergo dramatic social changes. Long-established institutions lost their standing in society. The war had been prolonged and painful.[48] The high price in dead and wounded affected the religious faith of many. Church attendance declined across the country and with it, the social standing of the Churches. The loss of influence for the Evangelicals would gradually be reflected in the decline of Christian Zionism in Britain in the decades ahead.

The slow decline of Evangelical influence after the war was especially notable in Wales. Jeremy Black, in his history of Wales, noted, "The decline of the Chapel as the centre of community life in Wales was itself particularly marked in the post-1918 period, and served to alter significantly the nature of Welsh society, Wales in essence becoming a more secular society as the pull of the Chapel declined."[49] This view is supported by other scholars and is particularly noted by Earle Cairns in his work "Christianity through the Centuries." Cairns summarized this period as a time of great decline for the Evangelical Nonconformists of Britain, but he did not see the war as the only source of the problem. He identified several other factors such as Scriptural criticism and the teaching of evolution which worked together to cause a national loss of faith.

> Criticism of the Bible, Darwin's theory of evolution, and other social and intellectual forces created religious liberalism in the late 19th century. Liberal theology has been greatly devoted to the scientific method and has applied evolution to

religion as a key that might explain its development. It has insisted upon the continuity of man's religious experience to such an extent that the Christian religion has become the mere product of a religious evolution rather than a revelation from God through the Bible and Christ.[50]

The decline was sometimes hard to measure, but Steven Koss, in his work, "Nonconformity in Modern British Politics," recognized the setbacks following the Great War.

However much a commonplace, it is no exaggeration to say that war, when it came unexpectedly in August 1914, dealt a shattering blow to organized religion. The Churches never recovered from the ordeal, either in terms of communicants or self-possession. Thereafter men looked elsewhere, if anywhere, for their moral certainties. Yet one must remember that here, as in other social situations, wartime experience only hastened and intensified trends that were already underway.[51]

In 1906, 185 Members of the House of Commons identified themselves as Nonconformists. By 1922, that number had been reduced to only 78.[52] Not only did the influence of Nonconformity wane, but also the energy of the movement dissipated politically. With few exceptions, Evangelicals at the turn of the century voted for Liberal candidates, but as early as 1910, there was a steady drift of these Christians to the Labour and Conservative Parties.[53] The election of 1918 was the most devastating for the Nonconformists. Only 88 Free Churchmen were elected to Parliament, the smallest number since 1880.[54] Koss believed that in postwar electioneering, political Nonconformity proved unable to define its reason for existence and so was denied one.[55]

Herbert Samuel's interest in Zionism was growing at this time.[56] In 1919, he traveled to Paris with Weizmann to help represent the Zionists at the Peace Conference.[57] In January 1920, the Foreign Office sent Samuel on a survey trip to Palestine. His instructions were to "Report upon financial and administrative conditions there, and to advise concerning the line of policy to be followed in future in these respects, should the Mandate fall to Britain."[58] During his survey of Palestine, Samuel came to believe that Britain must be the nation to champion the cause of Zionism. He diligently made note of what he saw and included in his report,

> It is now more than ever my firm conviction not only that Palestine will prove the best means of solving as a part of the world's peace the difficult and far-ramifying Jewish problem but that it will as the Jewish National Home prove a source of strength and satisfaction to its mandatory, Great Britain, and to all that Great Britain stands for in the East.[59]

The Jewish community of Palestine had been delighted with the Balfour Declaration and expected Jewish autonomy someday. This ambition stressed the relationship between the British government and the Zionists. Wasserstein noted, "Samuel saw it as his role to prevent the deteriorating relations between British officials and Jews in Palestine from upsetting the diplomatic negotiations in London and Paris."[60] Samuel wrote to Curzon to explain why some Arabs opposed the Declaration,

> The hostility against Zionism, which is so manifest six months ago, is due to various causes. First to ignorance of Zionist aims and methods. The Arabs were repeatedly told that the Jews were coming in masses into the country in order to despoil them of their land and property. Naturally, they became enemies of the Jews.

Samuel explained that the second reason was economic. Under the Turks, the privileged Arabs controlled "large numbers of fellaheen whom they bled white." The third reason for hostility, according to Samuel, was the "presence in Palestine of numerous agents of great European powers who try to influence the population…considerable and somewhat dangerous propaganda are the Italians-the Vatican." [61] In the same letter, Samuel admitted to Curzon that he was "not being unbiased." Regarding immigration, "The gates cannot be kept closed forever, and the sooner the regulated immigration is allowed, the easier it will be for the Zionist organization to allay the growing impatience of the masses and to control the flow of immigration in the future."[62]

At this time, Weizmann became close to Norman Bentwich, the Jewish Attorney General for Palestine and a Zionist, and his wife Helen. It surprised some that Weizmann's wife cared little for either Palestine or Zionism, allowing her husband to carry the banner of Zionism alone in his family. This was perhaps why he befriended eager young Christian Zionists like Orde Wingate and Ronald Storrs throughout his life. After a dinner party with the Bentwich family, Helen Bentwich, a critical observer, wrote, "The Weizmann's dined here... She doesn't like Palestine, either, and rather thinks the same about Zionism & living here as I do...I don't envy his job!"[63]

The Beginning of Violent Arab Opposition to Zionism

In March 1920, the Jews and Arabs of Galilee clashed violently. Since only a few Jews lived in this northern region, Ze'ev Jabotinsky was in favour of abandoning the area while David Ben Gurion advocated staying. The skirmish occurred at Tel Hai where about eight were killed. Despite the small scale of the incident, it was the first violent engagement between Jews and Arabs for land. This was a taste of what was to come. It would eventually become clear that the issue of territorial ownership in Palestine would not be determined by debate, but by force.[64]

The first large scale violent incident of the British Administration in Palestine occurred in early 1920. April 4 1920 was Nebi Musa, a festival for Moses celebrated by Christian Arabs. Muslims also came up to Jerusalem for the holiday, swelling the crowd that year to an estimated 50,000 or 60,000. Riots broke out for three days, which included destruction of property and violent attacks. The British had not understood the depth of Muslim resentment toward the Jews. By the time the riots were over, five Jews were dead and 216 wounded. Four Arabs were also killed and 23 wounded. Seven soldiers and police were wounded.[65]

After the attacks of Nebi Musa, the Jews began to train themselves in self-defense. Ze'ev Jabotinsky took leadership in this area, no longer believing the Jews would be safe from the Muslims by relying on British protection. The British arrested Jabotinsky and sentenced him to six years in prison. Richard Meinertzhagen intervened on behalf of Jabotinsky, succeeding in getting the six-year sentence reduced to six weeks plus a 12-month deportation order.[66]

The British conducted an inquiry into the causes of the Nebi Musa riots, finding Governor Storrs overconfident in his ability to control the people. It was also determined that British security forces were not sufficiently prepared and that the Jews were the main victims of the violence. The British were beginning to experience the complex challenges of a western power entering the Middle East to "help." Regardless of their true intentions and desire to objective, both the Jews and Arabs saw the British as a "Christian" power reentering the region. The British were to learn that the Middle East was a region of the world where religion and political power sometimes were perceived to merge into one imperial intention.

The Appointment of a Jewish Zionist as High Commissioner

In April 1920, on his way from Palestine, Herbert Samuel stopped in Italy to join the San Remo Conference where Lloyd George, Balfour, and Curzon headed the British delegation. The League of Nations was being formed, and would soon officially give the British the Mandate of Palestine, giving approval for the British to implement the Balfour Declaration. Samuel's stopover in Italy proved beneficial to his career. Perhaps Lloyd George and Curzon appreciated Samuel's recent report on Palestine. In any case, it was during the San Remo Conference that Lloyd George asked Herbert Samuel to become the first High Commissioner of Palestine's new civil administration.

It is probable that Lloyd George saw in Samuel a Zionism that was similar to his own. Moreover, it would have suited the Christian Zionist ideals of Lloyd George to appoint a Jew as the first High Commissioner of Palestine. It seems that Lloyd George was not overly concerned about the potential problems that might arise from appointing a Jew and a Zionist to be in charge of a territory that had a Muslim majority. It is also probable that Lloyd George purposefully made the decision in order to fulfill his personal desire to see a restored Israel. As a Christian committed to the restoration of Israel, it would make sense to appoint a Jew as High Commissioner in Palestine. As early as 1914, when Lloyd George was a Cabinet Minister, he had spoken privately to Herbert Samuel about the possibility of a Jewish administration in Palestine, telling Samuel that he "was very keen to see a Jewish State established there."[67]

Samuel immediately accepted the position. He was optimistic about the possibilities, writing the Prime Minister from the Royal Hotel in San Remo, "I am quite clear that if the government decided to invite me to fill that post, it is my duty to accept it." Samuel speculated to the Prime Minister how he believed the Arabs in Palestine could be won over.

> The objection which I mentioned to you, that measures which the majority of the population would accept from a non-Jew would be resented if they came from a Jew, could, I believe, be overcome. In the long run, their attitude would depend upon the reasonableness of the measures themselves and upon the manner in which they were presented.[68]

Samuel believed a Jewish High Commissioner of Palestine would have advantages. As part of his letter to the Prime Minister, he wrote,

> And there is an advantage on the other side. The fulfillment of the Zionist program must, from the nature of the case, be gradual and very considerate for the interests of the Arabs and Christians. Jews in Palestine and throughout the world would be more likely to practice patience, without losing enthusiasm, if the pace were set by an Administrator who was known to be in full sympathy with the ultimate aim.[69]

Upon parting company at San Remo, Lloyd George told Samuel, "You have got your start. It all depends on you."[70] Samuel did indeed have his start, although international authorization of the Mandate from the League of Nations would not be finalized until

1922. However, the problems in Palestine were already growing. Weizmann was also present at the San Remo Conference and was troubled by news of the riots against the Jews of Jerusalem, which preceded the San Remo Conference by two weeks. Allenby himself was being criticized by Colonel Richard Meinertzhagen who wrote to Lloyd George suggesting Allenby was not keeping to the spirit of the Balfour Declaration.[71]

Opposition to a Jewish High Commissioner

Allenby immediately opposed the appointment of Herbert Samuel as the first High Commissioner. For him, it was a major political problem that Samuel was Jewish. He wrote Foreign Secretary Curzon that the choice of Samuel was dangerous. Curzon took Allenby's warning seriously, but in the end, Allenby's objections did not prevent Samuel's appointment. In May 1920, Samuel was in London to meet with Curzon at the Foreign Office. According to Samuel's memoirs, Curzon explained Allenby's concerns, "The appointment of any Jew as the first Governor in Palestine would be likely to be the signal for an outbreak of serious disorder, with widespread attacks upon Jewish settlements and individual Jews, and perhaps raids from across the border."[72] The military administration in Jerusalem, through General Thwaites, also sent the Prime Minister a telegram protesting the appointment.

> Appointment of a Jew Chief Administrator…will precipitate crisis in Palestine which everyone is anxious to avoid at (great) cost of lives of British soldiers. Zionist Commission must be dissolved. Jewish Administration has been formed by Commission (into a) department (on parallel lines to) OETA and is functioning in spite of Chief Administrator. The position is impossible and dangerous and must not continue.[73]

Lloyd George responded by writing Allenby, asking him to "Kindly consider manner in which military should be replaced by civil administration…Effect upon natives population is an important factor in this consideration."[74] A week later, Allenby responded to the Prime Minister that he was still opposed to Herbert Samuel's appointment. "As regards effect on native population, I think that appointment of a Jew as first Governor will be highly dangerous." Allenby warned that the "indigenous Christian population...will also deeply resent transfer of government to Jewish Authority, and will throw their weight against Administration."[75]

In the end, Lloyd George decided Samuel would have the job. He would take over the administration of Palestine on July 1 1920. In London, Samuel met the King to be knighted and then departed for Palestine for a four-year term, with perhaps a fifth year if needed. Christian Zionist Ronald Storrs, Governor in Jerusalem, felt optimistic about the arrival of Samuel. He wrote to his family, "I doubt not that he will make of Palestine what it has never yet been in its calmest days, a radiating centre of prosperity and good sense. The work is trying but never dull, and I like it."[76]

In a way, it is astonishing that a Jewish High Commissioner should be appointed immediately following three days of Arab rioting. It must have seemed that Lloyd George and the British government were either stubborn, foolish or simply naïve. However, the fact was that the decision predated the events of April 1920, and the British were not easily intimidated. Certainly, it could be said that Samuel was well qualified for the position of High Commissioner. He had been the first member of the British Jewish community to sit in a British Cabinet and he had recently been involved at various stages of Zionist development; the Balfour Declaration, the Versailles Peace Conference, the Jewish Legion and negotiations over the nature of the Palestine Mandate.[77] Upon his arrival, Samuel stressed that there would be equal justice for all religions and persons, that taxation would be equitable, and that corruption would be suppressed.[78]

Christian Zionist Support in Britain

A few days after Samuel's arrival in Palestine, Arthur Balfour addressed the English Zionist Federation at Albert Hall in London. Five years after the Declaration that bore his name, Balfour was consistently promoting the restoration of Israel. In his speech, he linked the fortunes of the British Empire to those of the Jewish people. Balfour not only referred to a political tie, but to a deeper spiritual bond. He dreamed of a day when the concept of a Jewish National Home in Palestine would become a living reality. He wanted British Christian Zionists to play a role in fulfilling that dream. The foundational concept of his speech was, "We are partners together in this great enterprise." Balfour told his Jewish audience,

> If we fail you, you cannot succeed. If you fail us, you cannot succeed. But I feel assured that we shall not fail you and that you will not fail us; and if I am right, as I am sure I am, in this prophecy of hope and confidence, then surely we may look forward with a happy gaze to a future in which Palestine will indeed, in the fullest measure and degree of success, be made a home for the Jewish people.[79]

The Jewish community in Palestine appreciated the support of British Zionists. The Grand Rabbi Jacob Meir of Jerusalem wrote to Lord Curzon at the Foreign Office on October 16 of that year, "From the first elected assembly of Palestine Jews, convened in Jerusalem, We feel certain that, under Great Britain's experienced guidance, the children of Israel will return to their boundaries and country will develop for benefit of all its inhabitants."[80]

At this time, Nonconformist Christians were still an influential force in British politics, with Zionism as one of their highest values. Evangelical Churches and organizations communicated regularly with their followers, publishing a vast array of periodicals, including the *Methodist Weekly,* the *Baptist Times* and *Freeman and the British Congregationalist.* Besides such topics as biblical interpretation, godly living and world evangelism, these periodicals explained and promoted Christian Zionism. Koss called it "An efflorescence of literary monthly and quarterlies, theological reviews, children's and professional magazines and newsletters published at irregular intervals by individual chapels, leagues and committees.[81] Ben Gurion believed the British really wanted to assist the Jews. He once spent a week observing the British House of Commons and observed that he, "might as well have been at the Zionist Congress, the speakers had been so sympathetic to Zionism."[82]

Despite these displays of strength, the Evangelical movement was weakening, although many in the movement could not perceive the loss. Koss commented, "Belatedly, Nonconformists crossed the threshold into the new world of 20th century politics; some of them mistook it for the Promised Land."[83] It was clear that, to an extent, Lloyd George had made use of the Nonconformists for his own political purposes. For their part, Nonconformists had also linked their political fortunes to Lloyd George's Liberal Party. Koss noted that Lloyd George knew firsthand the theological and social tensions that prevailed within the Evangelical camp. "To an extraordinary extent, the political history of post-Victorian Nonconformity was linked, inexorably and avowedly, to the fortunes of this single and singular individual."[84]

Sometimes an outsider can articulate better what really happened. Edwin Montagu, a Jew, said of his own Liberal Party, "Ours is a Nonconformist Party, with Nonconformist susceptibilities and Nonconformist prejudices."[85] Koss recognized how Lloyd George exploited the support of Evangelicals. "Lloyd George assiduously enlisted Free Church dignitaries as confederates."[86] It was therefore inevitable that the decline in the fortunes of Lloyd George coincided with a loss of influence for both the Liberal Party and the Evangelical Nonconformists.

The Zionism of Weizmann and Samuel

In Palestine, Weizmann recognized the need to proceed slowly in the creation of a Jewish National Home. However, Samuel's vision of progress was even slower. Samuel foresaw gradual Jewish immigration, eventual Jewish rule, and perhaps someday, in the distant future, a Jewish State. He struggled to know how to proceed with his new civil administration. He had no predecessor to learn from and often others did not know how to relate to Samuel as a person or to the newly created office of High Commissioner. Weizmann initially showed Samuel a certain level of honour due to him, but he simply had difficulty respecting Samuel.

In the early years of his administration, Samuel worked hard to try to define his idea of Zionism, "By Zionist movement I mean the movement to re-populate as much as possible of the country with Jews, to revive the Hebrew language and Jewish institutions, to emphasize the intellectual and spiritual sides of life not less than the economic."[87] Initially, the Jews of Palestine were not equipped to assist the arrival of large numbers of Jews to Palestine. Upon his arrival, Samuel offered the Zionist Commission 16,500 new immigration permits. The Zionist Commission accepted only 1000. The Zionist Commission even sent a letter to its branches around the world telling Jews the time was not ready to immigrate to Palestine. Weizmann apologized to the Jews of Palestine for the timidity of the Commission. The Zionist Commission blamed the American Jews for not donating enough money to facilitate immigration.[88] At this time, Jewish immigration was anticipated primarily from Eastern Europe. Sephardic and Oriental Jews from the Arab countries were not expected.

It seems that, at first, Samuel conceived of an independent Jewish country in Palestine even while he was High Commissioner. In his memoirs, written in 1945, he calls his chapter dealing with his years as High Commissioner in Palestine, "Palestine: A State in the Building: 1920-1925." This is noteworthy, considering how few in 1945, let alone 1920, would use the word "State" for Palestine.[89]

In the early 1920's, Ruth Jordan was a young Jewish girl living in Haifa. She would later become an Israeli writer. As a girl, she held a high view of why the British were in Palestine because of what she had heard of the Zionism of Arthur Balfour. She wrote, "Now I learned that Balfour was a great Englishman (sic) who had been inspired from God to try to save the Jews all over the world from persecution and the exile of disgrace."[90] Jordan entered into her memoirs,

> I thought of Balfour as one of the thirty-six righteous men whom God plants among mankind at any given time and imagined him standing on a raised wooden platform in a large amphitheater, unrolling the declaration in full view and reading it out to thousands of cheering Englishmen who, as everyone knew, were brought up on the Bible and therefore aware of God's promise to Abraham.[91]

At this time, Lord Milner wrote an encouraging letter to Samuel, "I am confident that under you Palestine will make great progress and be the most successful of all our Mandates."[92] Later in the year, Milner visited Palestine as a guest of the High Commissioner. Samuel wrote, "At Jerusalem they spent some happy days sightseeing with Ronald Storrs as guide. Milner, who had been interested in Zionism since 1903, had warmly supported the implications of the Balfour Declaration, and was its draftsman and co-author."[93] In this revealing statement, Samuel credited Milner with being the "draftsman" of the Balfour Declaration. Although Milner certainly approved of the Declaration, there is also the possibility that he may have scripted it as well.

The Effect of Winston Churchill as Colonial Secretary

Early in 1921, Winston Churchill was appointed Colonial Secretary. At this time, various global political issues faced the British government. Turkey was in turmoil and Russia was engulfed in a civil war. These problems persisted until 1922.[94] Nevertheless, Churchill was keenly interested in the Middle East, particularly Palestine. He wrote to Herbert Samuel,

> I hope to take over Palestine from Foreign Office in about ten days...It is common talk in government circles how extraordinary well you have coped with the many difficulties of your problem and I need not say what pleasure it will give me to work again with you and help you to a long enduring result.[95]

According to Martin Gilbert, Lloyd George made Churchill Colonial Secretary in 1921 because he knew he could rely on Churchill's Zionism at a time when many politicians were already beginning to turn against the Balfour Declaration.[96] If this is true, it shows the determination of Lloyd George to appoint Zionists to key positions of influence where their sympathies might work for the cause.

Churchill's Zionism was deeply rooted. As a young child, his nanny and primary care giver, Elizabeth Everett, was a committed

Evangelical who had a great influence on Churchill. Growing up, Churchill witnessed his father befriend many Jewish colleagues. In 1898, when Emile Zola took up the cause of Captain Alfred Dreyfus, denouncing the French government and exposed the anti-Semitism of the French army, 24-year-old Churchill wrote his mother, "Bravo Zola, I am delighted to witness the complete debacle of this monstrous conspiracy."[97] Churchill's philosemitism was shown on other occasions as well. In 1904, while proofreading his mother's autobiography, he wrote his mother and told her to remove an anti-Semitic remark out of her book.[98] He even carried his beliefs into his marriage. While on his honeymoon, when his wife made an anti-Semitic comment, he told her to go to their room and not emerge until she had written a letter of apology to their host.[99]

As the new Colonial Secretary, Winston Churchill presided over the March 1921 Cairo Conference. During the Conference, word reached Cairo that Emir Abdullah was on his way from Arabia to Damascus, through Transjordan. T. E. Lawrence was still in the region, influencing events. Churchill desired the good will of the Arab community, particularly the favour of the Hussein family of Mecca. He quickly proposed a plan that called for Hussein to be the overall ruler of the Arabs. His three sons would then take their places in the three major centers of the region: Feisal in Damascus, Abdullah in Baghdad and Emir Zeid (the youngest son) over northern Mesopotamia.[100] If such a scheme worked, it could fulfill any obligations the British might have had toward the Arabs and the Hussein clan according to the McMahon-Hussein correspondence. This change of events cost the Zionist movement most of the land assigned to them by the Balfour Declaration and the San Remo Conference. In March 1921, following the Cairo Conference, Churchill visited Palestine. While in Jerusalem, he formally offered Emir Abdullah an Arab kingdom east of the Jordan.[101]

During his 1921 visit to Palestine, Churchill was impressed with the rebuilding of the country, indicating his favour with the ideals of Zionism. Speaking at the future site of Hebrew University, he declared, "Personally my heart is full of sympathy for Zionism. This sympathy has existed for a long time, since twelve years ago, when I was in contact with the Manchester Jews."[102]

In April 1921, while Churchill was still in Palestine, the Mufti of Jerusalem died. Samuel appointed Haj Amin al-Husseini as the new Mufti. Husseini was only 26, aggressive and bold. He was to make many problems for the British in the years ahead. His brother, father, and grandfather had all been the Mufti. Two Zionists were responsible for the appointment. Ronald Storrs recommended the appointment and Samuel implemented it. The appointment reflected local politics as the al-Husseini family expected to hold a balance of power with the Nashashibi family who held the position of Mayor of Jerusalem.

Despite the acceptability of the appointment of al-Husseini as Mufti, it was a risky move. It was a cruel twist of fate that Samuel, a British Jew, would appoint a man who would be responsible for so much unrest in the years to follow. Al-Husseini had been sentenced to ten years in prison by the British for inciting riots in 1920. He fled to Transjordan, but was later amnestied by Samuel himself, apparently in an effort to win Arab favour. In the following year, Al-Husseini was also appointed to lead the Supreme Muslim Council. Known later as the Grand Mufti, he was able to establish himself as the preeminent Arab authority figure in Palestine.

The Effects of Increased Violence

In the spring of 1921, new riots broke out in the town of Jaffa. The violence started with Arab attacks on Jews. There were beatings, killings and destruction of property. The riots spread to Petach Tikvah, Hadera, Rehovot and Kefar Saba. By the time the violence ended, 47 Jews were killed and 146 wounded. Forty-eight Arabs were also killed and 73 Arabs wounded.[103] The violence in Jaffa was far worse that the 1920 Nebi Musa riots. Some called it a pogrom while others called it a war. One of the results of the violence was that Tel Aviv grew to become less dependent on the larger community of Jaffa. Some Jews started to live in tents on the Tel Aviv beach, believing Jaffa was no longer safe. Norman Bentwich wrote of the 1921 riots,

> After the riots of 1921, Jews and Arabs became more and more separate...The Arab majority naturally wanted democratic constitution. A Parliament and Legislative Council, which

should be elected by equal franchise by Arabs and Jews. The Jews resisted the demand, fearing that the Arab majority in the Chamber would mean a check on Jewish immigration... They were prepared in 1923 to accept a part-time elected Council in which the official members and the Jews together would have a majority over elected Arabs. That was rejected by the Arab leaders and the elections were boycotted by Arabs.[104]

For the British, much of Palestine was simply impossible to control. The outlying countryside was difficult to police properly. Police Captain Reginald Moncton wrote, "The country between Ajlon and Jericho is full of thieves, in fact so much so that the police here were contemplating making a big raid on them with troops to try to mop up a few this week."[105]

In Jerusalem, the Nebi Musa celebrations of 1921 were quieter than the year before. The feeling among some was that perhaps Samuel was establishing law and order. On June 3 1921, he gave a speech from Government House in honour of the Kings birthday. In an effort to quell Arab anger, Samuel stressed the second part of the Balfour Declaration, that the establishment of the Jewish National Home would not endanger the Arabs. Samuel told the Arabs that the British government would never impose on them a policy that people had reason to think was contrary to their religious, political and economic interests.[106]

The Jews in Palestine felt betrayed. This was the first time the second clause of the Balfour Declaration was so interpreted. It seemed the Arabs were being rewarded for their violence. Wasserstein wrote, "A torrent of Zionist outrage burst forth in response to the speech, which was seen as a further concession to violence."[107] Many Jews in Palestine were displeased with Samuel, but realized he was at least a Zionist. Despite Samuel's efforts to calm Arab fears, he still advocated a Jewish home in Palestine. Writing to Churchill in December 1921, he wanted to convince Churchill of the benefits of the Mandate. In his view, the "plain duty" of the Mandate was to do what was necessary to make the Jewish National Home a reality. Samuel wrote,

It is, in my opinion, essential, in order to win the confidence and goodwill of the population of Palestine, that the Administration should be able to point to definite benefits that have followed from its establishment. It is, moreover, the plain duty of the Mandatory Power, in accordance with the Mandate, actively to promote the welfare of the present population, as well as to ensure the establishment in Palestine of the Jewish National Home.[108]

Churchill's Muted Zionism and the 1922 White Paper

The White Paper of 1922 preceded the endorsement of the Mandate by the League of Nations.[109] Although the 1922 White Paper, sometimes called the "Churchill White Paper," attempted to clarify the Balfour Declaration and open the door to Jewish immigration, it also was an attempt to pacify the local Arab population. Now the Jewish National Home would only apply to the land west of the Jordan River. The White Paper also stated that immigration would not exceed "the economic capacity of the country to absorb new arrivals." This promise appeased the Arabs somewhat and gave the British an excuse for a constant policy of immigration restrictions in the years ahead.

The attitudes and actions of Winston Churchill might seem inconsistent during this period. The question could be asked why Churchill did not behave as a committed Zionist when he became Secretary of State for the Colonies in 1921. He had expressed support for Zionism in the past, and in the years ahead, he would repeatedly stand with the cause of Zionism. In contrast to his open support of Zionism, Churchill rarely expressed sympathy with the Arab cause in Palestine. When a delegation of Arabs from Palestine traveled to London to complain to Churchill, he dealt with them in a curt manner. The delegation asked Churchill what the Balfour Declaration meant for them. Churchill would not entertain their complaints. He told the delegation, "Have a good talk with Dr. Weizmann…Try to arrange something with him for the next few years."[110]

In his work "Churchill's Promised Land, Zionism and Statecraft," Michael Makovsky attempted to explain the apparent contradictions in Churchill's actions and non-actions toward Jewish issues. One of these was Churchill's involvement in the 1922 White Paper. Makovsky's explanation has to do with Churchill's view of priorities. "Fundamental in Churchill's worldview was the belief that priorities had to be rigidly ranked. He inflexibly maintained perspective and prioritized his goals, especially when he was in government and was forced to make decisions."[111]

Churchill had responsibilities for all the British Colonies at a time when the Empire was at its zenith. At a more expedient level, he pushed for an efficient administrative system, telling the Chancellor of the Exchequer, "I am determined to save you millions."[112] In 1922, Churchill warned the government that the 8000 man garrison of Palestine would cost British taxpayers 3.3 million pounds per annum.[113] Churchill seemed determined to cut the costs of his department. This ability to prioritize goes a long way to explain his apparent occasional lack of action on behalf of Zionism.

It seemed that for Churchill, the purpose of the Cairo Conference was twofold. First, he wanted to establish territorial borders in the Middle East, and second, he desired to streamline British administration in the region. In Cairo, Hayward noted that, "Churchill succeeded in reducing the annual cost of administering the Middle East from 45 million pounds per year to 11 million."[114] He understood the political value of cost cutting. He had been Colonial Under-Secretary from 1905 to 1908. His next major Cabinet position was to be the Chancellor of the Exchequer, an office he held from 1924 to 1929.

Makovsky defended Churchill's support for Zionism as appropriate for the times, noting that, Churchill "...implemented the Balfour Declaration as Colonial Secretary in the early 1920's, which ensured continued Jewish immigration and Zionist development in Palestine. He publically championed Zionism in the 1930's, earning a reputation as one of the leading Gentile Zionists in England.[115] Makovsky saw Churchill's support for Zionism as more to do with civilization than religion. "He came to see Zionism as a cause that restored dispersed, persecuted Jews, a great ancient race whose heritage was integral to the foundation of Western civilization."[116]

Churchill did not respond well to Arab demands. In March 1921, the Executive Committee of the Haifa Congress of Palestinian Arabs sent Churchill a 35-page memorandum against Zionist activities in Palestine. Churchill replied, "You have asked me in the first place to repudiate the Balfour Declaration and to veto immigration of Jews into Palestine. It is not in my power to do so nor, if it were in my power, would it be my wish."[117] He did not view Islam favourably. As a young man, Churchill wrote, "Mohammedanism is a militant and proselytizing faith...and if it were not that Christianity is sheltered in the strong arms of science...the civilization of Europe might fall."[118]

In contrast to his negative view of Islam, Churchill believed in the good of Zionism. Responding to a memorandum from the Jewish delegation in Palestine, Churchill told them, "I am myself perfectly convinced that the cause of Zionism is one which carries with it much that is good for the whole world, and not only for the Jewish people, but that it will also bring with it prosperity and contentment and advancement to the Arab population of this country."[119]

Martin Gilbert, best known as the official biographer of Churchill, believed the 1922 White Paper to be positive for Zionism. "Serving as the basis of the British Mandate, the White Paper was emphatic in its support for Zionism."[120] Gilbert even credited the 1922 White Paper for fulfilling the Balfour Declaration. "With Churchill's active and persistent support, the establishment of a Jewish National Home in Palestine had become a reality."[121]

Testifying 15 years later at the 1937 Peel Commission, Churchill defended his Zionist motives in 1922. "We were trying to bring in as many as we possibly can in accordance with the original Balfour Declaration."[122] Churchill went on to tell the Peel Commission, "We were always aiming at the fact that, if enough Jews come, eventually it may be a great Palestinian State, in which the large majority of the inhabitants would be Jews"[123] James de Rothschild believed in the Churchill's good intentions for Zionism through the 1922 White Paper, "You then laid the foundations of the Jewish State by separating Abdullah's Kingdom from the rest of Palestine. Without this much opposed prophetic foresight, there would not have been an Israel today."[124]

Still, Weizmann and the Zionist Commission were not completely pleased. Even though only a handful of Jews resided east of the

Jordan River, it had been part of the Zionists dream that the east side of the river would also become part of the Jewish Homeland. Weizmann told Churchill that the lands east of the Jordan River were, "an integral and vital part of Palestine." However, it was to no avail. The decision for division was made and Weizmann and the Zionist Executive complied.[125]

When Richard Meinertzhagen, a fervent Christian Zionist, now employed as a military advisor to the Middle East Department, heard the east bank of the Jordan was severed from Palestine, he was in a rage. He accused the Colonial Office of "dishonouring the Balfour Declaration and sabotaging H.M.G.'s official policy."[126] Decades later, Meinertzhagen wrote an article for the Tel Aviv newspaper *Ha Aretz*. Part of his 1967 article read,

> The question is linked up with the severance of Transjordan from Palestine. Both Lloyd George and Balfour told me that in giving the Jews their National Home in Palestine they meant the whole of biblical Palestine, that is to say the whole of the country occupied by the Jewish tribes, including Moab and Ammon. But Churchill encouraged by Lawrence, gave the whole of Transjordan to that miserable Abdullah, thus depriving Israel of a vital territory and allowing a complete encirclement of Israel by Arabs.[127]

Weizmann did not dwell long on the loss of Transjordan. He believed the Jewish National Home could still be established in the remaining land west of the Jordan River.[128] In 1922, he said, "If only we go on working and working in Palestine, the time will come when there will be another opportunity of giving the Mandate its true value."[129]

Samuel's Responsibility for the White Paper

The question could be asked whether Samuel's influence was behind the 1922 White Paper. If so, it could have been related to the unexpected violence which began in 1921.[130] The British authorities reacted badly and in the end over 100 died with hundreds more injured.[131] According to Evyator Friesel, who researched the 1922

White Paper, Samuel did a "soul searching reassessment of his ideas regarding Zionism, the character of the Jewish National Home, and the conditions for collaboration between Jews and Arabs in Palestine."[132]

Before the 1921 riots, Samuel had been clear-minded in his Zionism. In January 1920, he wrote, "The Zionist idea is so much a part of my being that it naturally must influence my judgment."[133] In 1920, Samuel believed in a Jewish State in 50 years. He wrote to his sister-in-law Lucy Franklin, "In 50 years there may be a Jewish majority in the population, then the government will be predominantly Jewish, and in the generation after that there may be what might properly be called a Jewish country with a Jewish State."[134] However, after the riots of 1921, Friesel observed that Samuel now sought a more balanced perspective about the two cultures in Palestine. Friesel noted that now Samuel "…indicated his continual reflections on the balance between Jews and Arabs in Palestine."[135]

On June 3 1921, Samuel made a public political statement, approved by the Colonial Office, announcing changes in the policy of the Mandate.[136] In his statement, Samuel explained that Jews would find their home in Palestine "within the limits that are fixed by the numbers and interests of the present population."[137] Samuel was now advocating limited Jewish immigration. His new concept was the principal of the 'dual obligation' of the British toward the Arabs as well as toward the Jews.[138]

Friesel suggested that Samuel's Jewishness might have played a part in his change of mind. "Although Samuel never referred to his Jewishness as a handicap, he had experienced enough problems to be sensitive about it…He was certainly aware that many of the officials in his administration had a negative attitude to Zionist hopes in Palestine.[139] Even though Samuel was an important Zionist, he was never a formal member of the Zionist Organization. According to Friesel, although Samuel's relationship with Weizmann and other Zionist representatives were cordial, there was a certain distance between them. Samuel needed to realize his place. He was sometimes privy to government information that he could not share with Weizmann and his colleagues. He was "member of the Anglo-Jewish upper class, an important figure in the Liberal Party.[140]

Friesel believed Samuel had been living between his Britishness, his Jewishness and his Zionist sympathies without being forced to choose between them.[141] He needed to make decisions that would show where he stood, Samuel chose to identify with his Britishness first, and his Jewishness second. Both set limitations to his Zionism.[142]

Following the Arab violence of 1921, Samuel seemed to conclude that open Jewish immigration would not be wise. He wrote to the Colonial Office, "But it must be definitely recognized that the conditions of Palestine are such as not to permit anything in the nature of a mass immigration."[143] Samuel sent Churchill a letter proposing that Jewish immigration be limited by the "economic capacity" of Palestine to absorb newcomers.[144] This phrase made it into the text of the White Paper, seemingly derived from Samuel's letter to Churchill. Samuel was distressed by the unexpected Arab reaction to the Jewish presence. His calls for fairness may have pressured London and influenced an adjustment in policy, influencing the 1922 White Paper. This influence resulted in Samuel being, in a sense, the initiator of the 1922 White Paper.

Growth of American Evangelical Christianity

During the Great War, and into the 1920's, the Evangelical Christian movement in the United States grew rapidly. In 1918, the combined national membership of the three largest Evangelical denominations in the United States (Southern Baptist, Methodist and Presbyterian) was 10,461,000. This was an increase of 3,594,000 people in 18 years.[145] This is even more remarkable in that while the Catholic Church counted everyone present as members, including babies, most Protestant groups only counted baptized adults who made personal commitments to a local congregation.[146]

Despite challenges of the 1920's such as liberal theology, biblical criticism and evolution, most Evangelical denominations grew.[147] Sydney Ahlstrom, in his work, "A Religious History of the American People," noted that in the 1920's, for Protestants, "Never had the Churches been better attended, never had so many members been busily involved in the country's life and work."[148] In

1926, with a total population of approximately 114 million people, the United States had an estimated 54,576,000 Church members meeting in 232,154 congregations, representing about 47 percent of the national population. This indicates an overall national growth in Church membership of 2.2 percent in 10 years.[149]

From 1920 to 1929, the combined membership of the three largest Evangelical denominations in the United States (Southern Baptist, Methodist and Presbyterian) grew from 10,897,000 to 12,619,000, an increase for the decade of approximately 14 percent.[150] These three denominations are examples of the many related Evangelical denominations who did not keep such records or who refused to publish them.

During this decade, various American Evangelical Churches sent representatives to live in Palestine and establish a denominational presence there. This movement was consistent with the sharp interest in the Bible and the land of Israel as taught in the Churches. In 1920, representatives from the Church of the Nazarene arrived from the United States and established orphanages.[151] In 1926, the General Council of the Assemblies of God of the United States, a Pentecostal denomination, sent their first personnel to live in Palestine.[152] The Southern Baptists first entered Palestine in 1911 with permission of the Ottoman government, but a significant increase in personnel arrived in Jerusalem in 1923 and in Haifa in 1929.[153]

Increasing Christian Zionism in American Politics

In the United States at this time, a significant political breakthrough for Zionism took place. In 1921, the United States Congress passed several resolutions in favour of a Jewish National Home in Palestine. This was in contrast to the isolationist policy typical of the post Great War American attitude. The Americans were watching the Mandate begin, and Christian Zionists in America were seeking a political expression in the world. In 1921 United States President Warren Harding, a Baptist, declared, "It is impossible for one who has studied the services of the Hebrew people to avoid the faith that they will one day be restored to their historic National Home."[154]

In early 1922, Arthur Balfour addressed the Zionist Organization of America in Washington. He told the group that he still believed in what he had done for the Jewish people when he signed the Balfour Declaration in 1917. "You must do your work here. Great Britain is doing her work in Palestine; the two must cooperate...my desire to see the ideal of a Jewish home really rising in happy success before our eyes has not diminished."[155] Further developments favouring Zionism were taking place in the United States that year. On June 30, the 67th Congress of the United States unanimously passed Joint Resolution 322, already passed by the Senate, approving the Balfour Declaration. President Harding signed the Resolution on September 21 1922.[156] According to Lawrence Davidson, during the 1920's, the Zionist ideal became "firmly associated in the American mind with the Jewish National Home."[157]

In 1923, Calvin Coolidge became President of the United States. Coolidge remained in power until 1929, and through his years in the White House, showed consistent support for Zionism. For example, in 1924, Coolidge urged his government to sign a treaty with Britain recognizing her Mandate in Palestine. He identified himself with the Evangelical Christian community in America by joining the Congregational Church the year he became President. During his tenure, President Coolidge helped establish the Anglo-American Convention between the United States and Britain. This Convention assisted the establishing of the Rockefeller Museum in Jerusalem, the building of the YMCA in Jerusalem and safeguarded the activities of American missionaries in Palestine.[158] Coolidge, as an Evangelical Christian, personally supported Zionism. In 1924, he declared that he aligned himself "with the deep and intense longing which finds such fine expression in the Jewish National Homeland in Palestine."[159]

Political Change in London

In 1922, Lord Curzon expressed pessimism about the Mandate. He told Balfour, "Personally, I am so convinced that Palestine will be a rankling thorn in the flesh of whoever is charged with its Mandate that I would withdraw from this responsibility while we yet can."[160] Political and military reports repeatedly surfaced in

Britain related to "why" they were in Palestine. Several of the same ideas repeatedly came forward: to defend the Suez Canal, to protect Arabia and to guard the route to India. None of these reasons stood up well militarily or politically.

Still, in the early 1920's, British society in general seemed to view Zionism with favour. In 1921, Prime Minister Lloyd George continued to promote Zionism, suggesting to Balfour, "You ought to make a big speech again in the Albert Hall on Zionism."[161] In its 1922 edition, Encyclopedia Britannica included both Samuel and Churchill in its article about Zionism.

> There was every sign up to the end of 1921 that the government intended to proceed in full accord with the spirit and the letter of the Balfour Declaration. Mr. Winston Churchill, the Secretary of State for the Colonies, during his visit to Palestine in April 1921, emphatically declared that the Zionist policy of the government remained unchanged, while assuring the Arabs with equal emphasis that their rights would be fully respected. The first High Commissioner, Sir Herbert Samuel, had won the confidence of all sections of the population by his impartiality.[162]

In late 1922, significant political changes took place in London. Lloyd George was forced from office and was replaced as Prime Minister by Andrew Bonar Law.[163] Bonar Law was a Conservative, born in Canada and one of the authors of the Balfour Declaration. Like Lloyd George, he was raised in the home of an Evangelical Pastor. He looked with favour upon Zionism, and was widely considered a man of impeccable integrity. Lord Beaverbrook said of Bonar Law, "I have known one honest politician, Bonar Law. He was without guile."[164]

At the end of 1922, there was still reason for the Zionists to hope that the Jewish National Home in Palestine would eventually become a reality. Chaim Weizmann was influential, Churchill was still in charge of the Colonial office and Bonar Law was the new Prime Minister. On the other side, the ideal of Zionism was beginning to lose some of its popularity in Britain. Some even credited a pro-

Zionist position with contributing to the demise of the Lloyd George government in 1922. In the House of Lords, Lord Islington declared, "Zionist policy in Palestine contributed its share and no small share, I think to the downfall of the late Administration." Lord Islington went further to suggest that the Zionist policy of the government should be reconsidered. He believed the governmental downfall "would constitute a strong ground for early consideration of the whole policy."[165] In 1923, Colonial Secretary Lord Cavendish accused the 1917 Cabinet of attempting to win the favour of world Jewry. "The object of the Balfour Declaration was to enlist the sympathies on the Allied side of influential Jews and Jewish organizations all over the world."[166]

Other politicians shared this view. Lord Sydenham wrote to Churchill charging that the Zionists put pressure on the government to induce it to issue the Balfour Declaration, and that the administration in Palestine was effectively a Jewish one. Lord Sydenham rejected Churchill's contention that because Sydenham supported the establishment of a Jewish National Home in the past, he should not criticize the current efforts to bring it about.[167] Some considered how Britain might find a practical way to drop the burden of the Palestine Mandate. Herbert Sidebotham, Manchester Guardian's military correspondent and a Zionist, commented on the dilemma and the burden of the responsibilities. "It would have been easy for us to make no promises...but having raised those hopes, we must fulfill them to the best of our ability."[168]

In 1923, Philip Graves published a number of articles in the London *Times* voicing his opinion of the Mandate. He gave several clear reasons outside of Zionist ideals for remaining in Palestine. If Britain left, another power (Turkey or France), could invade. In addition, being there enhanced Britain's prestige, and gave Britain the support of Jews in Britain and America. In addition, supporting Zionism kept many Jews from embracing communism. There was also the issue of keeping promises. Despite these rational arguments, it was becoming evident that Britain was certainly not profiting in tangible ways from the Mandate of Palestine. In 1923, the British government further reduced the size of the potential Jewish National

Home when it ceded the Golan Heights to the French, who had a Mandate to rule Syria.[169]

Evangelical Christian Influence in British Politics

Even though Nonconformists had long constituted a minority in modern Britain, at times they influenced politics out of proportion to their numbers. This was especially true during the Victorian period and at the beginning of the 20th century. This concept can be seen by noting the religious affiliation of the ten Prime Ministers during the first half of the 20th. These were men born and educated during the middle to late Victorian period. The first eight Prime Ministers were raised as Nonconformist, while only the last two were raised in the Church of England.[170]

Despite the influence of Nonconformity on British politics of this period, the movement was in decline. In 1923, the Conservative *Morning Post* featured an article "The Nonconformist Conscience: A Fading Phenomenon."[171] That same year, three Church denominations needed to amalgamate in order to ensure their survival: the Primitive Methodists, the Wesleyans and the United Methodists. Anglican membership dropped by seven percent between 1925 and 1935. The Presbyterian Church of England reported 87,000 members in 1911, but only 84,000 in 1922.[172]

Despite their reduced numbers and influence, some Christian Zionists actively promoted their beliefs throughout the Mandate period. Wyndham Deedes is an example of this, first serving as an intelligence officer in Palestine. As an Evangelical Christian committed to the restoration of Israel, the Zionist Organization took notice of him. In April 1923, the Central Office of the Zionist Organization sent Deedes a letter of official appreciation. "You have firmly established yourself in affectionate regard of Zionists throughout the world, who are well aware how much your wise council and unfailing sympathy have contributed, in these early and difficult days, to the upbuilding of the Jewish National Home."[173]

Other Jewish organizations recognized Deedes for his Zionist beliefs. In 1923 he received a letter from the Keren Hayesod Fund, (The Eretz Israel Palestine Foundation Fund) that said in part, "I am instructed by the Board of Directors of the Keren Hayesod to express to you their warmest thanks for your generous advocacy and support of the work in Palestine."[174] Three decades later when the Jews had their own State, the Israelis named a street in Jerusalem after him.[175] Throughout 1924, Deedes took direct action to promote Zionism. He traveled to many countries in Europe, including Poland and Greece, to promote the cause. In his lectures, he encouraged the Jewish people of Europe to immigrate to Palestine.

The Loss of Andrew Bonar Law

In 1923, Stanley Baldwin became Prime Minister, taking over from the ailing Bonar Law. After serving as Prime Minister for less than a year, Bonar Law became seriously ill and would soon die of cancer. It will never be known what he would have been willing to do for the cause of Zionism. Although Baldwin had a Nonconformist Methodist background, he had changed over to the Anglican Church. Jill Hamilton, in her study of the restoration of Israel wrote,

> His father's family of Wesleyan Methodists in the north of England were circuit stewards, Sunday School superintendents, organists and general benefactors of the chapel in Stourport, Worcestershire. Baldwin was named after a great-grandfather, a Wesleyan Minister in Stourport, but by then his parents had gone the way of many successful Nonconformists and become members of the Church of England. Baldwin's mother was the daughter of Rev. George MacDonald, a Wesleyan Minister from Northern Ireland.[176]

Baldwin's first term as Prime Minister was short lived. In January 1924, Ramsey MacDonald defeated Baldwin and the Labour Party came to power. As a minority government, the MacDonald administration lasted only 11 months. Lord Passfield was the Foreign Secretary under this first MacDonald government, and did not favour a continued effort for a Jewish National Home.[177]

In October 1924, Baldwin was back as Prime Minister. Leo Amery was now Secretary of State for the Colonies. Amery would be the longest serving Colonial Secretary during the Mandate (1924-1929). Personally, he favoured Zionism. He was an Evangelical and sometimes spoke of his family's long standing devotion to the Congregational Church.[178] Of his mother, Amery wrote that she was, "deeply religious herself, and brought up in a somewhat narrowly Evangelical circle."[179]

Christian Zionists Help Establish Hebrew University

In the 1920's, both Jewish and Christian Zionists desired the advancement of the Hebrew language and Jewish education. One central manifestation of this idea was the opening of the Hebrew University in Jerusalem. Many Jews of Palestine believed that if the Hebrew language were to survive, they needed a University of their own.[180] On April 1 1925, the Hebrew University was officially opened. This was a great victory for Zionism and a practical example of British Christian-Jewish Zionist cooperation. Such displays of unity would be fewer in the years ahead. On this day, the atmosphere on Mount Scopus in Jerusalem was euphoric. Chaim Weizmann and Field Marshal Allenby were both present. Even though Hebrew University could have asked Albert Einstein, Sigmund Freud, Chaim Weizmann, or any number of Jewish academics to deliver the opening address of the University, they instead gave the honour to Arthur Balfour.

Balfour was beloved by many Jews as the man who restored Israel. He delivered his speech with passion and encouraged the Jews across Palestine to reestablish their land. He spoke at length without notes. Colonel Frederick Kisch, an Army Officer and Christian Zionist wrote of Balfour, "With his hands raised to the skies and his white hair floating in the wind, he looked like a prophet."[181] As Balfour toured the country, the Jews of Palestine cheered him wherever he went.

Bertha Spafford was present at the opening ceremony of Hebrew University on that day. She wrote of Balfour's participation, "The acoustics were perfect. The speeches were easily heard. I saw Lord Balfour, who was profoundly moved, with tears running down his face, deliver his oration."[182] Looking back 25 years later, Norman Bentwich wrote that the opening of the University was the greatest occasion of the entire Mandate.

> I remember the opening of the Hebrew University on April 1 1925. That was the greatest occasion of the many great occasions in the 30 years of the British Mandate for Palestine which I was privileged to witness. It took place in the open-air theatre of the Hebrew University on Mount Scopus which had been marked by Dr. Judah Magnes as the only possible place for a great ceremony which would gather the Jewish people in their thousands...They were gathered on the stage on that beautiful day of an early Palestine Spring, a wonderful galaxy of those who played a leading part in establishing the Jewish National Home.[183]

Bentwich went on to describe the array of dignitaries among the seven thousand guests present on that day. Balfour wore the scarlet robes of a doctor of Cambridge University. Samuel wore the gown of an Oxford graduate. Weizmann wore the gown of a doctor of Manchester University. Arthur Schuster, Secretary of the Royal Society of England was there. The chief Rabbi of the Empire, Joseph Hertz, was scheduled to pray for two minutes, but went on for 30. When Dr. Magnus tried to stop him, the Rabbi brushed Magnus aside "as if he was a fly."[184] Weizmann was delighted with the opening ceremonies. In a telegram to Wyndham Deedes, he wrote, "Inaugural ceremony successful inspiring Balfour had wonderful reception, regards, Weizmann."[185]

It is worthy of note that another Scottish Christian was commissioned to plan Hebrew University. Patrick Geddes (1854-1932) was a Scottish architect and Presbyterian Evangelical. In 1918, Geddes became involved in the Zionist movement, turning his interest to Jerusalem and Palestine. He was selected by Zionist leaders to design the Hebrew University in Jerusalem and to plan the enlargement of the city. After years of traveling back and forth between India and Scotland, the prospect of working in Jerusalem seemed to him a culmination of all his dreams. While working with Dr. M. D. Eder of the Zionist Commission, he suggested a comprehensive survey of Jerusalem that would recognize the past, present and future. Geddes's plan called for the University to follow his ideas of synthesizing knowledge and promoting an intimate relationship between university, city, and region. He also influenced the modern design of the city of Tel Aviv.

This 1925 trip was Arthur Balfour's first and only visit to Palestine and he showed a firm indifference to the protests of the Arabs. Many Palestinian Arabs closed their shops when Balfour passed through. Some sent him angry telegrams, which Balfour ordered destroyed. Days later, an angry Arab mob surrounded Balfour's hotel in Damascus to protest, but Balfour seemed to care nothing for their outrage. His commitment was to a Zionist restoration, not to Arab demands for "fairness."

The Legacy of Herbert Samuel, the Only Jewish High Commissioner

In 1925, Herbert Samuel completed his five years as the first High Commissioner of Palestine, feeling he had accomplished much. He left behind a functional administration system, relative calm, security, and a reasonably stable economy. Susanna Emery, an English schoolteacher on assignment in Palestine, wrote of the legacy of Herbert Samuel. She observed that Samuel ruled with patient justice, but received little thanks from the people. "The Arabs could not imagine that a Jew could possible treat them justly, and the Jews disliked him because he really was just."[186]

At the end of his term, Samuel received letters and telegrams of thanks from Jewish individuals and Zionist organizations. Chaim Weizmann wrote to Samuel as the President of the Zionist Organization, "You were privileged-to my great joy-to play a fundamental part in the laying of the foundation of the Jewish National Home." At the end of the letter, Weizmann wrote, "In the hope that we shall meet again in Zion rebuilt."[187] The Zionist Organization of America wrote of Samuel's "...devotion toward the rebuilding of the Jewish Homeland as he evidenced during the course of his administration."[188] The Executive of the Zionist Organization wrote that Samuel "...has brought Palestine the blessings of peace, order and good government, and has witnessed the completion of the first stage in the establishment of the Jewish National Home."[189]

The Arabs of Palestine resented Samuels's legacy. They saw it as the establishment of the foundation of a Jewish State. They did not see Samuel as impartial. Herbert Samuel left Palestine believing all was going well. Regarding Herbert Samuel and relations to Arabs, Charles Harington, the biographer of the next High Commissioner, Herbert Plumer, wrote of Samuel, "No Jewish administrator, however wise, could succeed in winning their confidence or overcoming their prejudice."[190] Bernard Wasserstein summarized what he thought of Samuels's personal beliefs during those first five years, "Zionism represented for Samuel a perfect synthesis of his Englishness and his Jewishness, his Liberalism and his imperialism, his political practicality and his religious sensibility-and the sentimental side of his nature that lay deeply buried behind his impassive public face."[191]

The Arrival of Herbert Plumer, Second High Commissioner

In 1925, Herbert Plumer arrived in Palestine as the new High Commissioner. Plumer was a Field Marshal and former governor-general of Malta. He had a quiet manner and stayed out of politics when possible. He was not Jewish, which was a relief to some. Palestine was relatively peaceful that summer. The first action Plumer took was to sketch a policy of quiet administrative reforms and the encouragement of agriculture. Plumer also believed the British garrison could be reduced from 700 to 500 British Gendarmes.[192]

Herbert Plumer was 68 when he began to serve in Palestine. His biographer, Charles Harington, mentioned no religious affiliation for the Plumer family, even though Plumer was Anglican and was comfortable referring to himself as a "Christian." As a professional soldier, his life was dedicated to the military. Throughout his career, he served in India, Sudan, South Africa and Ireland. After arriving in Palestine, Plumer traveled the country, visiting all the regions, often working 15 hours a day.

At times Plumer displayed significant sympathy with Zionist ideals. When the Arab leaders told him that they thought the Balfour Declaration made their situation hopeless, the High Commissioner told them, "You foolish people, do you think that I as a Christian am not at home in this Holy Land, with all the great memories of the Founder of our faith?"[193] According to Harington, Plumer told all parties, "There is room for all and whoever shows himself a useful citizen, whether he is Moslem, a Christian or Jew, will be employed."[194]

Plumer had an effective way of handling the challenges of the Muslim leadership of Palestine. On one occasion when the Mufti told Plumer that if he continued the policy of favouring Zionism he could not be responsible for the safety of Palestine. Lord Plumer retorted, "You responsible? Who asked you to be responsible for the peace of this place? I am!"[195] Through the mid-1920's, the Mufti generally co-operated with the office of the High Commissioner. The Mufti seemed to realize his position and the existence of the Supreme Muslim Council were dependant on the British, and that men like Plumer were not easily manipulated.

During his tenure, Lord Plumer made efforts to lower tensions and serve the Jews. He took an interest in the work of the St. John Eye Hospital, the Anglican Church, and the opening of the various Great War Cemeteries in Palestine. Plumer was committed to diligent work, fairness, ceremony, and agricultural development. He allowed Ze'ev Jabotinsky to return and live in Palestine even though condemned by a military court in 1920.[196] Norman Bentwich called the Plumer years, "The most tranquil period in the history of mandated Palestine...Field Marshal Lord and Lady Plumer were greatly beloved...During the years of Lord Plumer's administration there was peace in Palestine."[197]

Indeed, Plumer's rule was relatively quiet, giving rise to the feeling in Britain that Palestine was manageable. Plumer did not want Palestine to cost Britain money. He also did not want to do anything to encourage discord and violence. Plumer had a unique way of handling difficult problems between the Jews and the Arabs. If either side raised a touchy issue, he did nothing, declaring the problem to be "political" and "out of his jurisdiction."[198] In the 1920's, several Muslim-Christian Arab Associations were established. This was an early expression of Palestine Arab nationalism, but they lacked the vigour and organization of their Zionist counterparts.[199]

In 1926, a seemingly small incident occurred in Jerusalem that had a major impact. An effort was made by the Jews of Palestine to purchase a house near the Western Wall. Normally one Arab house could be purchased for about 5000 pounds. Enough houses to create a praying area around the Wall would cost about 100,000 pounds in total. Jews from around the world prepared to provide the money. Among the most prominent were Nathan Strauss of New York and Baron Rothschild of England. However, the purchase did not take place. The British Mandate administrations blocked the sale, desiring to preserve the religious status quo. The area around the Western Wall now had the attention of the Jews, the Arabs and the British.

As High Commissioner, Lord Plumer participated in public ceremonies whenever possible, especially Christian events. On December 22 1926, he laid the cornerstone for the new Jerusalem building of the British and Foreign Bible Society. It was significant statement that the High Commissioner would publicly endorse an Evangelical mission organization.[200] As Plumer laid the cornerstone, Muslim youths threw stones at the ceremony. The next day Plumer summoned the Mufti to Government House. The Mufti refused to take responsibility. Plumer told the Mufti, "Very well then, any more stones thrown by your people at a religious ceremony and I will appoint a new Mufti." The Mufti replied, "You cannot do that, it is impossible." Plumer responded, "Can't I? I warn you, now go away." There was no more stone throwing.[201]

Josiah Wedgwood's Complaints

In England in 1926, Member of Parliament Josiah C. Wedgwood campaigned vigorously for the cause of Zionism. As a wealthy Evangelical Christian, he had the means to conduct his own speaking tours for any cause that suited him. A colourful character, Wedgewood represented the ideals of Zionism well, but perhaps his eccentric personality and troublesome approach represented the new voice of British Christian Zionism. Rather than being debated in Cabinet, the restoration of Israel was becoming a noisy nuisance on the fringe of society. Despite all this, Christian and Jewish Zionists alike appreciated Wedgwood's efforts.

In January 1926, Wedgwood spoke in America on behalf of the Keren Hayesod fund of Palestine.[202] In October 1926, he toured Palestine to observe the progress of Zionism. He believed he had the ability to influence government policy in Palestine. He voiced his disapproval of what he saw to be the Mandate government's anti-Zionist policies, such as dividing Transjordan from Palestine. Wedgwood believed the Jews of Palestine were being held back in their political and national development. In December 1926, he sent 33 written criticisms of the Palestine government to Colonial Secretary Leo Amery. Copies were forwarded to Plumer in Jerusalem. Wedgwood charged that Plumer was not fulfilling the spirit of the Balfour Declaration. Plumer was angry and defensive. He called Wedgwood's criticisms "cowardly and wholly unjustified attacks...it is absolutely untrue to say that they do nothing and want to do nothing."[203]

The response to Wedgewood's criticisms in Britain was rather positive. The London *Times* thought his suggestions were sensible, "The author makes breezy suggestions full of good sense. Some, indeed, could probably be adopted by administrative decree."[204] The London *Observer's* comments were positive but questioned Wedgwood's impartiality. The paper reported that Wedgwood's report "...is written with an enthusiasm which raises occasional doubts as to the author's judgment."[205] Although Wedgwood's complaints were ineffective in bringing about real political change, they kept the issue of Zionism alive in Britain. The Zionist Organization in London approved of Wedgwood's report, and the Secretary of the Zionist Organization commended Wedgewood in a letter. "It is hardly necessary for me to assure you that what you are doing and the spirit in which you are doing it is warmly appreciated by the Executive and by the Zionist public as a whole."[206]

The Growing Burden of Zionism on the British Government

Looking back at this period in time, one might be tempted to ask why the British government simply did not apply itself more diligently to the problems in Palestine. Part of the answer lay in the fact that the Empire was far-flung and thinly manned. There simply were not enough resources to be active everywhere.[207] In 1927, the British government reluctantly had to resign itself to the fact that the Hashemite House of Hussein was gone for good from Arabia, having been expelled by the Saudi clan. Despite promises made to the House of Hussein, only the regime of Abdullah in Transjordan and Feisal in Iraq survived. In signing the Treaty of Jeddah with the Saudi family, Britain recognized the new regime of Saudi Arabia and its leader, Abdul Aziz Ibn Saud.

Some older British politicians who never embraced Zionism still virtually ignored its' existence. In 1926, Former Prime Minister Asquith published his memoirs. Despite the importance of Zionism and the Jewish National Home in British politics, Asquith made no mention of Palestine, the Balfour Declaration or General Allenby.[208] These omissions by Asquith are inexplicable as mere oversights. Asquith was Prime Minister of Britain through most of the Great War. The campaign in Palestine could have comprised a significant portion of any account of the war. General Allenby was arguably one of the most successful generals of the war, and to disregard him seems to be intentional. The importance of the Balfour Declaration in British foreign policy was indisputable, regardless of one's opinion of it. The only conclusion to be derived from these omissions is that they were deliberate, an attempt by Asquith to display his low regard for these matters.

In the summer of 1927, a powerful earthquake rocked Palestine. The most affected centers were Jerusalem, Nablus and Lydda. Hundreds of houses collapsed, about 400 people were killed and about 1000 injured.[209] Plumer immediately visited all the damaged regions. Government House, high on the Mount of Olives, was so badly damaged that Plumer and his wife had to consider a move. The Plumers entertained a great deal, so they decided a proper home needed to be built, both for themselves and for future High Commissioners. A site was chosen for the new Government House on the first ridge south of Jerusalem. The Jews of Palestine jokingly named the hilltop the "Hill of Evil Counsel" in reference to the political decisions made there.[210]

November 1927 marked ten years since the issuance of the Balfour Declaration and the entry of the British Army into Palestine under General Allenby. One of the political paradoxes of the 1920's was that more Arab land was available for sale than the Jews could afford to purchase. Throughout the 1920's, various Jewish groups, such as the Jewish National Fund, applied themselves to the task of land purchasing. If a master plan as to how to buy land ever existed, it was not published. Only in a general sense did the Jews know which land could be purchased, and the purchases were then made when and where possible.

The aim of the Jewish National Fund as clearly to buy the country, or any pieces of it that were for sale. In most cases, Arab landowners sold their land readily for the highest possible price. Among Arab landowners, motives sometimes were mixed. On one occasion an Arab, Aouni Abd al-Hadi, assisted in the land transactions of Arab land to Jews, yet at the same time went to the High Commissioner complaining about the land sales.[211]

The Continued Pressure of British Christian Zionism

In the late 1920's, Christian Zionists were still promoting their ideals. In November 1927, Richard Meinertzhagen again appealed to the British public about his continued passion for Zionism. He sent an open letter to the London *Times* declaring that he believed any "attempt to interfere with Jewry is to interfere with history... Enemies of Zionism can delay the ultimate destiny of Palestine, but they cannot prevent its ultimate fulfillment."[212]

In the late 1920's, Wyndham Deedes continued to be an energetic spokesman for Zionism. He typified the practical Christian Zionism of his day, travelling to Poland encouraging Polish Jews to immigrate to Palestine. For his speaking tour in Poland, the Zionist Organization created a poster to promote the lectures. The heading of the poster read, "Welcome to General Sir Wyndham Deeds." Part of the text of the poster read,

> It would be quite impossible within the space of this article to call by their names all the multitude of our friends, favourable to the Jewish cause, standing round Lord Balfour and the Jewish National Home. Their number increases constantly, comprising the noble minds of all political parties and professions in Great Britain. Moreover, this affection for Zion's cause on the side of our Christian friends is not at all platonic. A string of effective proofs followed since Balfour's declaration. Our noblest friend Sir Deedes can be assured that the Jewish race will set aside for him one of the

most honored places in the history of the reconstruction of Zion.[213]

Deedes knew the restoration of Israel would not be accomplished quickly or easily. In preparation for a speaking tour of Europe, he wrote a long letter to the Jews of Poland, thanking them for letting him speak about Zionism. Deedes wrote, "I should like to add this; Jews must remember that a movement of this nature which is taking place in difficult circumstances must expect to meet especially in its initial stages with obstacles occasionally with setbacks."[214]

Meanwhile in England, Josiah Wedgwood was working hard on a radical new proposal for the future of Palestine. In February 1928, he published a book entitled "The Seventh Dominion." (That same year Wedgwood became Chairman of the Parliamentary Committee for Palestine).[215] In his book, Wedgwood proposed that Palestine be declared a Crown Colony of the British Empire. Then Jewish immigration would be opened for a generation, to be followed by the granting of independence as a Dominion with the same status as Canada and Australia. The Colonial Office and the Mandatory government never issued official responses to Wedgwood's proposals. By advocating the idea of a "Seventh Dominion," Wedgwood believed Palestine should become a Jewish State, and the "Seventh Dominion" of the British Empire.[216]

Wedgewood's proposal was seen by some as a bold, innovative concept with an eye to the future. When asked about the Arab majority living in Palestine, he explained that Jewish immigration was a welcomed help to most of the Arabs. The Jews brought in needed professions, agricultural expertise and engineering skills to drain the malarial swamps. The Jews hired the Arabs and paid for land at prices far above market value.[217] When referring to his book, Wedgwood spoke of his personal family attachment to Israel and the people of the Old Testament. "When my ancestors hewed down the aristocrats at Wigan Lane and at Naseby they were armed with the names of Aaron and Abner; and they rallied to the charge, calling on the God of Izrael (sic) in the language of the prophets."[218]

Despite never achieving high political power, Wedgwood was a popular and influential Member of the House throughout his long political career. From 1906 until his last election in 1935, he received the votes of between 56-69 percent of the constituents in his riding. In his later years, few were compelled to contest his seat. In 1931 and 1935, he ran unopposed.[219] His efforts were noticed and appreciated by the Jewish leaders of Palestine. Chief Rabbi of Britain, J. H. Hertz wrote to Wedgwood that "Jewry around the world ever gratefully remember your sympathetic understanding of the Jewish cause, and the splendid support you have given it."[220] Nahum Sokolow wrote to Wedgwood, "At all events, your indefatigable zeal in our propaganda for a real Jewish National Home combined with the glory and the interests of Great Britain is for us a source of great delight and bright prospects for the future."[221] On May 16 1929, the Palestine Branch of the Seventh Dominion League was formed in Jerusalem. They wrote to Wedgwood, "To the Jews of Palestine, all without distinction, you are 'the friend' a courageous and faithful champion of Zionism."[222]

Wedgwood was not the only person to be forming new organizations in Palestine. Early in 1929, Samuel organized a new club in Palestine to bridge the Jewish and British communities. He called the new organization the Anglo-Palestine Club and declared it purpose was to establish and promote mutual understanding. When Balfour heard of the formation of this new organization, he sent his congratulations to Samuel, "The efforts of your committee have therefore my heartiest sympathy, and I hope they will be attended with every success."[223]

Some Zionists compared Wedgwood to the Jewish revisionist Ze'ev Jabotinsky. Both were dissatisfied with the status quo of British rule. Both men saw little value in negotiations with the Arabs of Palestine. Jabotinsky favoured direct action against both the Arabs and the British if Jewish liberties were threatened. Jabotinsky, like Wedgwood, was also opposed to partition. Joshua Stein wrote, "It is not surprising that Wedgwood, the man who refused to compromise, so often favored Jabotinsky, in many ways his Jewish counterpart."[224]

The Zionism of Ronald Storrs

Ronald Storrs served as the Governor of Jerusalem for seven years. As a committed Christian Zionist, he promoted the cause whenever he could. Eventually the Colonial Office told him he needed to leave Palestine. When told he would be "promoted" to Cyprus, Storrs wrote back, "There is no promotion after Jerusalem." Reluctantly however, Storrs accepted the appointment. Later, from Cyprus, Storrs wrote to a friend in Jerusalem, "I should be grateful if you could sometime send me a little news of The Land which always is my affectionate remembrance."[225] Storrs capitalized the words "The Land," clearly identifying with the Zionist custom of referring to Israel simply as "The Land."

In 1937, Ronald Storrs published his memoirs, which included much on his years in Palestine. Storrs was still a committed Zionist and hoped for a Jewish National Home in Palestine, believing that many people formed their opinions about Zionism based on their religious bias. He identified who the enemies of Zionism were, writing that the declared adversaries of Zionism are, "…all Palestinians who are not Jews, Roman Catholics (uninterested in the Old Testament) all over the world, and British sympathizers with Muslim or Arab views."[226]

Storrs blamed British society for not educating her young people about the history of the Jewish people. He believed only the Bible could reveal the truth about the Jews. He saw Zionism as an ideology embraced by Gentiles by choice through conviction, writing, "What does the average English boy know of Jews? As Jews, nothing…I never heard my father mention Jews save in connection with the Old Testament."[227] Storrs looked back at the optimism of the beginning of the Mandate. Regarding the arrival of the Zionist Commission in 1918, he wrote, "We believed (and I still believe) that there was in the world no aspiration more nobly idealistic than the return of the Jews to the Land immortalized by the spirit of Israel."[228]

Storrs believed that England above all other nations should be responsible for restoring Israel. His conviction was that the British connection to the Bible should convince her of her duty, writing, "Which of all was more steeped in the Book of Books or had pondered more deeply upon the prophecies thereof than England? The Return stood indeed for something more than a tradition, an ideal or a hope. It was The Hope, *Miqveh Yisroel*, the Hope of Israel."[229]

Lord Plumer Concludes His Term as High Commissioner

In July 1928, Lord Plumer completed his term as High Commissioner of Palestine. There was no new High Commissioner in place until Sir John Chancellor arrived in November 1928. It was not known at the time, but Plumer's term marked the end of relative quiet. Norman Bentwich wrote, "The three years' rule of Field Marshal Lord Plumer, who succeeded Sir Herbert Samuel, was the most peaceful period in the modern history of Palestine."[230] David Ben Gurion described Plumer as "first class...his relations with us were very good...he was a firm and wise governor."[231]

Susanna Emery wrote of Plumer's legacy, "Lord Plumer succeeded Lord Samuel as High Commissioner. He was every inch a soldier, tall, dignified, and perhaps rather stern, but also friendly and approachable." Norman Bentwich liked to say of the Plumer years, "and the land had rest."[232] Mr. E. Mills, served as Plumers Assistant Chief Secretary wrote that Plumers projected policy was "to be fair."[233]

Conclusion

The influence of British Christian Zionism played a key role in the establishing of the Mandate in Palestine. Between 1917 and 1922, Zionism had the support of major personalities in the government who were primarily motivated by their religious commitments. However, thereafter, the shift in British policy was, in great part, due to the decline in number and influence of similar personalities with such religious sentimentalities.

Politicians sympathetic to the restoration of Israel such as Lloyd George, Smuts, and Balfour were not replaced by likeminded politicians of similar caliber. Signs of a growing ambivalence toward Zionism were due largely to the fact that Christian Zionism was losing its influence. Evangelicals no longer filled enough key roles in London or Palestine. In broad terms, Samuel and Plumer were supportive of Zionism is their roles as High Commissioner. Likewise, Churchill and Amery supported Zionism as best they could from the Colonial Office. This situation gradually changed after 1928.

During his term as High Commissioner, Herbert Samuel retreated from his personal commitment to the ideal of Zionism once he was responsible for day-to-day events. When faced with Arab violence, he replaced his ideals with a political pragmatism that he hoped would better serve all the communities of Palestine. Winston Churchill, despite a lifetime of commitment to Zionism, once appointed Colonial Secretary, opted for a broader, more regional approach to Palestine. His 1922 White Paper was a shocking disappointment to Zionists, and in the end provided no appeasement to the Arabs. Yet, despite setbacks inherent in the 1922 White Paper, most Zionists still believed there was enough territory west of the Jordan River to establish a Jewish National Home. Martin Gilbert asserted that Churchill's time at the Colonial Office was good for Zionism.[234]

Throughout Britain, Nonconformist numbers and influence declined during the 1920's. This loss of influence included a decline in support for the restoration of Israel. According to Koss, the years 1924 to 1929 were the years when the situation for the Nonconformists "went from bad to worse...the Evangelical Free Churches, with their Puritan ethos, were most conspicuously out of touch with their times."[235] Not only were the Evangelicals in decline, but they were now more fractured in their voting patterns. In 1929, the *Church Times* postulated that before the war, probably 80 percent of Nonconformists voted Liberal, but following the war, for a variety of reasons, many more votes went to the Labour and Conservative parties.[236] The collapse of the Liberal Party paralleled the decline in Evangelical Christian political influence. The resulting fragmentation of votes translated into a less focused political influence for Evangelicals.

Despite these numerical declines, the cause of Zionism still enjoyed the support of many influential Britons. For example, Chancellor of the Exchequer Philip Snowdon and his wife were openly sympathetic to the Zionist cause. Malcolm MacDonald, the son of the Prime Minister, continued his involvement with Labour Zionists. Foreign Secretary Arthur Henderson, one of the original signatures of the Balfour Declaration, also still backed the ideals of Zionism. As encouraging as this was to the Zionists, these secondary personalities did not carry the political weight of the earlier proponents.

As the 1920's were ending, three of the original creators of the Balfour Declaration made their views heard once again by publishing a letter of support for Zionism in the London *Times*.[237] Among other issues, the letter raised the question of appointing a new Commission of Inquiry for investigating the issues of immigration, land and development in Palestine. Arthur Balfour, Lloyd George and Jan Smuts signed the letter. Despite this meaningful gesture, these men represented an influence from the past and not the current political power base.

The decline of British Evangelicals during the 1920's was correspondingly matched by the dramatic rise in the numbers and influence of Evangelicals in the United States during these years. With this rise in America came an increased interest in Zionism within the Churches and in politics. Although the American government still lacked the will and need to make its voice known, the day would come when American Christian Zionism would influence events in Palestine in a major way.

In the next chapter, the link between the decline of Christian Zionism in Britain and the relinquishing of Palestine will be examined. Violent Arab riots in Palestine in late 1928 and 1929 signaled a turning point in the Mandate. British security authorities were caught unprepared. Increasing numbers of British troops and police were sent to Palestine in an attempt to quell the violence. By the early 1930's, British society would be growing weary with the problems of Palestine. Most of the influential war leaders who backed the Balfour Declaration were out of power or deceased. There was no clear political procedure for how to implement the Balfour Declaration. Arab reactions were succeeding in making the British government more careful and pragmatic.

Chapter Three

The Challenges of the Mandate and the Decline of British Christian Zionism 1929-1939

❖ ❖ ❖

Introduction

This chapter will demonstrate the link between the decline of Christian Zionism in Britain and the gradual relinquishing of the British commitment to a National Home for the Jewish people in Palestine during the years 1929-1939. In order to do so, the increased Arab violence and the British response will be noted. The arrival of three new High Commissioners and their roles will be reviewed, along with the Christian Zionist response in both Britain and America. The growing interest in Zionism in the United States will be observed, especially in light of changing British foreign policy expressed by the Peel Commission of 1937. This chapter will conclude with the introduction of the White Paper of 1939 and the beginning of World War 2.

It has been seen that Christian Zionism in Britain played a significant role in the establishment of the Mandate in Palestine between 1917 and 1922. The ideal of Zionism had the support of major personalities in the government who, as we have seen, were primarily motivated by their religious commitments. In broad terms,

Samuel and Plumer were supportive of Zionism in their positions as High Commissioner. Likewise, men like Churchill and Amery supported Zionism from the Colonial Office when they held the role of Colonial Secretary.

After 1929, support for Zionism was no longer the single most important factor in determining British policy in Palestine. Such decisions were now determined more by political pragmatism than by religious ideals. This situation changed for two main reasons. First, the Arab protests in Palestine discouraged the British from pursuing the full intent of the Balfour Declaration. Second, the diminishing influence of Evangelicals and Christian Zionism at home weakened the resolve of the British government.

Violent Arab riots in late 1928 and 1929 signaled a turning point in the history of the Mandate. British security authorities were unprepared for the violence which initiated a time of disillusionment as British society seemed to grow weary with the problems of Palestine. Most of the influential politicians who backed the Balfour Declaration during the Great War were now out of power or deceased. Arab opposition to Zionism succeeded in making the British government more careful about supporting the restoration of Israel. To illustrate the change of policy, Foreign Secretary Austen Chamberlain, sent a circular through the Foreign Office in 1929 distancing his Ministry from supporting Zionism. Part of his memorandum read, "Any suspected intervention by His Majesty's government on behalf of Zionism would be liable to misconstruction."[1]

Evangelicals mourned the passing of Arthur Balfour in 1930. His death was a great loss to the Zionist movement. As a man who loved the Bible, Balfour arranged for Scripture to be inscribed on his tombstone, selecting some of the final words of the Apostle Paul, words that had meaning to British Evangelicals, "I have fought a good fight, I have finished my course."[2] At the end of a lifetime of high accomplishments, Balfour told his family on his deathbed that the work he did for the return of the Jews to Palestine was possibly the most worthwhile thing he had ever done."[3]

Despite this, the forces of Christian Zionism still had some influence in Britain, even though they were no longer initiating government foreign policy as they were in 1917. Norman Rose, in his work, "The Gentile Zionists," explains how the Christian Zionists promoted their cause during the years from 1929 to 1939. According to Rose, the Christian Zionists "attempted to mobilize government, Parliament and public circles through their Gentile supporters in an attempt to attain solutions more amenable to the Zionist idea."[4] However, during this time, a decline in numbers and influence of such men accompanied a shift in British policy away from Zionism. British Christian Zionism was losing its influence, as Evangelicals no longer filled enough significant roles in the government in London or in the bureaucracy of Palestine. The year 1929 represented a time of social and economic uncertainty in the western world.[5] In the decade to follow, various British governments would consider how they could reduce overseas imperial commitments while still fulfilling past promises. The Balfour Declaration and all its implications was a part of this conundrum. Twelve years had passed since the issuing of the Balfour Declaration and the situation in Palestine was now worse for the British than when they first conquered the region.

Despite the complexity of the problems in Palestine, the British government found it impossible to leave. They were attempting to facilitate the desires of both the Jews and the Arabs, but were failing on both accounts. Yet, there were reasons to stay. First, it would be a shameful thing within the international community to break a commitment to the League of Nations. Second, the British would be breaking promises to the Jews of Palestine, of Britain and the world. Third, Britain had to consider her strategic and imperial priorities. If she were to quit Palestine, another nation might enter, take responsibility for protecting Holy Sites and threaten the Suez Canal.

In the 1930's, the inconsequential influence of several noteworthy Christian Zionists such as Orde Wingate, Blanche Dugdale, Ronald Storrs, Josiah Wedgwood and Lloyd George illustrated the declining political role of Evangelicals in Britain. Instead of being central figures initiating government policy, as they had done in 1917 and 1922, British Christian Zionists were becoming peripheral players acting with a voice of protest and complaint. Christian Zionists and their Jewish colleagues now worked on the fringe of influence, satisfying themselves with letters in newspapers and dinner party dialogue.

The Eruption of Violence at the Western Wall

In the autumn of 1928, precisely when High Commissioner Herbert Plumer departed and his successor, John Chancellor, had not yet arrived, altercations at the Western Wall in Jerusalem set off a series of events that would shake Palestine for a year.[6] The incident involved a Western Wall partition screen on the evening of Yom Kippur, 1928.[7] The Jews had set up a temporary screen to separate the Jewish men and women who came to pray at the Wall. This had been the Jewish custom for many years during the holiday of Yom Kippur. Constable Douglas Duff was on patrol at the Wall and noticed the screen. He noted it as a simple wooden frame with a cloth on it. Some Muslims saw the screen, became alarmed, and started attacking Jews. They claimed the Jews were upgrading the prayer area to become a Synagogue.[8]

Edward Keith-Roach, the Jerusalem District Commissioner, became aware of the screen and the Muslim anger. He ordered Duff to remove the screen by the morning.[9] A skirmish with the Jewish worshippers resulted as the police destroyed the screen. On that day, Norman Bentwich was praying at the Ashkenazi Synagogue, and the situation still did not appear to be very serious, however, the problem did not resolve itself quickly.[10] The Mufti accused the Jews of plotting to take over the Wall, destroy the Al-Aqsa Mosque and rebuild the Jewish Temple. Arab rioting against Jews continued throughout Jerusalem.

John Chancellor was a 58-year-old Scot, having experienced many years in the Colonial Service. The Zionists were at first optimistic with the choice of Chancellor, as he seemed sympathetic to their cause. However, he was careful how his views on the subject might be perceived. He told a group of Zionists in London before his departure that he felt "particularly privileged to assist their great ideal." However, he asked that this statement not be made public.[11] Having no formal Church affiliation and little interest in religion, Chancellor was cool to Zionism. According to Wasserstein, "Chancellor had no firsthand knowledge of Palestine before his arrival in the country and no liking for it thereafter."[12] Leo Amery found Chancellor to be unsympathetic to Zionism."[13]

The Western Wall riots continued into the next year as Muslims renewed their attacks against Jewish worshippers at the Wall, throwing stones and beating drums in an attempt to disrupt Jewish prayers. The Arabs demanded an end to all Jewish immigration and the British authorities felt the pressure of those demands. Instead of diminishing, the Western Wall tension intensified through the summer of 1929. The traditional Jewish fast day of the Ninth of Av fell on August 14 in 1929.[14] On that night, thousands of Jews gathered at the Western Wall. Two days later, the Muslims held special demonstrations commemorating the birthday of Mohammed. The Muslims came out of the Mosque on the Temple Mount, down the ramp to the Western Wall and attacked the Jews who were praying there. Several people were injured and one Jew was killed.[15]

The Violence Shifts to Hebron

With Chancellor out of the country during the Ninth of Av riots, Harry Luke acted in his place. Luke, an experienced Colonial Official, met with both the Mufti and Chief Rabbi Kook, and later with other Jewish and Muslim leaders. The talks went on for hours but to no avail. Luke attempted to place himself in a position of mediator, not wanting to appear supportive of the Jews. Colonel Frederick Kisch, an Army Officer sympathetic to Zionism, believed Luke was strongly influenced by his fear of Arab violence, warning the Zionist Executive, "Mr. Luke appears to be intimidated by the rumblings among the Arab population."[16] Luke offered no support for Zionism, once calling the Balfour Declaration a "contradiction in terms."[17]

Luke's religious views were not clearly known. He did not identify himself with any Christian denomination, which fed rumours that he was Jewish. This may have been true. As early as 1923, the Colonial Office considered Luke for an administrative position in Palestine, but did not offer him the position. Colonial Office minutes recorded, "The only objection that I can see is that he is of Jewish extraction, but he is certainly not a professing Jew and does his best to keep his origin well concealed."[18] Apparently, these suspicions did not prevent Luke from being offered a position in Palestine later in 1928. Perhaps now in such an important role in Palestine, Luke was being careful to show no partiality to the Jewish position in order not to betray his heritage.

Unexpectedly, on Friday August 23 1929, the violence spread to the city of Hebron, south of Jerusalem. On that day, one of the Muslim preachers on the Temple Mount called on the Muslim faithful to fight the Jews to their last drop of blood. Some of the Muslims had weapons, and at least 23 gunshots were heard coming from the Temple Mount. The Mufti went to the Temple Mount but seemed to make the violence worse.[19] At the time, there were only about 1,500 police officers in the whole country, an insufficient number to quell the violence. By the end of day on Friday August 23, eight Jews were dead and 15 wounded. Five Arabs were dead and nine wounded.

Police Superintendent Raymond Cafferata had been recently posted to Hebron, which was home to about 20,000 Arab Muslims, about 700 Jews, as well as some Christian Arabs.[20] Only 32, and new to Hebron, Cafferata had not yet had time to become familiar with the local people.[21] During the rioting, Cafferata reported that he entered a Jewish house and watched an Arab man cut the head off a Jewish baby with his sword. Cafferata shot the man dead. Cafferata saw a second man, one of his own police constables, Issa Sherrif, standing over a dead Jewish woman with a dagger in his hand. Cafferata shot him dead also.[22]

The final report on the Hebron riots of 1929 indicated unprecedented violence. Sixty-seven Jews were killed, including 12 women and three small children, with many of the bodies mutilated. The report also indicated rapes, and hands and fingers cut off. The American Consulate reported that nine Arabs had been killed.[23] MP Richard Crossman concluded that the first sign of the Mandate not working was the poor British response to the 1929 riots.[24]

The violence continued until the last days of August 1929, encompassing Jerusalem, the surrounding villages and even reaching Tel Aviv. The Jews fought back, but in the end, 133 Jews were killed and 339 wounded. In addition, 116 Arabs were killed and 232 wounded. Feelings ran high. Living in Jerusalem at the time, future Nobel Prize laureate, Shmuel Yosef Agnon, wrote about the Arabs, "I do not hate them and I do not love them; I do not wish to see their faces. In my humble opinion we should now build a large ghetto of half a million Jews in Palestine, because if we do not, we will, God forbid, be lost."[25] When Chancellor returned to Palestine at the end of August, he published a proclamation condemning the violence against the Jews.

Proclamation

I have returned from the United Kingdom to find to my distress the country in a state of disorder and prey to unlawful violence. I have learned with horror of the atrocious acts committed by bodies of ruthless and bloodthirsty evil-doers, of savage murders perpetrated upon defenseless members of the Jewish population regardless of age or sex, accompanied, as at Hebron, by acts of unspeakable savagery, of the burning of farms and houses in town and country and of the looting and destruction of property…My first duties are to restore order in the country and to inflict stern punishment upon those found guilty of acts of violence.

Chancellor was shocked and discouraged. He considered bombing some Arab villages from the air. He wrote his son, "I am so tired and disgusted with this country and everything connected with it that I only want to leave it as soon as I can."[26] The violence of 1929 represented a new level for the British. Charles Townshend noted, "The riots of 1929 became a turning point in the history of Palestine…There was no military garrison. The police forces were overwhelmed, despite the enrolment of British residents – and even tourists – as Special Constables."[27]

The ramifications of the riots were complicated. A Commission of Inquiry was appointed after the violence of 1929 with Attorney General Norman Bentwich as the Chief Prosecutor at the trials, despite Chancellor's protests that Bentwich was a Zionist. Before the trials began, an Arab ambushed Bentwich, shooting him in the leg, forcing Bentwich to return to England for medical care. When the court proceedings began, 700 Arabs were put on trial. One hundred and twenty four were charged with murder. Fifty-five were convicted, with 25 sentenced to death. One hundred and sixty Jews were put on trial. Seventy were accused of murder, but only two were convicted and sentenced to life in prison. In the end, only three Arabs were executed, while the rest were given life in prison. Many Jews of Palestine blamed the British for what had happened.[28] Townshend believed the efforts of Chancellor to be fair minded following the Hebron massacre in 1929, in that he recognized the guilt of the Arabs. "He went further out on a limb by abruptly canceling the newly-activated constitutional plans, a deliberate attempt to punish the Arabs collectively."[29]

Recalling the event over 70 years later, survivor Rivka Burg blamed the British, "They (the British) certainly were on the Arab side. Because otherwise they would have come much earlier and my father and all the delegation went and asked for protection but they didn't help and the result was very tragic."[30] The London *Times* headline on September 2 1929 read, "Evidence of the Massacres." Part of the article read,

> Mr. Luke visited various houses where murders had been committed and went to the Jewish hospital, the synagogues and the Ghetto. Everywhere we met with the sight of blood... Finally we reached the synagogue, where not a piece of timber has been left intact. The floor is strewn with all sorts of wreckage and torn up Scrolls of the Law.[31]

Following the riots in Hebron, Raymond Cafferata returned to Britain where Christian Zionists received him as a hero, despite the fact that he did not openly express Zionist views himself. He received the Kings Police Medal and was interviewed widely as his story was reproduced in newspapers across Britain.[32] His personal revelation of events helped promote Zionism and show the injustice of the Arab violence. The British were obliged to call in reinforcements. At this time, Chancellor became the first High Commissioner to conclude that the Balfour Declaration was a blunder.[33]

Josiah Wedgwood's Reaction to the Events of 1929

At the time of the Hebron massacre, Zionist MP Josiah Wedgwood was active in his attempts to further the cause of Zionism by promoting his Seventh Dominion scheme throughout Britain. Unfortunately for Wedgwood and those who believed in him, neither the government, the Colonial Office, nor the Mandate administration took his Seventh Dominion idea seriously. To further illustrate the lack of attention he received, Wedgwood suggested a Parliamentary Commission be sent to Palestine to conduct an investigation. Even though he volunteered his services, his suggestion was turned down.[34]

Wedgwood's critics pointed out that Dominion status could not be achieved until there was a clear Jewish majority in Palestine, and that was not going to happen in the near future. However, Wedgwood's efforts were appreciated by the Revisionists in Palestine. In November 1929, at the All-Palestine Zionist-Revisionist Conference in Jerusalem, the delegates "endorsed and welcomed" a formal resolution in support of creating Palestine as the Seventh Dominion within the Empire.[35] Following the Conference, Jabotinsky sent "its heartiest greeting to the Hon. J.C. Wedgwood, as the true and noble friend of the Zionist idea."[36]

It was a sad commentary for British Christian Zionists that, at this time, one of the most outspoken advocates of Christian Zionism was an eccentric backbencher rather than the majority of the Cabinet Members as had been the case in 1917. There had been a great collapse of influence in just 12 years. Opponents to Zionism saw manifold problems with Wedgwood's proposal. In addition to the obvious obstacle of the Arab majority in Palestine, many of the Jews of Palestine were from countries like Germany, Poland and France and they did not naturally look with favour on Dominion status. They simply had no previous loyalty to the British Empire. As for Chaim Weizmann, he remained silent regarding Wedgwood's Dominion scheme. It could be that although he wanted full political independence in the long term, he could not speak plainly of his goals at this time. For Weizmann, Dominion status probably fell short of what he really hoped to achieve.

There were many public meetings about Palestine in Britain in late 1929, but the shock of the riots seemed to take attention away from Wedgwood. Perhaps his scheme seemed naïve compared to the harsh realities of the violence in Palestine. He wanted to see the restoration of a biblical Israel within the British family of nations. For Wedgwood, his beliefs were founded in the Old Testament teachings about the ancient nation of Israel, and the prophetic hope of national restoration.

The Unique Zionism of Leo Amery

Leopold Amery was a British politician who supported Zionism for many years in several different roles. His life and influence is worthy of note. Amery was born into an English Protestant family in Gorakhpur, India, and educated at Harrow and Balliol College, Oxford. A member of the Conservative Party, he was first elected to the House of Commons in 1911.[37] As the assistant secretary to the British War Cabinet in 1917, he may have been the person who actually wrote the Balfour Declaration.[38]

Amery was the longest serving Colonial Secretary during the Mandate (1924-1929). Personally, he favoured Zionism. He was an Evangelical and sometimes spoke of his family's long standing devotion to the Congregational Church.[39] Of his mother, Amery wrote that she was, "deeply religious herself, and brought up in a somewhat narrowly Evangelical circle."[40] Unlike most British politicians, Amery was willing to say that religion was the real cause of the tensions in Palestine. Regarding the 1929 riots, he wrote, "Purely religious to begin with...the measure of success achieved by them (the Arabs) in the destruction of Jewish lives and property inevitably encouraged the Arab political leaders to challenge the whole policy of the Mandate."[41]

Amery pursued the cause of Zionism from his various political appointments. He sometimes even made note of those who did not favour Zionism, writing, "Both the new High Commissioner, Sir John Chancellor, and the new Colonial Secretary, Lord Passfield, were definitely unsympathetic to the Zionist ideal."[42] When he finished his term of duty as Colonial Secretary in 1929, he was one of the last Evangelicals of influence in that role.[43] As Secretary of the Colonial Office, Amery pursued his role with idealism and dignity. No successor in his role would have the same political influence or commitment to Zionism than Amery in the years to follow.

However, Amery may have been a man with an extraordinary secret and another motive for his Zionism. In his autobiography, he stated that his mother, Elisabeth Leitner, (née Saphir) was a Hungarian exile who emigrated after the 1848 revolution, fleeing to Constantinople, and eventually to England. According to William Rubinstein, Professor of Modern History at the University of Wales, in his article "The Secret of Leopold Amery," this was not the whole story. Rubinstein believed she was in fact Jewish, and had married a Christian Englishman.[44] If this were true, it would make Amery Jewish.[45] Perhaps he was not aware of it, or if he were aware, he decided to conceal his background. Amery's possible reasons for concealing his Jewishness are open for speculation. Perhaps he was afraid of persecution, or perhaps he desired to assist the Jewish people from a concealed position.[46]

Chancellor Recommends Reduced Immigration

After his first 18 months in Palestine, Chancellor sent a lengthy report to the Colonial Secretary displaying a good comprehension of the situation. He acknowledged the civil unrest to be a serious problem and concluded with some severe recommendations. In response to Arab violence, Chancellor concluded that immigration and land buying rights of Jews must be restricted.[47] He recommended that the government, "Give consideration to practical reforms in such matters as the protection of the non-Jewish population, sales of land and control of immigration."[48]

Chancellor declared in his report that all the cultivable land in Palestine was now occupied. He believed if the Jews purchased any more land, then they would create a class of landless Arab peasants, writing, "In order to stop that process, the immigration of Jewish agricultural colonists must be restricted to the numbers required to develop and cultivate the land now in Jewish ownership."[49] Chancellor suggested only allowing into the country those Jews who could be accommodated on the settlements presently established. According to Kolinsky, Chancellor, "...was a strong advocate of limiting the development of the Jewish community by restricting immigration and land sales. In his view, this would "calm Arab fears and create the conditions for maintaining British authority."[50]

At the end of his report, Chancellor clarified that in fact the British had fulfilled their Balfour Declaration obligations to the Jews. "The bulk of the Jewish population of Palestine have little feeling of gratitude or loyalty toward Great Britain for what she has done for the establishment of the Jewish National Home."[51] He went on to say that if land sales are restricted, "I believe that there will be some hope for a peaceful future for Palestine."[52] He believed that,

> The wide-spread aim of Zionism...is to promote Jewish immigration in order that, as soon as practicable, there may be a Jewish majority and a Jewish government in Palestine... But I regard it as essential that the Jewish opposition to these measures should be resisted and that the Zionist leaders should be made to realize that the Mandate will be administered by Great Britain in accordance with His Majesty's government's interpretation of it and not in accordance with the interpretation of the Zionist Organization.[53]

Personally, Chancellor was in despair. He wrote gloomy letters home, articulating his feelings of hopelessness. He considered mass expulsions, or finding a way to cancel the Balfour Declaration. He thought too many Jews had been allowed into the country. Even though he had once declared that he felt particularly privileged to assist the great ideal of Zionism, he did little to promote that ideal.[54] Pragmatism rather than idealism was now the working policy of the High Commissioner.

The Response of the Christian Zionists in Britain

Following the violence of 1929, a British Commission of Inquiry was sent to Palestine headed by Sir Walter Shaw. The Commission's purpose was to determine the cause of the Western Wall riots of 1929 and investigate the problems facing the Mandate. Christian

Zionists in London were concerned about the possible outcome of the Commission.

In November, a Parliamentary pro-Zionist group was formed with Josiah Wedgewood as Chairman.[55] Twenty-one MP's attended the meeting, including Leo Amery, Herbert Samuel, Martin Conway and James de Rothschild.[56] According to Norman Rose, "The prime purpose of the group was to act as a watch-dog for Zionist interests; and in the delicate political balance of forces that had emerged since the formation of a minority (some would say captive) Labour government in May 1929 this factor took on an added significance."[57] The involvement of 73 year-old MP Martin Conway (1856-1937) in a way symbolized the kind lower level support Wedgwood and his group received. Having been raised in the home of an Anglican Minister, Conway was a backbencher who supported Zionism. Conway had himself considered a career in the Church while a student at Cambridge, but opted for politics instead.[58] At this time in his life, his influence was minimal. Due to his advanced age, his involvement in this cause would not continue for many more years.

On November 25 1929, Jan Smuts met with Weizmann in London. Smuts, one of the Cabinet members responsible for the Balfour Declaration in 1917 encouraged Weizmann to pursue his dream of a Jewish National Home.[59] Smuts also spent several days in late November with Arthur Henderson, the Foreign Secretary and Sidney Webb (Lord Passfield), the new Colonial Secretary. Smuts explained that the Balfour Declaration was not merely a platonic declaration but implied active assistance to facilitate the development of the National Home.[60] Smuts told Weizmann that Leo Amery, the previous Colonial Secretary, had asked him to take the post of High Commissioner of Palestine. Smuts had refused, citing his many other commitments.[61]

Wasserstein confirmed this claim that in 1928 Amery sought Smuts to be appointed as High Commissioner in succession to Plumer.[62] If this were true, Amery was clearly attempting to place a more pro-Zionist High Commissioner in Jerusalem. It remains unknown what might have happened for the cause of Zionism had Smuts taken the role in 1928 instead of John Chancellor. It may be that Smut's "other commitments" had to do with his role in South

African politics. He was Prime Minister from 1919 to 1924, an office to which he would later return. Perhaps it was unrealistic to expect a former head of a Dominion government to accept the role of High Commissioner of Palestine.

On December 17 1929, Weizmann met with a number of Christian Zionist friends to see what could be done about the expected findings of the Shaw Commission. At least 11 guests were present. The group decided that they must act to prevent the commission from transgressing its terms of reference.[63] The plan of action taken was to have a letter published in the London *Times* signed by Balfour, Lloyd George and Smuts. All three men agreed in the days following and the letter appeared in the London *Times* on December 20 1929.[64] Norman Rose called the meeting and the letter "A remarkable exercise in public relations, It was a vivid demonstration of the scope of Zionist's contacts, and the ability of the movement to conscript the most powerful support on its behalf during periods of government hesitation."[65] Despite the impressive display of support from these three men, it should be noted that they were all now past their years of real political power.

The four-member Shaw Commission delivered its report on March 26 1930. The report was critical of the Jews in Palestine, finding that the Arabs feared the political and national aspirations of the Jews. As Norma Rose put it, for the Zionists, it "confirmed all their worst expectations."[66] The Shaw Commission recommended an immediate statement of British intentions in Palestine and a re-examination of immigration policy. In order to placate the Zionists in London, Prime Minister MacDonald invited Passfield and some of the leading Zionists to lunch. MacDonald admitted that the report was "very bad, it will depress the Jews and elate the Arabs."[67] According to Gabi Sheffer, the Shaw Commission as of no great importance. "The only major outcome of its labour was the launching of further inquiry into Palestine's absorptive capacity in the realm of immigration and land questions-a task that later devolved on Hope Simpson. But at the time, the report caused a furor."[68]

On March 28 1930, Prime Minister MacDonald met with Lord Passfield to discuss how to handle the recommendations of the

Shaw Commission. According to Sheffer, Passfield was "allegedly unsympathetic" to Zionism.[69] The two decided to appoint a one-man commission to investigate the questions of land, development and immigration in Palestine. At first, Jan Smuts was considered for the task, but almost immediately, his appointment was reconsidered.[70] Smut's Zionist views would go against the positions of the Colonial Office and High Commissioner Chancellor.

After much consideration, Passfield was able to announce that, with the Prime Minister's approval, John Hope Simpson would lead the new inquiry. Sheffer observed, "By his decision, the embryonic 'Smuts threat' to Chancellor's authority and the possibility that the Colonial Office would be powerless to implement their commitment seemed to have been removed."[71] Sheffer concluded, "The appointment of Hope Simpson, rather than Smuts, temporarily restored the harmony between London and Chancellor that had been disturbed when the latter launched his proposals."[72]

One can only speculate as to the kind of report Smuts might have made regarding British policy in Palestine. His Zionist views would have compelled him to recommend policies consistent with the spirit of the Balfour Declaration. It is therefore not surprising that the Colonial Office and the Prime Minister decided to look to another man. A pro-Zionist report at this stage of the Mandate would have been unworkable to both the Colonial Office and to the position of the High Commissioner. The Hope Simpson report was made public on October 17 1930. The report attempted to define what the economic capacity of Palestine was and recommended the limiting of Jewish immigration into Palestine due to the lack of agricultural land to support such an increase in population.[73] The report was extremely damaging to the Zionist cause.[74]

After considering both the Shaw Commission and the Hope Simpson reports, the Colonial Office issued the Passfield White Paper on October 20 1930. The report was named after the Colonial Secretary at the time, Lord Passfield (Sidney Webb). Unlike some others in government at the time, Passfield had no religious training or connections. A long-time member of the left wing Fabian Society, Passfield was not disposed to be sympathetic to Evangelicals or to Zionism.[75]

It was apparent the Colonial Office initiated the Passfield White Paper to demonstrate their frustration with the cost of Zionism. The Commission blamed the Arabs for the violence, but suggested the Arabs were provoked by Jewish immigration and land purchases. Therefore, the report recommended that the British policies of Jewish immigration and Jewish land purchase restrictions continue. The report was well received by many British officials in Palestine, while the Jews of Palestine rejected the findings of the Commission. Ben Gurion was aghast at the Passfield White Paper, writing,

> The new policy he announced was the worst blow we had received up to then. For not only did it restrict Jewish immigration and the acquisition of land, but it was couched in terms which reversed the purpose of the Balfour Declaration and the League of Nations Mandate and condemned the Jews to be 'frozen' as a permanent minority.[76]

In the evening of October 20, Chaim Weizmann resigned as Chairman of the Jewish Agency and President of the Zionist Organization. Norman Rose summarized the situation by saying, "At one blow the whole framework of Anglo-Zionist relations had been shattered."[77] Following the publication of the Passfield White Paper, some Zionists in Parliament desired a full debate on the issue in the House of Commons, but this never happened.[78]

Leo Amery strongly disagreed with the recommendations of the Passfield White Paper. He wrote that the Colonial Office had "suddenly produced a White Paper which, in the restrictions it imposed on immigration and on Jewish acquisition of land, was a direct repudiation of the policy as set out in Churchill's White Paper of 1922, which we consistently followed."[79]

Zionist Protests and the MacDonald Letter

Immediately after the publication of the Passfield White Paper, Zionists in both Britain and Palestine strongly protested the Report. Prime Minister Ramsay MacDonald, sympathetic to Zionism, took care of the matter personally. He sent a letter to Chaim Weizmann promising that the recommendations of the Passfield White Paper would not be implemented. MacDonald even read the letter in the House of Commons, thus effectively neutralizing the Passfield White Paper.

The letter from Prime Minister Ramsay MacDonald to Chaim Weizmann, dated February 13 1931 was not equal to the Passfield White Paper in legality, but reiterated the Mandate's obligation to "facilitate Jewish immigration and to encourage close settlement by Jews on the land." MacDonald assured Weizmann that his letter was an "authoritative interpretation of the White Paper on the matters with which this letter deals."[80] This was surprising development. It seems the British government gave in to the Zionists. The Prime Minister explained to the House that it was not the intention of his government to stop Jewish immigration to Palestine. In fact, in the immediate years to follow, immigration would increase significantly. The Zionists had won a significant, albeit temporary political victory.[81]

The Macdonald letter emerged out of the work of a special Cabinet Committee chaired by the Foreign Secretary Arthur Henderson.[82] A prominent member of the Labour Party, Henderson became a Wesleyan Methodist as an adult.[83] He later became a lay preacher, having his own Church at Barnard Castle.[84] This deep, personal commitment to his faith and an already proven loyalty to Zionism may have motivated Henderson to play a role behind the MacDonald letter. This possibility may have been further shown by the fact that Henderson invited Weizmann to attend the Committee meetings.[85]

British Christian Zionism may have won this victory through internal pressure in the Labour Party. Lord Passfield was the Colonial Secretary of the Labour government that proposed the White Paper that carried his name. The conclusions of the White Paper were in contradiction to the stated policies of the Labour Party, which had supported Zionism and the Balfour Declaration up to this time. Alan Bullock, one of Ernest Bevin's biographers, noted, "Only a few days before, the Labour Party Executive at Llandudno had accepted the resolution of the affiliated Jewish Socialist Labour Party reaffirming Labour support for the establishment of a Jewish National Home in Palestine."[86]

Christian Zionism in Britain was never a class issue or a Party issue. Balfour was Conservative, Lloyd George was Liberal and Henderson and Barnes were Labour, but all supported Zionism. In 1930, Zionism found vocal support from the right wing of British politics. Three members of the Conservative Party wrote a letter in the London *Times* protesting the Passfield White Paper: Stanley Baldwin, Austin Chamberlain and Leopold Amery. Other influential Members of Parliament opposed to the White Paper were David Lloyd George, Winston Churchill, Herbert Samuel and Ernest Bevin. Speaking at Cowbridge, Glamorganshire, on October 23, Lloyd George assured his audience of Liberal support for Zionism. He claimed the Passfield White Paper was "a breach of national faith, a revocation of a solemn pledge."[87]

Richard Crossman, in his work, "A Nation Reborn, The Israel of Weizmann, Bevin and Ben Gurion," believed MacDonald himself made the decision not to proceed with Passfield's findings, not wanting to provoke a response from the Zionist movement.[88] Crossman wrote that MacDonald, "shrunk back when he saw the disastrous political effects of the policies recommended to him by his experts."[89] The unique letter had a powerful political effect. It greatly modified harsh government policy, and, according to Rose, "remained the legal basis for administering Palestine until the May White Paper of 1939."[90] According to Sheffer, the letter was referred to by some anti-Zionists as the "Black Letter." Sheffer noted that, "This letter governed the development of Palestine in the years that followed and was in fact only a return to traditional British policy.[91]

Ben Gurion was convinced the recommendations of the Passfield White Paper were dropped because of the influence of Zionists in various places. He wrote, "Only the combined efforts of the Jews of Palestine, the Zionist movement and other Jewish sympathizers in the world brought Passfield's efforts to naught."[92] The upcoming Whitechapel by-election may have also played a role in MacDonald's decision to write his letter. At the time, about a third of the voters in the riding were Jewish, and the Liberal candidate, Barnett Janner, was Jewish.[93]

MacDonald could have had another motivation for writing the letter. Perhaps he supported Zionism more than was commonly known, having been influenced from a young age by the Evangelical Christian community of his region. Born in 1866 Lossiemouth, Scotland, MacDonald was the illegitimate some of a farm labourer and a housemaid. He did not attend regular schools, but instead received his elementary education at the Free Church of Scotland in Lossiemouth and at the Drainie Parish Church. In 1885, at age 18, he was employed by a Church, serving as the assistant to the Minister at a Church in Bristol.[94] Such a role would not have been offered to a young man unless he displayed a high level of commitment to the belief system of the Church. It may have been that MacDonald drew from his Evangelical upbringing to do what he could to support the cause of Zionism as Prime Minister.

Although the Passfield White Paper never went into effect, it still had a lingering influence on the attitudes of the British government. Chancellor's gloomy reports may have inspired Passfield's suggestion that the Jews should remain a minority in Palestine, and they took the position that the Balfour Declaration implied equal obligation between Jews and Arabs and that Jewish immigration must not put Arabs out of work.

Despite a good outcome for Zionism, these events signaled a change in the relationship between Jewish Zionists and the Labour Party. According to Joseph Gorny, "In the period between the publication of the Shaw Commission Report and the October 1930 White Paper, the government and the Labour Movement became less sympathetic towards Zionist aspirations."[95] How did this come about? Since its inception, the Labour Party was committed to Zionism. This gradually changed throughout the Mandate. The explanation may lie in the fact that although some Labour Party members had Christian Zionist sympathies, the main bond between the Jewish Zionists and the Labour Party was Socialism. Gorny made a profound observation and asked two questions.

> The main ties between Attlee, Bevin and Ben Gurion, all socialists, might have been expected to be much stronger than those linking Lloyd George, Balfour and Weizmann. Yet history proved the reverse to be true. How did the rift between the two socialist movements occur? And why was

it the British labour movement which dealt Zionism one of its most bitter blows?[96]

Gorny's question is valid, and the answer to his question is that Socialism was only about politics. As soon as a political position was no longer beneficial, it was abandoned. Attlee and Bevin spoke in favour of Zionism when it suited them, and rightly so, since they viewed it as politics. When Zionism was no longer expedient for them, they no longer supported it. This is in contrast to how men such as Lloyd George, Balfour and Henderson viewed Zionism. They had an idealistic religious commitment to the cause that transcended politics.

Christian Zionism was a passion that not all in Britain could accept in the 1930's. Some saw Zionism as a worldwide clandestine Jewish movement, creating a hesitation to oppose the perceived will of the "Jews." Certainly, Weizmann's influence and friendships among the social and political leaders of Britain was impressive. By this time, he enjoyed great personal wealth due to royalties on his chemical patents. He could afford to divide his time between his homes in Rehovot, Palestine and London as he continued to persuade British politicians to promote Zionism. Lord Passfield complained that the influence of Weizmann gave an unfair advantage to Zionism. Crossman reported that Passfield said at this time, "It's very unfair that those Jews are so well represented. They have got Mr. Weizmann, whereas the poor Arabs haven't."[97]

In Palestine, Chancellor was in an awkward position. He had been politically outmaneuvered. The Jews of Palestine seemed to have their own personal direct links to the Cabinet and the Prime Minister. Chancellor was discouraged, revealing his feelings to his son that the world economic crisis required special caution because, he asked, "Who wanted now to get in trouble with 'world Jewry?'"[98] For his part, Weizmann supposed the British enemies of Zionism were defeated. He was so delighted at the outcome he referred to the victory as a "bluff."[99]

It is ironic to see Ernest Bevin so helpful to the Zionists at this point in 1931 since he would later aggressively oppose the efforts of Zionism. Ben Gurion speculated 30 years later why he supposed

Bevin was supportive of the Jews at this time. He thought Bevin was not yet very interested in Palestine, and was concerned the Christian Zionists in Britain would make political trouble for the government if the Passfield White Paper were approved. Ben Gurion thought that Bevin, "...knew very little about the problems involved at that time, but he was concerned about the political repercussions of the Passfield White Paper."[100]

The Christian Zionist Theological Struggle in Britain

Within the Churches of Britain in the 1930's, the ideology of Zionism was intrinsically linked to the doctrine of hermeneutics, (the interpretation of Scripture). This was a time in Britain when many Church denominations reevaluated their doctrinal views, especially how they interpreted the Bible. As the more liberal Protestant, Catholic and High Anglican Churches tended to reject a direct understanding of Scriptures, they found themselves in a position where they could not embrace Zionism. This belief was reflected in society as more people lost interest in Zionism. According to Church historian F. Michael Perko,

> For fundamentalists and many other conservative Protestants, Scripture is interpreted literally. Texts are to be taken as directly divinely inspired and, as a result, are to be understood as being literal truth. For liberal Protestants and Catholics, on the other hand, the Bible is to be interpreted according to the textual-critical method developed by the late 19th and early 20th century German philological and biblical scholars. Thus, texts are seen as divinely inspired but not necessarily literal truth.[101]

It is significant to note that Churchill believed in a direct interpretation of Scripture. He wrote an article about Moses in 1931, revealing his knowledge of the Bible and his admiration for Moses. In the article, Churchill claimed a preference for a plain interpretation of the Bible, rejecting the liberal notion of Moses being merely a legendary figure. Churchill wrote that he found "fullest satisfaction in taking the Bible story literally, and in indentifying one of the greatest of human beings with the most decisive leap-forward ever discernable in the human story...the greatest of the prophets, who spoke in person to the God of Israel."[102] According to Martin Gilbert, Churchill was fascinated by Jewish ethics. He read the Bible and was able to quote passages of Jewish Scripture speaking of their destiny.[103] Churchill's willingness to accept the direct meaning of the Bible was consistent with his support for Zionism.

Churchill also had a profound sympathy for Protestant worship. This was illustrated by his voluntary involvement in helping to prepare the combined British and American Church service on board the *Prince of Wales* off Newfoundland during World War 2. He wrote in his War Memoirs,

> The close packed ranks of British and American sailors, completely intermingled, sharing the same books and joining fervently together in the prayers and hymns familiar to both. I chose the hymns myself, "For Those in Peril on the Sea," and "Onward Christian Soldiers." We ended with "O God Our Help in Ages Past."...Every word seemed to stir the heart. It was a great hour to live.[104]

Throughout his long life, Churchill was open to Bible teaching. This was illustrated by a private meeting later in his life. In 1954, Churchill asked American Baptist Evangelist Billy Graham to visit him at 10 Downing Street. The two men met alone. Graham had been filling stadiums all over Britain with his gospel meetings and Churchill asked Graham how he did it. According to Graham's account, he told the 80-year-old Prime Minister, "It's the Gospel of Christ. People are hungry to hear a straight word from the Bible. Almost all the Clergy of this country used to preach it faithfully, but I believe they had gotten away from it." Churchill replied, "Yes, things have changed tremendously." Graham then read from the Bible and explained the way of salvation and God's plan for the future, including the return of Jesus. Graham recalled that Churchill was "receptive, if not enthusiastic, his eyes lighting up at the prospect." When the private meeting went overtime, Churchill instructed his secretary to let his next appointment wait. (The waiting guest was the former King Edward VIII, the Duke of Windsor).[105]

In 1931, a unique meeting took place in England that showed the sympathy of Prime Minister Ramsay MacDonald to the Zionist cause. Ben Gurion and other Jews from Palestine flew to England to meet with MacDonald at a breakfast meeting at Chequers. Ben Gurion recalled that MacDonald was positive toward Zionist aspirations and was negative in his opinion of Lord Passfield and John Chancellor, promising there would soon be a more sympathetic High Commissioner. MacDonald told Ben Gurion the Jews should not be content with parity. Some method must be devised to give them preference. MacDonald's son Malcolm wrote this down and the Prime Minster signed it. The statement was then sent to Chancellor.[106]

In Jerusalem, Chancellor was furious at the letter from the Prime Minister advising him how to treat the Jews. The policy of preference for the Jews over parity went against all that Chancellor believed. He saw the Jews in Palestine as living under the protection of the British since the Jews were still the minority. He believed if the British left, the Jews would be killed. He wrote his son, "The feeling among the Arabs against (the government) and the Jews is boiling."[107] He saw his role as impossible. Chancellor liked to say, "In Palestine only God in Heaven would make a good High Commissioner."[108] Wasserstein believed the difficulties of governing Palestine affected Chancellor personally, so that by the end he was "A discontented, self pitying, lonely, suspicious man, aloof toward his subordinates and hypersensitive to criticism."[109]

In the early 1930's T. E. Lawrence published two books that influenced British public attitudes regarding Zionism. Lawrence's books dealt with the conquest of the Middle East during the Great War. One book was "The Seven Pillars of Wisdom" and the other, "Revolt in the Desert." His perspective of the war challenged some of the conventional thinking many people in Britain had about the conquest of Palestine and Zionism. Immediately there was some controversy as to Lawrence's claims of the importance of the Arab Revolt in the defeat of the Turks. Besides this, Lawrence's personal role in the conquest and entry of Damascus was questioned. If

Lawrence's claims on behalf of the Arabs were true, then the importance of Zionism was reduced. Throughout his military and literary career, Lawrence showed no interest in Evangelical Christianity or Zionism. Politically, he favoured the Arab position.

The Growing Strength of American Evangelicalism

From 1930 to 1939, the combined Church membership of the three largest Evangelical denominations in the United States (Southern Baptist, Methodist and Presbyterian) grew from 13,106,000 to 14,469,000, an increase for the decade of approximately nine percent.[110] The numerous other Evangelical groups such as Pentecostals, Holiness Churches, Brethren, Independent Baptist and Gospel Churches, matched this level of growth. According to Kevin Phillips, in his work "American Theocracy," during the 1930's in America,

> For Fundamentalist, Holiness, Pentecostal, African American, and the New-Evangelical Churches and organizations, it was a time of expansion. The Southern Baptist Convention, the holiness Church of the Nazarene, the Pentecostal Assemblies of God, and the main black Baptist denominations all grew rapidly during this period."[111]

In the 1930's, gospel radio programs for evangelism and Bible teaching flourished in the United States. One of the largest was Charles Fuller's "Old Fashioned Revival Hour," broadcast from Los Angeles.[112] In 1936, with a population of approximately 127 million people, the United States had an estimated 55,807,000 Church members, representing about 44 percent of the total population. This indicates an overall growth in Church membership of five percent for the nation in ten years.[113]

In the 1930's, more American Evangelical denominations sent personnel to live and work in Palestine. This was viewed as a significant act in order to fulfill a desire to connect with the land of the Bible. The Pentecostal American Church of God's first representatives arrived in Palestine in 1934.[114] In 1936, the Zion Apostolic Mission was established in America with the goal of "biblical teaching and acts of loving-kindness." Later they sent their representatives to live in Palestine.[115]

As noted in previous chapters, there had long existed a religious sympathy for Zionism among these Evangelical Christian communities of America. As the United States was gradually growing in her strength and influence, this sympathy was being shown. Following the Arab riots of 1929, President Herbert Hoover, a Quaker and supporter of the restoration of Israel, sent a message of support to a special meeting of Jewish Organizations meeting in New York. As a Christian Zionist, Hoover desired to encourage the British in their work and make it known he wished for Palestine to become a homeland for the Jews.

> I know the whole world acknowledges the fine spirit shown by the British government in accepting the mandate of the Palestine in order that there might under this protection be established a homeland so long desired by the Jews. Great progress has been made in this inspiring enterprise over these last ten years, and to this progress, the American Jews have made enormous contribution. They have demonstrated not only the fine sentiment and ideals which inspire their activities but its political possibilities. I am confident out of these tragic events will come greater security and greater safeguards for the future, under which the steady rehabilitation of the Palestine as a true homeland will be even more assured.[116]

Slowly, Jewish Zionist groups and Evangelical clergy in America began working together. In 1930, Jewish leader Julian Mark and Christian Pastor Charles Edward Russell created a Pro-Palestine Federation of America, which enlisted a number of Christian clergymen in support of the Zionist program.[117] On the 50th anniversary of the Balfour Declaration, President Hoover wrote a positive letter to the Zionist Organization of America.

> I wish to express the hope that the ideal of the establishment of the National Jewish Home in Palestine, as embodied in

that Declaration, will continue to prosper for the good of all the people inhabiting the Holy Land....I have watched with genuine admiration the steady and unmistakable Progress made in the rehabilitation of Palestine which, desolate for centuries, is now renewing its youth and vitality through the enthusiasm, hard work and self-sacrifice of the Jewish pioneers who toil there in a spirit of peace and social justice. It is very gratifying to note that many American Jews, Zionists as well as non-Zionists, have rendered such splendid service to this cause, which merits the sympathy and moral encouragement of everyone.[118]

Another Christian group, the American Palestine Committee, created in 1932, counted Senators, Congressmen and other dignitaries among its sponsors. The APC was dedicated to Zionism and would continue to support the cause for many years to come.[119] For the most part, Jewish Zionists in America did little in the 1930's to exploit the sympathies of Christian Americans, despite the obvious willingness of Christian friends to support Zionism during the recurrent crisis precipitated either by Hitler or the British.[120] Zionism was not a popular notion among a large segment of American Jews in the 1930's. According to Allis Radosh of the City University of New York, "Before World War 2, most American Jewry thought Zionism was unnecessary and even dangerous."[121]

As the 31st American President, Herbert Hoover continued a long line of Protestant Christians who held the highest office in the United States. Every President and Vice President preceding Hoover had been affiliated with a Protestant Christian denomination, often with a personal support of Zionism.[122] In late 1932, he wrote to the American Palestine Committee expressing his own approval of the restoration of a National Home for the Jews.

I am interested to learn that a group of distinguished men and women is to be formed to spread knowledge and appreciation of the rehabilitation which is going forward in Palestine under Jewish auspices, and to add my expression to the sentiment among our people in favor of the realization of the age-old aspirations of the Jewish people for the restoration of their National Home land.[123]

The Arrival of High Commissioner Arthur Wauchope

In late 1931, John Chancellor finished his term of service and left Palestine. The new High Commissioner, Lieutenant General Arthur Wauchope, arrived in Jerusalem in November 1931 and would stay until 1937. He was a 57-year-old Scottish bachelor and had served in both the Boer War and the Great War. Ben Gurion was pleased at the choice and expected Wauchope would support Zionism. He believed the appointment was,

> ...intended as a sympathetic gesture to us on the part of an embarrassed British Labour government in 1931. I had been personally advised by Prime Minister Ramsay MacDonald of the plan to appoint "a good man, a fellow Scot," who would support Jewish immigration and land settlement.[124]

In his relations with the Arabs, Wauchope tried to deal properly with both the al-Husseini family and the rival Nashashibi family. In accordance with the recommendations of the Passfield White Paper, Wauchope set up a joint Arab-Jewish legislative council even though neither side wanted it. By now, both the Jews and the Arabs were set on victory, not cooperation. Wauchope seemed to like Palestine. He ruled with his personality, seemingly believing that all would be well again.

Wauchope appeared to be a moderate Zionist, but some thought his sympathy for the Jews went deeper. He wrote, "I am a wholehearted believer in the success of the National Home...I have the deepest sympathy not only with the Jews who settle in Palestine, but also with the ideals that inspire them."[125] Ben Gurion went so far as to declare, "He was the best High Commissioner we ever had."[126] Frederick Kisch believed the Zionism of Wauchope was similar to the Zionism of Balfour.[127] Wauchope supported the establishment of Jewish settlements, one of the keystones of Zionism. He wrote, "During my years in Palestine, one of my chief sources of encouragement has been the Jewish settlements and it is perhaps my chief hope now that by the time I leave their security may be permanently assured."[128] Wauchope showed the level of his Zionism by regularly communicating with Josiah Wedgwood.

> You and I think Arab and Jew, understand that I have real sympathy with the cause of Zionism...The Arab leaders hate, if not me, then my policy because I declared it more plainly a year ago than it had ever been put before. Arabs and many others believe that Jews rot the bough on which they are perched. I do not.[129]

Wedgwood responded with Christian passion to Wauchope's letter, encouraging the High Commissioner to serve the interests of the Jews. He even went so far as to instruct the High Commissioner that Zionism was a personal spiritual issue. Wedgwood wrote to Wauchope, linking the High Commissioner's soul to his policies, "If it would make any difference to you if Palestine were made a Crown Colony, then for your soul's salvation advocate a change which the Jews at least would welcome."[130]

In April 1933, General Allenby returned to Jerusalem as the guest of Arthur Wauchope. Allenby was well remembered by Christian Zionists as the general who dismounted before entering Jerusalem, declaring that he would not ride into the city into which his Saviour rode.[131] During his visit, Allenby dedicated the new YMCA building on King David Street. Part of his speech that day was preserved in blue ceramic tile in front of the building. "Here is a place whose atmosphere is peace, where political and religious jealousies can be forgotten and international unity be fostered and developed."[132] Despite these lofty words, practical solutions for peace were elusive.

In March 1933, Zionist Richard Meinertzhagen was discouraged with the progress toward a Jewish National Home. It had been 15 years since he had served with Allenby in the conquest of Jerusalem. Meinertzhagen wrote in his diary that he thought he, "...would not live to see the actual establishment of the Jewish State."[133] The reality was that the majority of the British officials in Palestine now tended to side with the Arabs. Valentine Vester of the American Colony recalled the situation in 1935,

Over the years of the Mandate, the British soldiers and officers stationed in Palestine became more and more pro-Arab, with fewer Zionists among them. I remember in 1935 most of the British officers I met at the King David Hotel were pro-Arab in their sympathies. But it was not something we talked about or seemed to think about a great deal.[134]

Under Wauchope, there were renewed Jewish hopes for British sympathies. Ben Gurion felt he had reason to speak well of the British, In 1934, Ben Gurion said, "We see in Great Britain the chief standard-bearer of this civilization in the world and Palestine should serve as the bridge between East and West. We do not see a better representative of western civilization than England."[135]

The Al-Qassam Affair and the Effects on Zionism

In November 1935, an incident occurred that would have political ramifications in Palestine for decades to follow. After this, not only would the British view Arab interests on a par with Jewish interests, they began to consult Arab leaders outside Palestine to determine British policy in Palestine. Sheikh Iz-al-Din al-Qassam left Haifa to live in the region around Jenin with his radical Muslim followers. Together they contemplated violent retaliation against the Jews. Some of al-Qassam's men clashed with the police and a Jewish police officer was killed. Al-Qassam was hunted down and killed, immediately becoming a martyr figure to the Arabs. Thousands of angry Arabs attended the funeral for Al-Qassam, in a show of Arab nationalism and anger. The al-Qassam incident ignited Arab passions that were already aroused because of increased Jewish immigration.

By early 1936, Arabs were striking all across Palestine. The strikes often turned violent. On April 19 1936, nine Jews were killed and four wounded in Jaffa. The riots became known to the Arabs as the "Arab Revolt." Bentwich believed that from that time on, the hope of a bi-national Jewish-Arab community and co-operation of Jews and Arabs disappeared.[136] The Mufti further complicated the issue by appealing directly to Muslim leaders throughout the Middle East. This began a trend whereby the Mufti learned he could effectively pressure the British government in London by appealing to foreign Muslim regimes. Kolinsky explained what the Mufti did.

> In April 1936, shortly after the Arab general strike began, he sent letters and telegrams to Muslim leaders, such as Ibn Saud of Saudi Arabia and to the press in Egypt and Iraq, appealing for support. He maintained contacts with Muslim leaders in India and as interest in the Palestine conflict grew in the Muslim world, his prestige grew correspondingly.[137]

The Mufti's new tactic worked effectively. Kolinsky noted that from this time on, the British government consistently consulted the Arab governments on issues in Palestine. Kolinsky wrote, "It was the first stage in a reversal of policy which led to the increased reliance of the British on the support of Arab governments in determining policy toward Palestine."[138] Thus, Foreign Secretary Anthony Eden "expressed concern that the general strike and violence which had raged in Palestine for the last two months could have negative effects on British relations with Arab countries."[139] The British authorities showed themselves to be weak and reactionary. Arab leaders, particularly the Mufti, were setting the agenda. According to Charles Townshend, "To most people, the British handling of the rebellion was a textbook example of vacillation."[140]

The New Government of Stanley Baldwin

In June 1935, Ramsay MacDonald gave up the office of Prime Minister to Stanley Baldwin.[141] From a wealthy family and having been educated at Harrow and Trinity College, Cambridge, Baldwin was a high Anglican who showed no interest in Zionism throughout his long political career. This lack of interest is manifest in Montgomery Hyde's biography of Baldwin, which has no mention of Zionism, the Balfour Declaration or Palestine.[142] In another Baldwin biography by Middlemas and Barnes, Palestine is mentioned only once, and that in passing. The reference is to "the troubles in Palestine."[143] Few Foreign Office records remain for Palestine from Baldwin's term as Prime Minister.[144] Neither are there Colonial Office records from the time when Samuel Hoare was his Colonial Secretary in 1935.[145]

The new Colonial Secretary in Baldwin's government was Malcolm MacDonald,[146] known at the time as a staunch friend of Weizmann and a firm advocate of Zionism.[147] Ben Gurion was pleased about some of the political changes in London. Arthur Ormsby-Gore was appointed Colonial Secretary and Anthony Eden was Foreign Secretary. Ben Gurion was so pleased with Ormsby-Gore that he wrote he was the only Colonial Secretary "who remained true to his earlier friendships and pursued policies according to his Zionist beliefs, and with the spirit of the Balfour Declaration and the Mandate."[148] This strong statement can be challenged in that Leo Amery also worked with a spirit of favour toward the ideals of the Balfour Declaration.

In the spring of 1936, the House of Commons discussed a proposal by the Baldwin government to set up a Legislative Council in Palestine that would give the Arab majority a decisive veto on any new Jewish immigration. Churchill spoke out passionately against the proposal, telling the House that Arab rule "would be a very great obstruction to the development of Jewish immigration into Palestine and to the development of the National Home of the Jews there." Churchill went on to say he could not conceive how the government could "reconcile...the development of the policy of the Balfour Declaration with an Arab majority in the Legislative Council.[149] As a result of having to heed Churchill's rebuke, Rose noted that the government suffered an overwhelming setback.[150] Wedgwood took some of the credit for the victory in Parliament writing his daughter, "I have had a successful week...actually slain the Palestine constitution. I got Churchill and Chamberlain and Amery and Sinclair all to speak, and they did."[151]

During these years, the political influence of British Evangelicals continued to decline. In 1931, there were only 23 lay clergy in Parliament, a dozen fewer than in the previous Parliament.[152] The last and most spectacular political effort of the Nonconformist movement was the "Council of Action" campaign, launched in 1935. The Council of Action campaign attempted to challenge the government on various moral issues. The effort did not achieve much recognition. According to Steven Koss, this failed effort revealed beyond any doubt that Nonconformity, once a force to be reckoned with in the national life of Britain, was not dormant, but dead.[153] In 1906, 185 Members of the House of Commons identified themselves as Nonconformists. By 1935, that number had been reduced to only 65.[154] In contrast, Cosmo Lang, Archbishop of Canterbury from 1928 to 1941, reflected the official Replacement Theology view of Anglican Church when he felt comfortable to suggest that the "Jews themselves" were to blame for "the excesses of the Nazis."[155]

In July 1936, Jan Smuts wrote to Lloyd George outlining his disapproval of the change in government attitudes. These were busy men living far from each other. Why would they be concerned about Zionism unless their interest was ideological? In his letter, Smuts inquired about rumours of the British government prohibiting Jewish immigration to Palestine. Smuts called this a "withdrawal of the Balfour Declaration and surrender to Arab agitation." Smuts urged Lloyd George to use his influence to stop it.[156]

The Arrival of the Peel Commission

Arab violence in Palestine spread to Jerusalem in the spring of 1936. Ronald Zweig, in his work "Britain and Palestine during the Second World War," believed the British were realizing by 1936 that they could not grant the wishes of both the Jews and the Arabs. Zweig wrote that it was apparent, "The dual task of encouraging the growth of the Jewish National Home, at the same time protecting the rights of Palestine's Arab inhabitants could no longer be implemented."[157]

The British government in London was looking for a solution to their dilemma. The Zionists saw their hopes and dreams being delayed. The Arabs complained their land was being taken from them. In late 1936, the Foreign Office sent Lord Peel and his five-member Commission to Palestine to investigate the situation.[158] Peel was a respected politician who had served in both Houses and had twice held the post of Secretary of State for India during the 1920's. From the beginning, Peel approached Palestine as a problem that needed to be solved. He and his team conducted extensive interviews with all parties involved and in the end submitted an extensive report. Lord Peel was a High Anglican who seemed impartial to the religious tensions involved, although his extensive experience with religious conflict in India prepared him for similar tensions in

Palestine. He was not a Zionist and carried out his work in Palestine without a dedication to the restoration of Israel.[159]

Some of the witnesses who testified to the Peel Commission were Weizmann, Ben-Gurion, Jabotinsky, the Mufti, Churchill and Lloyd George. The Mufti told the Commission there was no chance for co-existence between the Jews and the Arabs of Palestine. Lord Peel seemed to agree, writing, "The social, moral and political gaps between the Arab and Jewish communities are already unbridgeable."[160] Ben Gurion, as Chairman of the Executive Committee of the Jewish Agency for Palestine took the opportunity to defy the authority of the British government and affirmed a higher religious authority when he declared, "The Bible is our Mandate."[161] These words from Ben Gurion might have had an effect on the British Cabinet in 1917. They might even have had an impact in the 1920's. However, the Peel Commission was unmoved by Ben Gurion's attempt to rally religious sentiment. The Peel Commission did not see the Bible as authoritative in the politics of Palestine. Moreover, Ben Gurion was not a religious man and it is not surprising this unusual tactic on his part did not succeed.

When the Peel Commission consulted former High Commissioner Herbert Samuel, he testified that Prince Faisal's letter of 1919 was evidence of Arab acceptance of the Balfour Declaration, and that the British had not broken any pledge made to the Arabs. Samuel wrote to Lord Peel,

> It will be easy to judge whether the opinions there expressed by the head of the Arab Delegation at the Peace Conference are consistent with view that the Balfour Declaration, which was then in the forefront of the discussions on Palestine, was a betrayal of pledges that had previously been given to the leaders of the Arab movement.[162]

Despite noticing some limited success at coexistence, the Peel Commission concluded that the conflict in Palestine could only be resolved by the partition of the country. The Report read in part,

Partition offers a possibility of finding a way through them, a possibility of obtaining a final solution of the problem which does justice to the rights and aspirations of both the Arabs and the Jews and discharges the obligations we undertook towards them twenty years ago to the fullest extent that is practicable in the circumstances of the present time.[163]

The Peel Commission's report was a victory for the Arabs. The British had come to believe the Jews could not (and should not) have all of Palestine for their National Home. In less than 20 years, the British government had drifted far from the Zionist spirit of the Balfour Declaration. The idea of partition would now only give the Jews sovereignty over a part of the territory specified by the Balfour Declaration. The Peel Commission's report dealt with the hopelessness of Arab/Jewish political co-operation. The Commission concluded that the dream of the Balfour Declaration was unattainable. "We return then to partition as the only method we are able to propose for dealing with the root of the trouble...There seem to us to be three essential features of such a plan. It must be practicable. It must conform to our obligations. It must do justice to the Arabs and the Jews."[164]

The British idea of applied justice in this case was to attempt to please both sides in a spirit of fairness. The British seemed to believe the interest of both the Jews and the Arabs could be served through compromise. However, to these two different parties involved, compromise was impossible. The conclusion of the Peel Report included an old English proverb, "Half a loaf is better than no bread." The Report explained,

> Partition means that neither will get all it wants. It means that the Arabs must acquiesce in the exclusion from their sovereignty of a piece of territory, long occupied and once ruled by them. It means that the Jews must be content with less than the Land of Israel they once ruled and have hoped to rule again.[165]

The Peel Commission asserted the failure of both the Balfour Declaration and of the Mandate. "The Mandate for Palestine should terminate and be replaced by a Treaty System in accordance with the precedent set in Iraq and Syria."[166] The Commission also recommended the British remain in Palestine to administrate key cities. "A new Mandate therefore should be framed with the execution of this trust as its primary purpose." This special restricted new Mandate area was proposed to encircle Jaffa, Bethlehem, Jerusalem, Lydda and Ramle.[167]

During the final deliberations of the Peel Commission, Zionists, both Jewish and Christians, were active in London. Chaim Weizmann organized a dinner party for June 8 and invited Churchill as the guest of honour. Amery, Attlee, Wedgwood, Cazalet and James de Rothschild also attended. Lloyd George sent his regrets but expressed his willingness to abide by anything the assembly decided. During the long conversation after dinner, Amery and Churchill spoke the strongest on behalf of Zionism.[168] Despite the sincerity and quality of the gathering, it again symbolized how the British Zionism lobby was out of the circle of real power and influence.

The Peel Commission Report was published in July 1937. It was 404 pages long, with maps. The implication of the Report was that approximately two-thirds of Palestine would be an Arab State, and one-third a Jewish State. The British should administer certain "Holy Cities" such as Jerusalem and Bethlehem in a special reduced Mandate zone. Neither the Jews nor the Arabs of Palestine accepted the recommendations. It was not that the Jews rejected the concept of partition, the issue was how little the Peel Commission allotted to the Jews. In a way, the principle was accepted while the plan was rejected.[169] Despite these rejections, the Peel Commission entrenched the concept of partition in the minds of the various parties.

At the time of the Peel Commission, various Zionistic leaning British politicians communicated together to encourage each other in their views. The new Secretary of State, Ormsby-Gore, wrote his views regarding partition, "For the Jews it means a further drastic whittling down of the area of the National Home."[170] Leo Amery, as the former Colonial Secretary noted that Chaim Weizmann accepted the notion of partition, "in spite of the passionate indignation of most of his fellow Zionists."[171] Josiah Wedgwood wrote to Churchill, "You know the situation of the Jews in Poland. Public opinion here and in America still counts"[172] Herbert Samuel also appealed to Churchill, "You have always shown so complete an understanding of Palestine questions, and so much sympathy with the Jewish enterprise there."[173]

Although Herbert Samuel had been long removed from Palestine politics, he wanted to give his opinion of the Peel Commission report. He wrote to the Colonial Secretary that its recommendations not be imposed upon the two indigenous communities of Palestine.

> The fortunes of both the Arabs and the Jews of Palestine are to be decided, probably for a generation, perhaps for longer. Both communities are vitally concerned in the decision. Neither has accepted the Royal Commission as an arbitrator. By what right can the British government claim to determine, on the strength of the report of a Commission, the whole future of these two intelligent and politically-conscious communities, without even hearing their views upon proposals which may be entirely novel?[174]

Christian Zionist's spirits were down. At the end of 1937, Blanche Dugdale wrote sadly to Weizmann, "My uncle's document is now a historic piece of paper. It has given us 400,000 Jews and a few friends and that is all-but we must make that enough."[175]

Following the Peel Commission Report, the Arabs renewed their violence. The Jews in Palestine began in earnest to plan for a state of their own. Christian Zionism had hardly been a consideration during the Peel Commission deliberations. It was becoming clear that the British government no longer had the will to implement the restoration of Israel. Political pragmatism had replaced the religious idealism of Zionism as the government's primary motivation.

The Zionism of Orde Wingate

In contrast to the anti-Zionist tone of the Peel Commission's report, some individuals still kept the passion of Christian Zionism alive. Perhaps the best example of this passion was illustrated by the

British army officer Orde Wingate and his service for the Zionists in Palestine. Wingate was a fervent Christian Zionist who symbolized the zeal for the restoration of Israel that some British Christians still held. He arrived in Palestine in September 1936 as a British intelligence officer with the rank of Captain. Wingate was born in India and raised in various locations throughout the Empire. He was an Evangelical Christian with a love for the Bible and a knowledge of the history of the Jewish people in the land of Israel.

Wingate's father came from the Evangelical Free Church of Scotland, while his mother grew up in the Plymouth Brethren Church in England. According to one of Wingate's biographers, Trevor Royle, these factors had a "major influence in shaping the man. It was the crossing of the Bible with the sword."[176] Royle describes the Brethren as "A Calvinistic faith whose members interpret the Bible quite literally and believe in the second coming of Christ."[177] Wingate's family heritage was rich in Evangelistic enterprise. Orde's grandfather, William Wingate, was ordained by the Church of Scotland in 1842 and moved to Budapest the following year to begin a mission to the Jews there.[178] In 1910, Wingate's father, George Wingate, traveled to India at his own expense to "report on conditions facing Christian missionaries amongst the local Muslim community."[179]

At the age of seven, Orde Wingate loved to shout that he was Oliver Cromwell, off to war against the Catholics with a sword in one hand and a Bible in the other.[180] As a young man, Wingate volunteered to participate in social missions work in the Glasgow slums. There he encountered Jews and picked up his first words in Hebrew.[181] This early and passionate identity with the Bible and philosemitism played an enormous role through all of Wingate's life.

Upon arriving in Palestine, Wingate wrote, "Long before I reached Palestine I knew what the Jews were seeking, understood what they needed, sympathized with their aims and knew they were right."[182] Wingate did not merely have the opinion that the Jews were right; he was firmly convinced of it. On his first day in Jerusalem, Wingate met with Emmanuel Wilenski, the Chief Intelligence officer for the Haganah. Wingate told Wilenski, "There will be no free Palestine for the Jews unless you fight and win, and you will not win, my friend, unless I teach you how to fight and I lead you into battle."[183] Wilenski and Wingate worked closely together for the next two years. Wilenski coined the nickname "The friend," or *Ha'yadid* for Wingate.[184]

According to another of Wingate's biographers, Leonard Mosley, "Palestine for Wingate was a joy, in the beginning because it made everything he had learned from his Bible come true before his eyes."[185] By 1937, he had made friends with some of the most influential Jewish leaders in Palestine: Chaim Weizmann, Moshe Shertok, David Ben Gurion and Abba Eban.[186] In 1937, Wingate told Moshe Sharett, the future Israeli Prime Minister, that he had adopted Zionism as a religion.[187] Royle believed, "Wingate regarded Zionism as a cause for which all his previous training and experience had prepared him."[188]

Orde Wingate soon learned that if the Arabs attacked a Jewish community, the Jews would merely attempt to defend themselves. After the attack, the Jewish leaders were usually arrested for possession of illegal weapons.[189] Wingate also realized the retreating Arabs knew the British stayed to the roads and it was easy to take cover from the R.A.F. in the rocks and valleys.[190] Once he had this knowledge, Wingate advocated attack. He repeatedly warned his Jewish friends, "The Jews of Palestine are in bad condition. So long as you all sit in your settlements and wait to fight and die, you will die before you have a chance to fight."[191]

Wingate was well known among his fellow British officers for his passionate devotion to Zionism. He was constantly quoting the Old Testament, putting his biblical zeal into action. When he organized "Special Night Squads" in 1938 to attack Arab positions, Wingate taught new strategies to the Jews, showing them how to take the attack to the enemy, the non-importance of uniforms, leading from the front and reliance on a large reserve force. Wingate personally led these night raids against the Arabs. Operating usually with about 200 men, both British and Jews, Wingate's radical military style entered into the thinking of the modern Israeli Defense Forces.[192]

Ben Gurion thought Orde Wingate to be an excellent soldier and a man of conviction. "He was also a passionate Zionist…raised in an atmosphere of rigid Puritanism. The first things he read were the Scriptures, and from the Bible came his knowledge of and attachment to the Land of Israel and the Jewish people.[193] Wingate believed in promoting the symbols of modern Zionism. He told Chaim Weizmann that the first thing the Jews must do if they ever establish a State of Israel was to bring Herzl's bones from Vienna and bury them on Mount Carmel.[194] One of the men Wingate trained for night raids was Zvi Brenna.[195] Wingate appealed to Brenna to completely trust him. "Henceforth you must stop thinking of me as an Englishman and consider me as one of you, fighting the same fight as you, with the same goal as you. I am with you with every beat of my heart."[196] Wingate loved to quote the Old Testament verse to his Jewish comrades, "Go in this thy might and thou shalt save Israel."[197]

Wingate had a strong influence on Moshe Dayan, who would later become an Israeli general and Minister of Defense. Wingate was a hero to Dayan, as he inspired Dayan in forging the tactics that would later be used in the building of the Israeli Defense Forces.[198] According to Robert Slater, Dayan's biographer, "Every leader in the IDF was in effect a disciple of Wingate's, none more so than Moshe Dayan."[199] The first time Moshe Dayan met Wingate was at Shimron. Dayan wrote, "He looked you straight in the eye as someone who seeks to imbue you with his own faith and strength."[200] On a personal level, Wingate tended to be slovenly in appearance, rude, abrasive and fearless. What made a mark on Dayan was the sheer audacity of Wingate to believe he could teach the Jews how to defeat the Arabs. Dayan described Wingate as "mad and maddening."[201]

Wingate told the leaders of the Yishuv that there was only one important book on the subject of Zionism, and he was very familiar with it-the Bible. Slater wrote, "Before Wingate would undertake an action in Palestine he would read the appropriate biblical passage, trying to find evidence for an ancient Jewish victory in the locale of an upcoming Jewish attack."[202] Orde Wingate believed he was building a Jewish army for the future, even if the very people he was trying to help did not understand at first. Wingate envisioned his Special Night Squads as forming the nucleus of a burgeoning Jewish army.[203] Slater wrote,

Wingate was convinced that the only way the Yishuv could counter Arab violence was by building its own army. Throughout the 1920's and early 1930's such an idea was greeted with derision by the moderate elements of the Yishuv and the Haganah. But by 1938, Wingate's vision made sense.[204]

Wingate inspired confidence in the Jews. Even Moshe Dayan wanted to please Wingate. After a night raid where a small number of kibbutz fighters engaged a larger party of Arabs, Dayan wrote to his wife. "Everyone thinks our action was quite good. Captain Wingate praised our operation and we may be getting a citation. After all, we were just seven and there were 80 of them. Our boys behaved wonderfully."[205] Yossi Harel was a young Jewish soldier with Wingate. He was later Captain of the immigrant ship *Exodus*. Harel said of Wingate, "He was very pro-us, pro-Jewish. He commanded, and I was with him. He achieved more than any other unit in Israel...while working with us, he was very involved with the Bible. His idea was that he wanted to be the commander of the Jewish army."[206]

When news reached Palestine of the 1939 White Paper decision, Wingate was devastated. He asked Zvi Wilenski for a meeting of the Haganah leaders. Wingate declared to the Jewish leaders,

"Members of the Haganah, the White Paper has turned you down. There will be no Jewish State unless you fight for it, and it is the English you will have to fight." Wingate encouraged them to blow up the oil refineries in Haifa. The Haganah leaders were unwilling to comply. Clearly, the passion of Wingate's Zionism went far beyond the vows he had taken as a British officer.[207]

Despite his success in helping to crush the Arab rebellion, the independent activities of Wingate made problems for the British. Although his military activities met with the reluctant approval of the Mandate authorities, he compromised the impartiality of the British. According to Townshend, when the British allowed and cooperated with the Special Night Squads, they "signed the death warrant of the Mandate." Their cooperation "Skewed the symmetry of interests which gave British rule its claim to legitimacy."[208]

In late 1939, Wingate was transferred out of Palestine. His Commanding Officer wrote, "Orde Charles Wingate, DSO, is a good soldier, but so far as Palestine is concerned, he is a security risk. He cannot be trusted. He puts the interests of the Jews before those of his own country."[209] Wingate's Zionism was not popular among many of the British in Palestine in the late 1930's. Royle noted that Wingate's Zionism "did him few favours at a time when young officers were expected to be orthodox and seemly."[210] According to his friend Yossi Harel, Wingate was disliked by most of the British administration. When Wingate was transferred out of Palestine, his passport stamp read that the bearer should not be allowed to re-enter Palestine.[211]

Wingate was later killed in 1944 while serving in Burma, but his memory is still highly esteemed in Israel. The national sports training school in Israel was named after him. Had Wingate survived the war, it is likely he would have returned to Palestine to help the Jews achieve independence. Ben Gurion claimed that had Wingate lived, he would have been the natural choice to command the Israel Defense Forces during the 1948 War of Independence.[212] Wingate was passionate about Zionism and totally devoted to the cause. This was an encouragement and a help to the Jews in Palestine. However, there is a touch of the pathetic surrounding his efforts. Instead of Christian Zionism being promoted through the Cabinet or the Colonial Office, by the late 1930's, a low ranking Officer serving in Palestine had become the foremost British voice for the restoration of Israel.

The military activities of Wingate in the 1930's were far different from the high politics of Balfour in 1917 and the skilled diplomacy of Amery in the 1920's. Through men like Wingate, British Christian Zionism was championed in the lower levels of society. Despite the encouragement he was for the Jews in Palestine, and despite the symbolism he represented, he was mistrusted by most in the British administration in Palestine. His removal from Palestine illustrated his unpopularity among his colleagues and a desire to rid the country of such a man. His removal also illustrated the unpopularity of Zionism among the British officers and administration in Palestine.

The Sympathetic Cooperation of Arthur Wauchope

By 1937, with Nazi persecution in Germany and continuing pogroms in Russia, an increasing number of Jews were immigrating to Palestine. High Commissioner Wauchope accepted these high levels of immigration. In the face of Arab complaints about Jewish land purchases, the Jewish leaders in Palestine made a unique move. Jewish officials began to publish lists of Arab leaders who had sold land to the Jews. This was an attempt on the part of the Jews to show the hypocrisy of the Arab position. The list included Musa Kazim al-Husseini, former mayor of Jerusalem, the father of Mufti Haj Amin al-Husseini, Jerusalem's mayor Ragheb al-Nashashibi, the Dejanis family of Jerusalem, and the a-Shawa family of Gaza.[213]

As High Commissioner, Wauchope worked hard to stay fair minded and professional, but showed his personal favour to the Zionism. He wrote to the Colonial Office indicating he approved of partition because "it would give the Jews a chance at their own country...I am not by any means despairing of partition. It has had a set back and the sacrifices entailed by acceptance of Royal Commission can be severe for both sides."[214] In another letter to the Colonial Office, Wauchope even wished Jewish settlement to be expanded into Transjordan.[215]

Wauchope did not show the same benevolence to the Arab leaders in Palestine, once writing, "If the Mufti and Auni Bey are obstinate, they and their friends can be deported."[216] Arab violence expanded in September 1937 when Arab militants temporarily took control of large areas of the countryside. In October, the British dissolved the Arab Higher Committee and removed the Mufti as President of the Supreme Council. The Mufti fled from Jerusalem to Beirut and later surfaced in Berlin during World War 2.[217]

In contrast to the High Commissioner's distain for the Arabs, Wauchope had regular lunch meetings with Weizmann. The two men enjoyed a good relationship and the High Commissioner usually reported their conversations to the Colonial Office. The topics of conversation were order in Palestine, the plight of the Jews of Europe, impending war and Weizmann's hope of partition. Wauchope took a personal interest in Weizmann, writing, "I think Dr. Weizmann is not very well and he seems to have his days of cheerfulness and of depression."[218] Wauchope resigned as High Commissioner and left Palestine in February 1938. He was disappointed to see the relentless violence, "You can imagine how I hate retiring, especially at this juncture, when Palestine is in so bad a way…if Weizmann had not so constantly used the word, I'd say I was heartbroken."[219] Ben Gurion said of Wauchope,

> His term also coincided with the advent of Hitler and the desperate need to rescue German Jewry and bring them to Palestine. He supported our demands for a revolutionary change in the British Colonial Office's immigration policy, one that would enable us to take in tens of thousands of our fellow Jews…It was during Wauchope's administration that Jewish immigration reached its peak year-more than 60,000 in 1935.[220]

During his years as High Commissioner, Wauchope favoured Zionist ideals while faithfully carrying out his duties in a fair manner. He could be severe with the Arab leaders but did not show a corresponding coldness to the Jewish leaders in Palestine. Early in his term, he indicated his sympathies to Zionism and attempted to make decisions that would favour that sentiment. He wrote Ormsby-Gore that he had "the deepest sympathy not only with the Jews who settle in Palestine, but also with the ideals that inspire them."[221] Unfortunately for the cause of Zionism, Wauchope was given authority in Palestine at a time when political leaders in the Cabinet and the Colonial Office no longer had the same inclination to advocate Zionism.

The Arrival of Harold MacMichael as the New High Commissioner

Harold MacMichael became the new High Commissioner of Palestine in 1938 and seemed to be well prepared for the assignment. In his youth, MacMichael graduated from Magdalene College, Cambridge. After passing his civil service exam, he served in Khartoum, rising to the position of civil secretary in 1926. In 1933, he became governor of Tanganyika, serving in that role until 1937.

The following year he became High Commissioner of Palestine.[222] MacMichael seemed aloof to some, perhaps seeing himself as of a higher class than others around him. He anticipated a difficult time in Palestine. He said of his new posting, "I shall be lucky if I leave with one hair that is not white on my head."[223] Colonial Secretary Ormsby-Gore wrote to MacMichael in December,

> I am very grateful indeed to you for consenting to take on what I must admit is the hardest and toughest job under the Colonial Office. The various problems of Palestine are among the most difficult that the Empire has been confronted with in its history and require not only firm but wise handling...As I see it, we have to remain in Palestine for strategic reasons and for reasons of political prestige...Palestine is unique and of universal significance, and is at one and the same time the Holy Land of all Jews and all Christians and a holy land of the Arabs.[224]

In April 1938, an event occurred which polarized opinions of MacMichael. A Jewish teenager, Shlomo Ben-Yosef, and two of his friends, shot at an Arab bus traveling from Safed to Rosh Pina. There was no damage and no injuries. Even though the three were minors and had no previous offenses, Ben Yosef was given the death sentence. MacMichael refused to commute the sentence and Ben Yosef was hanged.[225] The Jews of Palestine were stunned at MacMichael's insensitivity.

In October 1938, General Bernard Montgomery arrived in Palestine to take command of security.[226] Montgomery was raised in Tasmania, the son of an Evangelical Minister who was serving as a missionary there.[227] Montgomery cared nothing for the claims of the Arabs to Palestine and compared the problems in Palestine to the religious troubles in Ireland. Colonial Secretary Ormsby-Gore agreed and called the comparison between Palestine and Ireland "singularly complete."[228]

The Slow Development of Zionism in America

In the United States during the 1930's, the government of President Franklin Roosevelt did not interfere in the problems of Palestine. As a member of the Episcopalian Church in America, he preferred higher Church liturgy, his beliefs not typical of some of the Evangelical Presidents who preceded him.[229] Although he personally seemed to have a hands-off policy toward the British Mandate, Roosevelt did make occasional statements supporting the Jewish cause in Palestine. In September 1936, he sent an open letter to the Jewish "United Palestine Yearbook," "It is a source of renewed hope and courage that by an international accord and by the moral support of the people of the world, men and women of Jewish faith have a right to resettle the land where their faith was born and from which much of our modern civilization has emanated."[230]

Also in 1936, Roosevelt commented on the traditional place Zionism had in American culture. "Every American knows of the love of the Jews for the land associated with the great beginnings of their history. Jews in the United States may well feel proud of the part they played in the rebirth of The Land."[231] In 1937, Roosevelt wrote to the United Palestine Appeal,

> The American people, ever zealous in the cause of human freedom, have watched with sympathetic interest the effort of the Jews to renew in Palestine the ties of their ancient homeland and to reestablish Jewish culture in the place where for centuries it flourished and whence it was carried to the far corners of the world. This year marks the 20th anniversary of the Balfour Declaration, the keystone of contemporary reconstruction activities in the Jewish homeland. Those two decades have witnessed a remarkable exemplification of the vitality and vision of the Jewish pioneers in Palestine. It should be a source of pride to Jewish citizens of the United States that they, too, have had a share in this great work of revival and restoration.[232]

Despite these positive statements, it is clear that Roosevelt's attitude toward Zionism, although officially supportive, was less than enthusiastic. Lawrence Davidson, in his work "America's Palestine," observed that during the 1930's, the general opinion of the State Department was that, "Open American support for the Zionist position in Palestine would only lead to disaster for both the United States and Great Britain."[233]

During the late 1930's, many independent Evangelical Christian groups in America promoted their support for Zionism. One of the most influential new groups was the "Friends of Israel Gospel Ministry" in New Jersey. In the beginning, their main purpose was to assist Jewish refugees escaping Nazi Europe and to promote Zionism. Their magazine *Israel My Glory* enjoyed a wide circulation.[234] One American Evangelical leader, J. Addison Bell, published a magazine, *The Christian Zionist*, in New York. His periodical was dedicated to encouraging Christian support for the restoration of biblical Israel. One 1937 article read, "Through Zionism a great opportunity offers itself to Christendom. To help God's people return to their ancient patrimony is to serve God's will."[235] An article in 1938 was more political, protesting the British policies of favouring the Arabs. "The official policy was indeed one of extreme favoritism toward a truculent minority of Arab religious and racial fanatics."[236]

In 1938, American diplomat James McDonald held the position of the League of Nations High Commissioner for Refugees. McDonald met several times with Hitler that year and predicted great trouble ahead for the Jews of Europe. As an Evangelical, McDonald sympathized with Zionism. He saw the coming world conflict as a spiritual battle, writing in 1938, "I had spent much time in Europe, talked much, read more and listened still more. I had met Hitler; and I had become convinced that the battle against the Jew was the first skirmish in a war on Christianity, on all religion, indeed on all humanity."[237] McDonald believed the plight of the Jews symbolized the problems of all mankind, writing, "The right of the Jew not only to life but to his own life is in its way a symbol of every man's right. It is in that spirit that I have sought, and still seek, to champion this right."[238]

Despite a carefully constructed, officially positive attitude toward Zionism, Roosevelt rarely expressed his personal opinion about the subject. Contemporary historian Selig Adler condemned

Roosevelt as, "caring little about the Jewish plight or Zionists plans for Palestine"[239] It does not appear that Roosevelt made much study of Zionism. In 1944, during World War 2, Weizmann was able obtain a private audience with the President. Weizmann was dismayed at the President's lack of knowledge on the subject of the Jewish National Home. Weizmann later related to his colleagues in Palestine, "The meeting actually resolved itself into a lesson on Zionism, with myself as teacher and the President as pupil." Roosevelt promised Weizmann that he would speak to Churchill about Zionism and the "righteousness of Jewish claims."[240]

There is no evidence that Roosevelt ever kept his promise to speak to Churchill about these matters. Despite his limited interest in Zionism, in March 1945, just before his death, Roosevelt seemed to favour a United Nations trusteeship over Palestine. Roosevelt told Hoskins of the State Department that, "He thought such a plan might well be given to the United Nations organization after it had been set up."[241]

The Effects of Changing Beliefs in Britain

During the Great Depression, Protestant Christians across the western world struggled to redefine their identity and doctrinal beliefs. As part of these changes, many ecumenical Christian Conferences were held in Britain between the wars. In 1937, two of the largest theological conferences ever convened in Britain were hosted in Oxford and Edinburgh. Unity of the denominations was of the highest importance. As the popularity of this new ecumenicism spread, doctrinal specifics such as Zionism were set aside for the sake of a more united Christianity. This contributed to new generations of Britons not understanding or committing to Zionism.

Through the 1920's and 1930's liberal Christian doctrine grew in popularity in the Protestant Churches of Britain. This was particularly true in the Anglican Church. One area of doctrinal dispute was related to an issue known as "Replacement Theology." This doctrine taught that the Gentile Church had replaced Israel as the Chosen People of God. It then followed that the Christian Church inherited the divine promises made to Israel. The implication of this belief was that the Jews were no longer the recipients of divine favour. One of the most practical implications of this belief was that the Jews had no claim to the land of Israel. The Catholic Church and the traditional Eastern Churches had long held this doctrine of Replacement Theology. Some Protestant Churches had also adopted this doctrine, notably certain higher elements in the Anglican Church. In contrast to this teaching, Nonconformist Evangelicals usually taught that the Jews were still God's Chosen People and that the Gentile Christians had been spiritually "grafted in" to the Jews.[242]

Through the late 1930's, the Anglican Church debated the doctrinal issue of Replacement Theology. This division was strongly felt in Jerusalem where the Anglican Church was separated into two camps. In East Jerusalem, St. Georges' Cathedral was pro-Arab and taught Replacement Theology. In contrast, Christ Church, inside the Jaffa Gate, was pro-Jewish and taught Zionism. Sometimes the issue went public. In an article for the London *Times* in 1938, Graham Brown, the Anglican Bishop of Jerusalem wrote, "It is the affirmation of the New Testament that the ancient Israel, 'Israel after the flesh,' has forfeited its claim to the promises."[243] As an Evangelical Anglican clergyman and a Zionist, Dr. E. Langston, challenged Bishop Brown's teaching. Langston answered Brown's article with a letter of his own in the *Palestine Post*. "Will the Bishop kindly inform us upon what authority he makes that statement?" Langston then quoted the New Testament book of Romans, the Torah, plus the prophets Zechariah and Isaiah. Langston responded, "No, the Bible in no place teaches us or leads anyone to believe that Israel has forfeited 'its claim to the promises.'"[244]

Immediately after Langston's letter appeared, Bishop Brown answered, declaring his authority was a statement entitled, "Doctrine in the Church of England-the Report of the Commission on Christian Doctrine appointed by the Archbishops of Canterbury and York in 1922."[245] Brown showed that the highest authorities in the Anglican Church upheld the opinion that the Jews had lost their claim to be "God's Chosen People." Regarding the issue of Replacement Theology, the lines between Church and State were sometimes muddled. Samuel wrote Colonial Secretary Ormsby-Gore warning, "The Anglican Bishop in Jerusalem is strongly opposed to any form of partition on religious grounds. He may perhaps have considerable support among the Christian communities."[246]

The British Labour Party had been linked to the Evangelical movement since its beginnings and this usually involved sympathy for Zionism. Despite the fact that the influence of the Evangelicals in Britain was waning, the Labour Party still tended to voice a positive opinion on Zionism. In October 1938, the Labour Party reiterated its support for the ideal of the Balfour Declaration, declaring, "As early as 1917 British Labour declared its support of the Jewish desire to establish a Homeland in Palestine."[247] Also in 1938, following his tour of Palestine, Ramsay MacDonald wrote a book about the Jews in Palestine. He called his work "A Socialist in Palestine." In his book, MacDonald defended Zionism, being impressed by the Socialism of the Kibbutz farms. He defended Zionism by writing, "Zionism has become the inspiration of Jewish labour."[248] MacDonald advocated Zionism with a strong dose of sentimentality, stating, "Israel, after many generations, has turned toward Palestine, as migrating birds obey the call of the seasons."[249]

During the 1930's Winston Churchill was experiencing life on the political sidelines. During these self-labeled "Wilderness Years," he occasionally spoke on behalf of Zionism. In the spring of 1938, he wrote an open letter in the London *Times* to the Jewish people, "You have prayed for Jerusalem for two thousand years, and you shall have it."[250] In 1938, Ormsby-Gore finished his service as Colonial Minister, his Zionist vision unfulfilled. Michael Cohen remarked, "Ormsby-Gore resigned from office a broken man, with Zionism the rock upon which his career had foundered."[251]

Throughout the 1930's Josiah Wedgwood was vocal in his protests of Jewish persecution in Germany. He ceaselessly promoted Zionism and continued to advocate his unique Seventh Dominion scheme. Wedgwood encouraged the British government to intervene in the anti-Semitism in Germany, calling for large-scale Jewish immigration into Britain.[252] He was so passionate in his beliefs he once called on the Jews in Palestine to attack British police.[253]

In 1939, former Prime Minister Lloyd George published his memoirs about the Peace Treaties following the Great War. By now, conventional thinking in Britain was that the Mandate was a mistake, a costly tragedy. Lloyd George played into this thinking, trying to convince the British public (and perhaps himself) that World Jewry pressured the 1917 Cabinet into their decision. He fed the idea that the influence of the Jews could determine the outcome of wars and topple regimes. Lloyd George explains that Britain simply had to "make a contract with Jewry."[254]

This new Lloyd George revelation of Jewish pressure was never substantiated or documented. Lloyd George became known in his later years as a man who could survive scandal, but really could not be trusted. He became looser with his opinions. Once, at a dinner party with Winston Churchill and others in 1936, he stated, "Success in politics depends upon whether you can control your conscience."[255]

The Shock of the 1939 White Paper

In 1939, the British government hosted a Round Table Conference in London, which became known as the St. James Conference. Some of the delegates in attendance were Prime Minister Chamberlain, Foreign Secretary Lord Halifax and Colonial Secretary Malcolm MacDonald. Jamal al-Husseini attended for the Arab side, but the Mufti was absent. David Ben Gurion and Chaim Weizmann headed the Zionist Delegation. The main demands of the Zionists were open Jewish immigration and a firm hand dealing with the Arabs.[256]

At the Conference, the British met with the Arabs and Zionists separately, even though there were some face-to-face Arab-Jewish meetings. Prime Minister Neville Chamberlain believed that if the Arabs were unhappy, they could make more trouble than the Jews could. He made his sentiments known to his Cabinet, telling them, "If we must offend one side, let us offend the Jews rather than the Arabs."[257] How different these Cabinet proceedings were from the Cabinet meetings of 1917 when Arthur Balfour expounded on the merits of making a "declaration favourable to the aspirations of the Jewish nationalists."[258] No longer were religious motivations a prime consideration for the government. Rather than seeking causes based on their ideals, the men of the Cabinet were now calculating how they could create the least amount of offence. Political pragmatism was now more important than idealism. Foreign Secretary Lord

Halifax, stressed that the Conference "must be so conducted to ensure that the Arab States would be friendly to us."[259]

When the Conference ended in May 1939, the British government announced that an independent State would be established in Palestine within ten years. This statement would take the form of a "White Paper." Lewis believed the failed conference in London was the last real attempt to forge peace in Palestine. The Jewish delegates walked out of the Conference and the "1939 White Paper" followed two months later.[260]

During the spring of 1939, the Zionists in London attempted to swamp the press with letters that would appear concurrently with the debate in Parliament.[261] Blanch Dugdale went to see Malcolm MacDonald at the Colonial Office and spoke her mind. "I mentioned then how he had broken the love and loyalty of the Jews...ruined the fair name of Britain-and I refer to his father and how he had once helped him repair a far lesser injustice."[262] Despite Dugdale's passion, it was a sad commentary for Christian Zionism that at this important moment in the movement's history, one of its main voices was an ineffectual plea at the Colonial Office.

The 1939 White Paper was officially published on May 17. Rose called it a "traumatic shock" for the Zionists.[263] In the Paper, the government attempted to reconcile the conflicting demands of the Arabs and Zionists for control of Palestine. This White Paper was a policy statement that took a very different position from the Balfour Declaration. Palestine was to be an independent State in ten years, clearly with an Arab majority. It stated that the British government would "not be justified in facilitating, nor will they be under any obligation to facilitate, the further development of the Jewish National Home by immigration regardless of the wishes of the Jewish population."[264] Louis believed the 1939 White Paper, "attempted to curtail and stabilize the Jewish population of Palestine at one-third of the Arab majority."[265]

The White Paper restricted Jewish immigration into Palestine for five years and permitted the free sale of land to Jews in only five percent of the country. Malcolm MacDonald had been Colonial Secretary since 1935 and some Zionist leaders blamed him for this restrictive policy. Some thought MacDonald had abandoned an earlier commitment to personal Zionism. Ben Gurion wrote of Malcolm MacDonald,

> We suffered more from him than any other Colonial Secretary. Before taking office, he had been pro-Zionist, like his father. But then he turned his back on us. And it was he more than anyone else who was responsible for the White Paper of 1939, which curbed Jewish immigration, and foresaw its total stoppage for five years, and restricted Jewish land settlement. This insidious policy was to last right up to the emergence of Israeli statehood.[266]

Zweig commented on the blame attributed to MacDonald,

> Ramsay MacDonald had been sympathetic to the Zionists when he was Prime Minister, and Malcolm was for a long while the favorite son of the Zionist lobby in Britain....Thus his subsequent role in Formulating the White Paper was seen as treachery, and everything he did afterwards has been judged in that light.[267]

According to Kolinsky, the purpose of the White Paper of 1939 was to propose an alternative to partition. Article six of the Mandate facilitated Jewish immigration, but the 1939 White Paper, "...confined the growth of the Jewish National Home so that Jews would remain locked in a permanent minority status."[268] However, Michael Cohen believed the British government had experienced a dramatic change of motivation. They would no longer be motivated by Zionistic ideals. "The White Paper reflected a dramatic change from the prior British policy in the area, in particular from the British attitude toward Zionism, which previously had been at worst bureaucratically neutral and at best openly sympathetic."[269]

Ben Gurion believed Malcolm MacDonald to be dishonest. "What I found distasteful about Malcolm MacDonald was his hypocrisy and his slyness in negotiation."[270] He claimed MacDonald deceived both he and Weizmann into joining the talks at St. James's

Palace in 1939, which ended with the White Paper. Ben Gurion wrote,

> Before the talks, he promised Dr. Weizmann and me categorically that Jewish immigration would not be stopped, that the Jews would never be turned into a permanent minority in Palestine, and that the terms of the Balfour Declaration and the Mandate would be safeguarded. It was with this guarantee that we agreed to join in the talks. The result was a complete betrayal.[271]

The White Paper stated it emerged out of the failure of the talks at St. James Palace.[272] The Esco Foundation for Palestine speculated on the reasons for the White Paper, claiming this was the last major British attempt to reconcile the Jews and Arabs of Palestine. The Esco Report read,

> The separate conferences had not brought matters any nearer a solution. The Arab position left no room for compromise since it denied the Jewish historical connection with Palestine, took an absolutely negative stand on the question of immigration and land settlement, and allowed Jews participation in the political life of the country only as a permanent minority.[273]

Leo Amery stated that the government's watchword had now become, "Appease the Arabs. Appease the Mufti. Appease them at all costs. Appease them by abandoning the declared policy of every government for 20 years past. Appease them by breaking faith with the Jews." Amery went on to say that "All the pledges and promises that have been given to them, broken."[274]

Churchill was appalled at the White Paper. He quoted in the House of Commons the words of Chamberlain in the House 20 years before, "A great responsibility will rest upon the Zionists, who, before long, will be proceeding, with joy in their hearts, to the ancient seat their people."[275] Churchill's attacks were creative, if ineffective. He read the names of 22 Members of the House who had supported the Balfour Declaration in 1917 and now voted for the 1939 White Paper, an embarrassment to the Conservative Party.[276] Churchill's condemnation was noticed by Ben Gurion who wrote, "During the 1939 debate on the White Paper, he condemned it as an act of betrayal. He even voted against it, in opposition to his own Conservative Party."[277]

Michael Cohen commented that the White Paper was unbearable to the Jews of Palestine. What was particularly unacceptable was that the Arabs were provided with a veto of further Jewish immigration after five years.[278] Referring to the part of the White Paper which said that there would be no further Jewish immigration after five years unless the Arabs of Palestine are prepared to acquiesce to it, Churchill told the House of Commons, "Now there is the breach; there is the violation of the pledge; there is the abandonment of the Balfour Declaration; there is the end of the vision, of the hope, of the dream."[279]

In Washington, the 1939 White Paper produced no official response. The American government had still not decided on a policy. Davidson observed, "Thus, at this point, the State Department and Congress were publicly at odds, and the resulting bickering meant that, on the eve of World War 2, there was really no single U.S. policy on Palestine."[280] Henry Feingold, in his work, "Zion in America," believed Roosevelt, while lacking an interest in Zionism, was also following the caution of his advisors. "He hesitated to intrude on what his foreign policy advisors insisted was a British sphere of interest."[281]

The summer of 1939 was a tense time throughout the world. The implications of the White Paper were being realized, and Arab violence in Palestine ceased temporarily. War in Europe seemed certain. Still in Palestine, General Montgomery did not believe the troubles in Palestine could be solved politically. He wrote to his friend Alan Brooke, "The Jew murders the Arab and the Arabs murder the Jew. This is what is going on in Palestine now. And it will go on for the next 50 years in all probability."[282] For many Zionists, the 1939 White Paper announced an end to the British commitment to the Jewish National Home. The British began to blockade 'illegal' Jewish immigration into Palestine. In 1938, the British built the

Atlit Detention Camp, south of Haifa. It would be a camp for illegal Jewish immigrants, holding up to 4,000 at a time. Between 1938 and 1948, the camp would intern over 40,000 Jews from Europe.[283] It had only been 22 years since the Balfour Declaration, yet British policy toward Zionism had taken a complete turnaround.

The question could be asked, "What did this 1939 White Paper accomplish for the British?" On a broad scale, it accomplished a number of things. It set a clear policy of containment at the beginning of another global conflict. The British government rightly seemed to sense it would have little energy to direct to Palestine in the years to come. The White Paper pleased the Arab Muslims of the Middle East, especially strengthening British relationships with King Abdullah in Transjordan and Ibn Saud in Arabia. These strengthened relationships were expected to fortify British interests in the Middle East during the coming period of global war. Published only six months after *Kristallnacht* in Germany, the White Paper was a catastrophe for the Jews of Europe. They were in a weakened, friendless position, but they could not afford to protest the White Paper too loudly. They saw the White Paper as a British betrayal of the Balfour Declaration. They were now facing the question of their survival, which was contrary to the popular theory of Jewish world influence. With war in Europe looming, the British clearly valued their friendship with the Arabs as more important than a continued commitment to Zionism. War seemed inevitable and the British were in a weak position.

On September 1 1939, Germany invaded Poland. Within two days, Britain and France declared war on Germany. Chamberlain asked Churchill to join his Cabinet by taking on the Admiralty. Palestine was temporarily out of the headlines of Britain. [284] From 1939, through the war years, Arabs in Palestine and elsewhere saw the 1939 White Paper as a sort of political pledge that Palestine would be closed to Jewish immigration. More importantly, it seemed to be a promise that the Arabs would always be the majority in Palestine. They did not thank the British for the White Paper, nor did the White Paper bring Arab respect for the British. Arab loyalty could not be bought with a shift in policy.

The Support of Old Christian Zionists

Richard Meinertzhagen had been Allenby's intelligence officer in 1917, becoming the Chief Political Officer in 1919. He wrote regarding the White Paper, "There has never, to my knowledge, been a single instance of Zionist progress at the expense of Arab religious rights" Regarding what he called trumped up charges by the Arabs, Meinertzhagen wrote, "This latter factor which is at the root of the evil in Palestine."[285] As a Christian Zionist, Meinertzhagen saw Islam as the root cause of the problems in Palestine.

Meinertzhagen, now retired, acted on his beliefs. In late 1939, shortly after the war began, he passed on to Vladimir Jabotinsky 200 jelly-like explosives, which Jabotinsky used to blow up German oil barges on the Danube River.[286] In London, Meinertzhagen compared his government's decisions to that of the Nazis. He wrote, "The action of His Majesty's government in Palestine is very near to that of Hitler in Germany. They may be more subtle, they are certainly more hypocritical, but the result (for the Jews) is similar-insecurity, misery, exasperation and murder."[287]

In December 1939, Weizmann and Churchill met at the Admiralty. They spoke about Zionism and the dream of a Jewish State. Weizmann told Churchill, "You have stood at the cradle of the enterprise. I hope you will see it through." Churchill replied, "Yes, indeed, I quite agree with that."[288] Five months later Churchill moved from the Admiralty to the office of the Prime Minister, but as Prime Minister, he would not make Zionism a high priority during the war. Despite the approaching war, the Jewish leaders in Palestine focused their attentions on their own problems. In August 1939, Ben Gurion, commented on the situation in Europe wrote, "It is the fate of Palestine that lies in the balance."[289] At this time, he still believed in the support of Churchill, writing, "He had always been a friend of Zionism, and on Zionism Churchill was absolutely consistent."[290]

By 1939, several facts were self-evident. The Jews of Palestine were too numerous and too well established to be expelled. The Jews and Arabs could not rule one country together. The Arabs were not going to leave, or comply with Jewish rule and the Jews were not going to expel the Arabs. Finally, the British were not able to defend all Jews of Palestine all the time. When the war began in Europe, world attention turned away from Palestine. In late 1939, some Foreign Office officials prepared a draft paper of their opinion of the situation. The statement articulates bitter frustration, "Palestine is a mill-stone around our necks at the worst crisis of our history. It hangs there because of our efforts to help the Zionists."[291]

Conclusion

In this chapter, the link between the decline of Christian Zionism in Britain and the relinquishing of Palestine between 1929 and 1939 was reviewed. The continued Arab violence, beginning with the Western Wall riots and the related violence in Hebron were particularly responsible for prompting the British government to abandon some of the ideals of Christian Zionism for more pragmatic responses. Kolinsky summarized how British sympathies had changed over the years. "The British sense of a moral commitment to the Zionist enterprise was quite strong until the late 1930's."[292]

It seems British government policy in Palestine followed three general phases. The first was a brief period of support for Zionism from the Balfour Declaration until Churchill's White Paper of 1922. The second was from 1922 until the Arab uprising in 1936-1939. During these years, the British seemed to pursue a policy of a Jewish National Home *in* Palestine, rather than Palestine *being* the National Home. The third phase followed the Arab uprising and was articulated in the 1939 White Paper. The British now were intent on curtailing Jewish immigration in the hopes of appeasing the Arabs.

The four High Commissioners of the 1930's: Plumer, Chancellor, Wauchope and MacMichael each had their unique influence, prompting various responses from Zionists both within and without Palestine. Plumer and Wauchope favoured Zionism while Chancellor and MacMichael were decidedly opposed to it. During these years, it was apparent that British government policy had changed. These years marked a growing rift between the Jews and Arabs of Palestine. Chancellor became the first High Commissioner to conclude that the Balfour Declaration was a blunder.[293]

A series of government reports attempted to analyze the situation in Palestine and recommend solutions. The Shaw Commission led to the Hope Simpson Commission, which led to the Passfield

White Paper. All three were unacceptable to the Zionists. The Passfield White Paper of 1930 was a stinging contradiction to the Balfour Declaration, but was overruled by Ramsay MacDonald's letter of 1931. MacDonald's motives for stepping in to negate the recommendations of the Passfield White Paper remain unclear. The Peel Commission Report of 1937 further distanced the government from the original intentions of the 1917 Cabinet. The Peel Commission Report illustrated changing British foreign policy in Palestine, policies that no longer represented the spirit of the Balfour Declaration.

During these years, Christian Zionism in Britain was being championed by elderly politicians past their days of real influence. Newer participants such as Wedgewood, Meinertzhagen, Wingate, Amery and Ormsby-Gore worked for the cause of Christian Zionism as they were able. Despite the fact that he was languishing in his self-described "Wilderness Years," Churchill continued to speak against government policies and on behalf of Zionism.

During this decade, the Evangelicals in the United States continued to expand in both size and influence. President Hoover was especially supportive of Zionism, as was career diplomat James McDonald. The establishment of the American Palestine Committee helped to move the cause of Christian Zionism from the Churches to the political arena. In the late 1930's the indifference of President Roosevelt to Zionism slowed the process of the movement in America. In Britain, the governments of Baldwin and Chamberlain showed little interest in Zionism. By this time, the Evangelical influence in Britain was of little politically significance and many of the Churches of Britain adopted the doctrine of Replacement Theology, a belief system that no longer counted the Jewish people as the divinely Chosen People.

In a sense, the 1939 White Paper was the government response to three years of Arab violence. It would be official government policy for the next five years. The outbreak of World War 2 in the autumn of 1939 delayed British consideration of departure from Palestine. Even if the British wanted to leave, the global nature of the war made it inconceivable to abandon any military position during wartime. At the beginning of the war, the Italians and the Germans had military footholds in North Africa. Their presence threatened the British in both Egypt and Palestine. Michael Cohen wrote, "By 1939 the 'Jewish National Home' in Palestine would be placed on a list of 'imperial luxuries' that had to be sacrificed."[294] According to Friesel, "Until 1939, British policy had hitherto considered the Balfour Declaration as binding and the Jewish National Home as its logical outcome. The 1939 White Paper revised this policy and assigned clear limits to the development of the Jewish National Home."[295]

The British government was adamant about the implementation of the White Paper, despite the hardships of the war. The next chapter will examine the diminished role of British Christian Zionism during the war years in Palestine as the British government focused its attention and resources on more urgent matters. The rise of American Evangelicalism will also be observed, with their growing interest in the cause of Zionism.

Chapter Four

Christian Zionism Waits through the War Years 1940-1945

❖ ❖ ❖

Introduction

This chapter will demonstrate that the diminishing influence of British Christian Zionism contributed to the British government's disregard for Zionist aspirations during World War 2. Throughout the war, the British strictly adhered to the 1939 White Paper. Despite the philosemitic sentiments of the Balfour Declaration, and other Zionistic gestures from the British during the earlier years of the Mandate, government policy was now cooler to Zionist hopes. Michael Cohen noted that the spirit of the 1939 White Paper was a departure from how the British had previously viewed Zionism. "The White Paper reflected a dramatic change from prior British policy in the area, in particular from the British attitude toward the Zionists."[1]

It has been seen that from 1929 to 1939, Arab protests prompted the British government to reduce its support of Zionism for more pragmatic responses. Despite their disappointment, Christian Zionists were still active in Britain in the 1930's, sometimes attempting to accomplish even more than their Jewish counterparts did. Norman Rose said of Christian Zionist activities in these years,

"The Gentile Zionists often outpaced the Zionist leadership."[2] Rose analyzed the situation well when he observed, "There can be little doubt that both the Zionists and their Gentile supporters saw the ultimate development of the National Home as a Jewish State."[3] Initially both parties were inhibited from openly declaring their desire for such a state, but now, Zionists had waited over 20 years since the Balfour Declaration to see this dream become a reality.

In Britain through the 1930's, the Cabinet and Colonial Office gradually took less of an interest in Zionism. In Palestine, the three High Commissioners of these years each had their unique influence, prompting various responses from Zionists both within and without Palestine. Despite the noteworthy efforts of some individual Christian Zionists, it was clear the political influence of Evangelicals in Britain was on the wane. The growing expression of interest in Zionism among Christians in the United States, particularly men such as Senator Harry Truman and James McDonald has been noted.

By 1939, both the Jews and the Arabs of Palestine wanted the British out of Palestine. Even the British themselves wanted to leave, but because of the global nature of the war, it was inconceivable to abandon any military position during this time. At the beginning of the war, the Italians and the Germans had military footholds in North Africa.[4] Their presence threatened the British in both Egypt and Palestine as life in Palestine continued under wartime constraints.[5]

It will be seen that by the 1940's, Christian Zionists in Britain were usually no longer people of significant contemporary political influence. This chapter will examine the further decline of Christian Zionist influence during the war as the British government focused its attention on the urgent matters of national survival and winning the war. Zionists believed they had reason to be optimistic when Churchill became Prime Minister in the spring of 1940. As the war came to a close, Zionists had additional reason for optimism with the appointment of Lord Gort as the new High Commissioner.

The growing interests of American Christian Zionism will be documented, realizing the United States did not yet hold a place of international political importance which would enable her to intervene on behalf of Zionism. While Evangelicals and Christian Zionists continued to experience declining influence in Britain, their counterparts enjoyed increased political relevance in the United States.

Consequences of the White Paper

High Commissioner Harold MacMichael was entrusted with the difficult task of implementing the White Paper. At first it seemed he was merely a pawn sent to carry out a difficult assignment. Yet, upon closer examination, it became clear he approved of the policy. More than that, he harbored a distain for Zionism. In 1940, John Chancellor wrote to MacMichael to congratulate him on his success in upholding the Arab cause.

> I must write you a line to congratulate you on your success in securing the passage of the Palestine Land Transfer Regulations. It is a real triumph for you...In the last twenty years, as you know, attempts have been made to protect the Arab peasants...but on each occasion H.M.G. yielding to Jewish pressure, has refused to sanction any measures designed to achieve that object...I conclude that the Jewish propaganda has been overdone and that the members of the House are now realizing that there is an Arab cause... At any rate this is the first occasion on which the House of Commons has shown some sympathy with the Arabs; & I hope that it marks a turning point in our Palestine policy.[6]

In early 1940, Jewish protesters across Palestine held demonstrations against the White Paper land transfer restrictions.[7] The laws pertaining to land transfers meant that no Jew could buy land from an Arab in most regions of the country.[8] Still, some Jewish leaders refused to relinquish their sympathetic ties to the British. Weizmann told the press that Jews would remain loyal to the Allies, but would continue to struggle for Palestine.[9] He wrote to MacMichael encouraging the High Commissioner to respect the British pledge to a Jewish National Home, pointing out that 64 percent of the land of Palestine was not open to Jewish purchase. "Jewish land purchase is forbidden as completely as it was in Tsarist

Russia outside the Pale of Settlement, or as it is at present in Nazi Germany."[10]

Renewed Hope for Zionists as Churchill Becomes Prime Minister

By the spring of 1940, it was clear to most Members of House of Commons that Neville Chamberlain was not the man to continue leading the nation. As Churchill was being considered for Prime Minister, the issue of his Zionism mattered to some. In May 1940, Samuel Hoare, the former Foreign Minister, wrote in his diary his reasons why Churchill should not become Prime Minister. One of his reasons was because of Churchill's stand on Jewish land purchases in Palestine.[11]

Nevertheless, the Labour Party indicated they would follow Churchill's leadership and the King asked him to form a government. So on May 10, Churchill became Prime Minister.[12] His appointment gave hope to Zionists since he had voted against the 1939 White Paper and had spoken out against it. Ben Gurion was so encouraged he declared, "We will not fight England."[13] However, at least one opponent of Zionism wrote of his fears of what Churchill might do. Harry St. John Philby, a close advisor to Ibn Saud, regarded Churchill as "the principal champion of Zionism in the Cabinet... and relied on the Jew's power of persuasion to secure Great Power sponsorship for his plan."[14]

Despite Churchill's previously declared support for Zionism, it was clear he was not going to take significant action in Palestine during the war. He was fully aware of the weight of the law and the power of British legislation. Despite his personal feelings, the White Paper would be respected for the five years stipulated. However, Churchill was never comfortable with the permanence of the legislation, telling the Cabinet in 1943, "I cannot agree that the White Paper is 'the firmly established policy' of His Majesty's government. I have always regarded it as a gross breach of faith... in respect of obligations to which I was personally a party...it runs until it is superseded."[15]

In 1940, Churchill surprised some of his Zionist friends by appointing Lord Lloyd to be the new Colonial Secretary. Although a respected politician, Lord Lloyd did not look with favour upon Zionism. In the summer of 1940, Lord Lloyd met with Weizmann, Ben Gurion and other Jewish leaders in London. Weizmann reported that Lord Lloyd suggested raising an Arab military force of equal size with a Jewish force in Palestine. Weizmann objected to such a course. Lord Lloyd then suggested the introduction of conscription. Weizmann replied it "would mean the worst of both worlds."[16] Despite his alarming views toward Zionism, Lord Lloyd had a reputation as an honest man. Ben Gurion said of him, "There was a man who was an avowed anti-Zionist, and yet I respected him...I found him a sincere and honest man, who spoke his mind straightforwardly."[17]

Early Indication of Ernest Bevin's Anti-Zionism

Churchill appointed Ernest Bevin Minister of Labour in the wartime coalition Cabinet. Early in 1941, Weizmann and Arthur Creech-Jones met with Bevin at the Dorchester Hotel in London. Weizmann and Creech-Jones were hopeful Bevin would support the concept of a Jewish National Home, but were disappointed in Bevin's apparent high regard for Arab relations. Part of Weizmann's memorandum from the meeting read, "Mr. Bevin said that he personally would greatly like to see the Jewish people firmly established in Palestine. However, there was another important factor in the situation-the Arab factor...We could not afford to do anything which might make our relations with the Arab countries more difficult."[18]

Even though Bevin indicated some support for the Jews at this time, he did nothing that was truly helpful for their cause. In the future, as Foreign Minister, he would work against the efforts of Zionism. However, at this time, Zionists might have expected Bevin would have been sympathetic to their cause because of Weizmann's contribution to the war effort. Throughout the war, Weizmann continued to undertake scientific research both in England and in Rehovot, near Tel Aviv. As in the Great War, Weizmann supplied the British government with practical ideas of applied science. For example, in March 1942, Weizmann showed Bevin and other members of the Cabinet how he could make synthetic rubber from starches found in Africa.[19] Weizmann also developed synthetic oils and other research patents for the British war effort, communicated through many secret contracts between Weizmann and the Ministry of Supply.[20]

Despite Weizmann's contributions, Bevin did not seem to appreciate Weizmann's scientific research. Weizmann's archives in Rehovot contain copies of the wartime correspondence between the two men, nearly all of it from Weizmann. It seemed Bevin rarely responded. For example, in 1943 Weizmann wrote Bevin asking to speak with him. Weizmann wrote a note to himself, "As usual, there was no response from Bevin."[21] Sometimes Weizmann was exceptionally determined in his efforts to get Bevin's attention. In one letter, he explained how he was forced to leave a message with Bevin's wife. "I have tried several times to telephone to you at the number you kindly gave me, but unfortunately have failed to reach you. I did, however, reach Mrs. Bevin this morning, and have explained to her as follows…" (What followed was a five-page memorandum)[22]

The Exile of the Mufti of Jerusalem

Christian Zionists and Muslim leaders shared a similar principal in their ideologies. They both viewed control of Palestine as essentially a religious issue rather than a political one. However, the difference was in how their ideologies were implemented. Christian Zionists did not usually resort to violence and would accept the rule of law, while the Mufti was not constrained by such values. To the Mufti, land sales to Jews and Jewish immigration were unacceptable to Islam. In September 1937, the British dismissed the Mufti of Jerusalem from his official position. Throughout his 16 years as the Mufti, Haj Amin al-Husseini had incited the Muslims to violence and feigned cooperation with the British authorities. He facilitated riots against the Jews in both 1929 and 1936.

According to Kolinsky, following his escape from Palestine, the Mufti "…arrived in Rome in mid-October 1941 and secured Mussolini's apparent agreement to his political aims, which he defined as the independence of Palestine, Syria and Iraq, and their unity."[23] In November 1941, the Mufti arrived in Berlin as the guest of Hitler. During the remainder of the war, the Mufti made his home in Berlin.[24] Hitler assured the Mufti that once Germany conquered southern Russia, "Germany's objective would then be solely the destruction of the Jewish element residing in the Arab sphere under the protection of British power. The Mufti would be the most authoritative spokesman for the Arab world."[25] He also asked Hitler for German support for an Arab State in Palestine and for German military assistance. Hitler agreed in principle.[26] As the war was ending in 1945, the Mufti escaped from Berlin as the Russians were entering the city.[27]

The Continued Decline of British Christian Zionist Influence

In Britain during the 1940's, the advocates of Christian Zionism were fewer and less vocal. It was generally accepted that the first goal of the government was to win the war. Political policy changes for Palestine during the war were not openly called for. In 1942, Viscount Cranborne, the Colonial Secretary, retorted that Weizmann was under a "complete misapprehension" if he expected the status quo in Palestine to be altered as long as the war lasted.[28] He had voted for the White Paper in 1939, and during the war declared that the government's "primary consideration must be to win the war."[29]

By 1942, even though Josiah Wedgwood was ailing, he still proposed some unusual Zionist ideas. In May of that year, Wedgwood advocated that the Palestine Mandate be transferred to the United States.[30] His reasoning was that the United States would be in a stronger position than a beleaguered Britain to help restore Israel. Even though his own nation would be relinquishing power, Wedgwood placed higher value on fulfilling Zionist goals. The government did not act on his suggestion. Arthur Creech Jones, a lifelong Christian Zionist, wrote to Wedgwood "My dear Comrade, You have taught us much, your courage independence and burning sense of injustice and conscience. We thank you."[31]

On July 26 1943, Josiah Wedgwood died.[32] He had been a Member of the House of Commons for five decades, but had only served once in the Cabinet.[33] Leonard Stein said of him, "He had traded the power to affect change for the power to criticize."[34] On hearing of Wedgwood's death, the British Chief Rabbi J.H. Hertz declared he was sure that "Jewry around the world ever gratefully remembers your sympathetic understanding of the Jewish cause, and the splendid support you have given it."[35] During his life, Wedgwood believed Dominion status the best policy for the Jews in Palestine.

Even though support for his Seventh Dominion Scheme faded in the 1930's, many Jews appreciated his efforts. Upon his death, the London *Jewish Chronicle* wrote of Wedgwood, "It may well be that in his steadfast support for the Seventh Dominion policy, the grand soul who has so splendidly earned his 'equal share in the world to come' would reveal himself to future generations not only as full of good deeds but as similarly honored for far-seeing political wisdom."[36] Norman Rose devoted a chapter of his work, "The Gentile Zionists" to Wedgwood's Seventh Dominion scheme. Rose summarized that although Wedgwood was well intentioned and appreciated; his idea fell short of reality. Instead, "Weizmann, and his inner circle of Jewish and Gentile advisors, took a more realistic view."[37]

In 1944, Christian Zionists appeared from a new source, Canada. A group of Canadian Protestant Christian Zionists appealed to their government on behalf of the Jews of Palestine. These Gentile Canadians formed the "Canadian Palestine Committee," with the goal of helping the Zionist cause. In 1944, they sent a delegation, headed by Arthur Roebuck, to meet with Prime Minister Mackenzie King. The delegation presented the Zionist case to King, asking him to urge the British government to ease Jewish immigrations restrictions. The Prime Minister made no promise. A Canadian Jew, Benjamin Dunkelman recalled, "Despite their powerful links of loyalty to Britain, its members did not waver in their support for the Jewish people, nor did they tone down their criticism of British policy in Palestine."[38] Although the group earnestly believed in their cause, their influence was small and produced no measurable effect.[39]

In 1944, word reached Palestine that Orde Wingate had died in Burma. He was well remembered in Palestine as a great friend of Zionism. Weizmann wrote a letter to Wingate's wife telling her they needed to decide how to best honour the memory of Orde Wingate.[40]

Churchill's Personal Wartime Efforts for Zionism

According to Martin Gilbert, Churchill performed a great service for Zionism in 1941. The matter had to do with working with Roosevelt on the Atlantic Charter, which would be the basis of the new world order after the war. The Charter stipulated that following the war, all the nations of the world would be compelled to form governments based on majority democratic votes. Churchill insisted that Palestine be excluded and Roosevelt reluctantly agreed. According to Gilbert, Churchill knew such a policy would threaten future Jewish autonomy in Palestine where the Arabs were still a majority.[41] If Gilbert's claim was true, Churchill's timely intervention saved the Zionist cause a great deal of potential trouble.

Following his political maneuvering with the Atlantic Charter, Churchill dealt with the same issue from within the Cabinet. He knew the White Paper would expire on May 16 1944, rendering political control of Palestine to the Arab majority. In order to avert such a crisis (for the Jews), he convinced the Cabinet to agree to a clause that the government would only support a regime in Palestine that had a Jewish majority.[42] Gilbert believed Churchill took a personal risk in taking this action knowing that since the White Paper was passed by a majority of the members of the House of Commons, it could not be overruled by the Cabinet. According to Gilbert, "This was certainly unconstitutional. But it ensured that the Jews would not be subjected to the rule of those whose aim was to deny them statehood in any form."[43]

Churchill also spoke on behalf of the Jews regarding another matter. In the midst of the war, there was a unique outburst from both Churchill and the Archbishop of Canterbury, William Temple, regarding the plight of the Jews in Europe. In 1943, Churchill wrote to Temple with a text for a public speech to express outrage at Nazi atrocities inflicted on the Jews.[44] Temple agreed and sent his own open letter to the London *Times,* declaring the Church of England's "burning indignation at this atrocity."[45] Further to this, Temple asked in his letter whether Palestine and England could receive more Jews from Europe. "In comparison with the monstrous evil confronting us the reasons for hesitation usually advanced by officials have an air of irrelevance."[46]

The next year, as a member of the House of Lords, William Temple again strongly advocated opening Palestine for Jewish immigration. He appealed to the House on moral principles, "We at this moment have upon us a tremendous responsibility. We stand at the bar of history, of humanity and God."[47] During these years, Temple was a powerful voice in the Church and in British society. He was a unique Anglican leader in that he mixed easily with all classes and showed sympathy for Evangelical enterprises. As a young man, he was actively involved with both the Workers Educational Association and the Student Christian Movement, which was established to send British students on overseas Christian missions.[48] It was a loss for Jewish causes when Temple died suddenly in 1944.

As further evidence of his philosemitism, Churchill worked closely with his son Randolph during the war to assist Jews in Europe when possible. On several occasions, as a paratrooper with Tito in Croatia, Randolph made extraordinary efforts, with his father's encouragement, to save Jews from the Nazis in that region.[49] These efforts took part of Churchill's attention at a time when he could have easily excused himself by saying he was occupied with the war effort. However, these gestures showed that philosemitism was one of his priorities. Gilbert noted that it was "…astonishing to me that this little country and Zionism, with the great issues of Fascism and Communism to deal with, how it dominated the Allied discussion, and how Churchill had to convince Roosevelt."[50]

Through his role as Prime Minister during the war, Churchill was occasionally able to influence events in Palestine. According to Gilbert, on several occasions, civil servants in the Colonial Office and the Foreign Office held secret discussions regarding the interception of Jewish immigrants fleeing the Holocaust. Knowing the sympathies of the Prime Minister, they conspired to not to tell Churchill or the Cabinet. However, on occasion, Randolph found out and told his father, who was then able to intervene and let some ships through to Palestine.[51]

In a more personal way, Churchill displayed his support for the Jews during the war by speaking out against anti-Semitism. In 1942, he warned General Edward Spears, then British Minister-Resident in Lebanon, against "drifting into the usual anti-Semitic channel which is customary for British officers to follow."[52] Many years later, in 1968, after Churchill's death, Spears told Martin Gilbert his opinion of Churchill, "He had one fault; he was too fond of Jews."[53] During the final years of the war, a high proportion of British Army Officers and Civil Servants in Palestine spoke negatively of Zionism, and many were openly anti-Semitic. Churchill wanted to make an example of them, to bring some of them home and have them dismissed, making the reason for dismissal known.[54] Churchill observed, "Of every 50 officers who came back from the Middle East, only one spoke favourably of the Jews."[55] Churchill's wish was not carried out.

Growing Christian Zionism in the United States

The United States entered the war in December 1941. With her vast resources, it would only be a matter of time before the Allies would be victorious and America's influence in the world would be felt, even in Palestine. During the war years, the Evangelical Christian communities in the United States continued to grow. Between 1939 and 1945, the combined national membership of the three largest Evangelical denominations in the United States (Southern Baptist, Methodist and Presbyterian) grew by 1,958,000 members. This was an increase of 14 percent in just six years.[56] The American response during times of war seemed to be an increase in Church attendance and involvement, contrary to the British experience where spiritual activity suffered during wartime.

During the war, Jewish Zionists in America increased their efforts to court the favour of Christian Zionists. According to Melvin Urofsky, the ZOA (Zionist Organization of America) spent over $70,000 annually during the war years to crystallize the sympathy of Christian America for their cause.[57] In 1941, the American Palestine Committee was reconstituted with many new members. The APC was a Christian organization supportive of Zionism, established in 1932, which now had an impressive membership of three Cabinet Members, 68 Senators (including Harry Truman) plus nearly 200 Members in the House.[58] Emanuel Neuman, in his work, "In the Arena," described the remobilization of the APC as a new political offensive-an intellectual and emotional effort which rolled on with ever-increasing momentum during the next seven years that followed."[59]

On May 9-10 1942, the American Emergency Committee for Zionist Affairs (an organization representing all major Jewish Zionist organizations in the United States) held a meeting at the Biltmore Hotel in New York. There they approved an eight-point program. The sixth point called for the fulfillment of the original purpose of the Balfour Declaration. According to Evyatar Friesel, "The creation of the Jewish State had become the immediate goal of the Zionist movement."[60] Friesel believed the Biltmore Conference and its resolutions were a clear watershed in Zionist policy...the thrust toward the creation of a Jewish State had now been proclaimed."[61]

Although this meeting of Jewish Zionist leaders was of great significance, and although their unity was impressive, certain political realities need to be recognized. The Biltmore Conference and the resulting resolutions were meaningful to those in attendance, but Jews working alone did not possess the political influence to create a Jewish State. The reality was that there would be no Jewish State without Gentile support, and this meant American Gentile support.

November 2 1942, was the 25th anniversary of the Balfour Declaration, which caught the attention of politicians in Washington where Zionist support was high among the Protestant dominated Congress and Senate. On that day, the American Palestine Committee presented President Roosevelt and Cordell Hull, the Secretary of State, with a declaration entitled "The Common Purpose of Civilized Mankind." Harry Truman was one of the politicians who signed the statement along with 67 other Senators, 194 Congressmen and 18 out of 23 Members of the Senate Foreign Relations Committee.[62]

The statement called for a reaffirmation of the "traditional American policy" supporting the Balfour Declaration and expressed "deep seated sentiment in favor of the Jewish Homeland in Palestine." Tens of thousands of copies of the statement were circulated throughout the United States, effectively silencing the Jewish anti-Zionism lobby. According to Thomas Kolsky, in his work, "Jews Against Zionism," "By this time, American Jewish anti-Zionists, despite their noisy fulminations, had become a small minority."[63] In

1943, Senator Truman was gradually revealing a personal interest in the plight of the Jewish people, declaring,

> Through the edict of a mad Hitler and a degenerate Mussolini, the people of that ancient race, the Jews, are being herded like animals into ghettos, the concentration camps, and the wastelands of Europe...Today-not tomorrow, we must do all that is humanly possible to provide a haven and place of safety for all those who can be grasped from the hands of the Nazi butchers. Free lands must be opened to them. This is not a Jewish problem. It is an American problem-and we must and will face it squarely and honorably.[64]

In January 1944, the American Congress passed a Resolution calling for the opening of Palestine to Jewish immigration and eventual Jewish autonomy. The Resolution read in part,

> Resolved, That the United States shall use its good offices and take appropriate measures to the end that the doors of Palestine shall be opened for free entry of Jews into that country, and that there shall be full opportunity for colonization, so that the Jewish people may ultimately reconstitute Palestine as a free and democratic Jewish commonwealth.[65]

Even President Roosevelt, who was usually silent on Zionism, wrote in March 1944 to Dr. Wise and Dr. Silver, co-Chairmen of the American Zionist Emergency Council, "The American government has never given its approval to the White Paper of 1939."[66] Despite these few letters and statements regarding Zionism, Roosevelt usually followed a policy of inaction toward Zionism. His reasons remain unclear. Perhaps he was aware of the presence of some anti-Zionist and anti-Semitic feeling in America. Perhaps it had something to do with the American King-Crane Commission of 20 years earlier, which reported that the Arabs had a right to resent Jewish immigration. Perhaps it was simply a personal indifference to the cause.

Growing Jewish Anger in Palestine

In February 1942, the refugee ship *Struma* sank off the coast of Turkey, resulting in the deaths of 768 Jewish immigrants escaping the Holocaust. Posters appeared throughout Palestine proclaiming MacMichael to be a murderer. Although he was not directly involved, and although he attempted to explain that this was British government policy, some blamed MacMichael. Bernard Wasserstein believed the case was not simple. He observed that the personal policies of the High Commissioner could influence London. "The Colonial Office view faithfully mirrored that of the men on the spot."[67] Of the position of High Commissioner, Ben Gurion wrote, "A High Commissioner might not be able to change the broad lines of policy laid down in London, though he could try…his powers were considerable. There was a great deal that he could do-either well or badly."[68]

In the case of MacMichael and the Colonial Office, this was one instance when the two seemed to agree. Wasserstein viewed the British government as persistently wary of the spirit of the Balfour Declaration, and believed they were pleased with the 1939 White Paper, writing. "The Colonial Office…had, since the inception of the mandate, been, with rare exceptions, dubious about the value to Britain of the Jewish National Home; to them the White Paper appeared as a welcome relief from some of their burdens."[69] Wasserstein also noted the High Commissioner's view, "MacMichael was a staunch advocate of the White Paper policy and rigidly restrictive in the implementations of its immigration provisions."[70]

The British Government's Weak Wartime Efforts for Zionism

During the war, there were a few small but noteworthy efforts by the British government for the cause of Zionism. Despite his busy wartime schedule, Churchill kept in constant contact with Weizmann. In October 1942, the Prime Minister wrote a short letter marked "private" to Weizmann. It was a personal statement of hope for the fortunes of the Jewish people. Churchill wrote, "Better days will surely come for your suffering people and for the great cause for which you have fought so bravely."[71]

Early in the war, Churchill supported the cause of the Zionists by appointing sympathetic Colonial Secretaries. During his brief time as Colonial Secretary, Lord Lloyd showed interest in policy development in Palestine, but died suddenly in February 1941. Zweig wrote of Lord Lloyd, "The loss of his personal interest removed much of the impetus within the Colonial Office for constitutional progress in Palestine."[72] Early in 1942, when Churchill appointed Lord Cranbourne to be the Colonial Secretary, the Cabinet looked again at a workable plan to partition Palestine.[73] Later in the war, Churchill appointed Oliver Stanley to the post. These appointments seemed to indicate a helpful posture on Churchill's part toward the Zionists. Ben Gurion wrote positively of Cranbourne and Stanley, "Both were good and friendly people, and were certainly better for us than either Lloyd or Moyne, but neither had the power to press for a major strengthening of our position in Palestine."[74]

Finally, in January 1944, the Cabinet approved a partition plan for Palestine, but the Foreign Office representative, Richard Law, dissented. Churchill described the plan as a "fine piece of work," but it was agreed that no action be taken until the defeat of Hitler.[75]

The Troubled Departure of High Commissioner MacMichael

The wartime relationship between Harold MacMichael and the Jewish leaders in Palestine had deteriorated significantly. In August 1944, MacMichael wrote the Colonial Office of his discouragement in Palestine. "It is perhaps inevitable that in leaving Palestine one should feel conscious of disappointment at having been able to achieve so little in a land that has such immense claims upon endeavour..."[76] A few days later, a bomb was thrown at his car in the Givat Shaul neighbourhood of Jerusalem. The driver was seriously hurt, MacMichael was slightly injured and his wife was unharmed.[77] Ben Gurion sent a letter of condolence to MacMichael, "My colleagues and myself are very happy that no serious harm occurred to you and that fortunately Lady MacMichael escaped unscathed."[78]

By late 1944, High Commissioner MacMichael was weary of his work. He spoke of his failure to rule. He conversed with Ben-Gurion about his frustration with the London government and the situation in Palestine. He claimed he did not like or understand politics.

MacMichael told Ben Gurion, "You have much more power than we do." Ben Gurion was unimpressed. Privately, he called MacMichael a "small man."[79] He believed MacMichael to be unsuited for the job of High Commissioner, writing. "MacMichael was both inept and malicious, and he showed this soon after his arrival when he recommended the hanging of Shlomo Ben Yosef on June 29 1938.[80] An undated Irgun memo instructed its members that MacMichael, "...symbolized the distain with which England treated the Palestine problem. Who was MacMichael before he was sent to take the place of the High Commissioner in Palestine?"[81] In 1965 Ben Gurion wrote of MacMichael,

> He was dreadful. Very bad indeed...He was petty minded, arrogant, bureaucratic, full of himself and his power; he behaved as a potentate toward 'natives'; and, which was the most grievous sin in a man of affairs, he had a closed mind... As Chairman of the Jewish Agency at the time,...I naturally had frequent business meetings with him. I cannot recall a single one which was not distasteful...His appointment and his whole term of office were a disaster-a disaster for us, and for Palestine and for Britain.[82]

MacMichael left Palestine in the autumn of 1944. Primarily the Jews remembered him as the man who turned away refugee ships and executed young Shlomo Ben Yosef. Norman Bentwich remembered MacMichael as the High Commissioner whom, "...the Jews could not forgive for his part in the rejection of the 'coffin ships' bringing fugitives from Europe's charnel house."[83]

Lord Gort, a High Commissioner Sympathetic to the Zionists

Conscious of the fractured relationship between the British government and Zionist ideals, the Colonial Office consulted the Jewish Agency to help them find a suitable man to be the next High Commissioner. This represented a return to a closer working relationship between the Colonial Office and Chaim Weizmann. In the summer of 1944, Oliver Stanley explained to Weizmann what kind of man would be suitable for the role. Stanley wrote, "You will remember that once we were having a talk about the sort of man who would make a good High Commissioner."[84]

Throughout the summer of 1944, letters, memos and telegrams passed between Weizmann and the Colonial office regarding the next appointment. Clearly, the Colonial Office was seeking another soldier. It would seem they also wanted someone more sympathetic to Zionism. Plumer and Wauchope had worked out well before.[85] Perhaps another similar man would serve the role well. Finally, the appointment of Lord Gort was announced.

In October 1944, Lord Gort arrived in Palestine as the new High Commissioner. He came from an old English Anglican family and was raised as a Victorian gentleman, becoming a Lord at age 16. As a young man, he attended Harrow and Sandhurst and dedicated his life to the Army.[86] On his way to Palestine, he stopped in Cairo to discuss current issues with the new Minister Resident Lord Moyne.[87] Gort possessed a sharp sense of humour. Upon arriving in Palestine, he was driven in his car along with his assistant John Shaw. Gort asked Shaw, "I suppose that at any moment we may be shot at?" Shaw replied, "Yes sir, we may. The trouble is that they will aim at you and hit me."[88] Gort replied to General Spears, "They daren't shoot me, they will get something much worse."[89]

Lord Gort was similar to Herbert Plumer in his outlook, wanting to learn all he could about the people of Palestine. In October 1944, soon after his arrival in Jerusalem, Gort wrote to his friend Captain Arthur Fitzgerald, "I am spending a lot of time chasing round the country looking at everything that goes on and being seen by those who are disposed to see me, whether of friendly or unfriendly disposition."[90] Gort wrote to MacMichael, "I feel it is only by personal contact with the people and the country that we can begin to understand the problems."[91]

In October 1944, in a publication by Irgun Zvai Leumi, Lord Gort was called a "worthy High Commissioner." The memorandum called all Gort's predecessors commencing with Sir Herbert Samuel to Sir Harold MacMichael "bad High Commissioners."[92] Norman Bentwich wrote of Gort, "He brought to Palestine, and kept, a reputation like Plumer of being the father of the people. Again happy relations were restored with the Jews after the stormy years of MacMichael."[93] Gort respected the ideals of Zionism, telling Norman Bentwich that the Zionists must preserve the purity of their enterprise. "The end cannot justify impure means. I must confess that I doubt whether the Messiah will come to the sound of bursting bombs."[94] Ben Gurion believed Gort to be a sensitive man who cared deeply about the plight of Holocaust survivors. He recalled, "And as I spoke, I saw the eyes of this tough soldier well with tears. He was a rare and good man. It is sad that he should have died so soon after, at a comparatively early age."[95] Christopher Sykes, in his work "Crossroads to Israel," commented on Lord Gort,

> Considering the state of Palestine in 1944 and 1945, he may be said to have added to his many titles to fame that of being a respected High Commissioner in the most difficult of all posts at the most difficult of times…virtual suspension of terrorist activity …was greatly helped by the fact of Lord Gort being the man at the head of affairs.[96]

In November 1944, Chaim Weizmann returned to Palestine. The moderating effect of Weizmann and Lord Gort together helped ease some of the tensions between the Zionists and the British. Gort wrote soon after arriving in Jerusalem, "I have been used to hard work for years and years, but so far this place holds the record."[97]

The Assassination of Lord Moyne and the Damage to Zionism

On November 4 1944, Churchill had his last wartime meeting with Weizmann, promising the Zionist leader a "generous" partition of Palestine once the war with Germany was over.[98] Two days later an event in Cairo affected this pledge. Lehi sent agents to Cairo to assassinate Lord Moyne, Britain's senior representative in Egypt. The assassination was carried out on November 6, damaging the reputation of Zionism and the Jews of Palestine. Crossman believed the assassination hurt the Prime Minister personally, noting that Churchill was not inclined to help the Jews at that time.[99]

Following the assassination, Churchill instructed his secretary to remove from the Cabinet's agenda the Partition Plan tabled by the Cabinet Committee on Palestine. Churchill did not receive

Weizmann again throughout the war.[100] Cabinet colleagues noted that for six months after the assassination, it was impossible to approach Churchill about the topic of Palestine.[101] He was angry and hurt. To Churchill, the people he was trying to assist had murdered a friend. He seemed to take the assassination as a personal betrayal of trust.

Despite his profound understanding of political matters, Churchill seemed to choose not to distinguish between the Jewish Agency, Lehi and the Haganah. He refused to consider that men like Weizmann would have had nothing to do with the assassination. Further to this, despite Churchill's claims of friendship with Lord Moyne, there is little evidence to indicate they were close. It seems possible that Churchill was primarily disappointed that his personal friendship with the Jewish Zionist leaders had been betrayed.

New Hope for Zionists as the Global War Comes to an End

Even as World War 2 was ending, Weizmann preferred not to pressure the British government for a solution in Palestine. As the President of the World Zionist Organization, he addressed his Executive on November 19 1944, pointing out his regret over Jewish violence, telling his Executive that it caused "great political damage, and robs us of energy we could turn into more fruitful channels."[102] Weizmann excused British inaction on Palestine. "The moment was not convenient to press upon Great Britain to change her Palestine policy, because the military situation demanded the attention of the London politicians almost exclusively."[103] In a display of cooperation with the British authorities, in December 1944, Weizmann sent a letter to the police with the names of approximately 500 Jewish resistance fighters. The British police made over 250 arrests. Ben Gurion was enraged.[104]

At this time, General Alan Cunningham had no idea he would someday be involved in Palestine. In December 1944, he wrote a letter to former High Commissioner MacMichael about the hope that the British would be remembered well in Palestine. "However that may be, I am sure that what the British have done for this country is far too deep rooted to be destroyed, and that anyway will emerge from the wreck of the future and be recognized at last."[105]

In April 1945, President Roosevelt died unexpectedly. Berlin was about to fall to the Allies and the war in Europe was nearly over. In Palestine, there was much anticipation as to what might happen after the global fighting ended. During the war, Zionists, both Jewish and Christians, kept up their appeals to the British government, realizing that the government was adamantly waiting for the end of the war before they would take action in Palestine.

Conclusion

The continued implementation of the 1939 White Paper throughout the war hampered the progress of Zionism, but it was generally accepted by Zionists that Britain had to first win the war before her attentions could return to Palestine. Zionists viewed High Commissioner MacMichael negatively as he abided by the White Paper and at times seemed extreme in the carrying out of his duties. As the new Prime Minister, Churchill focused his attentions mainly on the war effort, but occasionally attempted to make some token gestures for Zionism. Most noteworthy was his intervention in delaying a majority vote in Palestine and his voicing of outrage at Nazi atrocities against the Jews in Europe.

During the war years, the decline of influence of British Evangelicals corresponded with a similar decline in the voice of British Christian Zionism. By the end of the war, two eccentric but significant Christian Zionists, Josiah Wedgewood and Orde Wingate died. Meanwhile in America, Evangelical Christians were growing in numbers and increasing their vocal support for Zionist aspirations. The public political work of the American Palestine Committee was very important during the war, and set the stage for future American political involvement in Palestine.

As MacMichael left Palestine, the arrival of Lord Gort as the new High Commissioner was mildly effective in soothing tensions. At the death of Roosevelt, Vice President Truman automatically became President. At first he simply adhered to Roosevelt's policy of non-involvement. With the growing influence of the United States in the world, Zionists tried to anticipate how the new President might view their cause. There was already some evidence to consider. In 1939, while a Senator, Truman had condemned the White Paper.

Truman's remarks were published as an article in the *Washington Post*, where Truman addressed Roosevelt, "Mr. President, the British government has used its diplomatic umbrella again, this time on Palestine. It has made a scrap of paper out of Lord Balfour's promise to the Jews."[106]

In 1937, Truman had commented in a letter about the harsh treatment the Jews were receiving at the hands of the Nazis in Germany, "You are perfectly correct about all the technicalities that the German government is using to harass the Jewish people. I don't approve of it and I am morally certain that they will be properly taken care of for their attitude at some time in the future."[107] Although Truman sympathized with Jewish suffering in Europe, he had not yet actively supported the Zionist cause. The next chapter will look at the British government's continued disregard of Christian Zionism and the developing interest of the Americans in Zionism during the years 1945-1947.

Chapter Five

The British Abandon and America Assumes the Mantle of Christian Zionism 1945-1947

❖ ❖ ❖

Introduction

This chapter will demonstrate that during the immediate post war years of 1945-1947, the decline in the influence of Christian Zionism in Britain was a primary reason for the British departure from Palestine. A gradual reduction of numbers and influence of British Evangelicals was linked to a reduction in political support for Zionism, which was no longer a foreign policy priority to the government of Britain. As the Allies discovered the Nazi death camps near the end of the war, they realized how the Holocaust had decimated the Jewish communities of Europe. Many of the surviving Jews of Europe dreamed of moving to Palestine, and had little patience for the intricacies of British foreign policy. However, there would be much opposition from the British Foreign Ministry.

By the end of the war, both the British and Americans anticipated a complicated situation in Palestine. Arab oil was now a major issue to the western developed nations. It was understood in both London and Washington that the Arabs in Palestine would react violently to any increase in Jewish immigration. During these years, from 1945 to 1947, the British shaped their policy in Palestine with cautious pragmatism, disregarding their previous commitment to Zionism. Some Jews suspected other motives, that British anti-Zionism was an excuse for something darker. Looking back, Martin Gilbert observed, "British hostility to Zionist enterprise was so often a mask for anti-Semitism.[1]

Roosevelt's Legacy

On April 12 1945, President Roosevelt died unexpectedly. No previous American President had been less interested in Zionism than Roosevelt. Compared to the personal enthusiasm of Presidents Harding, Coolidge and Hoover for the restoration of Israel, Roosevelt was a disappointment to Zionists. Although he had made some tepid statements in favour of what the Jews were doing in Palestine, he showed no passion or personal support for the cause. Weizmann lamented that he had to instruct Roosevelt about Zionism like a pupil.[2] Compared to the Evangelical backgrounds of Harding (Baptist), Coolidge (Congregationalist) and Hoover (Quaker), Roosevelt's High Church (Episcopalian) experience seemed to have left him indifferent to the notion of Zionism.[3]

In contrast to Roosevelt, despite the pressures of the war, Churchill attempted to assist the Zionist cause when possible. Following the Yalta Conference in February 1945, both Roosevelt and Churchill travelled to Saudi Arabia for talks with Ibn Saud. Roosevelt met first with Ibn Saud three days before Churchill arrived.[4] A few days later, Churchill met with Saud.[5] Churchill tried to convince the Saudi monarch to support a Jewish State, but he was cold to the idea, leaving Churchill confused. According to Gilbert, Churchill later discovered that Roosevelt had, only days earlier, told Saud of his antagonism to a Jewish State, promising, "I will do nothing to assist the Jews against the Arabs."[6] Ibn Saud could well afford to rebuff Churchill's request for support of a Jewish State in that he knew Roosevelt's intentions.

Gilbert assessed the situation that, "Churchill was outmaneuvered by Roosevelt and departed Saudi Arabia with virtually nothing to assist the Zionists."[7] In the end, Roosevelt had gone beyond being indifferent to the restoration of Israel; he had actively attempted to prevent it. Gilbert summarized that Roosevelt, unknown to Churchill, simply decided not to support the Zionist hopes of Statehood.[8]

At the death of Roosevelt, Vice President Harry Truman automatically became President.[9] He had been sworn in as Vice President on January 20 1945, having served in that office for only 82 days. With little experience in foreign affairs, Truman was immediately under pressure to comprehend the issues facing him as quickly as possible. Roosevelt had not made it a priority to involve Truman in foreign policy. During his brief time as Vice President, Truman had not even been informed of the existence of the Manhattan Project.[10]

Although Truman had made some pro-Jewish remarks in public in earlier years as a Senator, his personal views toward a National Home for the Jews remained largely unknown. At a Chicago rally in 1944, then Senator Truman said, "Today, not tomorrow, we must do all that is humanly possible to provide a haven for all those who can be grasped from the hands of Nazi butchers. Free lands must be opened to them."[11] The shock of attaining high office so quickly caused him to be cautious in his early Presidential decision-making. At first, he maintained Roosevelt's policy of non-involvement in Palestine, as he considered the advice of his White House advisors and State Department.

The Conservatives Lose the Opportunity to Facilitate the Jewish National Home

With the surrender of Germany in May 1945, the Labour Party insisted on an end to the coalition government and a return to party politics. When Britain went to the polls to elect a new government, Churchill believed he would remain as Prime Minister. He informed Weizmann that his government's position in Palestine could not be considered until the "victorious Allies are definitely seated at the Peace Table."[12] Churchill promised an impatient Weizmann that after the Conservative election victory, one his first tasks will be that of reaching a "full and just" settlement in Palestine.[13] Clearly, he expected to win the election and form the next government.

Churchill was aware of the diminished financial strength of Britain. He also knew that Christian Zionism had a reduced influence in both the Conservative and Labour Parties. In light of this, he considered asking the United States to assume the Mandate in Palestine. In June 1945, he wrote to Weizmann, telling him he was considering passing the Mandate to the United States. "I need scarcely say I shall continue to do my best for it (Zionism). But as you will know, it has very few supporters in the Conservative Party, and even the Labour Party now seems to have lost all zeal."[14] Churchill's instincts were correct. By the time the war was over, the Americans desired to be consulted on all matters of foreign policy, even on Palestine. In June, Lord Stanley informed Lord Gort that before any new policies could be developed in Palestine, America and other countries would be consulted.

> It is essential that we should be in possession of information as to the probable reactions to each of the courses mentioned of the Arabs and Jews in Palestine and of the Arabs in the neighbouring Arab States and of the probable repercussions of each course in the sphere of international politics, with special reference to America and Russia."[15]

Churchill did not have the opportunity to act on this idea because the Labour Party won a landslide election victory and enjoyed a clear mandate to lead Britain. Even though Churchill was out of power, Zionists had hope in the Labour Party, which had long supported the idea of a Jewish National Home. At the 1944 Labour Party conference, only a year before, the Party accepted a resolution in favour of a Jewish National Home, which would eventually become a self-governing state.[16]

The Implications of the New Post War Order

At the end World War 2, the Arabs were becoming important players in world politics. In March 1945, the Arab countries in the Middle East formed the League of Arab States.[17] In a way, the League was the Arab political answer to the Jewish Agency, but lacked the idealism of the Zionists. Moreover, its membership did not include the Arabs of Palestine[18], a group it claimed to represent. Crossman suggested that in 1945 the Arab position was actually a weak one in that the Arabs had backed the losing side during the war.[19] To add to this, at the end of the war, British military power was enormous.[20] In contrast, to a large degree, the Jews of Palestine had backed the British war effort. About 30,000 Jews of Palestine had enlisted in the British military during the war, and many more had volunteered in other capacities.

With a clear majority in the House of Commons, the Labour Party would now set foreign policy in Palestine and elsewhere. While in opposition, the Labour Party had declared its support of Zionism, and initial indications after the election were that this policy would continue. As the war was ending, the Labour Party endorsed a Resolution favouring unlimited Jewish immigration to Palestine.[21] Labour MP Hugh Dalton, in May 1945, even attached a memorandum to the masthead of the Labour Party's policy, which read, "It is morally wrong and politically indefensible to impose obstacles to the entry into Palestine now of any Jews who desire to go there."[22] However, by July 1945, when the new Labour government was forming, they began to reexamine their policy in Palestine.

In forming his cabinet, Clement Attlee appointed Hugh Dalton Chancellor of the Exchequer. Zionist hopes were high as they related to the Labour Party in general and Dalton in particular. As a Christian socialist, Dalton supported Zionism. However, when the Labour Party realized power in 1945, foreign affairs were not at first high on their political agenda. Martin Jones noted, "For most people in 1945, Palestine was a distant problem made more remote by the many difficulties nearer home."[23]

On a personal level, Clement Attlee was not a typical Labour politician in that he attended Public Schools and Cambridge University.[24] He had been active in high levels of politics for many years. He was the Private Secretary to Ramsay MacDonald from 1922 to 1924, and leader of the Labour Party since 1935, a position he would hold until 1955. In 1940, Attlee became part of Churchill's Wartime Cabinet where he held several Cabinet posts.[25] As a political leader, Attlee was not a powerful personality but rather skillfully steered groups of talented men. Throughout his life, Attlee showed little interest in religious matters and revealed little of his spiritual beliefs, although he and his family were members of the Church of England.[26] In his autobiography, Attlee mentioned clergymen and missionaries in his family, but did not elaborate. Regarding his religious upbringing, Attlee wrote, "Our family were strong supporters of the Church of England and Sunday was strictly observed. There was much Church-going, special readings and no games."[27]

Attlee chose Herbert Morrison to be both Home Secretary and Deputy Prime Minister, positions he held from 1945 to 1951. Morrison had a long history with the Labour Party since he was first elected to the House of Commons in 1923.[28] He wrote the Manifesto on which the Labour Party campaigned in 1945, "Let Us Face the Future." As the son of a London police constable, Morrison left school at the age of 14. Through his life, he revealed little about his religious convictions or his views of Zionism. However, he did make a speech in 1939 condemning the White Paper. "The White Paper is not in harmony with either the Balfour Declaration or the Mandate, is not in harmony with their wording, is not in harmony with their spirit."[29] Morrison concluded his 1939 speech by declaring, "We cannot prevent this evil thing being done. We cannot prevent this White Paper being approved. Honorable Members opposite alone can stop this thing happening, and I appeal to them. I ask them to remember the sufferings of these Jewish people all over the world."[30]

It should be noted that Morrison appealed to the House on the basis of sentimentality and honour. His reasons were not religious. There is no evidence that the ideal of Zionism appealed to Morrison personally. His speech in 1939 reflected the official position of the Labour Party of the day, but the Labour government did not maintain this position when they came to power in 1945.

Foreign Minister Ernest Bevin and Zionism

Following his Party's election win in 1945, Attlee appointed Ernest Bevin to be the new Foreign Secretary. Martin Jones believed, "Attlee made the decision to appoint Bevin Foreign Secretary mainly because he felt that he would stand up to the Russians better than Dalton, and because he felt Dalton may not possess the right temperament for the Foreign Office."[31] Bevin was to hold the post of Foreign Secretary until 1951 and would have significant influence in the foreign policies of the postwar government. He seemed to want to keep a strong Britain, but believed Britain was overextended in the world. Because of the significant role he played in Palestine policy, it is worthwhile to take a close look at Bevin's background. It is especially noteworthy to observe the radical transformation Bevin experienced as a young man.

Ernest Bevin was born in Winsford, Somerset in 1881. His mother, Mercy Bevin, was a widow with six children. Having no husband when Ernest was born, she left the father's name off the parish register, rendering Ernest illegitimate. Bevin's mother died when he was six and he was sent to live with his married sister Mary and her husband George Pope in East Devon. The Popes were active members of the dissenting United Methodist Chapel.[32] Like most men of his class, Bevin left behind no diary and few personal letters. Despite this, much is known of his early life.

Bevin started working at various jobs at age 12, but eventually settled into driving a delivery van. From his early childhood, he was deeply involved in Evangelical Chapels. Bevin's biographer, Alan Bullock, wrote, "Bristol was a stronghold of Nonconformity and Ernest Bevin attended a number of Chapels before identifying himself with the Manor Hall Baptist Mission in St. Mark's Road, Easton."[33] Bullock noted, "Bevin joined the Mission as a Sunday School teacher, but soon became active in other ways as well. His first address to the Christian Endeavour Society (appropriately enough, on the history of Israel) is still remembered."[34]

In 1902, at age 22, Bevin was baptized by immersion at Bethesda chapel in Great George Street, Bristol where he remained an active member until 1905.[35] At this time, the Nonconformist Chapels took men of low birth with no formal education and instilled in them passion, cause and conviction. This was the "education" Bevin received. Bullock states, "The contribution of Nonconformity to the British Labour movement is commonplace: a chapel upbringing has been as characteristic of British trade-union leadership, for instance, as a public school education of the leaders of the ruling class."[36]

Bullock observed that Chapel not only gave Bevin a religious faith and moral principles, it quickened his latent intellectual powers. Bevin began to discover his capability to think, to argue and to speak.[37] George Wallis, a friend from those days remembered the Sunday classes when 300 men would sing, hear a Bible lesson and debate. According to Wallis, "My impression is that it was in the Adult School that Ernest Bevin learned how to stand on his hind legs and express himself in public."[38]

While still a van driver in his early 20's, Bevin grew angry about the social conditions in Britain. He observed the lives of working people as he drove his horses through the streets of Bristol. He was aware of the economic inequality in Britain. In 1905, half the wealth of the country was in the hands of only five million people. The other half of the nation's wealth was distributed among the other 38 million.[39] Bullock noted Bevin's thinking at this time,

> In his eyes, an economic and social system which produced such results stood self condemned; it could and should be changed. Finding such radical opinions looked at askance in chapel circles, he became more and more critical of the timidity of organized religion on social questions. He began to look elsewhere, to listen to those who not only attacked the evils they saw in society as outspoken as himself, but claimed to have found in the teachings of socialism an alternative method of social organization which would get rid of them.[40]

Bevin considered joining different group that could offer him real power and the potential for a role in social change. The turning point in Bevin's life came one Sunday morning when he organized a group of unemployed men to march into the Anglican Cathedral Church of Bristol. As an active member of an Evangelical Chapel, Bevin would have seen the High Church Anglican Cathedral as the religious enemy; in much the same way as Lloyd George viewed the Anglican Church as a young man. On that Sunday morning, Bevin had his men line the side isles of the Church, flanking the wealthy business people of Bristol. Bevin's intention was to shame the people into providing work for the unemployed.[41] Following that action, Bevin left the Chapel movement, and his personal faith. He never preached the Bible again. From that time on, his passion was all social politics. Sunday mornings were now taken by the Right-to-Work Committee.[42] Bullock wrote of it as a "conversion."

> Bevin's conversion to socialism was accompanied by the transfer of his interests from the chapel to politics, and was completed between the beginnings of 1905, when he left the Manor Hall Mission, and the beginning of 1908, when he became secretary of the Right-to-Work Committee.[43]

Bevin made a full transition from Chapel to trade unionism. The message of the two groups was different, but the systems were similar. New recruits were drawn in through the persuasive powers of open-air speakers. Idealism then offered both a cause and companions to share the cause. Bullock wrote, "Although Ernest Bevin was later to turn away from what he regarded as the narrowness of chapel folk on social questions, he carried over much that Nonconformity had taught him into his socialism and trade unionism."[44] Following years of organizing street corner meetings and strikes, Bevin became known as "Boss Bevin."[45]

When Bevin abandoned his place in the Evangelical movement, he left behind a number of values. Two of them were philosemitism and support for Zionism. Although he gave occasional token support to Zionism as a Labour Member of Parliament, once he became Foreign Minister, he opposed Zionism with great energy. In the world of international diplomacy, Bevin was an uncouth Foreign Minister. As an adult, he rarely revealed he had been a lay Bible preacher as a young man. More than this, he did not indicate an interest in the Holy Land or sympathy for the Jewish people. In the post war years, Bevin was to become an unpopular figure with the Jews of Palestine. However, Bevin saw himself as a spokesman for the common people of Britain. Norman Bentwich noticed that Bevin liked to speak with great democratic authority. To Bentwich, it seemed that Bevin, "... spoke always as if he had behind him a large section of the British people."[46] Ben Gurion saw the appointment of Bevin as a hostile act. "The most bitterly hostile action against Palestinian Jewry was taken when Ernest Bevin was Britain's Foreign Secretary and directly responsible for Palestine Policy.[47]

Ben Gurion knew Attlee backed Bevin, and that Bevin was a powerful personality. It was clear that with Attlee's support, Bevin would allow no other Cabinet Minister to interfere with the formation or execution of his policies. Ben Gurion wrote that this was "confirmed to me by several of his Cabinet colleagues."[48] Ben Gurion reflected on Bevin, "I do not think he was a man who read widely, since his conversation did not give this impression, nor a man who thought out problems from first principles. I am sure he had convictions; but I fancy that some of what he thought were convictions were simply prejudices.[49] Ben Gurion was reluctant to judge Bevin's motives. When asked if he thought Bevin was anti-Semitic, Ben Gurion responded, "I prefer to consider Bevin simply as an anti-Zionist."[50] Bevin's biographers deny the charge of anti-Semitism. One biographer, Peter Weiler, states, "Bevin was accused at the time of being anti-Semitic, a charge denied by Alan Bullock and other historians who contend that he was merely heavy handed and insensitive."[51] Only Bevin himself was in a position to realize his own motives. Whatever sympathies he might have once had for the Jews of Palestine in the 1920's and 1930's were apparently based on a common commitment to socialism. What is clearer is that Bevin's commitment to the restoration of Israel was something he only briefly held in his youth and later completely abandoned.

In a defense of Bevin, Martin Jones explained that Bevin was not alone in his views. "Bevin considered the Middle East as a single region…Bevin's views were in harmony with the department's outlook here."[52] To further explain Bevin's approach to the Middle East, Jones believed that Bevin had a wider view of the Middle East than just Palestine, "Bevin in fact linked the importance of Middle Eastern oil to global power, which in turn, he perceived as the necessary accoutrements of a Welfare State."[53] The foreign policy agenda for the Labour government was full and complicated in the post war years, and Bevin had little patience for Zionistic ideals.

Changes in the Labour Party's View of Zionism

In 1939, the Labour Party had voiced their clear opposition to the restrictive immigration policies of the 1939 White Paper. Because of this, when the Labour Party finally came to power in 1945, Jews around the world rejoiced in the hope that Jewish immigration to Palestine would be opened. Martin Jones explains, "When the Labour Party came to power in 1945 it had publicly placed on record its support for the Jewish National Home, a support that went back some years."[54] However, the new Labour government of 1945 proved to be no better that their coalition predecessors in lifting the restrictive immigration policy of the 1939 White Paper. The Labour government now had a variety of pressing issues to deal with, both domestic and foreign, and Christian Zionism had lost influence in the British government. According to David Charters, in his work "The British Army and Jewish Insurgency in Palestine, 1945-47," by late 1945, only 90 members of the House of Commons, of whom only 26 were Jewish, went on record supporting the Zionist movement.[55]

In November 1945, Bevin told the House of Commons that the restrictions of the 1939 White Paper policy would continue in Palestine. He took charge of policy for Palestine as Foreign Secretary even though it was traditional for the Colonial Office to assume the role. Ben Gurion was familiar with this shift in roles. "This certainly happened when Bevin was Foreign Secretary and Arthur Creech Jones was the Colonial Secretary. Creech Jones had been very friendly to Zionism before he joined the Cabinet, but then he found that he was not master in his own house."[56] Regarding the history of power sharing between the Foreign Ministry and the Colonial Office, Ben Gurion added,

> Actually, both the Foreign and Colonial Offices exercised a decisive influence on Palestine policy throughout the period of the Mandate, and I think it's true to say that for most of that period, the Ministers and permanent officials of both Ministries were not friendly to Zionism. Most of the officials were certainly pro-Arab and thought Britain had made a great mistake in committing herself to the Balfour Declaration and the Mandate.[57]

Clement Attlee's Labour government (1945-1951) brought significant changes in British foreign and domestic politics. One of these changes would be a policy of rejection of support for Zionism and the ideal of the Balfour Declaration. However, it would not come without protest. Martin Jones noted that both Attlee and Bevin underestimated the force of Zionism. "But of Zionist aspirations Bevin had no past experience and he tended, like Attlee, to regard the Jews as a religious group only, thereby underestimating the influence of the holocaust and the strength and messianic quality of the Zionist movement."[58] In Palestine at this time, Golda Meir was a committed socialist. She believed the Labour Party of Britain would support Zionism, but was surprised and hurt by the change in policy in 1945.

> We believed in these organizations in their programs and policies, and we were certain that they, above all, in moral sympathy with our purpose, would help us...Perhaps that is why the blow we have lately suffered (the anti-Zionist attitude of the British Labor government under Bevin) has been felt most keenly by the labor movement.[59]

Meir wrote of the personal disappointment she felt regarding Ernest Bevin,

> We had truly hoped that a better world would emerge when the war was over, and that then the rights of the Jewish people would be recognized. This did not happen. Instead, the British government began to make declarations 'proving' that a schism existed among Jews. Bevin set out to divide the Jews into Zionists and non-Zionists, extremists and non-extremists.[60]

As Prime Minister, Attlee had virtually no personal involvement with Palestine or with Jewish Zionist leaders. Likewise, Weizmann had few dealings with Attlee. In his 600 pages of memoirs, Weizmann referred to Attlee only once. The lone reference had to do with Weizmann noting that Attlee did not agree to Truman's request for 100,000 European Jews to be permitted to settle in Palestine.[61] The fact that this lone account was the sum total of Weizmann's references to the man who was the British Prime Minister at the time of Israeli independence illustrates the gulf that existed between the British government and the leader of the Jewish Zionist movement. This lack of interaction illustrates the extent to which relations had declined in the 30 years since Weizmann enjoyed close contact with Prime Minister Lloyd George and Foreign Minister Balfour.

After 1945, Harold Beeley became Bevin's principal advisor on Palestine, where he exerted his influence on Bevin. This was unfortunate for the Jews in that Beeley was decidedly pro-Arab in his views. Abba Eban wrote that Beeley was "regarded by the Zionists as Bevin's pro-Arab Rasputin."[62] In 1939, Blanche Dugdale confided in her diary that she believed Beeley had never been to Palestine, was ignorant of its affairs and had been won over to the Arab side.[63]

Zionist Considerations in the United States

After 1945, the political influence of the United States expanded rapidly. The isolationist policy of the 1930's was replaced by a new role of self-appointed responsibility for the world. Within America, society was changing with the growth of the Evangelical Christian communities. From 1940 to 1948, the combined Church membership of the three largest Evangelical denominations in the United States (Southern Baptist, Methodist and Presbyterian) grew from 14,435,000 to 17,406,000. In eight years, these three Church groups added nearly three million members, increasing their total Church membership by approximately 17 percent.[64]

Evangelical Christian magazines were popular in America between World War 1 and the 1950's. These journals promoted conservative Protestant Christian teaching which included a support for Zionism. Some of the best-known magazines were *Moody Monthly,* published by Moody Bible Institute in Chicago, *The Presbyterian Journal, Revelation, Eternity, Decision* and *Christianity Today.* In Britain, two similar Evangelical publications were rescued from near bankruptcy by American Christians: *The Christian* and *Church of England Newspaper.*[65]

Although President Truman was inexperienced in Middle East affairs in 1945, he was inclined to support Zionism. His Baptist background lent to this and he had spoken favourable of Zionism on several occasions as a Senator. Now as President, Truman had the benefit of a number of advisors both in the White House and in the State Department to assist him in his decision-making. Since these advisors varied widely in their opinions on what American policy in Palestine should be, and since they represented different religious backgrounds and experiences, they constantly maneuvered themselves to influence the new President.

James Byrnes, Truman's first Secretary of State, was a Catholic who consistently advised Truman to be sensitive to the Arab perspective.[66] Undersecretary Dean Acheson was an Episcopalian and was also pro-Arab in his advice. Loy Henderson of the Office of Near Eastern Affairs, despite being a Methodist, was also pro-Arab in his views. It should be noted that these men did not necessarily articulate anti-Jewish or anti-Zionist sentiments. The issues they dealt with immediately following the war were to determine what American foreign policy would be regarding the displaced Jews of Europe and how the United States might assist the British in settling the question of Palestine.

In contrast to this advice, Truman had a number of advisors who advocated support for the Jews. Earl Harrison, special emissary for Harry Truman, was a Methodist and an outspoken advocate of assisting the Jewish displaced people of Europe in finding a new home in Palestine. Special Counsel to the President, Clark Clifford, was an Episcopalian, but was sympathetic to Zionism. Truman's Administrative Assistant, David Niles, a Jew, was also strongly supportive of Zionist ideals.[67]

Truman began to make his presidential voice heard regarding Palestine in the autumn of 1945. After the Potsdam Conference, he addressed a press conference where he told the journalists he "...had asked the British to admit to Palestine as many Jews as possible."[68] Following this, Earl Harrison said of the Jewish refugees in Europe, "Only in Palestine will they be welcome and find peace and quiet and be given an opportunity to live and work."[69]

The Jews of Palestine React to Labour Government Policy

When the new Labour government in Britain announced their intention to continue the policies of the 1939 White Paper,[70] the

Jews of Palestine responded violently. They felt the position of the government was incompatible with the desperate need of European Jewish refugees. In response, General Barker ordered "Operation Agatha." Thousands of British troops and police entered Jewish homes and kibbutzim at night searching for weapons and illegal Jewish immigrants.

Lord Gort, High Commissioner in Jerusalem, felt control slipping away from him. He wrote in March 1945, "I could not agree more than I do about the weariness of having no compass course to maintain-it is really hopeless."[71] He wrote to Harold MacMichael, "I rather fancy Weizmann is getting more and more worried; he sees Zionism, despite his efforts, losing ground and getting more and more into the hands of the hotheads."[72] In this letter, Gort revealed his fears about Arab successes and the possibility that Arab oil might be more important to the Americans than Zionism.

> The Arabs are also becoming more and more difficult and nothing will induce them to co-operate with Jews about anything. That is just to be expected-both sides are raising their bids and the Arabs, with their newly formed Arab League and with their success in Syria against the French, think they are on top of the world...I cannot help thinking that American oil interests will best Zionism in the race on that side of the Atlantic.[73]

Doctor Julius Kleeberg was a Jewish physician living in Jerusalem in the 1940's. As the head of Internal Medicine at Hadassah Hospital, he wrote of the disappointment he felt with the Labour Party.

> Labour had always supported Zionism, and its election Party platform included that the position in Palestine would change. It did, but for the worse. Ernest Bevin, an ignorant anti-Semite, became Foreign Secretary, and launched what Winston Churchill described as 'Bevin's squalid war' against the Jews.[74]

In his memoirs, Dr. Kleeberg complained of curfews, raids, arms searches and deportations. As part of his job, he was charged with looking after the medical needs of eight Jewish resistance leaders who were on a hunger strike in the British prison in Jerusalem. Kleeberg recorded his disdain for Bevin and for the commander of the British Forces in Palestine, General Barker, writing, "Bevin's war against the Jews was led in Palestine by a neighbour of ours, General Evelyn Barker. He was commander-in-chief of the very considerable forces there. Like Bevin, he was a notorious anti-Semite."[75]

New Hope for Zionism with the Establishment of the Anglo-American Committee

During the immediate post war period, Truman had other foreign policy issues to deal with than just Palestine. The two foremost foreign policy concerns of the American government in these years were the Cold War and European reconstruction, not a peaceful solution in Palestine. For his first two years as President, Truman heard from all perspectives on Palestine, but took little action.

On October 4 1945, Bevin proposed the idea in Cabinet of an Anglo-American Committee on Palestine. He hoped the Americans would receive many Jewish Displaced Persons from Europe, thus alleviating problems in both Europe and Palestine. This was a significant step for Zionism. The Americans were now officially involved in determining the future of Palestine.

During the autumn of 1945, Truman learned that not all American Jews were Zionists. The American Jewish Committee, with Judge Joseph Proskauer as President, opposed Zionism and Jewish statehood. Jacob Blaustein was the AJC's Executive Committee Chairman at the time. These two American Jewish leaders met with President Truman asking the President to oppose Zionism.[76] In the years to follow, Truman needed to keep this unique Jewish perspective in mind.

The *Palestine Post* carried a story on October 19 1945, which reported a conversation between President Truman and Prime Minister Attlee. Truman reportedly asked Attlee to admit 100,000 Jewish refugees into Palestine, but the British Prime Minister refused.[77] The 100,000 number would become meaningful over the next three years. It would reappear later in the Commission's recommendations. Bevin was angered by what he saw as Truman's interference. According to Ronald Zweig of New York University, the British had another motive. They wanted the Jewish refugees in Europe to be categorized with all the other Europeans, not as a separate group. Any overt Jewish identification could translate into more trouble for the British in Palestine. Zweig claimed, "In the autumn of 1945, a revival of Jewish identity, or Zionism, in Europe was one thing the British did not want."[78]

Bevin launched a media attack against Truman, accusing the President of speaking on behalf of the Jews for the sake of obtaining Jewish votes.[79] However, Bevin's claim was unfounded. In making such a statement, he revealed his lack of knowledge of the American political system. Truman had no immediate need to seek votes. The next presidential election was over three years away.[80] Furthermore, the results of the next presidential election in 1948 show that Bevin's accusations against Truman were baseless for another reason. In reality, Truman did not gain Jewish votes after his recognition of Israel; he actually lost Jewish votes. In 1944, Roosevelt, who showed little interest in Zionism, received 90 percent of the Jewish vote in America. In 1948, Truman, just six months after recognizing the new State of Israel, received only 75 percent of the Jewish vote. In addition, Truman lost the State of New York, the home of the largest concentration of American Jews.[81] The reality was that many American Jewish voters did not reward Truman's recognition of Israel with their support. These statistics suggest that American backing for Israel was not based primarily on Jewish support, but rather on the sympathies of the Gentile Christian Zionist population.

On November 13 1945, the decision to form a Joint Anglo-American Committee on Palestine was announced. Bevin put great hope in the Committee's work, declaring in the House, "I will stake my political future on solving the problem."[82] Churchill was skeptical, replying, "No more rash a bet has ever been recorded in the annals of the British turf."[83] The Commission of six British and six American representatives began conducting hearings and receiving evidence in Washington, Europe, Palestine and other centers in the

Middle East. Bevin agreed to abide by the recommendations of the Commission.

The Sudden Departure of Lord Gort

In September 1945, High Commissioner Gort was ill. His doctors diagnosed a mild infection, but in fact, Gort was suffering from cancer of the liver.[84] On the night of October 31 1945, Jewish extremists and moderates cooperated in escalating the struggle by sinking ships, breaking railway lines and bombing bridges. Gort was too sick to respond. It fell to Major General John d'Arcy to take charge of events. During a visit by General Brooke and General Montgomery, Gort collapsed unconscious to the floor. His doctor ordered him to England.[85]

Upon his departure from Palestine, Gort wrote his brother Robert, "It is disappointing to end up 40 years of service this way and especially so as I was particularly anxious to see Palestine through her present troubles."[86] Gort's illness was a serious blow to order in Palestine. It was also a setback for Zionists in that Gort had been sympathetic to their ideals. He had enjoyed a long and distinguished career in the British Army. He had been the commander of the British Expeditionary Force in France in 1940, overseeing the evacuation of the beaches of Dunkirk. He was the Governor of Malta where he endured years of bombardment without surrendering. However, he lasted less than a year in Palestine.

Upon his arrival in London, Gort wrote to the Jewish Agency, "I take with me from Palestine many happy memories and I shall look back with pride on the twelve months I have spent there."[87] Sir George Gates, the Permanent Under Secretary at the Colonial Office wrote to Gort, "I fully believe that your personality alone has been a barrier to serious disorders in Palestine...your departure now, on the eve of a new policy, is a national calamity."[88]

The Arrival of the New High Commissioner Alan Cunningham

High Commissioner Alan Cunningham arrived in Palestine in November 1945.[89] Norman Bentwich noted Cunningham had enjoyed good relations with Jews in the past when he commanded Palestine Jewish units in East Africa, defeating the Italians there in

1941.[90] Personally, Cunningham showed little interest in spiritual matters and did not indicate a religious support for Zionism. His daughter-in-law, Penny Tancred, who took care of Cunningham during the last 18 years of his life in London, claimed Cunningham never spoke of spiritual things or indicated an interest in religion.[91] She believed he had no Church denominational affiliation.[92] In a way, Cunningham was somewhat typical for his generation. After serving in both World Wars, he had adopted a moral secular mentality outside of religious affiliation. He represented the trend of the British nation to secularism. He was fair-minded, acting without prejudice or religious motivations.

Bentwich noted that Cunningham knew he stood little chance of winning the favour of the Jewish leaders in Palestine. Too much had happened over the previous 28 years. Bentwich wrote of Cunningham, "His efforts to establish friendly relations with the Jewish leaders and the Jewish population were poorly requited. By this time the tension was too great, and the Jews were openly or tacitly in revolt."[93] Soon after his arrival, Cunningham met with Arab leaders from all over Palestine. Their main concern was preventing the establishment of a Jewish State. Abdul Hadi, an Arab spokesman, told Cunningham,

> For 25 years, the Arabs have been deprived of their rights. Another community persecuted in Europe and on the strength of having been here 2000 years ago, now asked that a million Arabs should be deprived of their rights, capping one injustice by another. A Jewish state can come in two ways, by killing all the Arabs or by expelling them. The Arabs would never live under Jewish authority.[94]

Cunningham's leadership was hindered for another reason. Under Bevin, he had no real powers of decision as other High Commissioners had enjoyed, nor was he given the authority to communicate with the external meddling factors. Twice he attempted to put forward his own proposals but they failed each time to gain support.[95] Both Lord Gort and Alan Cunningham were dignified, fair-minded military men. They shared the misfortune of history of being the last of the

High Commissioners in an unpopular setting. Bentwich said of Gort and Cunningham, "Both were personally sympathetic to Jews and anxious to foster friendly relations. But their friendliness could not prevail against the British government's obstinate negation of the Jewish demand for a home, or against the anti-Zionism of things."[96] Ben Gurion wrote that Cunningham,

> ...had the misfortune of presiding at Government House at a time when events were just too much for him and it was clear that he was just running a holding operation. Policy was pretty exclusively in the hands of London-and that meant Ernest Bevin...In all my dealings with him, I found him a courteous and friendly individual, and he knew and I knew that he was merely going through the motions of being an administrator.[97]

In November 1945, Bevin and the Foreign Office sent Cunningham advice on Palestine. The High Commissioner was reminded of the "dual obligation" of Palestine, a concept contrary to the spirit of the Balfour Declaration, but which was now official Foreign Office policy.

> The lack of any clear definition of this dual obligation has been the main cause of the trouble which has been experienced in Palestine during the past 26 years. The fact has to be faced that since the introduction of the Mandate it has been impossible to find common ground between the Arabs and the Jews.[98]

The Foreign Office instructed Cunningham that the 1939 White Paper was still to be enforced. "Ships and immigrants intercepted would be dealt with under Palestine law under which ships can be confiscated, master and owner can be liable to fine and imprisonment and immigrants can be detained."[99] Cunningham was a career soldier and obeyed his orders. Although some Jewish Holocaust survivors succeeded in entering Palestine, many others were caught. Some ships were turned back within sight of Palestine to internment camps in Cyprus. However, the world was watching, as Palestine was now the focus of international interest, particularly American interest.

The Zionist Response to Bevin

On November 13 1945, Bevin made a public statement that offended Jews around the world and showed some of Bevin's personal attitudes when he announced at a press conference, "If the Jews, with all their suffering, want to get too much at the head of the queue, you have the danger of another anti-Semitic reaction through it all."[100] Weizmann considered the remark "gratuitously brutal, even coarse." He suspected Bevin had been friendlier with him during the war in order to benefit from his scientific inventions. Weizmann wrote,

> There was not the slightest effort to understand our point of view; there was only an overbearing quarrelsome approach. An earlier contact with Mr. Bevin, when he had been Minister of Labour during the war, had been somewhat happier; but then Mr. Bevin had wanted my services.[101]

In Palestine, the Jews were outraged at the restrictions against their fellow Jews reaching Palestine. Abba Eban recalled, "Jewish fighters blew up British installations in protest against Bevin's persecutions."[102] On December 28 1945, Cunningham had a difficult meeting with Ben Gurion. Ten British soldiers and police had recently been killed while on duty. Despite the painful realities of the situation, both men were able to communicate with mutual respect. Cunningham recalled that Ben Gurion spoke of abhorrence at the violence and told the High Commissioner, "The Agency was no more associated with these acts than was the government. They deeply regretted the loss of life, but more than that they regarded it as a tragedy for this country and their people."[103]

American Zionist Policy Begins to Emerge

Near the end of 1945, Truman sought advice about Palestine from a variety of sources. In December, he met in Washington with influential Jewish leaders: J. David Stern, publisher of the

Philadelphia Record, Lessing J. Rosenwald, President of the AJC and Chaim Weizmann, president of the World Jewish Organization. Truman listened as he considered his own position on Zionism. It was a critical time in world events and Truman was carefully weighing the potential ramifications of any decision he might make. Cohen noted, "Truman made it abundantly clear to all three he was preoccupied with the fear that Zionist aspirations would lead to a racial or theocratic state, a possibility totally at odds with Truman's (American) model of a pluralistic, secular society."[104]

In Washington, in October 1945, Senator's Taft and Wagner introduced their own independent Resolution on Palestine. They wanted to express their Christian Zionism with an official political voice. Their independent Resolution called for Palestine to be opened for the free entry of Jews. Their Resolution also called for Palestine to be "a free and democratic Commonwealth."[105] This statement represented the feeling of some Americans that Palestine was not a complicated issue. The two Senators believed Palestine was the ancient home of the Jewish people and that Jews should be allowed to live there. On December 7 1945, the Taft-Wagner Resolution passed in the Senate, while on the same day the concurrent Wright-Compton Resolution passed in the House. The identically worded Resolutions called for open Jewish immigration into Palestine and for Palestine to be "a free and democratic Commonwealth."[106] Even without Presidential approval at this stage, the swift passage of these two Resolutions by the mostly Gentile Congress and Senate must have had an effect on Truman. Gradually, during the months and years ahead, the President began to solidify his personal position on Zionism.

Another important consideration for Truman was the broad Christian support for Zionism in America. Cohen observed, "There was a widespread belief in the moral claim of the Jewish People to the Holy Land and a 'wish to help realize scriptural prophecies,' made the more urgent by the universal revulsion against the horrors of the Holocaust."[107] From 1945 to 1948, Truman faced a variety of opposition to Zionism: the State Department, the Military, the Arab League and the new British government. When comparing the Jewish community in Palestine to the potential of the Arab oil reserves, the State Department favoured pleasing the Arabs. Cohen noted that at this time, "The State Department viewed Palestine as an integral part of the Arab world."[108]

Despite strong grassroots support for Zionism in the United States, American religious groups, both Christian and Jewish, opposed Zionism. One of the most prestigious Jewish organizations in the United America, the American Jewish Committee opposed the establishment of a Jewish State in Palestine. The American Council for Judaism also zealously opposed the idea of a Jewish State.[109] In their study of Truman during these years, Weinstein and Ma'oz observed, "Throughout 1946, President Truman had been under tremendous pressure from the British, the Arabs (especially the Saudi Arabians) and his own State Department. At times during 1946, he wavered and seemed ready to accept a binational state of some sort."[110] If Truman had ignored the issue of partition and Zionism, it probably would have brought little trouble to his administration. As President, he held considerable power. For the time being Truman would not take action.

The Labour Government Seeks a Compromise in Palestine

Ernest Bevin was well aware he had stepped into the role of Foreign Secretary nearly 30 years after the Balfour Declaration. British society had changed along with attitudes toward Zionism, so Bevin was motivated to seek a negotiated solution in Palestine. According to Weiler, "Bevin initially insisted that the conflict 'must be settled by discussion and conciliation,' not force."[111] However, the situation in Palestine in the late 1940's was not conducive to discussion or reconciliation. There was little ground for compromise on either side in Palestine. Harris commented,

> When Hitler began to persecute the Jews in Germany in the early thirties, the rate of Jewish immigration into Palestine increased. So did the resistance of the Arabs, rising to a level of violence with which Britain, dependent on Arab support for oil and her strategic position on the Suez Canal, found it difficult to deal.[112]

Harris believed the Labour Party's dilemma was a moral one. "Britain's main interests in the Middle East predicated support for the Arabs…To support Zionist aspirations would achieve comparatively little for British or for Western interests but would risk immense loss."[113] Harris pointed out other pressures on Britain. The Soviet Union had taken on an expansionist policy, both the British Foreign Office and the American State Department believed the Arabs would win a war against the Jews and support for Zionism would achieve little for Western interests while risking immense loss.[114]

Clement Attlee, unlike his predecessor Churchill, was not interested in assisting the cause of Zionism. When Attlee moved into 10 Downing Street in July 1945, he found a letter from Truman to Churchill in which Truman expressed, "the hope that the British government may find it possible without delay to take steps to lift the restrictions of the White Paper on Jewish immigration into Palestine."[115] Attlee did not take action to fulfill Truman's request. Perhaps Attlee never believed the Jews were a true nation who deserved a home of their own. Hugh Dalton reported that both Bevin and Attlee expressed the opinion that the Jews were a religion and not a race, Dalton noted, "In this attitude, Bevin and Attlee were a long way from the traditionally sentiments of the Labour Party."[116]

The Recommendations of the Anglo-American Committee

The Anglo-American Committee met from November 1945 until April 1946. The main point of interest in their Report was the recommendation that 100,000 European Jews be released to Palestine by the end of 1946.[117] The Report also recommended the creation of a binational state in which neither side would dominate the other and called for a trusteeship under the United Nations. To the Zionists, the support for immigration was good news, but the opposition to a Jewish State was devastating. The two strongest Zionists on the Committee were the Americans James McDonald and Bartley Crum. Both believed they had served Zionism well as members of the Committee. Immigration would now be open, and they believed Jewish statehood would come later.

At the inception of the Committee, Bevin had reluctantly promised to endorse whatever recommendations the Committee made. However, he was angry when he realized the Committee recommended 100,000 Jews be allowed to enter Palestine immediately. Begin observed, "Macdonald and Crum reminded Bevin that he had solemnly promised the members of the Commission that if the recommendations were unanimous, they would be implemented. Bevin did not reply."[118]

Former High Commissioner MacMichael also disagreed with the Committee's recommendation. He compared what such a number would represent if compared to the population of the United States. "I worked out President Truman's 100,000 for immediate entry into Palestine as 1 in 16 of the present entire population here. On the same figure the U.S.A. should open her doors to 8,100,000 –the distressed Jew problem is then solved."[119]

In April 1946, Bevin asked the United States government not to publish the report until the two governments had consulted together on the matter. Truman agreed, but then changed his mind and released the Committee's recommendations. Apparently, Truman saw no good reason to reconsider the matter. Truman had personally endorsed the entry of 100,000 Jewish immigrants and was pleased the Committee recommended it. Bevin was outraged.[120] At this time, Truman's support for Zionism was evolving. Even though he advocated massive Jewish immigration to Palestine, he was still not an advocate of the idea of a Jewish State (or an Arab State) in Palestine. On April 30 1946, Truman officially backed the Committee's recommendations.[121]

Attlee reacted, immediately telling the House that his government could not implement the Commission's recommendations.[122] Bevin seemed to take the report personally. At the Labour Party conference in June, he declared to the Party that a propaganda campaign was being carried out in the United States, especially in New York, for the admission of 100,000 Jews to Palestine.[123] In order to resolve the tension between the two governments, a new committee was formed to find a solution. Ambassador Henry A. Grady of America and Deputy Prime Minister Herbert Morrison of Britain cooperated on the so-called Morrison-Grady Plan.[124]

According to James McDonald, Bevin never intended to cooperate with the proposals of the Anglo-American Committee of Inquiry. McDonald described Bevin's theory of how Truman was responsible for the British rejection of the recommendations. Bevin said to McDonald, "There were ten points in your program. I accepted all ten. President Truman accepted only one." McDonald wrote, "I was aghast. For the moment, I felt as if I had heard the echo of Hitler's words about telling a big lie.[125] For the truth in this matter was exactly the contrary. If any fact was beyond dispute, it was the fact that Bevin had rejected virtually all of them."[126]

McDonald recalled Bevin's behaviour, "What extraordinary demagoguery! Banging his fist on the table, at times almost shouting, he charged that the Jews were ungrateful for what Britain had done for them in Palestine."[127] McDonald wrote of Bevin, "In his resentment he had used his browbeating technique, arrogantly taking the offensive to put the man he was dealing with at a disadvantage."[128] McDonald classed Bevin with some of the worst dictators of the period, "Bevin, like Hitler and Mussolini in my interviews with them when I was League of Nations High Commissioner in the 1930's, had impressed me with a complete sense of ruthlessness."[129]

Attlee also spoke against the recommendations of the Anglo-American Committee, claiming there were "illegal armies" in Palestine and so large a body of immigrants could only be admitted if "these formations have been disbanded and their armies surrendered."[130] Richard Crossman, a Labour MP who supported Zionism, answered with an article in the *New Statesman and Nation*.

> If the policy is adopted, we may well find ourselves drifting involuntarily into an Anglo-Jewish war...In that case, a Labour government, solemnly pledged to right the wrongs of the White Paper, and to support Zionism, will be brought into armed conflict not merely with the small minority of terrorists, but with the whole Jewish population of the National Home.[131]

In a speech to the House of Commons, Crossman challenged his own Labour Party to abandon the White Paper policy and adopt the recommendations of the Committee.

When the war ended and the Labour government came into power, the White Paper still remained in force. The Jews, who had expected an immediate fulfillment by the Labour government of the Labour Party program with regard to Zionism, felt a sense of outrage when no change of policy occurred…We have drifted without contract until we are in grievous danger. So I beg the house to agree that here, and here alone, lies the way out of the difficulty-acceptance in principle of that report, and then to work out with the American government and with the Jewish Agency the way to implement all those ten clauses of the report which hang together and without which we can have no peace in Palestine and no peace in the Middle East.[132]

The American Government Maintains Pressure on the British

In Washington, Truman began a new campaign to pressure the British government to implement the entry of 100,000 new Jewish immigrants into Palestine. Truman wrote Attlee requesting the "early immigration of 100,000 Jews into Palestine."[133] Seemingly, in an attempt to show understanding, Truman added, "I also join with you in the hope that law and order will be maintained by the inhabitants of Palestine while efforts are being made toward a solution of the Long Term Policy."[134]

On June 26 1946, Truman's Jewish friend and ex-business partner, Eddie Jacobson, visited him for the first time at the White House, bringing with him some American Zionist officials. This was the first of many such visits by Jacobson.[135] What was motivating Truman's interest in Jewish affairs at this time? Ronald Zweig of New York University believed the Truman administration was interested in the Jews out of sympathy for Holocaust survivors and in order to obtain Jewish votes for the Democratic Party. He also noted that the American Army was surprised by how many Jewish survivors there were in Europe, which were considered by the Army to be a threat to civil order and public health.[136]

There was another factor influencing Truman during this immediate post war period. Apparently, the State Department was informing the President that Saudi Arabia would go to war if Palestine were given to the Jews. Although Truman had not yet backed the concept of a Jewish State, he supported Jewish immigration to Palestine. He feared a Jewish State would require an American military commitment to defend it. He wrote to Senator Joseph Ball of Minnesota on November 24 1945 urging caution and patience.

> I told the Jews that if they were willing to furnish me with five hundred thousand men to carry on a war with the Arabs, we could do what they are suggesting in the Resolution [favoring a state]... otherwise we will have to negotiate awhile..It is a very explosive situation we are facing, and naturally I regret it very much, but I don't think that you, or any of the other Senators, would be inclined to send half a dozen Divisions to Palestine to maintain a Jewish State...What I am trying to do is to make the whole world safe for the Jews. Therefore, I don't feel like going to war for Palestine.[137]

After the Anglo-American Committee's report, Truman's personal views became more sympathetic to the Jewish position. He showed this view in a speech on the eve of Yom Kippur, October 4 1946. On this, the most important day of the year in the Jewish calendar, Truman pledged American support for Jewish immigration and partition. Despite the fact that the Yom Kippur date was dismissed by the White House as coincidental, Truman's timing had great meaning to Jews everywhere. Part of Truman's speech referred to Jewish autonomy in Palestine. Truman declared, "I cannot believe that the gap between the proposals which have been put forward is too great to be bridged by men of reason and goodwill. To such a solution our government could give its support."[138]

The timing of Truman's speech meant that every Rabbi in the country could mention it their synagogues on Yom Kippur. Regarding the so-called Yom Kippur speech, Allis Radosh believed, "Truman could not come to an agreement with the British and was only stating the reality of the situation."[139] The British government was dismayed by Truman's remarks, but Zionists saw hope. Certainly, it was a pivotal point in the American posture toward Jewish statehood.

From now on, Truman would gradually lean more toward support for Jewish statehood.

Jewish Discouragement and Retaliation in Palestine

With the Labour government set against immigration, it was now nearly impossible for the Jews of Palestine to conceive of how the British would facilitate the founding of a Jewish National Home. Christian Zionists in Britain were fewer and quieter than in decades past. From Palestine, Cunningham reported the challenges of administrating Palestine.[140] In March 1946, Weizmann told the High Commissioner that he saw partition as "the only practical solution."[141] Cunningham replied to Weizmann, "It is of some importance to note that Mr. Churchill, as a Zionist, would support partition if proposed as a solution."[142]

Despite Cunningham's friendly relationship with Weizmann, he believed Weizmann no longer held significant power within the Zionist movement. In April, Cunningham sent a telegram to the Foreign Office, saying of Weizmann, "It is plain that he has lost authority with the Yishuv...It is generally believed that he will not long continue on the political scene."[143]

In the spring of 1946, the British finally completed part of their long-standing obligation to the house of Hussein. On March 22, Britain recognized the sovereign independence of Transjordan with Abdullah as King. [144] With British recognition, the descendants of the Sherif of Mecca now had a State to rule, but they looked warily across the Jordan River to Palestine. Abdullah wrote, "Palestine is the subject of Jewish ambitions and is still directly controlled by England."[145] Clearly, he still saw any future Jewish State as something that would be determined by Britain.

Weizmann Seeks Christian Support for the Jewish National Home

In 1946, Chaim Weizmann appealed to two of the longest standing Christian Zionists, Winston Churchill and Jan Smuts. In his letter of appeal, Weizmann expressed his fear that all might be lost, that there might be no future immigration, no National Home, and the last hope of thousands of Jews in the world might be destroyed.

Weizmann wrote that if there were no Jewish State, it would mean, "in fact, a destruction of the 'Third Temple' built up with so much effort and devotion on the basis of Britain's pledged word."[146]

Weizmann was relentless in his personal appeals to any who might have influence. He wrote to Attlee of the untenable position of the Jewish survivors in the Displaced Person's Camps of Europe. The majority wanted to go to Palestine since there was no future for them in Europe. Weizmann told Attlee that 100,000 new immigrants was a reasoned application. "I would urgently plead that H.M. government may see its way to grant this application...The Balfour Declaration was part of a general Middle Eastern Settlement offering a sub-continent to the Arabs, and a 'small notch' –as Lord Balfour put it- to the Jews."[147] There is no record of a response from Attlee.

Weizmann even invited Bevin to visit him in Palestine, but Bevin did not accept the invitation.[148] Weizmann's charm seemed to have no effect on Bevin, despite the fact that he and Weizmann had had a close working relationship through World War 2. The weight of Bevin's rejection was heavy on Weizmann. Bevin was a man with an education only to age ten, with the personal knowledge of only one language and one culture shunning the invitation of a world-renowned diplomat and scientist fluent in eight languages.

During these days, James McDonald tried to encourage Weizmann. As a pro-Zionist member of the Anglo-American Committee, McDonald knew something of what Weizmann had been experiencing, writing to him, "The struggle has been intense and at times exhausting. I hope, however that when you learn of the resolution you will not feel that all the efforts have been put into preparations for these hearings and the hearings themselves have been lost."[149]

British Anti-Semitism in Palestine

Another factor that revealed the decline in British sympathy for Christian Zionist was the increase in anti-Semitic attitudes among the British in Palestine. By 1946, such behaviour was widespread in the military.[150] Begin took note of the antagonism of some of the British soldiers in Palestine. He recalled one incident when soldiers of the 6th Airborne wrote a threat on a copy of the underground newspaper *Herut*, "Oh Gee, oh Gee, Hitler killed 6,000,000 Jews. The 6th Airborne will kill 60,000,000 if you don't bloody well behave yourselves."[151] At the time, McDonald attempted to convince Begin to be more cooperative with the British, but Begin wrote, "Mr. McDonald is undoubtedly a friend of our people...but he is mistaken if he thinks that it is possible to secure a change in British policy in Eretz Israel.[152]

According to Holocaust survivor Shalom Lindenbaum, who arrived in Palestine from Auschwitz in 1945, the anger of the British soldiers increased near the end of the Mandate. "In Palestine after the war, there were a few British soldiers who were sympathetic to us. They did not shoot to kill, but only to graze us. But in the last years (of the Mandate) most of the British officials and soldiers were opposed to us."[153] Rita Mouchabeck was born in Jerusalem in 1925 into a Christian Arab family. Because of her language skills, she worked for the British police at the Russian Compound Police Station in Jerusalem. Throughout her time working for the British, she remarked, "If there were Zionists among them, they kept it to themselves."[154]

Bevin was concerned about offending the Arabs by appearing to be too friendly with the Jewish Agency. He was troubled about rumours that Weizmann might soon meet with Attlee. Bevin sent Attlee a warning, "These reports are bound to create the impression in Arab countries that we are consulting Dr. Weizmann but intend to reach a final decision before we have consulted any Arab leaders or even answered their invitation to negotiate"[155]

In June 1946, in order to protest, and to display their resolve, the Haganah carried out a night operation of destroying bridges.[156] As a response, the British raided the Jewish Agency Headquarters in Jerusalem on June 29 1946. The *Palestine Post* headline read, "Army Seize Jewish Agency, Hold Leaders, 1000 Others in Dawn Swoop."[157] The Jews of Palestine called this day "Black Sabbath." The new British raids, under orders from General Barker, resulted in the arrests of about 3000 Jews. The situation in Palestine had never been worse for the British. After the Black Sabbath of 1946, more Jews than ever in Palestine were united in their resolve to oppose the British. Golda Meir saw these events as a signal for the end of the Mandate, as the British no longer had a rationale to stay.

"The 29th of June, when the British government arrested the leaders of the Yishuv, was a turning point in Palestine. In this action the government overreached itself."[158] Meir recalled,

> On the 29th of June, the government set out to break the spirit and backbone of the Yishuv in Palestine by one concentrated blow. That day the government fell upon us; the troops it sent against us assaulted the Jewish Agency building, occupied it, and held it for a week; that day, on a Saturday morning, the members of the Executive and of the National Council were led off as prisoners.[159]

Meir believed these attacks united the Jewish people.[160] She wrote, "Above all, these blows strengthened our determination to demand that full measure of political independence which can be attained only through the establishment of a Jewish state."[161] After the summer of 1946, the British no longer pushed for full control of Palestine. Bevin's policies had forced the Jews of Palestine to abandon any hope of British cooperation to establish a Jewish State. Weizmann was distressed at this turn of events. For 29 years, he had courted the favour of the British. On the day of the Black Sabbath raid, he visited High Commissioner Cunningham to complain.[162]

Four weeks after Black Sabbath, on July 22 1946, Jewish extremists detonated a bomb in the King David Hotel in Jerusalem, which at the time, housed the government secretariat.[163] The bomb destroyed a portion of the hotel, killing 91 people, including Jewish employees. The Irgun claimed responsibility.[164] Cunningham sent detailed telegrams to the Secretary of State explaining what had happened.[165] Following the bombing, Herbert Samuel addressed the issue in the House of Lords. He condemned the bombing and blamed the attack on the frustration caused by the "…cruel policy of His Majesty's government in closing the doors of Palestine to the few remaining survivors of Nazism."[166]

The King David Hotel bombing and the Black Sabbath raids were exceptionally violent events in the history of the relationship between the British and the Jews in Palestine. General Montgomery, the Chief of the Imperial Staff, was angered and motivated to action.

He wrote two days after the bombing, "We shall show the world and the Jews that we are not going to submit tamely to violence."[167] Despite these strong words, the resolve of the British in Palestine was now in question. The breakdown of trust and respect shown by these incidences indicate how grim the situation was. Thurston Clarke noted, "The Irgun's revolt-in particular, the King David bombing and the hanging of the two sergeants-accelerated, but did not cause Britain's departure from Palestine."[168]

The tensions between the British administration and the Jewish residents intensified because of the events of the summer of 1946. One specific example concerned a neighbour of General Barker. In the autumn of 1946, Dr. Kleeberg of Jerusalem was told he would have to move out of his house in three days. His house was needed by the military authorities, as well as the house of another Jewish family next to General Barker's house. The order came personally from Barker, but Barker refused to see Dr. Kleeberg. Barker's aide-de-camp spoke with Kleeberg instead, telling him, "Did you not treat the eight Jewish Agency leaders during the hunger strike in April? The Agency leaders would certainly have chosen a sympathetic doctor. Birds of a feather flock together."[169] Kleeberg wrote, "I heard later that General Barker had commented sardonically, 'Who would like to live next to two Jews?'"[170]

General Barker ordered the trees cut down in Dr. Kleeberg's yard for the sake of security. Kleeberg was forced to remove and store his belongings from his six-room household and six room clinic. Kleeberg wrote, "People in misery and need quickly become objects, first of pity, then of resentment. The world loves a winner, and avoids a loser."[171] At this time, Golda Meir spoke to Kleeberg and he wrote of the conversation. Meir told him, "You are looking so sad. Why? Now you know *dafka* that you must fight them."[172] Kleeberg noted she offered no consolation."[173] He wrote, "It meant my complete financial ruin…British anti-Semites had expelled us from our home, my place of work as a physician and healer of the sick. I felt that Job had had trifling troubles compared to mine."[174]

At this time, General Barker went too far in displaying his contempt for the Jews. Abba Eban was working in the offices of the British Army when he noticed an order on the bulletin board signed by General Barker. Eban described the order as "a vulgar anti-Semitic tract urging troops to avoid Jewish shops in order 'to hit the Jews where it hurts them most-in their pockets. That is the only language that the race understands.'"[175] Eban secured a copy of the order and sent it to John Kimche, a British journalist who published it in several British newspapers.[176] The open prejudice of Barker fueled the rage of the Jews of Palestine. Barker was eventually recalled to Britain. The usually open-minded Weizmann said to Bevin, "I do not want to waste any words on a man like General Barker."[177]

The Morrison-Grady Plan and Truman's Intervention

On July 25 1946, the British introduced the Morrison-Grady Plan for Palestine. This was the follow-up plan of the Anglo-American agreement, and represented British pressure on the Americans. Attlee wrote to Truman suggesting that obstacles "…should not deter us from introducing a policy designed to bring peace to Palestine with the least possible delay."[178] The Morrison-Grady Plan gave sympathy to the Jewish refugees, hoping that many would resettle in Europe and America. For Palestine, they recommended an Arab Province, a Jewish Province, a Jerusalem District and a District of the Negev. They also endorsed the immigration of 100,000 Jews to Palestine.[179] The new plan was a compromise, reducing the amount of land given to the Jews. Truman at first thought the plan fair. Undersecretary of State Dean Acheson approved of it. It was the closest Truman and Bevin ever came to agreeing. However, in the face of intense Jewish disapproval, Truman abandoned the Morrison-Grady Plan.

In August, Truman suggested his own compromise solution of Palestine in two States, one Jewish and one Arab.[180] The suggestion was not immediately acted on, but the idea grew in the months ahead. This development is significant in that Truman was beginning to assume personal responsibility for the issue of Palestine as the State Department was apparently having a diminished influence on the President. In July 1946, Truman's first Secretary of State, James Byrnes, wrote to David Ben Gurion to say he wanted Ben Gurion to know that the Palestine issue was out of the hands of the State Department and in those of President Truman. Byrnes resented

Zionist criticism of the State Department's Palestine policy and welcomed being relieved of the responsibility.[181]

The British Struggle for Order in Palestine

During the autumn of 1946, the Jews in Palestine continued their resistance as the British detained ships and sent thousands of Jewish refugees to detention camps in Cyprus and Atlit, near Haifa.[182]

In Britain, the voice of Christian Zionism could still be heard. In August, the magazine *Time and Tide* published an article entitled, "Leadership in Israel: Chaim Weizmann."[183] *Time and Tide* was a left-wing political left-wing magazine, founded in 1920. Part of the article read,

> Compare Weizmann to Joseph or Moses-a spokesman rather than a leader. Weizmann said in 1937 to Britain, "You shall not play fast and loose with the Jewish nation…this trifling with a nation bleeding from a thousand wounds must not be done by the British whose Empire is built on moral principles."[184]

Sympathy for the Jews and support for Zionism, while in decline, was still widespread in Britain. In Palestine, the British were reluctant to treat the Jews as harshly as they treated the Arabs. The British used arrests, curfews, interrogations, threats, prison and even death sentences. However, they were reluctant to punish Jewish neighbourhoods the way they would punish Arab villages. Many of the Jews were European, and considered to be "civilized," not like the Arab villagers. Besides, the Jewish Agency and the Haganah were officially opposed to the violence.

It was clear what the Jewish leaders in Palestine were seeking: open immigration, political control and eventually independence. But what did the British in Palestine want? They wanted order. They wanted the Jewish Agency to oppose Jewish violence. They wanted a solution that would please both the Jews and the Arabs. Norman Bentwich believed both a prejudice against Jews and a fear of the Arabs were motivating Bevin. Bentwich wrote, "For Bevin, the step from anti-Zionism to anti-Jew was instinctive…his aim-as it turned out, a futile aim-was to salvage for Great Britain Arab goodwill out of the wreck of the Mandate for Palestine."[185]

No longer were Jews and Arabs speaking about a future together in Palestine. In September, a Palestine Conference was held in Lancaster House, London. Delegates from seven States of the Arab League as well as Azzam Pasha, Secretary General of the Arab League, were present. Prime Minister Attlee personally welcomed the Arabs delegates. At the end of the sessions, no recommendations were made.[186] Throughout the autumn of 1946, Bevin blamed the Jews for the slow progress and he still desired the participation of the Americans to solve the stalemate in Palestine. In October 1946, he wrote to the American ambassador in Britain claiming, "... responsibility for this delay rests mainly with the Jews...It seems unreasonable that we should be castigated for delay when the Zionists are in fact so largely responsible for it."[187] In Washington, Truman still desired that the displaced Jews of Europe soon find a suitable home. He believed that for many of the Jewish Displaced Persons, Palestine was the answer. He wrote Atlee,

> My feeling was that the announcement of the adjournment until December 16th of the discussion with the Arabs had brought such depression to the Jewish displaced persons in Europe and to millions of American citizens concerned with the fact of these unfortunate people that I could not even for a single day postpone making clear the continued interest of this government in their welfare.[188]

Truman went on to advocate again that 100,000 European Jews immigrate immediately to Palestine and promised that the American government would finance the transfer. Truman told Attlee, "In our view the development of the Jewish National Home has no meaning in the absence of Jewish immigration and settlement on the land as contemplated in the Mandate."[189] Attlee answered,

> It would be impossible for His Majesty's government to propose that Palestine should accept a large number of displaced persons in advance of effective international action

on the general problem...And it has not yet been possible, largely owing to the reluctance of the Jews themselves to enter into negotiations with His Majesty's government to reach this general decision.[190]

During these post war years of hardship, the British people were questioning why their soldiers were still in Palestine. Questions were raised about the strategic value of the region. In November 1946, Bevin sailed to New York where he had several intense conversations with James Byrnes, the Secretary of State. Bevin persisted with his posture of blaming the Jews, telling Byrnes, "Americans agitated for Jewish immigration to Palestine because 'they did not want too many Jews in New York.'"[191] Biographer Weiler defended some of Bevin's supposed anti-Jewish statements, but concluded, "It is also the case, however, that Ernest Bevin held anti-Semitic views."[192] Weiler also noted of Bevin, "Various of his colleagues privately noted what Ian Mikardo called 'the pejorative and often vulgar language of many of Bevin's references to Jews.'"[193]

Bevin finally met with Truman on December 8 1946. Bevin emphasized that provincial autonomy in Palestine was "a very fair and practical solution."[194] The United States gave no encouragement to the idea of assuming the Mandate from the British. In December 1946, Colonial Secretary Arthur Creech Jones made it clear that he personally favoured partition in Palestine, which he believed was beneficial to the Zionists. On December 10 1946, Weizmann and Jewish Agency announced that the National Home must become a Jewish State.[195] This was the first time the Jewish Agency clearly stated this purpose. Of these days, Vera Weizmann, the wife of Chaim Weizmann wrote, "My husband's encounters with Bevin, so warm and friendly in the first years of the war when Bevin required his scientific services, became acrimonious and harsh."[196]

Bevin felt he had little room left in which to maneuver on the issue of Palestine. It seemed impossible to continue in Palestine, yet how could the British quit their commitments in Palestine with dignity? Even though the British still had the power to impose their will in Palestine, they no longer had the rationale or the heart to continue. Crossman wrote, "At any time during 1946, Ernest Bevin could have smashed Jewish resistance and imposed British rule on Palestine for another ten or fifteen years. But Bevin believed Britain could no longer 'go it alone.'"[197]

The British Seek a Solution in 1947

By 1947, Bevin was diligently seeking any workable solution for Palestine. He believed that a settling of the Palestine problem would bring peace, stability and a continuation of Britain's prestige to the Middle East. He was keenly aware of the damaged reputation of British foreign policy because of Palestine. In January 1947, Bevin said he feared that "the impression seemed to be growing that we had lost the ability, and, indeed, the will, to live up to our responsibilities."[198]

In Britain at this time, some Zionists were still raising their voices in Parliament. In the spring of 1947, Richard Crossman received a three-page letter of thanks from Chaim Weizmann for his work in the House of Commons. The letter spoke of the problems of martial law and the renewed violence, but was filled also with thanks to Crossman. Weizmann wrote of his "...heartfelt thanks for the wonderful article, various speeches and kindness. I think we shall all be indebted to you."[199] He had been a member of the Anglo-American Committee of Inquiry. In 1947 he published his account of his visit to Palestine searching for a way to still fulfil the Balfour Declaration and facilitate a Jewish National Home.[200] It seems that Crossman's Zionism was a unique combination of values based on socialistic principals supplemented by a Christian sense of justice.

By the late 1940's, Crossman realized many in Britain were tired of the problems in Palestine. He wrote, "Palestine had for many years been one of those wearisome subjects which were always cropping up in the papers."[201] The ideals of Zionism were also weakening within the Jewish community in Britain. Crossman noted that in 1947, out of 25 Jewish Labour MP's, few supported Zionism. He believed, "It is doubtful whether a single Jewish MP owed his election to the fact that he was a Jew or had championed the Zionist cause. British Jewry, some 300,000 strong, is too small to form an effective pressure group."[202]

In the spring of 1947, Weizmann wrote a lengthy summary of the situation on describing the plight of the Jewish Displaced Persons in

Europe, the need to end immigration quotas and the continuation of refugee boats being intercepted.[203] In London, Bevin wanted Jewish Holocaust survivors viewed as part of the world refugee problem, to be settled throughout the world. He did not want a special status allocated to the Jews, believing this approach would appease the Arabs both in Palestine and throughout the rest of the Middle East. William Roger Louis wrote,

> The key to the problem of Britain and the end of the Palestine mandate lies in an understanding of the thought and motivation of the Foreign Secretary Ernest Bevin... Bevin was in overall control, and he followed developments with a grasp of detail and force and personality unrivaled by his British contemporaries.[204]

Throughout his years as Foreign Minister, Bevin tended to promote the Arab cause. He claimed he believed that under Jewish rule in Palestine, the Arabs would not be given equal rights. Besides this, there was also the issue of oil. A contemporary Cabinet paper stressed the importance of Middle East oil to Britain and the Empire.[205] Norman Bentwich observed that the personal dominance of Bevin was able to squelch any influence the Christian Zionists might have had. "Neither the High Commissioner in Jerusalem nor the Labour Colonial Secretary in London, Arthur Creech Jones (whom Helen and I had known as an ardent friend of Zionism) could exercise any influence. The Foreign Secretary, Mr. Bevin, and the soldiers had taken charge."[206]

By 1947, Bevin's power to make policy was enormous. Louis noted, "Bevin himself was the architect of Britain's foreign policy."[207] He did not agree with the concept and implications of Zionism. Bevin felt pressured by both the Americans and the Arabs, but was not responsive to Zionist ideals. Churchill called Bevin a "working class John Bull."[208] Bevin knew he could make policy unilaterally and impose his will on the situations around him. Louis observed, "Bevin was careful to square his ideas with Attlee's before Cabinet meetings. Together the two of them often made an unbreakable combination."[209]

A third key figure in foreign policy making at this time was Arthur Creech Jones. He was Parliamentary Under-Secretary for the Colonies from July 1945 to October 1946 and then Colonial Secretary until 1950. Usually Creech Jones worked well with Attlee and Bevin, but in this matter he personally favoured Zionism. By 1947, Creech Jones preferred partition, but was forced to submit to Bevin's lead. Herbert Morrison could also be counted on to support government policy. Palestine was simply not a controversial issue within the Labour Cabinet in the autumn of 1947.

Various facets of the Palestine problem continued to be addressed in London. Churchill challenged the government to safeguard the reputation of Britain. He expressed to the House of Commons, "I earnestly trust that the government will, if they have to fight this squalid war, make perfectly certain that the will power of the British State is not conquered by brigands and bandits."[210] The debates were intense and sometimes personal. Attlee, Morrison and Bevin had all supported Zionism before the war, now they opposed it. The influence of Zionism was now almost eliminated in the House of Commons. According to Martin Gilbert, between 1946 and 1948, Churchill was shouted down many times in Parliament, often with anti-Semitic taunts.[211]

Apart from the political problems, there were other practical reasons for the British to exit Palestine. Elizabeth Monroe calculated, "The bill for Palestine between January 1945 and November 1947 was 100 million pounds- a poor return for money in a year in which the British were finding it financially necessary to ration bread at home."[212] Aside from the financial obligations, three governmental departments could be free of Palestine: the Colonial Office, the War Office and the Foreign Office. During these years, the situation in India absorbed much of the attention of the Foreign Office. Bevin kept the Prime Minister informed about the region, sometimes calling the situation in India "alarming."[213] As Foreign Secretary, Bevin saw a link between the Muslim colonies and the problems in Palestine, telling the American ambassador that the Arab-Jewish quarrel concerned the whole Moslem world including India and South East Asia.[214]

Norman Bentwich called 1947 the "Year of Anger" in Palestine.[215] In January of that year, the British administration in Palestine ordered all British women and children to leave Palestine. In February, Cunningham wrote to London, "The past months, December 1946 to February 1947, have been characterized in Palestine by deterioration in public order arising from an extension in the scope and number of terrorist outrages."[216]

At this time, some British soldiers lost their sympathy for the Jews. To illustrate, in 1946, 18-year-old Anthony Wright joined the Palestine police force. When asked by a recruiter in England why he wished to join and what he knew of the country, Wright cited his Christian upbringing and his interest in the land of Israel. He wrote in his diary, "Years of Scripture lessons, backed up by a firm Christian upbringing proved invaluable and seemed to satisfy my lone examiner."[217]

Months later, 19-year-old Constable Anthony Wright was shocked by the reality of what he experienced in Palestine. The Jews were unfriendly and the Arabs taunted him. He wrote in his diary that the Arabs told him, "We have no argument with you. Go home 'Inglisi' (sic) and we will push the Jews into the sea."[218] A few weeks later, he wrote in his diary that his sympathies were changing towards the Arabs. "After all, it was the Jewish terrorists who were causing us grief."[219] This personal testimony illustrates the hard realities the British were facing in Palestine. Thirty years after the Balfour Declaration, the British and the Jews in Palestine had little ideology left in common.

Bevin Declares, "Balfour is Dead"

In February 1947, one last attempt was made in London to secure an agreement between the Jews and the Arabs of Palestine. The talks ended in failure as no compromise could be reached.[220] In light of this, the Cabinet decided to turn the issue of Palestine over to the newly formed United Nations. At this time, in a speech in the House of Commons, Bevin declared, "Balfour is dead."[221] His blunt statement displayed his personal frustration over Palestine. William Roger Louis was kind in his assessment of the statement's meaning. He believed Bevin meant that further debate about the meaning of the Balfour declaration of 1917 would be of little help in resolving post-1945 dilemmas."[222] Eban was appalled at Bevin and wrote, "We are seeing British policy at its lowest level of expression."[223] Crossman noted, "Bevin's handling of Palestine had become heavily clouded by anti-Semitism."[224]

Eban realized that Bevin was no longer meeting with any of the Jewish leaders of Palestine. He wrote, "This is the first time ever a British Foreign Secretary refused to see Weizmann."[225] In response to Bevin's comments, Churchill emerged from out of his silence.[226] He challenged the Colonial Secretary, Arthur Creech Jones, in the House,

> How long does the Secretary of State for the Colonies expect that this state of squalid warfare will all its bloodshed will go on, at a cost of 30 million or 40 million pounds a year, keeping 100,000 Englishmen away with the military forces? How long does he expect that this will go on, before some decision is reached?[227]

In his work on Churchill's Zionism, Michael Makovsky believed that Churchill had complicated personal reasons for being relatively passive about his Zionism during these years. However, when given the opportunity, he once more would rise to champion the cause. Makovsky wrote, "From 1945 through 1948, the wider picture was hazy and conflicting, and for personal, political and psychological reasons he ignored Zionism even though it tugged on his conscience. He reverted back to supporting Zionism from 1949 until the end of his political career."[228] Whatever his personal reasons for his silence, from this time on, Churchill would be more engaged in speaking out on behalf of Zionism.

Following Bevin's announcement, the United Nations immediately began plans to send its own Commission to investigate what they called the "Palestine Problem." In April 1947, the Colonial Office prepared a 52-page document detailing their partition plan, calling their document, "Palestine, a Study of Partition."[229] This plan offered the initiative for the United Nations to follow. On May 13 1947, the United Nations appointed a special committee to study the problem of Palestine and report back in three months. Sir Donald MacGillivray was appointed the Liaison Officer of this United Nations Special Committee (UNSCOP). The purpose and role of the Special Committee was announced with some optimism in the *Palestine Post*.[230]

Weizmann testified before UNSCOP in October 1947. He told the Committee that Arab territorial demands in the regions were satisfied. He reminded the Committee that in 1918, he and Emir Feisal signed a treaty stipulating that if the rest of Arab Asia were free, the Arabs would concede the Jewish right to freely to settle and develop in Palestine, which would exist side by side with the Arab State. Weizmann pointed out to the Committee that the condition which Feisal had stipulated, the independence of all Arab territories outside Palestine, had now been fulfilled.[231] The Committee did not act on Weizmann's testimony.

In the end, the UNSCOP Report recommended unanimously that Britain end the Mandate and grant Palestine independence. Seven of the countries involved recommended partition into three areas: one Jewish, one Arab and Jerusalem. Three other countries on the Committee recommended the establishment of an "Independent Federal State."[232] Churchill told Weizmann how closely the UNSCOP Report was to Lord Moyne's Committee report before Moyne was assassinated in 1944.[233]

Martial Law and the *Exodus* Incident

Throughout 1947, the Colonial Office and the High Commissioner communicated daily about the problems of governing Palestine.[234] Cunningham wrote of frustrating meetings with both Arab and Jewish leaders.[235] On March 2 1947, he declared Martial Law in Palestine. The next day the *Palestine Post* carried the headline, "Tel Aviv Outlawed, Martial Law over Half Yishuv." The *Post* article explained how most of Jerusalem and Tel Aviv are under curfew.[236] Martial Law lasted until March 16. Through all this, as much he was able, Cunningham attempted to maintain order in Palestine.[237]

In the summer of 1947, the Jews of Palestine were encouraged by the *Exodus* ship incident. More than 4,500 European Jewish survivors of the Holocaust arrived in Palestine on board an old ship hastily renamed *Exodus*. It was a moral triumph to bring the ship to port in Palestine. However, Bevin ordered the ship back to Europe, not Cyprus. The *Exodus* sailed to France, and then to Hamburg where the refugees were detained. The international press condemned Britain, while the plight of the refugees received world attention. Christopher Sykes wrote, "When these things happened, the incident gave rise to a general and uncritical sympathy with Zionism and an extravagant notion of English cruelty. Bevin has fallen into an enormous trap indeed."[238] Nearly 60 years later, Yossi Harel, commander of the Exodus recalled, "It is a dark, dark stain on the British authorities. Even the Arabs would not go mad if a few ships would arrive at night and unload people."[239]

At least three Christian Zionists attempted to influence events when the *Exodus* was denied entry into Haifa. Rev. John Grauel, volunteered to be a crew member on the *Exodus*. After witnessing the British assault on the ship off Haifa, he travelled to Jerusalem to testify before UNSCOP. He told the Committee how British soldiers boarded the ship and clubbed and shot those who resisted. Grauel testified, "The *Exodus* had no arms. All they fought with were potatoes, canned goods and their bare fists."[240] The other source of assistance came from Rev. William Hull, an Evangelical Alliance Minister who had worked in Palestine since 1935. He appealed directly to Justice Ivan Rand, one of the 11 members of UNSCOP to support the Jews. Hull later followed up the meeting with a letter to the entire Committee, setting out the case for biblical Zionism.[241]

Cunningham Summarizes the Problem in Palestine

In July 1947, High Commissioner Cunningham sent to the United Nations an 18-page report on Palestine. The Report outlined the history of the Mandate and explained the present situation. Part of the report read,

> The British were the planners of the National Home and the prime movers in its establishment. Between 1918 and 1939 the Jews increased from a few thousands to 600,000 and this in the face of the most intense and bitter opposition of the Arabs…Had the British cracked in the year 1940/41 when

they stood alone there would not have been a single Jew left in Palestine…Few of whom could in fact have got to Palestine at that time even if entry had been open."[242]

In summation, Cunningham reported on the present realities of Palestine: the problems, the brutality and the security issues. In the past two and half years, there were 316 British deaths, plus 960 wounded. So far, it had cost three million pounds to operate Cyprus Detention Camps. Property damage in Palestine exceeded one and a half million pounds for the previous year.[243] It seems Cunningham's report had an effect on the government. In the United Nations, Colonial Secretary Arthur Creech Jones informed the General Assembly of the termination of the British Mandate in Palestine. The British would withdrawal. Creech Jones said in part, "I have been instructed by His Majesty's government to announce…that in the absence of a settlement they must plan for an early withdrawal of British forces and of the British administration from Palestine."[244]

Certainly, the British felt that their international reputation was threatened. The idea of turning the problem of Palestine over to the United Nations was abhorrent to many British politicians. In his role as Colonial Secretary, Creech-Jones told the House of Commons, "We are not going to United Nations to surrender the Mandate."[245] However determined his words, this was exactly what the British were doing. The decision was a shock to many in Britain. It was hard to understand at first. The announcement went against 30 years of British foreign policy. Despite the fact that people at home had grown accustomed to the news of violence and trouble from the Holy Land, there was a sense of failure about the entire enterprise.

The Americans Consider their Commitment to Partition

For months, President Truman had been silent about Palestine. Now with the publication of the UNSCOP Report, he decided to increase his involvement. He still hoped for a solution other than partition, and was dedicated to helping the European Jewish immigration problem. At this time, Christian Zionists in the United States were increasing their commitment to assisting the Jews in Palestine. In 1947, American based "Christian Council on Palestine" declared its' support for Zionism, This Christian organization had a membership of almost 3000 Protestant clergy, and was a political force useful to the Jewish Zionists.[246] In addition, within the general population, support for a Jewish Homeland was solid. A poll taken in late 1947 indicated that 65% of Americans supported partition.[247]

As a leader, Truman preferred to arrive at his own decisions in his own way. He detested being pressured. He was especially irritated by the flood of support for a Jewish State from Jewish Zionists. On October 17 1947, Truman wrote to Senator Claude Pepper regarding mail he received during the deliberations of UNSCOP.

> I received about 35,000 pieces of mail and propaganda from the Jews in this country while this matter was pending. I put it all in a pile and struck a match to it — I never looked at a single one of the letters because I felt the United Nations Committee was acting in a judicial capacity and should not be interfered with.[248]

There was much debate in Washington about this issue, and it became clear the Republican Party would probably back partition. In September 1947, the leaders of the Democratic Party of New York also expressed to Truman their support for partition.[249] During these days, as the Cold War was beginning to intensify, it was apparent that the Communist Bloc countries might vote against partition. In September 1947, Truman was still undecided about his position toward the issue. Even in the beginning of October, he had not made up his mind. He had many foreign policy issues to consider. He was concerned about the implications of possibly sending American troops to the Middle East.

While considering the matter of partition, Truman's advisors included David Niles, the son of Jewish immigrants. Niles was a Zionist and had been kept out of the Roosevelt administration. Another Truman advisor was Max Lowenthal, a Jew who kept a low profile and was a friend of Judge Louis D. Brandeis. Michael Cohen believed these two men played a major part in influencing Truman to favour Zionism. Another Presidential advisor, Oscar Ewing, recalled that Truman told him,

I was in a tough spot. The Jews are bringing all kinds of pressure on me to support the partition of Palestine and the establishment of a Jewish state. On the other hand, the State Department is adamantly opposed to this. I have two Jewish assistants on my staff, David Niles and Max Lowenthal. Whenever I try to talk to them about Palestine, they soon burst into tears because they are so emotionally involved in the subject. So far, I have not known what to do.[250]

In early October, Truman's old Jewish friend and former business partner, Eddie Jacobson, traveled to Washington to appeal personally to Truman. Michael Cohen noted that Jacobson requested of the President, "If it were possible for you, as leader and spokesman for our country, to express your support of this action, I think we can accomplish our aims before the United Nations Assembly...Harry, my people need help and I am appealing to you to help them."[251]

On September 17 1947, Secretary of State George Marshall, addressing the United Nations, indicated that the United States was reluctant to endorse the partition of Palestine. However, as the Soviet Union had now come out in favor of partition, Truman, having previously supported it, could certainly do no less. On October 11, Herschel Johnson, United States deputy representative to the United Nations Security Council, announced United States support for the partition plan. However, Truman's support for a potential Jewish State remained cautious and conditional. He was especially irritated by the torrent of support for a Jewish State from Jews, and became more so as time went on.

On September 22 1947, Loy Henderson strongly warned Secretary of State George Marshall that partition of Palestine into Arab and Jewish states was not workable and would lead to untold troubles in the future. [252] He also warned Marshall that partition would eventually drive the Arabs over to the Soviets.[253] Henderson's advice was politically sound and provided a perceptive insight into the future problems that partition would bring. Despite this advice, Marshall and the State Department, seemed to want partition, mostly because it might outmaneuver the Soviets.[254] Ambassador Warren Austin, a Congregationalist Christian, was pessimistic about partition, primarily because he did not see how an autonomous country could be carved out of such a small piece of land.[255]

On October 5 1947, Truman made his final decision and instructed Secretary of State Marshall to publicize American support for partition. The American announcement was made at the United Nations on October 11. Two days later, on October 13, the Soviet Union announced their official approval of partition. Why did both the Soviet Union and the United States both agree on the issue of partitioning Palestine? Certainly, Cold War strategy played a role. According to Friesel, the Soviet Union's reason was to force the British out of Palestine as part of a general strategy of weakening the position of Britain and the western powers in the Middle East.[256] Another related factor could have been that the Soviets hoped that perhaps Israel might become a communist client State in the future.

Regarding the appeal of Jacobson, some historians have dismissed his role as a myth. However, Frank Alder of Kansas City discovered that White House records indicate Truman received Jacobson 24 times in the Oval Office. This is in addition to several visits in other cities and three days aboard the presidential train.[257] While it cannot be accepted that Truman would have decided for partition as a favour to Jacobson, the evidence suggests that Jacobson influenced his old friend to consider the cause of Zionism. The final decision belonged to Truman, however the American reasons were complex. Friesel pointed out that until 1947, Palestine did not represent a major American political interest. The State Department and the oil interests were contradictory pressures against helping the Zionists.[258] Friesel also suggested that American refusal to back partition could spark a Jewish-Arab war which would be detrimental to western interests in the region.[259] In his reasoning, Friesel failed to note the idealistic influence of Christian Zionism at work in the United States at the time.

At this time, Abba Eban recalled a remarkable incident which showed the secular mentality of the early leaders of Israel. Eban told how Weizmann and his colleagues were working in their New York hotel room on October 16 1947, writing a speech to deliver to the United Nations General Assembly. Weizmann suggested he end his speech with a biblical verse about Zionism, but no one had a Bible.

After looking for a while, they found a free Bible in their hotel room supplied by the *Gideons*, an Evangelical Christian organization that named itself after one of the Judges of ancient Israel.[260]

It took the men half an hour to find a suitable passage but they eventually chose Isaiah 11:12, which described how the Lord "... shall assemble the outcasts of Israel and gather the dispersed of Judah from the four corners of the earth."[261] Weizmann concluded his United Nations speech by reading the passage to the General Assembly. This incident revealed the fact that Jewish Zionists could have secular motivations for their Zionism. However, this was not true of Evangelical Christians, who relied on biblical reasons for their desire to the restoration of a Jewish National Home.

The British Plan to Withdraw as the UN Votes

On October 2 1947, the Foreign Office informed Cunningham that a date for British withdrawal would soon be announced. "Situation may well develop at General Assembly in which we shall obligate to state a definite date for completion of withdrawal of British Forces and Administration from Palestine."[262] Cunningham responded that the order of events for the withdrawal would be complex and dangerous.[263]

On November 29 1947, the United Nations General Assembly passed Resolution 181, approving the partition plan for Palestine. As was required, more than two thirds of the nations of UN voted for the Resolution, which called for a Jewish State and an Arab State to be created in Palestine. The vote count was 33 in favour, 13 against with 11 abstentions.[264] There are several possible explanations as to why the majority of the other countries of the world voted for partition. Worldwide, there was sympathy to the Jews because of the Holocaust. Some new nations may have had feelings against the legacy of British colonialism. The Soviet Union voted for partition, probably in the hope of obtaining the future loyalty of any Jewish State that might be declared. The eastern European Soviet satellite countries voted for partition out of obligation to the Soviet Union.

Some countries were influenced by the new international status of the United States. According to Forrest Pogue, enormous American political pressure was brought on Latin American delegates to vote for partition.[265] In a sense, this was an extension of American Christian Zionist influence, that the American government pressured other nations to vote alongside the United States. Most of the nations who voted against the Resolution were Arab countries. Iraq had become independent in 1932, Lebanon in 1943 and Syria in 1944. One of the reasons the Arab League was formed was to oppose the establishment of a Jewish State. After a presence of 31 years in Palestine, the British government abstained from voting. The Labour government declared they would not remain in Palestine to enforce the partition. Bevin was angry, telling the Cabinet that partition would be "manifestly unjust to the Arabs" and would "precipitate an Arab uprising."[266]

In Palestine, the result of the UN vote was received with joy by the Jews, but was rejected by the Arabs. The passing of the Resolution was a bittersweet victory for the Zionists even though the Jews were allocated only about 13 percent of the territory originally implied by the British in 1920. Besides Transjordan, which became an independent Arab State in 1946, a second Arab State was now possible on the west side of the Jordan River. Nevertheless, there was universal Arab rejection of the Resolution. About 500,000 Arabs would be within the Jewish section, while 10,000 Jews would be within the Arab section. The border would be nearly impossible to defend.

In London, Attlee was disappointed in how events had unfolded. Crossman offered him a report on Palestine which Attlee rejected, telling him, "I'm disappointed in you Dick. The report you have produced is grossly unfair." Crossman asked if unfair to Jews or Arabs. Attlee replied, "No, unfair to Britain, of course. You've let us down by giving way to the Jews and Americans."[267] Attlee's views on the Jews were as harsh as Bevin's, but he refrained from crudely proclaiming them to the public.

Truman's Motivation for Backing Partition

In the United States, President Truman supported the 1947 partition plan against the advice of part of his administration including the Defense Secretary and the Joint Chiefs of Staff. George Keenan, head of the State Department planning staff wrote, "U.S prestige in the Muslim world has suffered a severe blow, and U.S. strategic interests in the Mediterranean and the Near East have been seriously prejudiced."[268] In voting for partition, the United States risked a great deal. The Arabs of the Middle East controlled most of the world's oil supplies. It was conceivable that in the future the Soviet Union could align herself with these Arab countries. Although this did not happen in the 1940's, it did happen temporarily in the 1960's and early 1970's. Besides this, the new Jewish State with its predominant socialist politics might incline itself toward the Soviet sphere of influence.

Regarding partition, Truman found his sympathies to be with Zionism as he made an idealistic decision contrary to the wishes of most of his advisors. Truman was a leader who made decisions carefully. He took his conscience and beliefs into account when he wrestled with important issues. Two years earlier, Truman had made the difficult decision to use two atomic bombs against the Japanese. In the future Truman would make the lonely decision to dismiss the popular general, Douglas McArthur for overstepping his authority in Korea. Together with his decision to support Zionism, these were possibly the three most important decisions of Truman's presidency.

Michael Cohen believed Truman's motives for supporting partition were political. He wanted to be assured of Jewish votes in the next election, particularly Jewish votes in New York. Cohen claimed that ten days before the UN partition vote, Clark Clifford wrote a memorandum to Truman telling him that he must have the New York Jewish vote in order to be elected President in 1948. (In 1948, the Jews of New York did not vote for Truman in strong numbers, but he won the election anyway).[269]

Israeli historian Zeev Sharef believed Truman's decision was of great political significance. "By this act, President Harry S. Truman not only atoned for all the retreats and fluctuations in the policies of his government in the Palestine context, but he also took a step of the first political magnitude."[270] It could be argued, however, that Truman's decision also benefited his own country in the long term. American influence is strong in the Arab world today not despite but partly because of the American-Israeli alliance.

Stanley Taylor of Brigham Young University recognized a common misconception among Americans that Truman decided to support Zionism simply because he had more Jewish voters than Arab voters to think about.[271] Taylor explains that such a motivation was completely opposed to the nature of Harry Truman. "Truman's core character was not one prone to pander or cater to political expediency."[272]

A closer look at Truman's personal background explains why he chose to help the Jews in Palestine at this critical time. Truman was born in 1884 into a farming family in Lamar, Missouri. He had a rich Evangelical Christian upbringing. At the age of six, Truman began to attend a Presbyterian Church where he met his future wife Bess Wallace at Sunday School.[273] Truman developed an early love for the Scriptures. Michael Cohen noted, "He liked to boast that he had read the Bible through twice by the time he was twelve years old."[274] Truman made his faith a personal matter, choosing his own denomination as a young man. "By the age of 18 Harry joined the Baptist Church at Grandview, a membership he retained throughout his life."[275]

Cohen pointed out, "For Truman, the Bible was neither legend nor myth, but literally the story of everyday, God fearing people."[276] Truman told one biographer, "The stories in the Bible, though, were to me stories about real people, and I felt I knew some of them better than *actual* people I knew."[277] Rev. H. L. Hunt lived across the street from the Truman family in the town of Independence. Hunt remembered that Truman read and studied the Bible and often referred to its teachings when he became President.[278]

Besides his love for the Bible, Truman displayed a pattern of strong philosemitism all his life. In earlier days, Truman owned a clothing store he opened in 1919 with his Jewish partner, Eddie Jacobson. The store failed in 1922, but Truman and Jacobson remained close friends. Years later, Jacobson and another Jewish friend, Abraham Granoff, visited Truman in the White House to speak again to the President about supporting Israel. Jacobson had little connection to the Zionist cause throughout most of his life, but he later claimed, "The President always listened to me because he knew I would tell him the truth. But I want to make it clear that whatever President Truman did for Israel he did because he thought it was the best thing for this country."[279]

Jacobson's sudden interest in Zionism is somewhat curious. It could be asked why he was not active for the Zionist cause sooner, perhaps in 1939, or throughout the war. Perhaps he was prompted by other Zionists, or maybe he simply decided to seize the opportunity to appeal to his old friend who now held such high authority. Stanley Taylor explained that Truman was personally motivated at this time to assist the Jewish people regardless of the pressures against him. "Truman emerges out of the historical record as a man acting out of moral, ethical and sympathetic impulses on behalf of a persecuted Jewish minority despite both international and domestic strategy arguments made to the contrary."[280]

The Effects of the Partition Decision

Immediately following the partition announcement, fighting broke out between the Jews and Arabs of Palestine. In a few weeks, nearly 200 people were killed. Reports began to filter in of Arab resentment to the American backing of partition. In 1947, it was rumoured that Syria delayed ratification of the Tapline Agreement, an oil pipeline through Syria to the Mediterranean, because of the American backing of partition. Colonel William Eddie, a State Department official, gave a warning in late 1947,

> All Arabs resent the actions of the present United States Administration as unfriendly to them...The prestige of the United States government among the Arabs has practically vanished, while that of Great Britain has greatly increased... Popular Arab resentment against the United States is at present greater than fear or dislike of the U.S.S.R.[281]

From Jerusalem, Cunningham reported to the Secretary of State of the effect of the partition vote on the people of Palestine. He told the Colonial Office that the Jews were delighted and the Arabs were in shock. Cunningham wrote,

The U.N. decision was received with jubilation by the Yishuv generally, even those factions of the extreme Left and Right who are in principle opposed to partition joining in the general rejoicing...The Arabs almost to the last had expected that they could muster sufficient support to avert a two-thirds majority, and the vote of the Assembly, which showed the virtual isolation of the Moslem bloc, came as a shock.[282]

By the end of 1947, Britain still had 100,000 troops in Palestine. The annual security cost for Palestine was now 40 million pounds. Michael Cohen believed that there were three major factors responsible for the British leaving Palestine: American intervention, undermining of British rule in Palestine and the escalation of illegal immigration. Cohen noted, "These combined had by the summer of 1947 broken the British will to stay on in Palestine."[283] Zweig concluded that the new post war relationship with America contributed to the British exit of Palestine. "Britain's increased dependence on the United States as a result of the war greatly complicated her problems in Palestine."[284]

Conclusion

Dramatic political changes took place in the world during the post war years of mid-1945 to 1947. President Roosevelt was dead, but his passing would not harm the cause of Zionism. He had taken little interest in Zionism, less than any previous President. In Britain, Churchill's wartime coalition government was replaced with a new Labour government under Prime Minister Clement Attlee. At first, there seemed to be some hope for Zionists because the Labour Party had a tradition of supporting Zionism. However, the Labour Party had new priorities. Attlee and his new Foreign Minister Ernest Bevin displayed a new attitude of antagonism to Zionism.

In mid-1945, the new Labour government in Britain was faced with domestic problems at home and international challenges abroad. Palestine was only one of their responsibilities that needed to be addressed with diminished resources. Added to this was a fearful desire to appease the Arabs, who now had autonomous countries of their own and a growing influence in international affairs with their oil reserves. In Britain, the voice of Christian Zionism was muted as Churchill took his place on the sidelines of power and men like Creech Jones in the Colonial Office were cut out of political influence. As a Member of the House of Commons, Richard Crossman made speeches in favour of Zionism, but to little avail. The political influence of Evangelical Christian Zionism in Britain continued to diminish. Their position was so weak that Bevin was able to declare in the House of Commons, "Balfour is dead."

In contrast, the Evangelical Christians in the United States continued to grow in numbers and influence during these years. Contrary to Roosevelt's indifference to Zionism, Truman's evolving interest in the cause would come to represent America new foreign policy. The British decision to involve the Americans in deciding the future of Palestine resulted in the formation of the Anglo-American Committee and the Morrison Grady Plan. Still, Truman was taking his time to make his decisions. He resisted political lobbies and self interest groups, including Zionists who often requested private meetings. He invited opinions but valued the time and space he needed to make up his mind.

In Palestine, Lord Gort's departure and Cunningham's arrival as High Commissioners were little more than formalities. Both were competent, fair-minded men who somewhat favoured Zionism, but were attempting to hold control over a lost enterprise. In Palestine, during these last years of the Mandate, there was growing anti-Zionism and anti-Semitism among the officers and bureaucrats of the Mandate.

After months of intense debate and diplomacy, the work of the Anglo-American Committee eventually led to the United Nations Resolution for the partition of Palestine in November 1947. Truman risked a great deal supporting partition as he acted to a large degree on his religious faith. The Arab nations were opposed to partition, but fortunately for the cause of Zionism, the Soviet Union and the nations under her influence backed the motion. When the United Nations partition vote passed, the way was open for both the Jews and the Arabs of Palestine to each have political autonomy. Within six months, the British would be gone.

Partners Together in this Great Enterprise

Arthur Balfour, Foreign Minister of Great Britain who signed the Balfour Declaration

David Lloyd George, Prime Minister of Great Britain at the time of the Balfour Declaration and Christian Zionist

Partners Together in this Great Enterprise

Andrew Bonar Law, A Canadian who became the Prime Minister of Great Britain and co-writer of the Balfour Declaration

General Allenby entering Jerusalem, December 1917

Partners Together in this Great Enterprise

Herbert Samuel, First High
Commissioner of Palestine

Winston Churchill was a
lifetime Zionist

Partners Together in this Great Enterprise

Harry Truman, President of the
United States 1945-1952,
was the first World Leader to
recognize the State of
Israel in 1948

Israel Independence proclaimed
by David Ben Gurion in Tel Aviv,
May 14, 1948

Partners Together in this Great Enterprise

A Street in Jerusalem named for Arthur Balfour

A Street in Jerusalem named for David Lloyd George

A Street in Jerusalem named for Jan Smuts, Christian Zionist and co-writer of the Balfour Declaration

A Street in Jerusalem named for Josiah Wedgwood, British Politician and Christian Zionist

Partners Together in this Great Enterprise

A Square in Jerusalem named for Orde Wingate,
British Officer and Christian Zionist

British Mandate Inscription, King George Street and
Jaffa Road, Jerusalem

Partners Together in this Great Enterprise

The Augusta Victoria Hospital in Jerusalem.
Built by the Kaiser, but home of the first British
High Commissioner of Palestine

British Government House Front Gate, Jerusalem

Partners Together in this Great Enterprise

British Mandate Mint on Hebron Rd, Jerusalem

The American Colony Hotel in Jerusalem, home of the Spafford family

Partners Together in this Great Enterprise

West Jerusalem YMCA, a meeting place for the British during the Mandate

The British Mandate Central Post Office in Jerusalem, now used by the State of Israel

Partners Together in this Great Enterprise

British Mandate Pillbox on Hebron Rd., Jerusalem

British Mandate Prison Entrance, Jerusalem

Partners Together in this Great Enterprise

British Mandate Prison Interior, Jerusalem

British Military Cemetary, Mount Scopus, Jerusalem

Partners Together in this Great Enterprise

British War Cemetary, Beer Sheva

Home of Chaim Weizmann, First President of Israel, Rehovot, Israel

Israeli War Museum at Latrun, Israel

Monument to the British Capture of Jerusalem in 1917, adorned with Crusaders

Partners Together in this Great Enterprise

British Mandate Mail Boxes, still used in Jerusalem
in the 21st Century

House on Disraeli Street, Jerusalem, where some
Peel Commission interviews were conducted in 1937

Partners Together in this Great Enterprise

The Palace Hotel in Jerusalem, built by the Mufti and home of the 1937 Peel Commission

King David Hotel South Wing, Jerusalem

Chapter Six

The End of the Mandate and the Significance of Christian Zionism in the American Recognition of Israel 1948

❖ ❖ ❖

Introduction

This chapter will demonstrate that Christian Zionism was a significant factor behind the American recognition of the new State of Israel in May 1948. The growing Zionism within American Evangelicalism influenced this political decision, while the personal faith of President Truman was a contributing reason why he decided the United States would recognize the new Jewish State. For many years, the significance of these factors remained largely unrecognized. Sixty years after the founding of the Jewish State, the prevalent thinking in Israel was still that American recognition in 1948 was exclusively a Jewish accomplishment. To illustrate this, an article in the 60th anniversary edition of the *Jerusalem Post* in 2008 called American recognition Israel's "first significant diplomatic achievement." The *Post* article cited four factors behind American recognition: humanitarianism, sympathy for Jewish DP's, Jewish votes, and Jewish pressure on President Truman. Noticeably absent was any reference to Christian Zionism in America.[1]

In 1948, despite many significant news events happening around the world, the creation of Israel was a major international news story in the United States.[2] This was consistent with the importance that millions of American Christians gave to the restoration of Israel. Zionism was a vital component in American Evangelical thinking, that the Jewish people would someday return to the Land of Israel and restore Jewish autonomy there. American Evangelicals believed that this restoration would fulfill the biblical promises of the Jewish prophets. Moreover, they were willing to help facilitate that restoration.

In the late 1940's, the British government were confirming their indifference to the cause of Zionism. In January 1948, Anthony Eden visited the Middle East as a prominent member of the opposition Conservatives. His extensive tour took him to most Arab countries, but not to Palestine. Eden carried with him a letter of reference from Prime Minister Attlee.[3] It was clear the attention of the Foreign Office was now focused on good relations with the Arab countries. In a speech in Egypt, Eden declared to King Farouk that the British "…wanted firm friendship with his Majesty and second that all Arabs should be friends one with another."[4] In his report to the Foreign Office, Eden claimed that of all the countries he visited, he was most encouraged by Iraq, which had "good prospects for development and cooperation."[5] The priorities of the trip represent a dramatic change from Balfour's visit to Palestine in 1925 when he lauded the achievements of Zionism and ignored the complaints of the Arabs.

The Continued Decline of Evangelical Influence in Britain

For decades, most of the Evangelical Churches in Britain taught Zionism as a biblical value. Through the first half of the 20th century, this brand of Christianity declined significantly, along with the political influence of Christian Zionism. Yaakov Ariel observed that in Britain, where Evangelicalism was in constant decline from the late 19th century onward, the teaching of biblical prophecy in the Churches had become increasingly peripheral.[6]

In 1948, four major Church denominations in Britain continued to experience a steady decline in attendance. Based on the Easter Sunday attendance records of 1911 and 1948, the Church of England recorded a 1948 attendance of approximately 2,046,000, or a decline of about 11% since 1911. The Baptists in England declined from 419,000 to approximately 319,000, a reduction of about 24%. With 314,000 in attendance in 1948, the Congregationalists measured a decline of approximately 36%, while the Presbyterians in Scotland had slightly over 2.2 million attendees in 1948, representing a decline of less than two percent since 1911.[7]

In 1955, on Easter Sunday, the Church of England counted about 2 million Church attendees. In addition, there were 300,000 Baptists, fewer than 300,000 Congregationalists and about 1.2 million Presbyterians in Scotland. These numbers represent a drop in attendance since 1911 of about 13 percent for the Church of England, 29 percent for the Baptists, 40 percent for the Congregationalists and 1.6 percent for the Presbyterians in Scotland. This represents an average reduction of Protestant Church attendance by about 21 percent over a 44-year period, during which time the population of Great Britain had risen moderately.[8]

The decline of Evangelical Christian culture in Britain continued into the late 20th century. In 1970, the Church of England counted only 1.75 million Church attendees. The Baptists now were 293,000 and the Congregationalists were 265,000. When measured against the Church attendance records of 1911, the Church of England attendance was 23 percent lower, the Baptists were 31 percent lower and the Congregationalists were 47 percent reduced.[9]

Over a longer time span, the number of Chapels in Wales declined from 1,755 in 1920 to 1,142 in 1990.[10] The Baptist Union in the British Isles declined from a membership of 419,000 in 1910 to 202,000 in 1998.[11] The Congregationalists in the United Kingdom declined from 494,000 in 1910 to 165,000 in 1971.[12] The Methodist Church of Britain declined from 868,000 members in 1910 to 394,000 members in 1995.[13] The Presbyterian Church of England reported 87,000 members in 1911, but had declined to only 70,000 members in 1965.[14] These statistics represent not only a large loss in real numbers, but also a somewhat greater loss in the proportion of the population. No longer were British Evangelicals sufficiently numerous to influence the politics of the nation.

According to Steven Koss, between 1910 and 1966, the Methodist population in Britain dropped from 1,168,415 to 700,000. During the same years, Baptists declined from 400,000 to 280,000, while Congregationalists lost even more members, declining from 456,613 to approximately 200,000. Smaller groups such as the Salvation Army and Quakers dropped similarly.[15] Koss observed that instead of precipitating political change, as they had intended, the Evangelicals were overtaken by it.[16]

On June 21 1972, the House of Commons paid tribute to the historic tradition of Evangelical influence in the House during a debate on the United Church Reform Bill. The Bill itself was not of high importance, but many Members of the House took the opportunity to acknowledge their indebtedness to a religious tradition that had played so prominent a part in the nation's political history.[17] Despite the warm tribute paid to the influence of Evangelicals in British politics, it was a sad recognition for those who still held to its values.

The Source of Christian Zionism in America

A look at the roots of Christian Evangelicalism and philosemitism in America sheds light on this matter. Soon after the Puritans arrived in America in 1620, they began to establish schools, education being one of their highest values. The Puritans established Harvard University in 1636 with the primary goal to prepare men for the Protestant Church ministry. Hebrew was one of the essential courses of the University. A love for the hope of the restoration of the Jews to Israel and a knowledge of the ancient Hebrew language were values of those early Americans.[18] Henry A. Atkinson, the founder of the Christian Council on Palestine, and a Congregationalist Minister, taught the importance of Zionism. He favoured the idea of establishing a Jewish Commonwealth in Palestine. Atkinson did not believe Zionism was primarily a Jewish issue. He declared in 1942, "It (Zionism) is something far greater. It is an attempt to answer what is basically not a Jewish problem, but rather a Christian problem."[19]

In the United States, an interest in biblical prophecy in the late 1880's accompanied the emergence of Christian Zionism as a dominant force in 20th century American Protestant culture.[20] Ariel observed, "An important segment of American Evangelical Protestantism favoured the idea of the restoration of Palestine to the Jews."[21] During the 31 years from the Balfour Declaration to the American recognition of Israel, Evangelicalism had grown in numbers and influence in the United States, and with it a support for Christian Zionism.

During these years, the combined Church membership of the three largest Evangelical denominations in the United States (Southern Baptist, Methodist and Presbyterian) grew from 10,461,000 to 17,406,000. This represented an increase of nearly seven million people, and a growth of approximately 40 percent.[22] The number of training institutions for the movement's leaders also increased. Besides the traditional Christian Seminaries and Bible Colleges, from 1930 to 1950, the number of independent Bible Institutes in the United States for training Ministers and Church workers increased from 49 to 144.[23]

The majority of these American Christians were advocates of Zionism, and were increasingly making their views known. Yet, their support of Zionism was often overlooked. David Arnow researched the various factors behind the establishment of the State of Israel and cited eight factors which led to the creation of the Jewish State. Except for his mention of the American Palestine Committee, a Christian Organization dedicated to Zionism, he noted nothing about the influence of Christian Zionism.[24] This oversight fails to give credit to the widespread support Evangelical Christians gave to Zionism and to religious motivation behind the actions of Harry Truman.

The strength of the Evangelical culture in America in the 1940's can be illustrated by the popularity of the Billy Graham evangelistic campaign in Los Angeles during the autumn of 1949. The meetings simply consisted of gospel music and Bible teaching. Graham, a Baptist evangelist, preached daily for eight weeks that summer. In total, 72 meetings were held, sometimes with 10,000 at a time attending. At the end of two months, about 350,000 people had attended at least one meeting, with several thousand becoming Christians.[25] Soon after, Graham and his team conducted similar meetings in New York City with over two million people attending the meetings over 16 weeks.[26]

After thoughtful consideration and research, the Graham organization decided to call their meetings "Crusades," a term that referred back to the medieval military conquest of the Holy Land.[27] Meanwhile, Graham became a friend and advisor to every American President from Truman to George W. Bush.[28] In 1950, Graham visited Harry Truman at the White House to pray with the President where they found they had much in common. Graham wrote, "Truman was a fellow Baptist and a fellow Democrat, which meant the same thing in the South."[29]

The United States Reconsiders Support for Partition

In February 1948, the American government seemed to doubt the ability of the United Nations to carry out the partition of Palestine. Warren Austin, the United States representative to the United Nations, announced the United States was "not prepared to impose partition by force."[30] The situation looked serious for the Jews of Palestine if the United States were to back out of her promise to support partition. It appeared impossible that the new Jewish State could survive without American backing.

At this time, the situation was made worse for the Zionists due to the intense behaviour of Rabbi Abba Hillel Silver.[31] As co-chairman of the American Zionist Emergency Council during World War II and chairman of the American section of the Jewish Agency for Palestine, he and his entourage were granted a meeting in the Oval Office. Silver outraged Truman when he pounded his fist on the President's desk. Truman told the Rabbi, "No one, but no one, comes into the office of the President of the United States and shouts at him, or pounds on his desk. If anyone is going to do any shouting or pounding in here, it will be me." Truman had them ushered out of the Oval Office, telling his staff, "I've had it with those hotheads. Don't ever admit them again, and what's more, I also never want to hear the word Palestine mentioned again." Truman later remarked that many of the problems of Palestine were due to terror and Silver.[32]

In early March, with American support for partition wavering, Weizmann sailed to America to see if he might present the Zionist case before the President, but Truman refused to see anyone related to the issue, including Weizmann. However, the president of B'nai B'rith, Frank Goldman, contacted Truman's old friend Eddie Jacobson, encouraging Jacobson to speak to the President again. A few days later, on March 13, Jacobson visited the White House and asked Truman to meet with Weizmann. Jacobson saw for himself how furious Truman was over the pressure tactics applied by Zionist leaders. Jacobson recalled later,

> I suddenly found myself thinking, that my dear friend, the President of the United States, was at that moment as close to being an anti-Semite as a man could possibly be, and I was shocked that some of our own Jewish leaders should be responsible for Mr. Truman's attitude... after all, he had been slandered and libeled by some of the leaders of my own people whom he had tried to help while he was in the Senate and from the moment he stepped into the White House.[33]

Nonetheless, after considerable persuasion, Truman said to Jacobson, "You win, you baldheaded son-of-a-bitch. I will see him."[34] So on March 18 1948, Truman met with Weizmann who explained to the President that partition was the best solution for the Jews. Truman accepted what Weizmann said and promised American backing of partition. He also reassured Weizmann of American support for a Jewish State, promising to recognize the State whether or not it was declared under UN auspices.[35]

All seemed well for the Zionists, but suddenly for a second time, it looked as if the United States government might withdraw her support for partition. On March 19 1948, in the United Nations Security Council, American Ambassador Austin called for an end to partition efforts. Further to this, he called for a special meeting of the General Assembly to approve UN trusteeship.[36] Austin's proposal caught Truman by surprise and outraged Jewish groups. Although he had given instructions for such an announcement, Truman did not know when it would be introduced.[37] This trusteeship idea was short-lived because no neutral power was willing to accept the task.[38] A Special Session of the UN General Assembly met to discuss

Palestine on April 1, and again on April 16 1948. The American proposal of trusteeship was not accepted. Partition remained the only plan for Palestine.

Background to American Recognition

Following his decision to support partition, the next major issue for President Truman to consider was official recognition of the new Jewish State. According to British withdrawal plans, the earliest possible day for recognition would be May 15. On May 11 1948, one of Truman's advisors, David Niles, showed the President polls that indicated popular American support for recognition of Israel.[39] Despite this, Truman was under political pressure not to recognize the new Jewish State. White House advisors Clark Clifford and David Niles supported recognition while Secretary of State George Marshall and his staff stood in opposition, advising against it.

According to Forrest Pogue, George Marshall's biographer, Marshal played a major role in the issue.[40] Marshall was an Episcopalian and indifferent to the ideal of Zionism. He believed the Arabs would defeat the Jews in Palestine and cut off oil supplies to America. In April, Marshall stated that if the Jews gambled to continue fighting and lost, they should not come to the United States for help.[41]

Truman called a meeting in the Oval Office on May 12 to discuss possible recognition of the new Jewish State. The State Department was represented by Marshall, Lovett, Robert McClintock and Fraser Wilkins. Clifford, Niles and Matt Connolly of the White House staff were present.[42] Marshall entered the room. He had been an Army General and the Chief of Staff during World War 2. He could be an intimidating man. He asked Truman, "What the hell is he (Clifford) doing here?" Truman replied, "I asked him to be here."[43]

When the meeting began, Lovett of the State Department cautioned the President that recognition would damage the American position in the United Nations. In addition, according to international politics, the United States had never before recognized a country lacking defined borders. [44] According to Marshall's biography, the President called on Clark Clifford, (General Council on Domestic Affairs to the President) who advocated recognition of the new

Jewish State as soon as independence was proclaimed. Clifford's arguments were that he believed recognition would bring Jewish votes, and the Americans needed to beat the Soviets to recognition for the sake of influence among Jews in Palestine and throughout the world.[45]

Marshall was not pleased, telling Clifford that "...if domestic politics were not involved, Clifford would not be at the conference."[46] Marshall then told Truman that if the President took Clifford's advice, then he would vote against Truman in the next election.[47] Despite this warning by his own respected Secretary of State, Truman decided to proceed with recognition.

In Tel Aviv, the Provisional Council waited through May 12, not knowing for certain what Truman would do. They were afraid that Marshall would have his way. As a profound military strategist, he knew the Arabs held the high ground in Palestine in greater numbers the Jews. For the next day, Truman kept his intentions secret. On May 13, at a Press Conference in Washington, when Truman was asked what he would do the next day, he replied, "I will cross that bridge when I come to it."[48]

On May 14, the Jewish National Council and the General Zionist Council met in the Tel Aviv Art Museum. There, Ben Gurion proclaimed the establishment of a Jewish State to be called "Israel." He read a 979 word Declaration of Independence to the small audience and announced, "The State of Israel is established! The meeting is ended."[49] Ben Gurion told those assembled that the new State of Israel would be a free and independent country among the nations of the world. It is noteworthy that the Israel Declaration of Independence did not contain any reference to God. This was because most Jewish Zionists were secular, some of them militantly so.[50] In contrast to this, Christian Zionism was a religiously based concept, dependant on the biblical beliefs of those who advocated it.

On the day of the announcement of independence, Ben Gurion was appointed Prime Minister, and Weizmann was elected President of the Provisional Council. Weizmann had hoped for more, but the reality was that although he was perfectly suited to events in 1917, and although his intervention with Truman in March 1948 was invaluable, his style was now inadequate for handling the deteriorating military situation in Palestine itself. Ben Gurion, on the other hand, had adapted to the times and was the clear choice to be Prime Minister.[51] In addition, Ben Gurion proved himself to be a practical man. Along with Golda Meir, he had planned for an inflow of arms as soon as the Jews were free from British control. The Arabs did not attempt to declare a State of their own on the land allocated to them.

Ben Gurion announced the independence of the Jewish State on the hour of the termination of the British Mandate, at midnight on May 14 (Tel Aviv time was six hours ahead of New York time). The United States then granted the new State of Israel *de facto* recognition in an announcement in the United Nations 11 minutes after Ben Gurion's declaration of independence, at 6:11 pm Eastern Standard Time. Professor Jessup rose in the United Nations to read the following statement issued from the White House, "The government has been informed that a Jewish State has been proclaimed in Palestine, and recognition has been requested by the Provisional government itself. The United States recognizes the Provisional government as the *de facto* authority of the new State of Israel."[52]

Following the election of a permanent government in 1949, the United States granted Israel *de jure* recognition on January 31 1949.[53]

Chaim Weizmann felt this recognition "set the seal on America's long and generous record of support of Zionist aspirations."[54] Weizmann wrote in his memoirs that his first official act as the President of Israel in 1948 was to accept an invitation from the President of the United States to be his guest. While visiting the White House, he presented Truman with a Torah scroll.[55] Michael Pragai, in his work, "Faith and Fulfillment," wrote,

> It was an historic moment indeed. The head of the largest Christian country in the world receiving the Holy Scriptures inscribed on the traditional hallowed parchment, from the first President of the modern State of Israel-a token of the strong spiritual and moral bond between these two nations, both so richly rooted in the biblical heritage.[56]

After visiting Truman, Weizmann wrote, "I expressed our gratitude to the President for the initiative he had taken in the immediate recognition of the new State."[57] Three days after the American recognition of Israel, Secretary of State Marshall was still furious with the President. He told Truman that the handling of the affair was "a hell of a mess." He warned the President that the reputation of the United States had hit an all-time low in the United Nations and "had better be careful what it did in the future..."[58] Marshall considered resigning, but his friends talked him out of it. He reluctantly conceded that the President "who, had a constitutional right to make a decision, had made one."[59] In June, both the Democrats and the Republicans pledged full recognition of the State of Israel.[60]

Truman's Reason's for Recognition

From the moment of American recognition of the State of Israel, it became clear what a crucial role Truman played in the process. Still, his personal motivations were at first hard to determine. Michael Cohen wrote, "From 1947 to 1948, President Harry Truman arguably played the decisive diplomatic role in the birth of the new State of Israel. On this most historians would agree; but they would disagree in their analysis of his motivation."[61]

One of the best pieces of evidence for Truman's religious motive came from a statement in 1953 when Truman and his old friend Eddie Jacobson were invited to visit the Jewish Theological Seminary in New York. While there, Jacobson told several professors, "This is the man who helped create the State of Israel." Truman replied, "What do you mean 'helped create?' I am Cyrus, I am Cyrus."[62] Truman was referring to King Cyrus of Persia, who in the Old Testament facilitated the return of the Jews from their Babylonian exile. In this lighthearted setting, Truman was eager to claim credit for his accomplishment in facilitating the restoration of Israel.[63]

Rather than seeing a religious motivation, Michael Cohen believed that Truman's reasons were instead a desire to gain electoral votes and campaign money for the 1948 presidential election.[64] Cohen did not see Truman as a spiritual man. "Truman was a product of his mid-century Missouri background: struggling, xenophobic and racist."[65] However, Cohen's views are not shared by all those who study the records. Richard Kirkendall of the University of Washington believed Truman was significantly motivated by his religious background to recognize Israel.[66] As to Cohen's claim that Truman was a racist, it should be noted that Truman was the President who ended segregation in the United States Armed Forces and the Civil Service.[67]

Similarly, Melvin Leffler of the University of Virginia observed, "Truman had a personal belief in the Bible. He believed that the land of Israel was the biblical home of the Jewish people."[68] Leffler concluded that Truman believed Israel had a right to exist. "He believed this was the land God promised to the Jews. His first reason was religious, based on his Evangelical beliefs. Secondly, he had significant Jewish friends and they were influential."[69] According to Lawrence Davidson, an independent Jewish State in the world made a lot of sense to the religious side of Truman. "In his mind Palestine was really an extension of the Judeo-Christian world and the proper home of the Jewish people…He had studied the Bible and read much of the available English language (Christian) literature on the subject."[70]

Since Truman was a Baptist by choice, and since Evangelical Christianity in America enjoyed great influence at all levels of society in the 1940's, perhaps Truman's support for Israel was not so difficult to understand. In the early 1950's, Ben Gurion told Truman that Truman was in "constant sympathy with our aims in Israel, your courageous decision to recognize our new State so quickly, and your steadfast support since then had given you an immortal place in Jewish history." Ben Gurion recalled that as he said these words, "…tears suddenly sprang to his eyes, and his eyes were still wet when he bade me good-bye. I have rarely seen anyone so moved."[71] In 1952 Truman wrote, "I had faith in Israel before it was established, I have faith in it now. I believe it has a glorious future not just as another nation, but as an embodiment of the great ideals of our civilization."[72]

Truman credited his knowledge of the Bible for inspiring him to assist the Jews. In 1959, he said in an interview, "As a student of the Bible I have been impressed by the remarkable achievements of the Jews in Palestine in making the land of the Holy Book blossom again."[73] In 1966, Israeli ambassador Yehuda Avner interviewed Truman about the 1948 American recognition of Israel. Truman explained to Avner his struggle with the State Department.

> Those State Department fellows were always trying to put it over on me about Palestine, telling me I really did not understand what was going on there, that I ought to leave it to the experts. Some were anti-Semitic I'm sorry to say. Dealing with them was as rough as a cob. They didn't want instant recognition of statehood.[74]

Truman made a difficult decision in 1947 to vote for partition. He made an even more difficult, lonely decision in 1948 when he decided that America would be the first nation to recognize the new State of Israel. In 1966, Prime Minister Levi Eshkol sent a letter to Truman thanking the President for what he had done. Truman responded, "Very kind of the Prime Minister to give me such credit for your nation's independence in '48. But the man to really thank is Eddie Jacobson."[75] Truman explained that Jacobson personally appealed to Truman to see Chaim Weizmann when Truman had been reluctant to give Weizmann an audience. Truman had hoped the United Nations could solve the Palestine problem on its own. Truman explained to Yehuda Avner,

> Let's cut the crap, I'll tell you exactly why I was upset with Eddie-because the Zionists were badgering me. Some were disrespectful and mean…They wanted me to stop Arab attacks, keep the British from supporting the Arabs, furnish American soldiers to do this, that, and the other…My patience was being drawn so tight I issued instructions that I didn't want to see any more spokesmen of the Zionist cause. I even put off seeing Dr. Chaim Weizmann. My attitude was that as long as I'm President I'll see to it that I made policy, not the second or third echelons at the State Department. So on the day the Jewish state was declared, I gave those officials about 30 minutes notice. And then, exactly 11 minutes after

the proclamation of independence, I had the press secretary, Charlie Ross, issue the announcement that the United States recognizes Israel.[76]

The role of Jacobson is so unique, it is worth looking into further. Jacobson was not a man who would normally have had access to the President. However, he did have access because he was the President's friend, and Truman placed a high value on old friends. It may even be that Jacobson was not a committed Zionist through the process. According to Ronald Radosh of City University of New York, Jacobson was not a Zionist at first. However, as soon as Truman became President, the Jewish Agency sought him out. At first he said no, but later agreed to help. He visited Truman 24 times at the White House, 13 times off the record.[77] Michael Cohen stated his opinion in a more direct manner. "Eddie Jacobson was not a Zionist. He was enlisted."[78] Whether or not he was enlisted, Jacobson's role in calming Truman was essential. The President was incensed at Rabbi Silver's direct manner. According to Ronald Radosh, "Silver nearly succeeded in turning Truman against Zionism."[79]

The question could be asked, "Why did Truman need to be persuaded to recognize Israel?" If he was predisposed to Zionism, then why did he not simply act on his own? According to Leffler, there are several reasons. He detested Rabbi Silver and hated to be pressured. More than this, he was receiving credible advice from the State Department and the British not to support a Jewish State. The Jews were not expected to successfully defend themselves and Arab oil could be lost. He was bothered by the issue of Jews and Palestine. He wished they would go away. He had more important things to do.[80]

Truman was an emotional man who expressed anger or sadness easily. He could be blunt. In his diary entry for July 21 1947, Truman wrote his thoughts after a conversation with Henry Morgenthau about Jewish ship in Palestine. His opinions could seem anti-Semitic if his character was not understood.

> The Jews have no sense of proportion nor do they have any judgment on world affairs...The Jews, I find are very, very

selfish. They care not how many Estonians, Latvians, Finns, Poles, Yugoslavs or Greeks get murdered or mistreated as D[isplaced] P[ersons] as long as the Jews get special treatment. Yet when they have power, physical, financial or political neither Hitler nor Stalin has anything on them for cruelty or mistreatment to the underdog. Put an underdog on top and it makes no difference whether his name is Russian, Jewish, Negro, Management, Labor, Mormon, Baptist he goes haywire. I've found very, very few who remember their past condition when prosperity comes...[81]

Besides the personal religious factor, there were other reasons to favour recognition. Truman would soon face an election against Dewey, his Republican opponent. The Republicans had criticized his administration for lack of support for Israel. Truman also wanted to relieve the suffering of the Jewish refugees left in Europe. Finally, there was no real alternative since the British were unwilling to continue the Mandate. No other country in the world was willing to send troops to enforce a Trusteeship. A binational State or a single State were untenable.

In light of all these reasons, and since it was apparent the Jews in Palestine were willing to attempt to defend themselves, Truman gave them the independence they were asking for. Melvin Leffler saw the complexities of the situation for Truman. "Truman was beleaguered by military, religious and geo-political factors. He appeared inconsistent, but he was practical and sensible."[82] Truman also believed that the promise of the Balfour Declaration needed to be kept. He wrote in his memoirs,

> The question of Palestine as a Jewish homeland goes back to the solemn promise that had been made to them [the Jews] by the British in the Balfour Declaration of 1917 - a promise which had stirred the hopes and the dreams of these oppressed people. This promise, I felt, should be kept, just as all promises made by responsible, civilized governments should be kept.[83]

When he became President, Truman had not had much experience in international affairs. Although he was magnanimous in recognizing the influence of Jacobson and Weizmann, he made it clear that, as President, the decision was his. With a multitude of factors before him, Truman had to find a political way to make a wise decision. One of the factors he chose to consider was the biblical faith within him.

The Significance of Truman's Decision

Truman knew he had the backing of a large segment of American society when he recognized Israel. Davidson believed American recognition of Israel made sense to the majority of Americans who were Protestant and biblically literate. "It is apparent that Americans, schooled in the Bible and in their own history, readily see the birth of modern Israel as a new Exodus and a return to the Promised Land."[84] Ronald Stockton, in his work "Christian Zionism: Prophecy and Public Opinion," observed that for American Evangelicals, "Christian Zionism centers on the belief that the emergence of a Jewish state in Palestine in 1948 was the fulfillment of biblical prophecy."[85]

In her memoirs, Golda Meir wrote of what American recognition meant to her. "I think what President Truman did that night may have meant more to me than most of my colleagues because I was the 'American' among us."[86] Ben Gurion regarded Truman highly and esteemed Truman's contribution to Zionism, writing, "For us Israelis of course, his most memorable act was in recognizing the State of Israel within minutes of my proclamation of independence."[87] After investigating many of Truman's private letters and diaries, Cohen concluded,

> This is primarily an American story, which tells of a unique conjunction of circumstances that, seemingly against all odds, persuaded the President of the United States, against the advice of all the official 'experts' to lend his diplomatic support to the Zionist cause when it was needed most.[88]

During the next few days, other nations recognized Israel, including the Soviet Union, Poland and several South America countries. Britain at first did not recognize Israel since Bevin was still trying to influence the Dominions and the countries of western Europe to withhold recognition.[89] On May 15, Weizmann sent a request for recognition to South Africa to the last surviving author of the Balfour Declaration, Prime Minister Jan Smuts. South African recognition followed soon after.[90]

In late May, Weizmann sailed from America to Israel. He wanted to stop in London, but did not feel he could. Britain was backing the Arab Legion of Transjordan, which was attacking Jerusalem. Weizmann wrote, "I had always believed that an anti-Zionist policy was utterly alien to British tradition, but now an atmosphere had been created in which the ideals of the state of Israel, and the policies of Great Britain, under Mr. Bevin's direction, were brought into bloody conflict."[91]

On May 14 1948, the day the Mandate was terminated, the Jews controlled Tiberius, Safed and Haifa. On that day, six Arab States attacked the new country of Israel: Transjordan, Syria, Iraq, Egypt, Saudi Arabia and Lebanon. King Abdullah of Transjordan wrote, "We for our part promise sincerely that our sword will flash side by side with your swords in defense of truth, justice, and the will of Allah."[92] Abdullah wrote to Cunningham telling the High Commissioner that the Arab League was building up their men and weapons for the opening stages of the operation.[93] Abdullah wrote, "I am fed up, my dear friend, of hearing even the name of Palestine... Abdullah."[94]

The Arabs did not fight well, lacking leadership and organization. Serving with the Arabs, General John Glubb wrote to D'Arcy, "If I were Emperor of all the Arabs-or better still Dictator-I could arrange their affairs very well! But when one tried to maneuver-not only Transjordan-but six other Arab governments, it is not so easy."[95]

The purpose of the Balfour Declaration and the Mandate had been to establish a National Home for the Jewish people in Palestine. Although this goal had been accomplished, discouragement and resignation were the chief emotions in political circles in London in the spring of 1948. Opposition leader Winston Churchill faced

Ernest Bevin in Parliament during these days. As one of the last of the Balfour era politicians, Churchill voiced his views with confidence. Ten years earlier Churchill had made his position clear. To the Jewish people he had written in the London *Times*, "You have prayed for Jerusalem for 2000 years, and you shall have it."[96]

At this time, Churchill was one of the few British politicians who still spoke openly of his support for the restoration of Israel. In the Commons, Churchill challenged Bevin to recognize Israel. Churchill asked, "I hope that the right Honourable Gentleman will bear in mind the great importance of our pursuing an even handed course of strict impartiality, at a time when we are resigning our responsibility in Palestine." Bevin responded, "I have done that. I have a clear conscience on that matter."[97] On June 10 1948, the House of Commons debated recognition of the State of Israel, but did not arrive at a decision.

Bevin felt personally insulted by events in Palestine. He blamed others. James McDonald wrote of Bevin, "His bitterness against Mr. Truman was almost pathological; it found its match only in his blazing hatred for his other scapegoats-the Jews, the Israelis, the Israeli government."[98] Tom Segev believed the British never really had a clear idea of what they wanted to accomplish in Palestine. In the final years, this lack of idealism made it impossible for them to remain. Segev wrote,

> Altogether, the British seemed to have lost their bearings in this adventure. They derived no economic benefit from their rule over Palestine. On the contrary, its financial cost led them from time to time to consider leaving the country. Occupying Palestine brought them no strategic benefit either, despite their assumptions that it did...There were early signs they were getting themselves into a political problem that had no solution.[99]

The British Exit Strategy

In the early months of 1948, High Commissioner Cunningham made his final withdrawal plans. He first planned to leave Gaza, then parts of Samaria, Jerusalem, Galilee and finally Haifa.[100] He reported a final annual government budget for Palestine of 24 million pounds, with eight million for security.[101] Clearly, there would be enormous financial benefits to leaving Palestine. In the end, much of the British equipment was abandoned, prisoners set free and documents destroyed. Some buildings and equipment were sold. Every weapon was to be accounted for, but this was not easy.

As the British prepared to quit Palestine, there was a feeling at home that the Balfour Declaration had been a mistake. It was difficult to feel anything else under the circumstances. By early 1948, the fighting had already begun between the Jews and the Arabs. Both sides claimed to be on the defensive as they maneuvered for the most advantageous positions. Cunningham received numerous reports of Syrian volunteers entering Palestine, as well as reports of Arabs from Palestine training in Syria.[102]

Even at this late date, some Jews in Palestine still violently resisted the British. Early in the new year, the Haganah detonated a bomb in the Semiranis Hotel in Jerusalem. Cunningham sent for Ben Gurion to discuss the incident. Cunningham wrote of the discussion, "I sent for Mr. Ben Gurion yesterday as a result of the blowing up of the Semiranis Hotel. I impressed on him the utter futility of such acts and told him if the Haganah continued this policy, they would find themselves increasingly engaged in action with British troops."[103] Ben Gurion responded to Cunningham, "I take the liberty to inform you privately that the Haganah officer responsible for 'Semiranis' was removed from his command."[104]

The Significance of the Ben Yehuda Street Bombing

With only months of the Mandate left, on February 22 1948, a massive explosion rocked Ben Yehuda Street in downtown Jerusalem. Most of the dead and wounded were Jews. The location and large size of the blast immediately marked the bombing as something extraordinary. This was not an Arab or British target. Eyewitnesses testified that British soldiers placed the bomb. The awful possibility that this might be true began to dawn. The next day, the *Palestine Post* ran the headline, "Street Bombed by Uniformed Men in Army Convoy; 44 Known Dead, More than 130 Hurt."[105]

The Ben Yehuda Street bombing was one of the largest terrorist attacks of the Mandate period, yet remained unsolved. With less than three months to go in the Mandate, there was no time for an investigation. Some Jews believed it was the work of departing British soldiers avenging their dead. Speaking 60 years later, Ben Zion Borohov of Jerusalem recalled hearing the blast and running to the scene to help the wounded. Borohov remembered survivors claiming to have seen British soldiers dropping off the bomb.[106]

R. M. Graves was the British Chairman of the Jerusalem Municipal Commission (Major) of Jerusalem from 1947 to the end of the Mandate in May 1948. Referring to the Ben Yehuda Street bombing, Graves believed the bombing was probably carried out by British soldiers, even though the British government issued a statement that it was unbelievable that such a crime had been committed by British servicemen. Graves believed, "Sympathisers with this policy might have lowered themselves to commit the Ben Yehuda Street outrage, but we may never know the truth."[107] Graves pondered, "I wonder if the authorities responsible for the government statement know what bitter feelings there are against the Jews among many British policemen and a few British soldiers... some members of the police force openly approve of the policy of Hitler."[108]

The bombing was a tragic commentary of how far British-Jewish relations had fallen in 30 years. The bombers knew that the British administration lacked the time and inclination to act. They also knew that the Jewish authorities had no means to properly investigate the incident.

In a Personal Way

As the British prepared to depart, many Jews turned against them in ways Arthur Balfour and David Lloyd George would have never imagined. Some of their personal stories illustrate the deterioration of British/Jewish relations. Shlomo Hillel was a member of the Irgun. He later went on to be an Israeli Cabinet Minister for the Labour Party, and a Knesset Speaker of the House. He recalled that after 1945, "The British attitude became more and more negative; this became clear in their behaviour to the immigrants."[109]

Dov Chaikin was a Jewish teenager who joined the British Army in 1942. He was one of about 30,000 Jews from Palestine who volunteered. During the war, he was proud to serve, but when he was discharged in 1947, he saw the British attitudes toward Jewish independence and decided to fight the British. Until the end of the Mandate, Chaikin served in the Jewish resistance against the British.[110]

Zvi Kalisher arrived in Palestine from a Displaced Persons Camp in Poland in 1948 after spending seven months in a British detention camp in Cyprus. Having lost all his family in Warsaw, the 19 year-old Holocaust survivor had little patience for British authority. He had difficulty seeing the difference between the British soldiers in Jerusalem and the German soldiers who patrolled the streets of Warsaw. Kalisher was typical of many eastern European Jews in that he knew little of the Balfour Declaration or Christian Zionism. He now had to live in Palestine according to what he could see for himself. According to Kalisher, High Commissioner Cunningham was considered a reasonable man, a professional soldier with a difficult assignment. Kalisher recalled standing alongside the road outside Jerusalem on May 14 watching the last British convoy leave the city. He remembered feeling pleased, that now the Jews will have independence. He felt the Jews were ready to defend their independence. Kalisher believed Ben Gurion was the right choice for Prime Minister, because he had stood up to the British. He thought that Chaim Weizmann was not qualified to be the President because he had been too friendly with the British and had lost his connection with the Jewish people.

In his 11 months living under British authority in Palestine, Kalisher knew British soldiers who favoured the Arabs, but he did not meet any who favoured the Jews. When he fought the Arab Legion at Latrun and the Egyptians at Ramat Rachael, he noted that both armies used British weapons and equipment. Kalisher told himself that the British treated the Jews no differently than the Germans did.[111] Sometimes personal testimonies illustrate how much government polities changed. It is difficult to believe Arthur Balfour would have expected such an impression when he signed the Balfour Declaration 31 years earlier.

The Last Days of the Mandate

As the British prepared to quit Palestine, debate raged in London as to what might happen immediately following their departure. Now a member of the House of Lords, Herbert Samuel wrote to his old friend Chaim Weizmann, predicting a civil war between the Jews and the Arabs that "...may last for months, possibly for years."[112] However, Samuel spoke of the advantage of having a Jewish-only State as opposed to Jews ruling over Arabs. "Zionism would be freed from the burden of governing, against their will, some hundreds of thousands of Arabs."[113] Samuel also wrote to Attlee, telling the Prime Minister of the probable open and unrestrained civil war about to break out across Palestine.[114]

In the final weeks of the Mandate, Cunningham received a variety of letters from Jews in Palestine. More than a few expressed thanks to the British for their efforts in Palestine. One letter is particularly positive for such difficult days. A Jewish woman in Jerusalem, Rachel Yanait, who had lived through the Mandate, sent a hand written letter of thanks to Cunningham, She wrote in part, "My grandfather had planned of coming to Palestine. My husband's family too, had for generations dreamt of the return to Zion. Since the days of our childhood, Great Britain was dear to our hearth. We looked up to Britain's great men, who were amongst the truest friends of Israel."[115]

On the other hand, Cunningham also received numerous negative and accusative Arab complaints. The Supreme Arab Committee sent a letter to Cunningham complaining about the Zionist policy of the British. Part of the letter read,

> Whilst the Arabs fought during the world war on the side of the Allies, expecting the fulfillment of their national aims of liberty and independence, the British government surprised them with the undesirable declaration known as the Balfour Declaration, which aims toward the establishment of a Jewish National Home in Palestine...The Arabs have done their best, since the publication of this declaration to convince the British government by various means of the unwisdom of the Zionist policy. They have sent many delegates to England

for this purpose, but the widespread Zionist propaganda has always prevented the just claims of the Arabs from reaching the proper authorities.[116]

The violence in Palestine was approaching war conditions. Susanna Emery was evacuated from Haifa on April 12 1948, having lived in Palestine throughout the Mandate. She wrote of shootings and bombings leading up to her departure.[117] Dorothy Norman wrote from Jerusalem that the Jews were firing mortars in the streets and the Arabs were shooting back.[118] She wrote of her friend being shot on King George's Street in Jerusalem,

> Suddenly there was a shot and Mildred fell down in the road. I knelt beside her and then as somebody kept on firing, I lay down beside her and kept my head as low as I could...after a long time a policeman came running up the road shouting in Arabic to the snipers that we were English and they should stop firing, and by and by they did. British soldiers later arrived and helped the women out.[119]

In the House of Commons, Bevin kept the House informed of the situation in Palestine. He was openly pro-Arab in his sentiments, declaring, "We must remember that the British sergeants were not hanged from the tree by Arabs."[120] On the same day, Bevin told the Commons, "I do not despair. Britain will be withdrawing on 15th May and when everyone has faced that fact, much may happen."[121] Christopher Mayhew, Bevin's Parliamentary Under Secretary, noted in his diary Bevin's low view of the Jews,

> There is no doubt in my mind that Ernest detests Jews. He makes the odd wisecrack about the 'Chosen People,' explains Shinwell away as a Jew; declares the Old Testament is the most immoral book ever written...He says they taught Hitler the technique of terror-and were even now paralleling the Nazis in Palestine. They were preachers of violence and war-'What could you expect when people are brought up from the cradle on the Old Testament?'[122]

According to Louis, "Bevin was not anti-Semitic, but his pro-Arab and anti-Zionist sentiments made him vulnerable to charges of pursuing an anti-Jewish course."[123] Due to his strongly held views, Bevin sometimes suffered from a lack of credibility. In 1948, Bernard Montgomery was Chief of the Imperial General Staff. According to Montgomery, at a meeting at 10 Downing Street, Bevin became, "...very worked up. He said 23,000 Arabs had been killed, and the situation was catastrophic. He demanded to know what I was going to do about it. I said that as the War Office had received no reports, it was clear to me that he must be greatly exaggerating the situation in Haifa."[124]

Finally, the British announced they would hand authority of Palestine to the United Nations by May 14. The British would try to preserve peace until midnight. Most government agencies would be given to the Jews.[125] On May 13, the Haganah hosted a farewell dinner for the last of the British officials in Jerusalem. Chief Secretary Gurney left the King David Hotel with his staff of 17. Their convoy drove out of Jerusalem, with some tanks along the road. A few people on the streets waved goodbye. As one of the last acts of the British administration, the British donated 14,500 Pounds to the Hebrew University.

On the morning of May 14 1948, the British flag was lowered from Government House in Jerusalem. Cunningham surveyed his last honour guard and raised the Red Cross flag over Jerusalem. Most of his staff flew out of the airport in Lod, but Cunningham traveled to Haifa by convoy to depart from there. The British held a small enclave around Haifa for several days as they loaded their ships for departure, but Cunningham sailed from Haifa at 11:30 that night. The British Mandate of Palestine was finished.

British Indifference to a Likely Outcome

Besides Arab numerical superiority in Palestine, and six Arab States surrounded the country, the Labour government took no action to arm the Jews for their own defense. Shlomo Hillel believed of Bevin, "The mere fact that he did not change his attitude, and knowing that we are going to be attacked by the Arab armies. And he knew exactly what the Arabs were telling their people, that they are not coming for a parade, but to exterminate the Jewish people in this part of the country."[126] The British General Sir John Glubb was the military commander in Transjordan. After the British departure from Palestine, Glubb's Arab Legion was the best-trained and equipped fighting force in the region. Besides this, the British had supplied Egypt with tanks and aircraft, while the Jews had none.[127]

Clement Attlee seemed to care little for Zionism. In his autobiography, published in 1954, Attlee made no mention of Zionism, Zionists, Arthur Balfour, Chaim Weizmann, Ben Gurion or Israel.[128] Cyril Clemens, in his biography of Attlee, referred to Palestine only three times. Clemens wrote that, "The Palestine problem continually impinged on the Egyptian aspect of the matter."[129] He also noted that Attlee referred to the "...romantic adventure of the Palestine experiment,"[130] complaining, "In dealing with the Palestine question we sought to hold a fair balance between the rival claimants to this little territory, and, as usual, got small thanks from either side."[131] Clemens only seemed to see Palestine as either a problem, an experiment or a question.

Richard Crossman noted that both Bevin and Attlee had years of experience with Jewish Trade Union groups in the East End of London. As a result, both men got it firmly into their heads that the Jews of Palestine should be treated as a religious group, on a par with the Christians and the Muslims. The Arabs, in their view, had a right to national self-determination, because they were a nation. However, the principle did not apply to the Jews, since they were only a religious community.[132]

Crossman recalled how he once told Bevin, "The Palestine Jews have grown into a nation and, if you refuse them partition, they will fight for their lives." Bevin responded to Crossman, "No, there's only a Jewish religion, not a Jewish nation. And if those Jews in Palestine aren't religious, they ought not to call themselves Jews."[133] It seems Bevin was unable to give credence to a theological system he abandoned as a young man. He was unwilling to return to a faith-based opinion he once held as a young Bible preacher in Bristol. As Secretary of State, he would not allow himself to believe that the Jewish people were a valid nationality deserving of a country of their own. Instead, Bevin challenged, "Are we in the United Nations as a religion or are we in the United Nations as a people geographically situated, or how are we in it?"[134]

Truman's Zionist Ambassador

In the spring of 1948, James McDonald did not realize he was being considered to be America's first ambassador to Israel. In early June, Truman phoned McDonald asking him to take the job. More than that, Truman asked McDonald to agree immediately.[135] MacDonald complied and became the first American ambassador to Israel. As Truman's personal choice, McDonald was an Evangelical Christian, and a committed Zionist. In circumventing the State Department, Truman was able to install a fellow Christian Zionist into this significant role.

James McDonald was a committed Evangelical who viewed his service in Israel as a divine appointment. On one of the days in which he was preparing to depart for Israel, he chose to read Isaiah chapter 12 for his morning devotion. "So, thou, son of man, I have set thee a watchman unto the house of Israel; therefore hear the word at my mouth, and give them warning from me."[136] During his years of public service, McDonald rarely spoke openly of his personal beliefs. However, in his memoirs, he tells of how he began every day, even as ambassador in Tel Aviv. He called it his "unbreakable rule." He read aloud one chapter from the Old Testament and another from the New Testament. McDonald thought personal Scripture reading necessary for his work. He wrote,

> In modern Israel, which perhaps sometimes placed too much stress on physical problems and too much confidence in their solution by strength of arm, it is good to be reminded of the lessons of another day, of the destruction of the golden calf, of the warnings of Jeremiah, of the submission and the crucifixion.[137]

In his role, McDonald reveled in the biblical significance of what had been accomplished, writing, "Weizmann remained in my mind the unique symbol-the restoration of Zion and the 'ingathering of the exiles,' of the fulfillment of the two-thousand-year Jewish dream."[138]

When Truman appointed James McDonald to be the first United States Ambassador to Israel, it was a unique appointment in that the entire process took only one telephone call. Truman believed McDonald uniquely qualified to take the job. He was a Christian Zionist and Truman's only choice. In his memoirs, McDonald saw the immigration of Jews to Israel as a fulfillment of the prophecies of Isaiah. McDonald called Isaiah chapter 23, "Isaiah fulfilled: the ingathering of the exiles."[139] He often quoted Isaiah chapter 27, "And ye shall be gathered one by one, O ye children of Israel…and they shall worship the Lord in the holy mountain at Jerusalem."[140]

The appointment of McDonald greatly pleased Ben Gurion. Menachem Begin also approved of the appointment of McDonald, writing,

> Before the Committee left for Switzerland Mr. McDonald sent me a message in which he expressed the belief that there was a 'good fighting chance' to secure a radical change in British policy toward Palestine and Zionism…Mr. McDonald is undoubtedly a friend of our people. I had heard this already from Vladimir Jabotinsky at the time McDonald was appointed Commissioner for the Refugees from Nazi Germany. However, he was mistaken in thinking that it was possible to secure a change in British policy in Eretz Israel.[141]

Old Zionists Congratulate Each Other

In the months following the founding of the State of Israel, Zionists recognized and congratulated one another. Israeli President Weizmann wrote to Churchill in August 1948.

> My mind goes back to the time when British Statesmen like Mr. Lloyd George, Mr. Balfour and yourself had laid the foundations of the Jewish National Home…It is a matter of deep distress to me, who laboured for a quarter of a century

for cooperation between the Jewish and British peoples, to see this work at any rate temporarily jeopardized.[142]

Churchill held to Zionist sympathies all his life. In an undated letter from Churchill to Josiah Wedgwood, Churchill revealed his agreement with the Zionist passion of Wedgwood, "There is nothing you could tell me about the Palestinian question that I do not probably know, and very little you would be likely to say with which I am not in general agreement."[143] Churchill's Zionism may have been encouraged through his friendship with Lloyd George, who had a significant influence on Churchill. When Lloyd George died in 1945, Churchill told the House of his old friend and the influence Lloyd George had on him. Churchill said of Lloyd George during the time of the Great War, "I was his lieutenant and disciple in those days."[144]

In Canada, Christian Zionists and Jews worked together to assist Israel. In the summer of 1948, Lorna Wingate, the widow of Orde Wingate, traveled to Toronto to see Benjamin Dunkelman. Wingate's purpose was to recruit Dunkelman to fight for Israel. Dunkelman was a Jewish Canadian and a retired Canadian Army officer who had once lived in Palestine. Dunkelman wrote,

> Her message was simple: she wanted me to leave the peace of Toronto and go back to Palestine as a soldier. She was very direct: "Were my husband alive, he would not take no for an answer. He would demand that you go to Palestine and volunteer your services"! But what caused me to make up my mind was a speech by an American clergyman-an Arab sympathizer-who described in lurid detail what the Arabs would do in the inevitable military showdown.[145]

Lorna Wingate succeeded, and Dunkelman agreed to travel to Israel to fight for the new Jewish State. He first set out to recruit other men in Canada to help the Zionist cause in Israel. More Gentile Christians than Jews volunteered to fight for Israel. Dunkelman wrote of the volunteers, "Most of them came with a clear sense of purpose, perhaps best expressed by the Canadian fighter ace George

'Buzz' Beurling, who said, 'I believe...that the Jews deserve a state of their own after wandering around homeless for thousands of years. I just want to offer my help.'"[146]

Canadian George Beurling was an accomplished fighter pilot with 32 enemy "kills" to his credit. Although he was raised Presbyterian, he joined an Evangelical Brethren Church as a young adult. With a strong faith, Beurling was committed to regular Bible studies and Church attendance. He always flew into combat with a Bible in the cockpit of his fighter. Although not Jewish, he was committed to helping the new Jewish State fight for independence. Besides committing to go himself, he recruited other Canadian fighter pilots to fight for Israel.[147] In a twist of fate, Beurling did not make it to Israel. He died on May 20 1948 when his plane crashed leaving Italy. Nevertheless, Beurling had made his mark with his recruiting of other pilots for Israel. About a thousand Canadians fought for Israel in 1948 and 1949, mostly Gentiles. Dunkelman was pleased to write, "There was a strong body of opinion in Canada that supported the Zionist cause."[148]

To illustrate the passion of some Christian Zionists, in the final days of the Mandate, Richard Meinertzhagen, Allenby's intelligence officer in 1917, returned to Palestine to fight alongside the Jews. On April 23 1948, Meinertzhagen came ashore in Haifa. It had been over 30 years since he had first entered Palestine and he never wavered in his passion for Zionism. Although he was 70 years old, he joined the Haganah in their fight against the Arabs around the Haifa Harbour. Wearing a borrowed uniform of the Coldstream Guards, Meinertzhagen took up a position at the front of the line. In the fighting, he shot seven Arabs and participated in the capture of another. After being ordered to return to the ship, he cleaned his kit, opened a bottle of champagne and toasted, "Altogether I had a glorious day. May Israel flourish!"[149]

During the rest of 1948 and most of 1949, the Arabs of Palestine fought the new State of Israel. Transjordan, along with five other regional countries assisted the Arab cause. By the spring of 1949, the fighting decreased in Israel, but there was not any real peace or surrender. After a failed cease-fire, the United Nations arranged a final cease-fire for July 20 1949. Besides the land allotted to Israel by the partition plan, she gained about 2,500 more square miles. However, Israel no longer occupied the Jewish Quarter of the Old City of Jerusalem. The Jewish State lost about one percent of her population in the fighting, about 6000 killed out of a population of 600,000. The year 1949 ended with the British out of Palestine and a new State of Israel occupying about half of the land. Transjordan had been somewhat militarily successful. She ended the war in occupation of Judea, Samaria and East Jerusalem, with Egypt in control of the Gaza strip.

The Difficult Relationship between Israel and Britain

For the next few years after the end of the Mandate, British relations with the State of Israel were strained. Bevin suffered from a sense of profound loss, telling the Commons he saw failure in what had occurred. The goal of the British had been to "persuade Jews and Arabs to live together in one State as the Mandate charged us to do. We failed in this. The State of Israel is now a fact."[150] Arthur Balfour, Lloyd George and other Christian Zionists did not live to see the creation of the State of Israel. However, had they been alive in 1948, it is doubtful they would have viewed the establishment of Israel as a "failure."

The British government continued to delay its recognition of Israel. An Israeli provisional government headed by Ben Gurion was functioning in Tel Aviv, occupied mostly with the War of Independence. The Israeli government sent Joseph Linton to London, but only as a representative of the Israeli government, not as an ambassador. The British government refused to grant Linton any official status. He confided his frustration to James McDonald, "I've almost reached the point where I can no longer continue to be merely tolerated here as an unrecognized 'agent.'"[151] A similar diplomatic problem occurred in Israel. In 1949, the British government appointed Cyril Marriot to be the British representative to Israel. He had an office in Haifa, but even the most basic communication was difficult. When attempting to write to the provisional Israeli government, Marriott addressed his letters to the "Jewish Authorities, Tel Aviv." The letters were returned unopened.[152]

In London, Bevin was frustrated that America was now so powerful in world politics, quietly forcing Britain to play a secondary role in world affairs. Bevin was particularly angry about American support for Israel. According to Bevin, the American attitude was "let there be an Israel and to hell with the consequences."[153] He even compared the new Israelis to the Nazis of Germany, telling the House, "I think that the driving of poor innocent people from their homes, whether it is in Germany by Hitler, or by anyone else, and making the ordinary working people of the place suffer, is a crime, and we really ought to join together to stop it if we can."[154] Despite Bevin's strong opinions, the United States and most of the other nations of the world desired to recognize the legitimacy of the State of Israel. The United Nations accepted Israel into membership on May 11 1949, with a vote of 37 to 12, making Israel the first new nation accepted into UN membership.

What was Churchill's response during these days about the breach between Britain and Israel? According to Weizmann, "He was as friendly as always but, because of limited energy, could not personally intervene in the Palestine issue." However, Churchill spoke of the "terrific mess" that Bevin and his colleagues had made.[155] After delaying for two years, Britain finally granted full diplomatic recognition to Israel in April 1950. In September 1951, Prime Minister Churchill received Israel's first ambassador to Britain, Eliahu Elath. On this occasion Churchill said the creation of Israel was "...a great event in the history of mankind." He told Elath he was "proud of his own contribution towards it, and he had been a Zionist all his life."[156] For the rest of his political life, Churchill was viewed well by the Israeli people.[157]

Conclusion

Nineteen forty eight was a pivotal year for Zionism. During the 31 years from the Balfour Declaration to the American recognition of Israel, Evangelicalism and Christian Zionism had grown in size and influence in the United States, while at the same time these beliefs had significantly declined in Britain. This is an important factor in understanding both the British abandonment of Palestine and the American recognition of Israel in 1948.

Following the 1947 United Nations vote for partition, High Commissioner Cunningham had a difficult time containing the growing violence between the Jews, the British and the Arabs in Palestine. Increasingly, British soldiers expressed their frustration with the Jews in violent acts of retaliation. Despite these challenges, Cunningham maintained enough control to plan a strategic British retreat.

The American government reconsidered its support for partition in March 1948, hoping that the United Nations might find a new country to assume a trusteeship for Palestine. None was found. Rabbi Silver's attempts at persuasion failed to move Truman. Instead, Eddie Jacobson was enlisted to convince the President that he should meet with Weizmann. The resulting meeting was crucial to Zionist aspirations.

As the British departed from Palestine on May 14, Ben Gurion proclaimed the establishment of a Jewish State to be called "Israel."[158] The Arabs did not attempt to declare a State of their own on the land allocated to them. From Washington, President Truman gave instructions to recognize the new State of Israel immediately. News of the American recognition reached the provisional government gathered in Tel Aviv Art within minutes. On that same day, Truman immediately invited Weizmann to visit him at the White House.

In contrast to the goodwill shown by the American leader, Weizmann refused to stop in Britain on his way home travelling from America to Israel. In the next few days, the Soviet Union and several other countries give official recognition to Israel. Jan Smuts, the last surviving writer of the Balfour Declaration, and the Prime Minister of South Africa, had South Africa recognize Israel soon afterwards. In London, the British government decided not to recognize Israel. Ernest Bevin was angry and felt personally insulted by events in Palestine. He blamed others. He compared the new Israelis to Nazis. In the House of Commons, Churchill expressed his delight at the new nation of Israel.

Part of Truman's motivation to recognize Israel was his commitment to biblical beliefs. Jewish lobbying on its own would not have persuaded him. He was a forthright man of high ethical standards thrust into a role of complex decision-making. Truman was given the responsibility of great power and he took his responsibilities seriously. Throughout his presidency, Truman had a sign on his desk which read, "The Buck Stops Here." He was a man who knew how to consider his options and make difficult decisions. Following recognition, Truman continued to act to help the new Jewish nation. He asked James McDonald to be the first American ambassador to Israel. As Truman's personal choice, McDonald was an Evangelical Christian, and a committed Zionist. In circumventing the State Department, Truman was able to install a fellow Christian Zionist into this significant role.

The form of Zionism Truman was raised with was long established in Evangelical American culture, and contributed to a mindset of philosemitism and support for the restoration of Israel. At this time in the United States, Zionism was a strong grass roots conviction of many of the people. Furthermore, it was not a belief merely based on historical memory, but rather it was a mindset that was alive and growing. Truman shared this religious conviction, and after long reflection, used this belief to make the decision to recognize Israel.

The new Israelis nation was indebted to the United States and to the personal intervention of Harry Truman. The American experience corresponded with the long decline of Evangelicals in Britain and the growing indifference the British nation felt toward Zionism.

Chapter Seven

Various Christian Denominations and their Views on Zionism

❖ ❖ ❖

Introduction

This chapter will examine how various Christian denominations view Zionism and some of the exceptions within their communities. Since the Evangelical movement has been identified as predominately Zionistic in other chapters, this chapter will deal with how the mainline liberal Protestant Churches, the Catholic Church and the Mormon Church view Zionism. It will be seen how the varied interpretations of eschatology and hermeneutics are key determining factors in how a Church denomination regards Zionism.[1] For the Catholic Church, it will be seen that Catechism is a primary vehicle for articulating denominational doctrine.

In addition, it will be seen that specific material exceptions exist as to why individuals are motivated to support Zionism, in spite of their denominational theology. On a personal level, these exceptions include humanitarianism, familial tradition and sympathy for the plight of post-Holocaust European Jewry. On a political level, Cold War posturing, foreign policy and American pressure also were sometimes motivations for governments and politicians.

Wide differences exist in the belief systems of the various Christian Church denominations in the United States regarding the Jews and the Restoration of Israel. Mainline liberal Protestant Churches such as Anglican/Episcopal, Lutheran, and some Presbyterian Churches tend to teach Replacement Theology, with the accompanying doctrinal position that opposes support for Zionism. By contrast, Evangelical American Churches such as most Baptist, Nazarene, Methodist, some Congregational and some Presbyterian Churches tend to hold to a more direct and non-allegorical hermeneutical interpretation of the Bible that encourages Zionism.

As was previously pointed out, the way a denomination interprets prophetic Scripture is a critical factor in determining its view of Israel. A more allegorical approach to eschatological hermeneutics will tend to result in a Replacement Theology position, in which the "Church" has replaced "Israel" in the divine plan of the end times. If however, a more direct historical and grammatical understanding of prophetic Scripture is taken, Israel and the Church are usually seen as separate entities. Israel will then be still viewed as a valid nation in God's future prophetic plans. However, even within denominations, there is room for local congregations and individuals to arrive at their own conclusions regarding Jews and the Restoration of Israel.

Some Exceptions in the Evangelical Denominations

While most Southern Baptists are Christian Zionists, a minority would not consider themselves to be so. This was because they were free to interpret the Bible more allegorically and arrive at a Replacement view. The Southern Baptist denomination is not only the largest Protestant denomination in the United States, it is also one of the most evangelical denominations. Their influence is still noteworthy in that the Southern Baptist Convention experienced consistent growth during the post-War period. According to the research of Roger Finke and Rodney Stark in their report, *The Churching of America, 1776-1990*, the Southern Baptist Convention grew 32% between 1940 and 1985.[2]

The Church of the Nazarene is another significant American Evangelical denomination. Rev. Lindell Browning, Representative of the Church of the Nazarene in the Middle East, explained that although his denomination was primarily supportive of Zionism, they believed it was necessary to be sensitive to the spiritual needs of the Arab Christians in the region. This was due largely to the fact that the majority of Middle East converts to the Nazarene Church originated from the Arab population.[3] According to Finke and Stark, the Church of the Nazarene grew 42% between 1940 and 1985.[4]

The American Congregational Church emerged out of the Puritan movement in England, and as such was both philosemitic and Zionistic. As a Church denomination, they held to the principle that the Jewish people were still God's Chosen people, not replaced by the Church. Although the Congregational Church supported Christian Zionism, it would not necessarily have the same commitment to supporting the policies of the government of Israel. The Congregational denomination allowed individual members to have freedom of opinion, so it was possible that some might hold to differing views on this subject. Once the largest denomination in the United States, the Congregational movement is now divided into a number of smaller denominations. According to Finke and Stark, Congregationalists declined 56% from 1940 to 1985, losing approximately 12% of their members in the 1960's alone.[5]

Non-Zionistic Motives behind Support for Zionism

The question is sometimes raised why some non-Evangelical Churches and individuals might be inclined to display support for the cause of Zionism. The material motivations for Christian Zionism in Britain and the United States during the time period outlined earlier in this book can be summarized as follows: imperial expansion of the British Empire, desire for expanded economic trade, the winning of worldwide Jewish favour and securing Jewish votes at home. Later, following Israeli independence, some wanted to support Israel as the weaker party in what was seen as a "David and Goliath" struggle with the Arabs. For others, there was a desire to support what was often promoted as the only democracy in the Middle East.

Furthermore, the devastation of the Jewish communities of Europe during the Holocaust prompted many people in the west to call out for justice for the Jewish remnant of Europe. According to Paul Charles Merkley, in his work, "Christian Attitudes toward the State of Israel," Merkley believed that this concept of "justice" was a primary rationale for the United Nations partition vote in November 1947. "As the United Nations was approaching its decision in 1947, most of the speechmaking of politicians and diplomats, and most of the arguing of editorialists, was couched in the rhetoric of 'justice.'"[6]

The desire for justice may have been prompted by admiration or sympathy for the Jewish people or a sentimental belief that they deserved a home of their own. This felt need for justice was based both on the 2000-year Diaspora and the recent Holocaust. The physical requirements of hundreds of thousands of Holocaust survivors added to the urgency of the cause.[7] Merkley believed also, that in part, loyalty to the converts of their denomination influenced some to side with the Arab viewpoint against Israel. "The fundamental theological bias in American Protestantism against Jewish Restoration and against Zionism is the fact that Protestant missionary efforts in this part of the world have been successful only among the Arab population."[8] Merkley explained that the result was that the sponsoring Churches became accustomed to seeing the local situation from the perspective of their Arab clients.[9]

The beginning of the Cold War in 1945 provided a temporary setting for both the western nations and the communist bloc to vie for Israel's favour. Following the establishment of Israel in 1948, the tensions of the Cold War had tiny Israel playing the role of pawn in a new "Great Game" of world politics. In the immediate post-War period, Israel became a rare item of agreement for the two sides. "In 1947 and 1948, the creation of the State of Israel was the only issue that the superpower antagonists agreed."[10]

When political leaders were prompted to support Zionism for material reasons, their motives were not according to the religious, idealistic motive of Christian Zionism. Christian Zionism was more than merely Christians possessing a positive attitude Jews and Israel. It was not simply a support for Israel based on feelings of guilt for anti-Semitism, or sympathy because of the Diaspora and the Holocaust. Christian Zionism was not a political position based on Cold War posturing, or anti-Arab sentiments.

Despite the possibility that these motivations may have played a role in British and American policy decisions during the Mandate, these material motivations are not to be confused with the religiously inspired impulses of Christian Zionism. A commitment to Christian Zionism is based on an interpretation of Scripture that the Jews are forever God's Chosen People with the eternal right to possess the Land of Israel.[11]

The Diversity of Doctrines within the Anglican Church

The Anglican/Episcopal Church is unique in that it allows for wide differences of doctrinal positioning within its organizational structure. This holds true in its views regarding Zionism. Rev. William Broughton has served as a member of the Board of the Bishop's Committee of the Anglican Church in Israel at St. George's Cathedral in Jerusalem since the early 1960's.[12] Accordingly, Broughton has a rich understanding of the Christian theological spectrum in Israel and is eminently qualified to comment on this issue.

Broughton explained the difference between the two Anglican communities in Jerusalem during the time of the British Mandate. "St. George's Cathedral in East Jerusalem was part of the Anglican Church Mission Society. This meant they had a mission to bring the gospel to the whole world. Over the years, some of their clergy were somewhat Evangelical, but most were not."[13]

In contrast to St. George's Cathedral, Broughton pointed out that Christ Church at the Jaffa Gate in Jerusalem was under the authority of the Anglican "Christian Mission to the Jews." Not only were they Evangelicals, but they also had a unique mandate to bring the gospel message exclusively to the Jewish people. This exclusive mandate contributed to Christ Church being more supportive of Zionism than their Anglican counterparts in East Jerusalem.[14]

In response to the question why there is such diversity in theological opinions between different Anglicans, Broughton explained that within the Anglican Church, (Episcopalian in the United States), there are many Societies which serve as sub-sections with different mandates and doctrinal heritages. However, Broughton emphasized that all Anglican clergy are required to adhere to the 39 Core Articles of Faith and abide by the Scriptures as the last resort of appeal in settling matters of disagreement. Nevertheless, each individual has the freedom to hold to their own opinions and personal interpretations of Scripture. This applies to how they view Zionism.[15]

Broughton explained why the leadership of St. George's Cathedral appeared to be more positive toward Jews and Israel following the Six-Day War in 1967. By then, the leadership of the Cathedral had become nationalized. The resulting new Arab leadership did not want to appear anti-Semitic, even though they had become very political and anti-Israel. They were careful to guard their words, attempting to show honour by not revealing their anti-Zionist, anti-Israel agenda.[16]

Mainline Liberal Protestant Denominations and Zionism

Following the founding of Israel, some liberal Presbyterians in America tended to oppose Zionism. O. T. Ellis, Professor of Theology at Princeton Seminary (Presbyterian) wrote in 1956, "Does the Israeli cause deserve to succeed?... We believe the verdict of history will be, No!"[17] Rev. Clarence Musgrave, former Minister of St. Andrew's Presbyterian Church in Jerusalem explained that his denomination did not support the theology of the Restoration of Israel, but rather held to a Replacement Theology position.[18]

According to Rev. John Cubie, another former Minister of St. Andrews Presbyterian Church in Israel, "Arthur Balfour was a layman and not a typical Scottish Presbyterian in his beliefs."[19] Cubie believed that Balfour was influenced by his English education and studying the Bible for himself, thus arriving at his Zionist conclusion. Cubie supposed that Balfour's Zionist view would not be tolerated today in the Church of Scotland, emphasizing that "the Church of Scotland is pro-Palestinian and does not support Israel."[20]

The tension between Israel and her Arab neighbours in 1967 highlighted the differences of opinion that existed between various American denominations. In the spring of 1967, a number of Catholic and liberal Protestant clergy in the Boston area issued a statement against Israel entitled, "Declaration of Moral Principal." In the declaration, they asked Americans "to recognize that Israel might well be destroyed."[21] In response to this move, a group of American clergy, both Protestant and Catholic, including Martin Luther King Jr., J. C. Bennett, Robert McAfee Brown, Franklin Littell and Reinhold Niebuhr, published a counter statement that called upon "Our fellow Americans of all persuasions and groupings and on the Administration to support the independence, integrity and freedom of Israel."[22]

According to Merkley, beginning in June 1967, the anti-Israel posture of mainline liberal Protestantism became more overt with every passing month. In 1967, the *Christian Century*, one of the most popular liberal Protestant magazines in America, questioned whether Israel should have been granted statehood.[23] Over time, this trend continued. Merkley noted in 2001, "It has come to the point where many liberal Protestants feel free to openly question the wisdom of bringing Israel into existence in the first place."[24] When asked why the mainline Churches of America (Episcopal, Presbyterian, Lutheran, etc.) did not support Israel in the way the more Evangelical Churches did, (Baptist, Methodist, Pentecostal, etc.), Broughton responded that this was because "the Evangelical Churches had a 150 year old tradition of interpreting the Scriptures historically and literally."[25]

According to Broughton, the Evangelical Churches in America had a heritage of emphasizing prophecy and Paul's appeal in the Epistle to the Romans chapters 9-11, regarding the high place of the Jews in God's plan.[26] In contrast to this, Broughton explained that the liberal mainline Churches in America tended to interpret the Bible "in a theological manner, and not literally, resulting in the stronger possibility of Replacement Theology. This interpretation would invariably result in a negative view of Israel."[27]

Despite this, Broughton clarified that many Anglican Church leaders do not hold to a full commitment to Replacement Theology. Rather, they adhere to what they consider to be a modified version of this doctrine. They decline to make a full claim that the gentile Church has replaced Israel in the mind of God. These Anglican clergy still see Judaism as a legitimate, living faith. Furthermore, they would emphasize that it was not the Jews who killed Jesus, but rather all mankind who killed Jesus, thus averting accusations of anti-Semitism.[28]

The Lutheran Church and Zionism

Since the Lutheran Church derived her eschatology from the Catholic Church, Lutheranism, in general, did not look with favour upon Zionism. From Martin Luther himself, to the present day, Lutherans see the Church as having replaced the Jewish nation in the eyes of God.[29] An exception to this position was American Lutheran theologian, Reinhold Niebuhr, who supported Israel throughout his long life. According to Merkley, Niebuhr, "remained out of step with the Liberal company that he generally kept by displaying his firm pro-Israelism to the end of his life."[30] Commenting on American Lutheran teaching regarding Zionism, Halvor Ronen, raised a Lutheran and Director of the "Home for Bible Translators and Scholars," in Israel observed, "The Lutheran Church today in America is almost completely anti-Zionist and anti-Israel.[31]

In his article and lecture, "Toward a Lutheran Response to Christian Zionism," Lutheran theologian Rev. Robert O. Smith, Continental Desk Director for Europe and the Middle East, Evangelical Lutheran Church in America, stated, "Christian Zionism is a politically mobilized strand of Christian fundamentalism committed to preserving Jewish control over all of historic Palestine to ensure the realization of the movement's own end-times hope."[32]

Smith concluded in his summary of the Lutheran response to Christian Zionism, "It (Zionism) is not a vision of hope, but a vision of injustice; it is a threat I believe. I believe that we have something vital to say as Lutherans, both in response to the challenge of Christian Zionism, and also in the sphere of North American religiosity."[33] Further reading about the position of the Lutheran Church toward Zionism can be accessed at the following sources indicated in the footnote.[34]

The Uniqueness of Mormon Zionism

Although considered a cult by both liberal and evangelical Protestantism, American Mormon support for Israel stems from their unorthodox theology. Mormons consider themselves to be the descendants of the biblical Patriarchs Abraham, Isaac and Jacob. Accordingly, they see themselves as adoptees into the House of Israel. Mormons use the terms "House of Israel" and "House of Joseph" to refer to themselves.[35] As such, the Jewish people are foundational to the history of Mormonism, where Jews are looked upon as the Covenant People of God, held in high esteem, and are respected in the Mormon faith system. The Mormon Church is consequently strongly philosemitic in its position toward Jewish issues. Mormons believe they are members of one of the tribes of Israel, either by blood lineage or by adoption. Mormons and Mormon politicians can be counted on to support Israel.[36] In a sense, Mormon politicians voting in favour of Israel are voting for themselves.

One of the congressional supporters of the Bergson Group in the 1940's was a Mormon, Sen. Elbert Thomas (D-Utah). The Bergson Group challenged the Roosevelt administration's policies on the Jewish refugee issue during the Holocaust and later lobbied against British control of Palestine.[37]

Thomas, as a Mormon, believed his kinship with the Jewish people had been forged by both his community's experiences as a mistreated minority and his religious convictions about the Jews and the Holy Land.[38]

The World Council of Churches View of Israel

The World Council of Churches (WCC) was formed in 1948, within weeks of the independence of Israel. Since that time, many Evangelical denominations and the Catholic Church have remained outside the membership of the WCC.[39] Merkley noted that since the WCC has always been primarily a liberal Protestant organization, it has had great difficulty consolidating a collective view on Israel. "The one issue on which it has proved most difficult for the WCC to encourage unanimity among Christians has been the issue of Israel."[40] The exception to this occurred at their first gathering in August 1948, when the WCC recognized Jewish suffering during the Holocaust by declaring, "No people in this world has suffered more bitterly from the disorder of man than the Jewish people."[41] Despite this statement of sympathy for the plight of European Jews during the Holocaust, the WCC has never issued a statement of support for Zionism.

Protestant Liberals in the Roosevelt and Truman Administrations

During the 1930's and 1940's, President Franklin Roosevelt had a variety of Cabinet members, secretaries and advisors. Some were Christians and some were Jews. In his work "Hitler, the Allies and the Jews," Shlomo Aronson summarized that among Roosevelt's Jewish advisors, "Felix Frankfurter was declared 'Zionist,' Herbert Lehman was more sympathetic toward the Zionist idea, Bernard Baruch much less so, and Henry Morgenthau had been sympathetic."[42] Felix Frankfurter was a lawyer and was active in Zionist causes. He and Benjamin Cohen were members of the American Zionist delegation to the Paris Peace Conference in 1919. Roosevelt's personal secretary, Louis McHenry Howe, was an Episcopalian who apparently had little interest in assisting the Jews in Europe. Thomas G. Corcoran was an Irish Catholic and a lawyer. He was a long time advisor to Roosevelt but indicated little interest in Jewish issues. Evangelicals seem to have been almost absent from the Roosevelt administrations.

President Truman inherited Roosevelt's close advisors in the spring of 1945, but made changes almost immediately. At the State Department, Truman replaced Secretary of State Edward Stettinius, an Episcopalian, with James F. Byrnes. Byrnes was a Catholic who consistently advised Truman to be sensitive to the Arab perspective.[43] Undersecretary Dean Acheson was an Episcopalian and was pro-Arab in his advice. Loy Henderson of the Office of Near Eastern Affairs, despite being a Methodist, was also pro-Arab in his views. It should be noted that these men did not necessarily articulate anti-Jewish or anti-Zionist sentiments. The overwhelming humanitarian crisis they dealt with immediately following the war would determine what American foreign policy would be regarding the displaced Jews of Europe and how the United States might assist the British in settling the question of Palestine.

Truman had a number of advisors who advocated support for the Jews. Earl Harrison, special emissary for Harry Truman, was a Methodist and an outspoken advocate of assisting the displaced Jewish people of Europe in finding a new home in Palestine. Special Counsel to the President, Clark Clifford, was an Episcopalian, but was sympathetic to Zionism. Truman's Administrative Assistant, David Niles, a Jew, was also strongly supportive of Zionist ideals.[44]

Truman began to make his presidential voice heard regarding Palestine after the Potsdam Conference of 1945. At that time, he addressed a press conference, telling the journalists that he, "...had asked the British to admit to Palestine as many Jews as possible."[45] Following this, Earl Harrison, a Methodist, said of the Jewish refugees in Europe, "Only in Palestine will they be welcome and find peace and quiet and be given an opportunity to live and work."[46]

James Byrnes handled the opening rounds of negotiations at the postwar conferences of allied foreign ministers, but he proved problematic for the President. Truman replaced him in 1947 with George Marshall, an Episcopalian who predicted the defeat of the new Jewish State and feared antagonizing the Arabs. In 1949, Marshall was succeeded by Dean G. Acheson, a former Undersecretary of State. Acheson was also an Episcopalian and was consistently pro-Arab in his advice to Truman.

The question Truman faced in the autumn of 1947 was whether to accept the U.N. partition plan and the possible creation of a Jewish state. While Truman personally sympathized with Jewish aspirations for a homeland in the Middle East, the issue involved both domestic and foreign concerns. The President and his political advisers were aware that American Jews, a major constituency in the Democratic Party, supported a Jewish State in the Middle East. In an election year, Democrats could ill afford to lose the Jewish vote to Republicans. On the other hand, Truman's foreign policy advisers, especially Secretary of State Marshall, counseled strongly against American support for a Jewish State. They worried that such a course was certain to anger the Arab states in the region and might require an American military commitment.

The Question of Catholic Motivation

Father Michael McGarry of Jerusalem is well qualified to speak about Catholic philosemitism and apparent Catholic support for Zionism.[47] McGarry is the Rector of Tantur Ecumenical Institute in Jerusalem, which is administered by the Vatican. He is a well known Catholic scholar on the question of Jewish-Christian dialogue and has written extensively on Jewish-Christian relations, including "Christology After Auschwitz."[48] He has served on the Advisory Board for Christian-Jewish Relations for the United States Catholic Conference of Bishops.

McGarry claimed that invariably, some American Catholic politicians would support Israel. He believed it was understandable that some American Catholic politicians like Thomas D'Alesandro and his daughter, Nancy Pelosi, would be pro-Israel. However, their reasons were not because of their religion. "They have their reasons, but their reasons will not be theological."[49] McGarry speculated that perhaps they believed the Israeli position was advantageous to American foreign policy, or perhaps they had sympathy for the Jews because of the Holocaust or a large Jewish constituency to consider. McGarry was certain their reasons were not biblical, in the way the reasons of an Evangelical politician might be. "In Catholicism, doctrinal issues are the concern of the priest, not the laypeople."[50] McGarry summarized his thinking by stating, "I doubt any American Catholic politician who votes favourably for Israel would ever have any more than a ten percent interest in religion in his consideration of the decision."[51]

Dr. Christophe Rico of the Dominican Ecole Biblique in Jerusalem is uniquely positioned to comment on the Catholic view of Israel. Although not a Priest himself, Rico is a linguistic scholar dedicated to the biblical text and Catholic doctrine. He holds a PhD in Philology and Linguistics from the Sorbonne in Paris, and is employed by the Ecole Biblique in Jerusalem, which is administered by the Dominican Order.[52] In answering the question why some American Catholic politicians vote in favour of Israel, Rico, like McGarry, also stated that he believed "their reasons would have to be either political or sympathetic. Their reasons would not be religious."[53]

Rico pointed out, that in 1947, most Latin American countries voted in favour of the partition of Palestine because of American pressure and because of sympathy for the Jews following the Holocaust. He was certain their reasons were not religious.[54] Rico emphasized his point by stating, "The Balfour Declaration could never originate from a Catholic country."[55]

Catholic Exceptions in the Support of Israel

The example of Senator Thomas D'Alesandro Jr. of Maryland, later Mayor of Baltimore, a Catholic supporter of Israel, and his daughter Nancy Pelosi, later Speaker of the House of Representatives, should be noted. Rafael Medoff, Director of the David S. Wyman Institute for Holocaust Studies, wrote in 2007 how D'Alesandro opposed President Roosevelt on the issue of assisting the Jews of Europe. D'Alesandro was known as a Roosevelt Democrat and a committed Catholic, but broke ranks with the President on the issue of rescuing Jews from Hitler.[56]

D'Alesandro was one of the congressional supporters of the Bergson Group, a maverick Jewish political action committee that challenged the Roosevelt administration's policies on the Jewish refugee issue during the Holocaust.[57] The Bergson activists used unconventional tactics to draw attention to the plight of Europe's Jews, including staging theatrical pageants, organizing a march by 400 Rabbis to the White House and placing more than 200 full-page advertisements in newspapers around the country.[58]

D'Alesandro's involvement with the Bergson Group was remarkable because he was a Democrat who chose to support a group that publicly challenged a President from his own Party. D'Alesandro was otherwise a staunch supporter of the President and the New Deal. He even named his first son Franklin Roosevelt D'Alesandro.[59]

Until late in the war, the stance of the Roosevelt administration was that nothing could be done to rescue Jews from the Nazis, except to win the war. However, the Bergson Group was convinced that there were steps the United States could take to rescue refugees without impeding the war effort.[60] Bergson's motivation for changing U.S. policy was anchored in the hope that humanitarian-minded Democrats like D'Alesandro would break ranks with the White House over the plight of the Jews.[61] Pressure from the Bergson Group influenced Roosevelt. In early 1944, the President established the War Refugee Board. Despite its small staff and meager funding, the Board played a key role in the rescue of more than 200,000 Jews from the Holocaust. Its many accomplishments included sponsoring the heroic life-saving activities of Swedish diplomat Raoul Wallenberg in Nazi-occupied Budapest.

After the war, D'Alesandro continued supporting the Bergson Group as it campaigned for the establishment of a Jewish State in Palestine. This sometimes meant clashing with the Truman administration, which initially wavered on the issue of Jewish statehood.[62] D'Alesandro did not clearly state what his motivation was for supporting the Jews and Israel. He did not claim to be a Zionist. He was a Catholic and the son of Italian immigrants. In the spirit of the Democratic Party, his sympathy for religious minorities and refugees likely fueled his humanitarian instinct. Hearing of innocents being persecuted and in need of help, demanded a response, regardless of political considerations.

D'Alesandro took a significant political risk. He knew that by defying Roosevelt and Truman, he might make enemies in the White House. In 1947, at the moment he was breaking ranks with Truman over Palestine, D'Alesandro decided to run for Mayor of Baltimore. If the White House had chosen to retaliate against him for his dissent on Palestine, he might never have been elected.[63]

Each member of Congress who was part of the Bergson Group had their own reasons for offering their support. Rep. Andrew Somers (D-N.Y.) was of Irish Catholic descent. His resentment of British rule in Ireland likely strengthened his support for the Bergson Group's campaigns against the British shutdown of Palestine to Jewish refugees.[64] Some reasons for political support for Israel could be quite personal. For example, another important Bergson supporter, Rep. Will Rogers Jr. (D-Calif.), was part Native American. He attributed his interest in the plight of the Jews to his general concern for minorities.[65]

Thomas D'Alesandro's daughter, Nancy Pelosi, later became Speaker of the United States House of Representatives. While in this role, she maintained her family tradition of supporting Israel. In 2007, she spoke at a Knesset dinner in Jerusalem during a visit to Israel. She was well received by her Israeli audience. Not only was Pelosi the first female Speaker of the House to address Israel's lawmakers, she also addressed the Parliament of a country whose creation her own father championed at the risk of his career.[66]

Throughout her life, Pelosi was at the center of her father's intense political world. As a result, she was a political veteran long before she even entered politics. She was fortunate to have as her role model a man who courageously put his humanitarian principles above his narrow political needs. She "learned her politics at the elbow of her father," a Washington Post profile of the House Speaker noted.[67] In the early 1960's, President John Kennedy seemed to be personally supportive of Israel even though he had little opportunity to act on any views he might have had. As the only Catholic President in American history, and being largely untaught in biblical prophecy, Kennedy neither embraced nor rejected Zionism. To a large degree, he dealt with Israel as he would any other country.

New York Mayor Rudy Giuliani is another example of a Catholic political supporter of Israel. Profoundly influenced by the September 11 2001 terror attacks against the World Trade Center, he opposed the goal of successive White House administrations who proposed the establishment of a Palestinian State. In 2007, he warned "against the push by President George Bush and Israeli Prime Minister Ehud Olmert to establish a State in Judea & Samaria ruled by Fatah."[68]

Giuliani stated, "It is not in the interest of the United States at a time when it is being threatened by Islamist terrorists, to assist in the creation of another state that will support terrorism." Giuliani said Palestinians must show "a clear commitment to fighting terrorism, and willingness to live in peace with Israel." He argued that the problem for Palestinians was not a "lack of statehood" but good governance and that too much emphasis had been placed on Israeli-Palestinian talks which just brought up the same issues "again and again."[69]

Considering the Possibility of Changing Catholic Doctrine toward Zionism

In recent years, there has been an increase in dialogue between the Catholic Church and Jewish religious leaders. The question should then be asked if the Catholic Church has recently changed her doctrine regarding the Jews and Israel. Catholic Catechism teaches the role that the Jewish people have had in the plan of God. Of particular interest is the doctrine of the "Mystery of the Jews," and the belief that "Israel is the Priestly People of God who are called by the name of the LORD."[70] In addition, the Jewish People are called, "The first to hear the word of God," and the people of "Elder Brethren" in the faith of Abraham."[71]

However, Catholic Catechism also reveals that the core doctrines regarding the Jews have not changed. Although the Catholic Church holds the spiritual heritage of the Jews in high regard, Catholic Catechism does not recognize that the Jews are God's Chosen People, and nowhere suggests that the Jews still have a divine right to the Land of Israel. Regarding the doctrine of soteriology, Catholic Catechism still states that Jews need to accept Jesus in order to receive spiritual salvation.[72]

The Brothers of Zion at the Ratisbonne Institute in Jerusalem are unique as a Catholic Order. Because of their Jewish origins, they claim a particular interest in the Jewish people.[73] Since the 19th century, the Ratisbonne Institute has been a prominent Catholic academic center for Jewish Studies in Jerusalem. One of the Order's stated purposes is, "To witness in the Church and in the world to Jesus Christ's particular love for his people Israel."[74] The Brothers of Zion even acknowledge that, "The existence of the State of Israel cannot be without spiritual and religious significance. It calls forth our understanding, our sympathy, as well as our fervent desire and prayer that there be peace between Israel and its Arab neighbors."[75] Yet, despite the apparent philosemitism of the Brothers of Zion, they did not go so far as to acknowledge the spiritual salvation of Jews within Judaism.[76]

Father Stephen Kuncherakatt of the Ratisbonne Institute in Jerusalem explained that the Order's interest in the Jews has been often misunderstood. When asked if the Order was Zionistic, he responded "This has been a fixation of some Jews for many years. No, we are not Zionists."[77] Kuncherakatt explained that the Brothers of Zion dialogue with Jewish theologians "in order to appreciate Judaism and go to the roots of Christianity." He went on to describe how the Order showed love for the Jews by housing Jewish Deported Persons from Europe in the late 1940's and 1950's. Kuncherakatt saw this as a Christian service to the Jews.[78] The Ratisbonne Institute was also the venue for negotiations between the government of Israel and the Vatican in 1994, which resulted in Vatican recognition of the State of Israel.[79]

The Dominicans are another Catholic Order that dialogues with Jewish theologians, particularly the Dominicans who serve at the Ecole Biblique in Jerusalem. Dr. Christophe Rico of the Ecole Biblique recognizes that both the Dominicans and the Brothers of Zion have a unique interest in the Jews because of the Catholic teachings of the "Mystery of the Jews," and the "Mystery of Israel." However, Rico cautioned,

> This is not Zionism. It is much broader. We are not Zionists. The Dominicans and the Brothers of Zion have a regard for Jews because as Catholics, we realize that most of the Bible came to us through the Jews. We are well aware that Jesus was a Jew, as were the disciples and most of the early Christians.[80]

Regarding the Dominicans and the Brothers of Zion, McGarry also confirmed that these Orders have a strong identity with the Jews because of what Catholic theologians call the "Mystery of the Jews," and the "Mystery of Israel."[81] McGarry explained that these "mysteries" are related to the Catholic interpretation of Genesis chapter 12, that God blessed the world through the descendants of Abraham. According to McGarry, the Catholic view is that this blessing is now fulfilled and transferred through the Catholic Church, through faith in Jesus, Catholic baptism and Catholic Church membership. This theology negates not only Jews, but also Evangelicals and liberal Protestants.

McGarry conceded that the Catholic Church still teaches, and will always teach, exclusivism, meaning that for the Jews, there is only salvation in Jesus Christ through the Catholic Church. "The Jewish people have turned their back on Jesus. Without Jesus, Jews are incomplete." McGarry did not see this as anti-Semitic, but a clarification of the New Testament teaching of spiritual salvation.[82] According to McGarry, "There is no such thing as a Roman Catholic Christian Zionism. Christian Zionism is in the domain of the Protestants."[83]

When asked if he believed an individual Catholic could be a Zionist, Rico responded, "To recognize the State of Israel, yes. To support the State of Israel, yes. But, to be a Zionist in that they believe the Bible teaches that God gave this land to the Jewish people forever? no. This is not Catholic. Not even all Israelis believe this."[84] Rico considered other reasons for Catholic philosemitism, "Catholics may have sympathy for the Jews because of the Holocaust, and a respect for the theological "Mystery of the Jews," but they are not Zionists."[85]

It seems clear that despite an increase in rapprochement between Catholics and Jews in recent years, Catholics are still necessarily bound by anti-Zionist theological doctrines. However, McGarry named three Catholic theologians who have been well known supporters of Israel: Marcel Dubois, Bruno Hussan and Isaac Jacobs. However, in all three cases, McGarry identified the motivation for their views as sympathy for the Jews because of the Holocaust.[86] As a Catholic theologian involved in dialogue with Jewish leaders, McGarry explained three Catholic reasons for recent increases in rapprochement between Catholic and Jewish theologians: to break down stereotypes, to ask questions, because "we have some of the same questions" and to possibly understand the Old Testament better.[87]

When asked if the Catholic view toward Israel was Replacement Theology, McGarry responded, "Yes."[88] According to McGarry, "We are not Biblicists like the Evangelicals. We interpret the Bible theologically, not literally."[89] McGarry explained why this was so.

> Catholics understand Scripture through theological interpretation while Evangelicals use biblical proof texts. There is no Catholic doctrinal statement. We rely on the creeds, which say little about the Jews. There is no Roman Catholic Doctrinal statement. We hold to the Church Creeds from the early Church Councils. We make use of our Catechism to help define for laypeople our beliefs."[90]

To illustrate the unchangeable nature of Catholic doctrine, McGarry referred to Theodore Herzl's meeting with Pope Pius X in 1904. McGarry believed the Pope's response to a request to assist Zionism would be the same in the 21st century. The leader of the Catholic Church would have to reject such a request on theological grounds. McGarry believed that the Pope's 1904 reasons would be the same today, because Catholic doctrine does not change.[91]

Dr. Rico's opinion of the unchangeable nature of Catholic doctrine was similar. He believed that the Pope today would have to give the same response as the Pope did in 1904. Rico elaborated by explaining that the first reason for Pope Pius X's refusal was that he was not in a political position to accomplish this task. He did not establish new states. The second reason was that such assistance would be opposed to Catholic teaching, which teaches that God is working though the (Catholic) Church now, not through the Jews.[92] Rico also believed that the key issue was the interpretation of the Bible. "Evangelicals interpret the Bible literally. Catholics interpret the Bible theologically."[93] Rico illustrated his statement by explaining that although the Vatican now recognizes the State of Israel, this does not mean Catholic doctrine has changed since 1904. Rather, this simply means the Vatican accepts political realities.

According to Rico, within the Catholic Church, there is now a deeper understanding of these matters, a development of thinking about the Jews and Israel. However, this does not mean the Catholic Church has become Zionistic.[94] Rico believed it was essential to understand that the Catholic Church divides between the spiritual and the political. Despite having a mystical view of the Jews, Catholics would not be Zionists.[95]

Rico recognized that some Jews might misunderstand Catholic intentions. He explained why some Catholics and Priests seem to view Israel differently than other Catholics. "The various Orders and individuals in the Catholic Church are permitted to have their own opinions and express themselves. This is true about their opinions about Israel."[96]

Conclusion

Wide doctrinal differences have existed for centuries in the United States between the various Christian Church denominations regarding the Jews and the Restoration of Israel. The more Puritan inspired Evangelical Churches such as Baptist, Methodist, Congregational and some Presbyterian Churches tend to hold to a direct interpretation of Scripture when they study eschatology, which encourages support for Christian Zionism. By contrast, the Catholic Church and most mainline liberal Protestant Churches such as Lutheran, Anglican/

Episcopal and some Presbyterian Churches tend to teach Replacement Theology. This doctrinal position opposes support for Zionism because of an allegorical and theological interpretation of Scripture. As might be expected, even within each denomination, there was room for local congregations and individuals to arrive at their own conclusions regarding Jews and the Restoration of Israel.

With Christian Zionism defined as a gentile Christian commitment to the belief that the Jews are forever God's Chosen People with the eternal divine right to possess the Land of Israel, it was noted that sometimes governments and individuals could support Zionism for other reasons. These other reasons include fighting anti-Semitism, humanitarian sympathy because of the Diaspora and the Holocaust, anti-Arab posturing, responding to the wishes of a Jewish constituency and political positioning during the Cold War.

The doctrinal diversity of the Anglican Church and the agendas of sub-categories of its Mission Societies have been noted. The anti-Zionistic positioning of the liberal mainline Churches has also been surveyed. Special notice has been given to the doctrine of the Lutheran Church and the unique motivations of Mormon Zionism. The anti-Zionistic posturing of the World Council of Churches has been recognized.

A study of Zionistic activity during the 1930's and 1940's in the Roosevelt and Truman administrations revealed few Evangelicals and Catholics in positions of power. The abundance of representation from mainline liberal Protestant Churches resulted in little support for Zionism until President Truman himself made some personal decisions to support the cause of Zionism. The question of Catholic motivation for Zionistic support was examined using the examples of Thomas D'Alesandro, his daughter Nancy Pelosi and others.

Despite some indications that Catholic doctrine may be changing toward Zionism, it was seen that Catholic doctrine remains unmovable regarding its belief that Israel has been replaced by the Catholic Church. Positive Catholic overtures to Israel and Jewish religious leaders are based on motives other than Christian Zionism.

Chapter Eight

British Closure and American Christian Zionism Following Israeli Independence 1949-21st Century

❖ ❖ ❖

This chapter will demonstrate that Christian Zionism remained a significant factor behind American support of Israel through the second half of the 20th century. Gentile American Zionists continued to maintain an influence in their foreign policy toward Israel long after initial American recognition in 1948. Although this continuity of influence is not usually recognized, Evangelicalism and Christian Zionism have remained relevant factors in American culture and politics from the end of World War 2 through to the beginning of the 21st century.

In this chapter, the post-1948 British retreat from Zionism will be surveyed, as Britain gradually accepted the reality of the Jewish State. Then, Harry Truman's enduring passion for Zionism will be documented. The rational for the perpetual American support of Israel will then be examined, followed by a closer look at the backgrounds and beliefs of the various American Presidents in the second half of the 20th century. A brief review will be made of instances when American foreign policy went contrary to the wishes of Israel, and finally, several 21st century developments regarding Christian Zionism will be noted.

British Postwar Reassessment

The influence of British Christian Zionism peaked in 1917, and thereafter experienced a long gradual decline. This was largely linked to the reality that, in Britain, Evangelicalism progressively became irrelevant to society during the 1920's, 1930's, and 1940's. Through these years, the voice of Christian Zionism was heard less frequently and by the 1940's, only occasionally. One of these occasions was in January 1949, when Churchill pressed the Labour government to recognize the State of Israel. On January 29, the British government did so.[1] Four months later, on May 11 1949, Israel was admitted to the United Nations as its 59th member. Between January 1 1949 and May 11 1949, 32 nations recognized Israel. This was in addition to the 20 nations who had accorded Israel recognition prior to December 31 1948. It seemed Britain had been relatively alone in her delayed recognition of Israel.

Winston Churchill maintained his lifetime commitment to Zionism, despite the changing mood of his nation. In 1951, he wrote Chaim Weizmann of his long-standing loyalty to Zionism, "My Dear Weizmann, Thank you for your letter and good wishes. The wonderful exertions which Israel is making in these times of difficulty are cheering to an old Zionist like me."[2] When Weizmann died on November 9 1952, Churchill was addressing the Lord Mayor's banquet in London. Upon hearing the news, he departed from his planned speech and declared, "Those of us who have been Zionists since before the days of the Balfour Declaration know what a heavy loss Israel has sustained in the death of Chaim Weizmann."[3] Richard Meinertzhagen, another British Christian Zionist, also opposed the trend of his nation and remained a Zionist all his life. He wrote of Weizmann, "Chaim was a great chemist, a great Jew, a great man and a Prince of Israel. He and Smuts are the two outstanding figures of my generation and I am proud to have worked with them...I had no better or more loyal friend than Chaim Weizmann."[4]

It is noteworthy to observe the importance Weizmann gave to his Christian Zionist friends. In his Rehovot mansion in Israel, which is a museum today, his library was a prominent room. His wife's desk is next to his, and on their desks are only a few framed portraits: their two sons, Albert Einstein, Arthur Balfour and David Lloyd

George. In the large lobby there are two busts, one of Weizmann and one of Arthur Balfour. Clearly, these Christian Zionists were important men in Weizmann's life.[5]

Ernest Bevin resigned from the Cabinet in March 1951. When he died a month later, The London *Times* obituary stated that Bevin reflected "characteristically British qualities-courage, frankness, shrewdness and practicality."[6] Abba Eban had a different perspective on Bevin. "He immediately subjected the Jewish people to a shock of sadistic intensity…shattering all the hopes that Jews had invested in the prospect of better times after the war."[7] Peter Weiler believed Bevin's life personified the profound transformation Britain had experienced. Bevin had once been a vocal part of the British Evangelical community, but in his later years rejected those values, including Zionism. Weiler wrote, "Bevin's life came to be understood to exemplify the changes undergone by British society in the first half of this century.[8]

Truman's Continued Passion for Israel

Late in his Presidency, Truman still held to his Zionistic views, writing in 1952, "I had faith in Israel before it was established, I have faith in it now. I believe it has a glorious future not just as another nation, but as an embodiment of the great ideals of our civilization."[9] Even after the death of Chaim Weizmann, Truman stayed in contact with his widow, Vera. In January 1953, Mrs. Weizmann visited the Truman's in America. Vera Truman recorded in her diary that Truman told her, "Your husband was a great man, and I had looked forward to co-operating with him for many years to come." Mrs. Weizmann recorded that she replied, "My husband not only greatly respected and admired you, but he also had deep affection for you." At this, Vera Weizmann recorded, "tears filled Truman's eyes."[10]

It is interesting to note what was of value to Harry Truman. On her visit to Missouri in 1953, Vera Weizmann noted that Harry Truman had two portraits on his desk: Andrew Jackson, the seventh president of the United States and Chaim Weizmann, the first President of Israel.[11] Ben Gurion wrote to Harry Truman on the occasion of Truman's 80th birthday. "In the annals of our people you will always be remembered as the man who ensured the inclusion of the desolate and empty Negev in the State of Israel for the absorption of the remnants of the Nazi Holocaust."[12]

American Rationale for Supporting Israel

In contrast to the British experience, the influence of Christian Zionism in the United States reached a high point in 1948, and continued to strengthen thereafter. Rather than claiming that American political support for the State of Israel after 1948 was due to pressure from the Jewish lobby in Washington, or to Cold War political necessities, it should rather be realized that Christian Zionism was a dynamic force behind American foreign policy toward Israel during the second half of the 20th century. This force was sustained by the influence of the Evangelical communities of American society, which was an important component in American society during the post war years.

From 1948 to 1956, the combined Church membership of the three largest Evangelical denominations in the United States (Southern Baptist, Methodist and Presbyterian) grew from 17,406,000 to 20,876,000, an increase for the eight-year period of approximately 16 percent.[13] This was in addition to numerous Evangelical denominations in the United States who did not report their statistics. In America, as in Britain, political Party affiliation had little to do with support for Zionism. Citizens in both the Democratic and Republican Parties equally shared a commitment to the Bible and to Zionism.

Before Dwight Eisenhower was elected President in 1952, he sought the spiritual advice of Billy Graham. Following his election, Eisenhower continued to regularly meet with Graham for advice.[14] Eisenhower summoned Graham five days before his inauguration in January 1953, telling Graham, "I think one of the reasons I was elected was to help lead this country spiritually. We need a spiritual renewal."[15] Once President, Eisenhower proclaimed a National Day of Prayer and joined a Presbyterian Church in Washington, even complying with the new membership instruction classes.[16]

Dwight Eisenhower possessed a strong Evangelical faith. His early life revolved around worship. Every day, morning and night, the family members got down on their knees to pray. His father led the family in Bible reading twice a day.[17] As President, Eisenhower proceeded to introduce two Bills that he believed would strengthen America spiritually. First, he proposed a Bill to add the words "Under God" to the Pledge of Allegiance. The Bill was passed on Flag Day, June 14 1954.[18] Second, Eisenhower recommended to Congress in June 1955 a Bill that would "Provide for the inscription of 'In God We Trust' on all United States currency and coins." The Bill was introduced on March 22 1956, and was quickly approved and signed into law on July 30 1956.[19] The words "In God We Trust" have appeared on all United States currency issued after October 1 1957.[20]

Rather than merely representing a declining influence from the past, Evangelicalism in the United States kept growing through the second half of 20th century. While some might argue that Cold War posturing put America on the side of Israel, this argument fails to explain why American support for Israel continued after the end of the Cold War in the late 1980's.

In June 1967, Israel fought the Six Day War against Egypt, Syria and Jordan, gaining all of Jerusalem, the West Bank, the Gaza Strip, the Sinai and the Golan Heights. This momentous event influenced world politics for decades to follow. The Israeli victory was a catalyst for varying opinions within Christian Churches. Paul Charles Merkley noted how the war opened again the issue of Zionism within the Protestant Churches of the United States. Merkley wrote, "In most instances, however, the events of June 1967 served to revive and even amplify the Restorationalists zeal of 1948, seeping away doubts and reservations that many conservative Christians had had originally."[21]

Regarding the 1967 war, John F. Walvoord, a leading Evangelical theologian in the United States wrote in the Evangelical *Moody Monthly* magazine that they had just seen, "one of the most remarkable fulfillments of biblical prophecy since the destruction of Jerusalem in 70 AD."[22] The editor of another Evangelical magazine, *Christianity Today*, Nelson Bell (father in law of Billy Graham), wrote, "That for the first time in more than 2000 years Jerusalem is now completely in the hands of the Jews gives the student of the

Bible a thrill and a renewed faith in the accuracy and validity of the Bible."[23]

Following the 1967 war and the reuniting of Jerusalem, Evangelicals from all over the world voiced their opinion that a reunited Jerusalem must be the capital of Israel. Dr. Douglas Young, the son of Presbyterian missionaries to Korea, moved to Jerusalem in 1957 to establish the "American Institute," a graduate school for western Evangelicals desiring to learn more about Israel. Following the 1967 war, Young relocated the school to Mount Zion. In 1971 Young said, "Jerusalem has never been the capital of any people except the Jewish people. The unity of Jerusalem must be preserved."[24] Under Young's leadership the American Institute taught a love for Israel to thousands of young Evangelicals.

In 1969, Baptist evangelist Billy Graham published a book about Israel entitled "His Land." Graham later made the book into a movie. In both the book and movie, Graham explained how the Jewish return to the land of Israel was a fulfillment of Bible prophecy. Graham enjoyed great influence in American political circles for many years, advising and praying with every American President from Harry Truman to George W. Bush.

Following the Yom Kippur war, American Evangelical author, Hal Lindsay, wrote a book about Israel and biblical prophecy called "The Late Great Planet Earth." The book sold 15 million copies worldwide. In his book, Lindsay called Israel the "fuse of Armageddon."[25] The book was even translated into Hebrew for Israelis to read. So influential was the book that Ben Gurion had a copy. At his home at Sde Boker in the Negev desert, his Hebrew copy of the book still lies on his desk as it was left when he died.[26] In 1977, Billy Graham addressed the National Executive Council meeting of the American Jewish Committee and called for the rededication of the United States to the existence and safety of Israel.[27]

By the late 1970's, American Baptist leader Jerry Falwell linked the survival of the United States to the American defense of Israel.[28] In 1979, the government of Israel rewarded Falwell with a private jet to better do his work. Two years later, he received Israel's Jabotinsky Award for his support of Israel.[29] Evangelical influence in America during these decades was impossible to ignore. In a 1986 Gallop poll, 33 percent of Americans called themselves "Born-Again, Evangelical Christians." Although this percentage may seem low, it should be realized that Gallop used a narrow three-fold definition for Evangelicals: they believe that the Bible is the literal Word of God, they accept Jesus as their personal Saviour and they encourage others to accept Jesus.[30] Peter Gardella wrote,

> If these Evangelicals relate to Israel as a fulfillment of biblical prophecy, as most of them do, and if some Catholics, liberal Protestants, and others who do not pass Gallop's test nevertheless believe that God is ingathering Israel as part of the climax of history, there may well be eighty million Americans who look to Israel and think of the end.[31]

During the 1980's, Christian religious life continued to grow in America. In 1890 only about 34 percent of Americans were members of a formal Church. By 1989, the share of those who belonged was 60 percent.[32] Ronald Stockton, in his work "Christian Zionism: Prophecy and Public Opinion," researched American public support for Israel in the 1980's. He concluded, "...a major factor in that support is that religious doctrine commonly called Christian Zionism...it is an important component of how Americans-especially Evangelical Protestant Americans view Israel, Jews and their own country."[33] Stockton believed "Christian Zionism is a mainstream phenomenon firmly rooted in those religious and cultural groups from which it historically sprang, but also transcending them."[34]

Being more specific, Stockton's research noted that in the 1980's, "Acceptance of Christian Zionism is significantly higher among white, self-identifying Evangelicals that among Catholic or non-Evangelical Protestants..."[35] He concluded that Christian Zionism in America in the 1980's was very much a "mainstream cultural theme linked to American self-identity and to perception of America as a moral community. It is definitely not the pathological perspective of an extremist fringe as sometimes portrayed by its distracters."[36]

In the 1990's, various Evangelical Christian groups in America began to show their support for Israel in more independent ways. Sometimes individual local Churches decided to support Zionism on their own. John Hagee, Pastor of the Cornerstone Church in San Antonio, Texas, announced in February 1997 that his Church was donating over one million dollars to the government of Israel to resettle Jews from the Soviet Union in the West Bank and Jerusalem.

In 2005, a Baptist Pastor from Oklahoma, Jim Vineyard, purchased a full page in the *Jerusalem Post* to encourage the people of Israel to not relinquish any of their land to the Arabs. Quoting the Bible, the Balfour Declaration and various Rabbis, Vineyard wrote, "Don't give up one grain of sand of the Land which the almighty gave to you by everlasting covenant in Genesis 17." Reverend Vineyard personally raised $695,000 for the State of Israel during the previous two years, claiming he had the backing of 40 million Christian Zionists in America.[37]

Michael Benson, in his work, "Harry S. Truman and the Founding of Israel," noted that by the 1990's, America's relationship to Israel was based more on sentiment than strategy.[38] In March 1990, former Secretary of State George Shultz commented that some Israelis were uncomfortable with American support for Israel based on moral commitment.[39] In 1995 Henry Kissinger commented that above all, the survival of Israel had sentimental importance to the United States.[40]

Within the American electoral system, the influence of Christian Zionism could exert real political pressure. In December 2005, the Christian Coalition of America announced they would begin to publish the voting records of American legislators in regards to Israel. The Christian Coalition of America is an Evangelical Christian group with a membership of about two million. During the 2004 presidential elections, the Coalition distributed 70 million voter guides throughout the United States. Usually focusing on the issues of homosexuality, abortion and euthanasia, the Coalition also included politicians voting records on Israel.[41]

In 2008, a survey of how Americans felt about Zionism indicated that Evangelical Christians were the strongest supporters of Israel. Eighty-two percent of American Christians saw a "moral and biblical obligation to love and support Israel and pray for the peace of Jerusalem," while 89 percent of American Evangelicals agreed with the statement.[42]

The majority of the members of the United States Congress have been Protestant Christian in each of the 112 sessions of Congress. In the 111th Congress, 54.7% of seats were held by members of Protestant denominations. The top five religious affiliations in the 111th Congress (Jan 09 to Jan 2011) were Roman Catholic (30.1%), Baptist (12.4%), Methodist (10.7%), Jewish (8.4%), and Presbyterian (8.1%). Protestant denominations have held a large majority throughout congressional history, reflecting American's traditional demographics.[43]

Of the 535 members of the 112th Congress, (January 2011 to January 2013), 304 members (57%) were Protestant, 156, (29%) were Catholic, 15 (3%) were Mormon, 39 (7%) were Jewish, two were Muslims and 3 were Buddhist. Only 6, or 1.1% did not specify a religious affiliation.[44]

Members of the United States Senate in the 112th Congress, (January 2011 to January 2013), were 55 Protestants, 24 Roman Catholics, 13 Jewish, six Mormon, one Eastern Orthodox and one unaffiliated Christian. It could be said, in broad terms, that 87% of the Senate was Christian, compared with about 80% of the population. Thirteen percent of the Senate was Jewish and no Senator fell under the category of Atheist/Agnostic.[45]

The American Presidency and Christian Zionism

In the last half of the 20th century, the American tradition of having Protestant Presidents from Evangelical Churches continued. Dwight Eisenhower belonged to a family associated with the Brethren Church in Pennsylvania. As President, Eisenhower joined his family in contributing financially to "Messiah College," a Brethren Bible College near his home in Harrisburg, Pennsylvania. Shortly after his inauguration as President, Eisenhower asked to be baptized and joined the National Presbyterian Church in Washington. Although sparing in his public remarks about Israel, Eisenhower supported Israel during his presidency, from 1953 until 1961.[46]

Lynden Johnson was a member of the Disciples of Christ Church.[47] Because of the Baptist origins of the denomination, Johnson had a predisposition to favour Zionism. Johnson's grandfather had been a Bible Professor at Baylor University, and Johnson grew up in a home with regular Bible readings. Throughout his life, he rarely missed attending Church on Sundays.[48] Early in his Presidency, he spoke at a National Prayer Breakfast in Washington. "No man can live where I live, nor work at the desk where I work now, without needing and seeking the strength and support of earnest and frequent prayer."[49]

Johnson was the first President to invite an Israeli Premier to the White House for a state visit when he hosted Prime Minister Levi Eshkol in 1964. He supported Israel during the Six-Day War in 1967. Three weeks after the war, he related a conversation he had had with the Soviet leader Alexei Kosygin. "He couldn't understand why we'd want to support the Jews-three million people-when there are 100 million Arabs. I told him that numbers do not determine what was right. We tried to do what was right regardless of the numbers."

As President, he told a gathering of Jewish Americans in 1968, "Most if not all of you have very deep ties with the land and with the people of Israel, as I do, for my Christian faith sprang from yours....the Bible stories are woven into my childhood memories as the gallant struggle of modern Jews to be free of persecution is also woven into our souls."[50]

Richard Nixon was a life-long member of the Quakers, one of the oldest Christian denominations in America. As a young man, he taught a Bible class and played the piano in his Church. Billy Graham observed that, "His spiritual legacy from that quiet Quaker tradition of 'friendly persuasion' helped shape the way he looked at the world."[51] Nixon was uncompromising in his support for Israel.

In October 1973, Israel fought the Yom Kippur War against Egypt and Syria. Although Israel was losing the war at first, she eventually prevailed. At the time of the war, President Richard Nixon was entangled in the Watergate scandal. Nevertheless, Nixon personally backed Israel and kept his pledge to provide Israel with fighter aircraft and other equipment Israel needed. However, America's support for Israel came at an economic price. The resulting Israeli victory prompted an Arab oil boycott that shook the economies of the western world.

As an Episcopalian, President Gerald Ford's support for Israel was manifest in a formal, political style, without the Evangelical passion. In 1974, Ford told Prime Minister Rabin of Israel,

> The United States has been proud of its association with the State of Israel. We shall continue to stand with Israel. We are committed to Israel's survival and security. The United States for a quarter of a century has had an excellent relationship with the State of Israel. We have cooperated in many, many fields — in your security, in the well-being of the Middle East, and in leading what we all hope is a lasting peace throughout the world.[52]

In 1976, Jimmy Carter was elected President. As an Evangelical, Carter was open about his faith, calling himself a "Born-Again Christian."[53] A committed Southern Baptist, he continued to teach an adult Sunday School class in his Church even while President. In those days, Carter believed in the significance of Israel and worked to bring peace to the Middle East. He was successful in brokering a peace deal between Israel and Egypt, declaring, "We must recognize that the Israelis did not cause the Palestinian problem...commitment to a viable Israeli state must be a cornerstone of American foreign policy."[54]

Speaking of President Jimmy Carter in the late 1970's, Samuel W. Lewis, American Ambassador to Israel wrote, "...we have another American President reared on the Bible, who also has a personal and profound conviction about the unique nature of the State of Israel."[55] During his Presidency, at a White House briefing, Carter spoke of America's religious bond to Israel.

> We have a commitment to the preservation of Israel as a nation, to the security of Israel, the right of the Israeli people, who have suffered so much, to live in peace that is absolutely permanent and unshakeable. The ties that bind the people of the United States and the people of Israel together, the ties of blood, kinship, ties of history, ties of common religious

beliefs, the dream, centuries old, of the founding of the new nation of Israel have been realized.[56]

Near the end of his presidency, Carter told a United Jewish Appeal National Youth Leadership Conference, "I am opposed to an independent Palestinian state, because in my own judgment, and in the judgment of many leaders in the Middle East, including Arab leaders, this would be a destabilizing factor in the Middle East and would certainly not serve the United States interests."[57]

Ronald Reagan was raised in the Disciples of Christ Church, an offshoot of the Southern Baptist Church. At the age of 12, Reagan was baptized at his request at the First Christian Church in Dixon, Illinois. On that same Sunday, he joined the Church.[58] Throughout his teen and college years, Reagan taught Sunday School at his Church. In 1926, he led the Easter sunrise service.[59] As Student Body President in High School, he spoke at his graduation from the New Testament text of John 10:10, that Jesus promised an abundant life to his followers. He did some Bible preaching as a young man, and was known to have a personal biblical faith.[60]

Reagan grew up under the close supervision of his mother Nelle, a devout Evangelical. It was from his mother that Reagan acquired much of his native optimism and sense of divine providence.[61] Reagan wrote of his mother's influence, "I now seem to have her faith that there is a divine plan, and while we may not be able to see the reason for something at the time, things do happen for a reason and for the best.[62] Three years into his presidency, Reagan made a speech about the Bible to the Annual Convention of the National Religious Broadcasters Association. As part of his speech, Reagan asked the audience, "Nineteen-eighty-three was the year more of us read the Good Book. Can we make a resolution here today? –that 1984 will be the year we put its great truths into action."[63]

Although Reagan often kept his personal faith a private matter, he attended Evangelical Churches regularly throughout his life. Reagan wrote in 1967, "I believe the Bible is the result of Divine inspiration and is not just history...I believe in it."[64] Sometimes Reagan's faith surfaced publicly. In 1980, while a candidate for the presidency at a conference in Detroit, Reagan asked the crowd to pause and join him in a moment of silent prayer. The crowd fell silent and after a few minutes, Reagan ended with, "God Bless America."[65] While campaigning in 1980, Reagan made it known to the press that he did not believe in evolution, but instead believed in biblical creation, a view held by most Evangelicals. Even after the media called it Reagan's "biggest mistake" of the campaign, Reagan's popularity increased and he went on to win another presidential election.[66]

Throughout the 1980's, President Ronald Reagan supported Israel. As President, he wrote to the Zionist Organization of America in 1984, praising Zionism as "A fundamental aspiration of the Jewish people...I decry those who would equate the beauty of Zionism with the ugliness of racism...Yours is an organization very close to my heart, for since 1948, Israel's well-being has been of tremendous importance to me."[67] Reagan often spoke of the unshakable commitment the United States had for Israel. "America has never flinched from its commitment to the State of Israel—a commitment which remains unshakable."[68]

Reagan sometimes explained the mixture of motives that the United States had for her support for Israel. "Since the foundation of the State of Israel, the United States has stood by her and helped her to pursue security, peace, and economic growth. Our friendship is based on historic moral and strategic ties, as well as our shared dedication to democracy."[69] He also claimed, "The people of Israel and America are historic partners in the global quest for human dignity and freedom. We will always remain at each other's side."[70]

Following the Presidency of Reagan, George Bush served in the White House for four years. As a life-long member of the Episcopal Church, he also supported Israel. In 1991, with George Bush as President, the United States led a coalition against Iraq in the Gulf War.[71] The United States asked Israel stay out of the war, even if attacked. Despite the fact that Iraq launched missiles against Israel, Israel trusted their American allies enough to withhold retaliation. George Bush said,

> We also share a profound desire for a lasting peace in the Middle East. My Administration is dedicated to achieving this goal, one which will guarantee Israel security. At the

same time, we will do our utmost to defend and protect Israel, for unless Israel is strong and secure, then peace will always be beyond our grasp. We were with Israel at the beginning, 41 years ago. We are with Israel today. And we will be with Israel in the future. No one should doubt this basic commitment.[72]

In speaking about Zionism, George Bush said, "Zionism is the idea that led to the creation of a home for the Jewish people...and to equate Zionism with the intolerable sin of racism is to twist history and forget the terrible plight of Jews in World War II and indeed throughout history."[73]

Bill Clinton was another Southern Baptist President, and through the 1990's he followed the American pro-Israel tradition of Christian Zionism. Clinton said, "The United States admires Israel for all that it has overcome and for all that it has accomplished. We are proud of the strong bond we have forged with Israel, based on our shared values and ideals. That unique relationship will endure just as Israel has endured."[74] Clinton liked to speak of the things America and Israel had in common. "The relationship between our two countries is built on shared understandings and values. Our peoples continue to enjoy the fruits of our excellent economic and cultural cooperation as we prepare to enter the 21st century."[75]

George W. Bush became a Methodist as a middle-aged man following a Christian "born-again" experience. In his support for Israel, Bush said, "We will speak up for our principles and we will stand up for our friends in the world. And one of our most important friends is the State of Israel."[76] Commenting on Jewish biblical history, Bush spoke of the continuing divine history of Israel.

Through centuries of struggle, Jews across the world have been witnesses not only against the crimes of men, but for faith in God, and God alone. Theirs is a story of defiance in oppression and patience in tribulation- reaching back to the exodus and their exile into the Diaspora That story continued in the founding of the State of Israel. The story continues in the defense of the State of Israel.[77]

In speaking to a Jewish audience of what America and Israel had in common, George W. Bush declared,

> Our two nations have a lot in common, when you think about it. We were both founded by immigrants escaping religious persecution in other lands. We both have built vibrant democracies. Both our countries are founded on certain basic beliefs, that there is an Almighty God who watches over the affairs of men and values every life. These ties have made us natural allies, and these ties will never be broken.[78]

American Disagreements with Israel

On several occasions during the second half of the 20th century, the United State government followed policies contrary to the interests of Israel. These policies were usually manifest through the office of the President. This reality illustrates that the influence of Christian Zionism in America was not omnipotent, but rather was an important factor that often influenced American policy, though not always. For example, both Truman and Eisenhower maintained an arms embargo against Israel. It was not until the 1960's that the United States began supplying weapons to Israel.[79]

The first significant instance of disagreement between America and Israel was during the 1956 Sinai campaign. President Eisenhower opposed British, French and Israeli incursions into Egyptian territory in order to seize the Suez Canal. It is important to understand Eisenhower's reasons for siding with the Egyptians. First, he had an abhorrence of anything that resembled colonialism. Second, he had a keen sense of justice that prompted him to defend his concept of Egyptian nationalism. Finally, it should be realized that Eisenhower's decision was primarily against the British and French military action, not against Israel. He even ordered an oil embargo against the British during the duration of the conflict.[80]

In the early 1960's, President John Kennedy opposed the Israel government obtaining nuclear weapons. As the only Catholic

President in American history, and being largely untaught in biblical prophecy, Kennedy neither embraced nor rejected Zionism. To a large degree, he dealt with Israel as he would any other country. Similarly, in the 1970's President Gerald Ford asked the State Department to reassess American policy toward Israel, indicating his willingness to treat Israel as he would other nations.

Although President Jimmy Carter supported Zionist ideals during his presidency in the 1970's, in later years, Carter would rethink his personal views and become a spokesperson for Palestinian aspirations. This change of mind occurred around 2000 when Carter publicly left the Southern Baptist Convention and actively called for the creation of a Palestinian State. In 2006, Carter articulated his views in his book, *Palestine: Peace Not Apartheid*, where he criticized Israel, comparing her policies to the Apartheid laws of South African.

In the 1980's, President Ronald Reagan sold state-of- the-art weaponry to Saudi Arabia in spite of the protests of the Israeli government. In the 1990's, President Bill Clinton pressured Israel to embrace the Oslo accords which inadvertently led to the second Intifada. In the early 21st century, George W. Bush became the first President to speak of a two state solution and push for a Palestinian State. Although these events offended the Israeli government at the time, they did not represent a major change in American attitudes toward Israel.

Changing Twenty-First Century Christian Zionism

Several developments regarding Christian Zionism took place at the beginning of the 21st century. First, Christian Zionism became more international as Evangelical Christianity spread throughout the world. Christian Zionists from around the globe displayed their support for Israel in many ways. Some visited Israel as tourists, while others stayed to live in Israel in order to volunteer their time and resources to assist the Jewish nation. One of the best examples of this is the work of the International Christian Embassy in Jerusalem. The Embassy began in 1980, after the Israeli government announced that Jerusalem would be her eternal capital, and almost all foreign embassies relocated to Tel Aviv. In response, the International

Christian Embassy was founded in Jerusalem. This new Embassy sought to become the centre for worldwide Evangelical Zionism. Walter Riggins, the Secretary General of the International Christian Embassy in Jerusalem often declared, "We are more Zionist than the Israelis."[81]

Sometimes Jewish and Evangelical groups joined forces to support Zionism. The International Fellowship of Christians and Jews, led by a former Anti-Defamation League employee and Orthodox rabbi, Yechiel Eckstein, raised over $5 million, mostly from fundamentalist Christian Zionist sources.

A further development in the 21st century has to do with growing recognition and appreciation among Israelis for Christian Zionism. In early 2001, Israeli Knesset Members created the "Christian Allies Caucus" in Jerusalem. This new committee would work to coordinate common efforts between the Israeli government and Christian Evangelicals worldwide. Dr. Yuri Shtern, Chairman of the National Union Party, announced,

> Israel has no better friend in the world than the United States, and that is in no small part due to our Christian friends in America, and we hope to see the same happen in Europe and elsewhere. Our shared values and beliefs, based on our common Judeo-Christian heritage, are the source of the strong ties between us, and in the post 9/11 world, our long-standing relationship has become more important than ever before.[82]

Responding to the Knesset announcement, Malcolm Hedding, Director of the International Christian Embassy in Jerusalem said, "We welcome this initiative as an opportunity to further support Israel by making known to Knesset Members the vital work that Christian Zionists do for and on behalf of the State of Israel."[83] In May 2005, the Israeli Knesset in Jerusalem honoured the International Christian Embassy in Jerusalem for 25 years of Zionist work. Member of Knesset Yuri Shtern declared, "Christian support for the State of Israel has reached levels unimaginable 25 years ago."[84]

Another 21st century development has to do with the expressed opinions of Muslim religious leaders regarding Christian Zionism. It can be revealing what the enemies of Zionism say about the advocates of this view. In an interview published in a major Arabic newspaper in 2005, Mahmoud al-Zahar, a senior Gaza-based Hamas leader said that his organization did not regard the West as the enemy. He explained, "We do not consider the West as an enemy, but we believe Christian Zionism is criminal." Al Zahar went on to say that Christian Zionists are to be found mostly, but not exclusively, in the ranks of Evangelical Christianity. They not only believe that the God of Israel gave the Land of Israel to the people of Israel, but they also believe that they are to stand with Israel against those who are out to rob the Jews of their land. He warned his Arab readers that millions of Christian Zionists around the world support the Jewish claims to the Land of Israel and reject Arab assertions that they have national rights to this land.[85]

In early 2006, the Palestinian Supreme Islamic Judicial Council announced their displeasure with the Evangelicals. "Zionist Christian motivation is said to be 'Crusader motivation' and was behind not only the cursed Balfour Declaration, but is today behind the British and American policy in Palestine, Iraq, Afghanistan and other Arab and Muslim countries."[86]

A further 21st century development has to do with the attitudes of Christians in Britain where a remnant of Christian Zionism still exists. In 2006, Lord Carey, former Archbishop of Canterbury reacted to the decision of the Church of England to consider disinvestment from companies doing business with Israel. Carey called the Church decision "a most regrettable and one-sided statement. Carey went on to say he was "ashamed to be an Anglican."[87] Eventually, the relevant committee of the Church of England rejected the proposal. Speaking in the early 21st century, Andrew White, former envoy to the Middle East for the Archbishop of Canterbury observed,

> What we saw at the turn of the last century was the fact that many of the key Christians, certainly in our land, were

profoundly influenced by the Evangelical movement at the time because there was only one real form of Christianity which was prevalent in political circles and that was the form of Christianity which took seriously God's word and took seriously the injunction of the Jewish people to return to the Land.[88]

Since the end of the Mandate, some British Christians have believed the promise of the Balfour Declaration was forsaken by the British. They believed an apology was in order. Such an apology took place early in the 21st century, when on April 27 2006, a unique event took place at the site of the former Atlit British detention camp near Haifa. Representatives from over 20 British Evangelical Christian Church groups and organizations traveled to Israel to gather at the former site of the camp. A small cluster of invited former camp detainees were also present. The British delegation then publicly apologized to the Jews present and to the nation of Israel. A plaque was unveiled, which read, "In sorrow and shame we recognize the complete betrayal of the British Mandate for Palestine as represented by the Atlit Detention Camp. 'Father forgive us, we pray.'"[89] Andrew White commented on his perception of the moral and spiritual nature of the issue, "There is a real key issue where I think the people of Britain need to repent."[90]

Conclusion

❖ ❖ ❖

This book has demonstrated five main points. First, that Christian Zionism was a primary incentive behind British interest in the Holy Land in the early 20th century. Second, that Christian Zionism was a significant motivation for the British government to issue the Balfour Declaration in 1917. Third, that the gradual decline in the importance of Evangelicalism and Christian Zionism in Britain was a major rationale for the British departure from Palestine. Fourth, that Christian Zionism was a main factor behind American recognition of the new State of Israel in 1948. Fifth, that Christian Zionism remained an important influence behind American support of Israel through the second half of the 20th century as Gentile American Zionists continued to have a voice in their national policy toward Israel.

The Motivation for the Balfour Declaration of 1917

Christian Zionism was significant factor motivating the British government to issue the Balfour Declaration in 1917. Political explanations alone fail to explain the Cabinet's actions. They do not sufficiently account for the influence of certain religious beliefs maintained by a number of the Cabinet members at this time. Having examined these reasons, and the men who made the decision, it is evident that the various political factors were less important than the motive of sympathy for Zionism. Of the ten men in the Cabinet in November 1917, seven were Evangelicals.[1] Three were raised in the homes of Evangelical Pastors,[2] and one was an ordained Methodist

Minister.[3] No High Anglicans were in the Cabinet, and Edwin Montague, a Jew, cast the only vote against the Declaration.

The Balfour Declaration was not a sudden random act of a desperate government. It was a carefully considered statement that reflected the personal faith of several of the Cabinet members who commissioned it. The timing of events is noteworthy. On the day that British and Australian troops conquered Beer Sheva, October 31 1917, the Balfour Declaration was approved by the Cabinet in London. The Declaration was made public a few days later.

Party affiliation was irrelevant to this political decision since Christian Zionists were to be found in all the political parties of Britain. Balfour was a member of the Conservative Party throughout his political career. Lloyd George was a lifelong Liberal, and in the early 20th century, the Liberal Party was the Party of choice for many Nonconformists. The Labour Party embraced Zionism for much of its history, until the post World War 2 years under Attlee and Bevin. However, the Labour Party's commitment to Zionism was largely based on a shared interest in socialism that the Labour Party had with the Jewish Zionists in Palestine.

In 1917, there were political and military reasons behind the Balfour Declaration. The question can be asked whether these motives alone would have sufficed to bring about the Declaration. Being hypothetical, the question cannot be answered definitively, but a negative response would seem appropriate. In any case, the evidence indicates a strong religious motivation within the Cabinet. Although a variety of reasons were behind the Balfour Declaration, the Cabinet took advantage of the political circumstances in which they found themselves to publish a declaration that reflected the personal religious convictions of several leading members. They realized they were in a position of power to shape world history and facilitate their spiritual beliefs, and they seized the opportunity.

Although religious belief was a significant motivation behind the Balfour Declaration, career politicians like Balfour and Lloyd George would not openly make decisions for the Empire based on personal sentiments alone. The decisions they made had to make political sense both to themselves, and to the public. Blanche Dugdale commented, "The Balfour Declaration was the first constructive step toward a solution of the Jewish problem on a national basis, but it was not made under the pressure of pity or without proper consideration.[4] Ten years after the decision was made, Balfour gave the Declaration a high place not only in Jewish history, but also in world history. "If those efforts meet with all the degree of success which the Zionists hope for, 1917 will indeed be a date, a blessed date, not merely in the history of Palestine, not merely in the history of Jewry, but, as I think and believe most firmly, in the history of the world itself."[5]

The Balfour Declaration was a unique, positive gesture from the British Cabinet to World Jewry. Even though it was a political statement, it was given in a spirit of biblical belief. It was an attempt by British Evangelicals to cooperate with the Jewish community in the restoration of Israel. The Balfour Declaration could not have been completely a Jewish enterprise because the Jewish community lacked the necessary unity, military power, and world support to act alone. It could not have been a completely Gentile enterprise, because one group of people could not impose a selected destiny upon another people. It had to be a partnership, as Balfour told an audience of British Jews, "We are partners in this great enterprise."[6]

In the minds of the writers of the Declaration, there were political factors motivating them, but for many of them, it was either partially or primarily a religious decision. The complexities of the political situation at hand gave this unique group of men the opportunity to carry out what they perceived to be a great historic accomplishment. The men of the Cabinet of 1917 were in the position to do something unprecedented to help the Jewish people, a people that according to their biblically conditioned views constituted God's Chosen People. From the time of the publishing of the Balfour Declaration, it provoked hostile responses. John Marlowe called Arthur Balfour the "ruthless dilettante," without whom "there would have been no National Home."[7] Elizabeth Monroe wrote that the Balfour Declaration was "one of the greatest mistakes in our imperial history."[8] Arnold Toynbee wrote, "I will say straight out; Balfour was a wicked man."[9]

The British began their adventure in Palestine with energy and positive intentions. The conquest of Palestine in 1917 was a remarkable military achievement. The relative ease of the campaign was a relief to the British people. General Allenby was a hero. Litvinoff pointed out the political legitimacy the Balfour Declaration gave to Zionism, "It gave the Jews secular 20th century legality for the return to the Holy Land, when hitherto that legality rested only on an ancient presence, a majestic literature and a mystical idea."[10]

A Diminished Commitment to Zionism Influences a Change of Heart

During the prolonged peace talks following the Great War, the influence of British Christian Zionism continued to shape events. Lloyd George, Balfour and other Zionists were still in power. They played a key role in the establishing their rule in Palestine between 1917 and 1922, as they succeeded in obtaining the Mandate from the new League of Nations. They even appointed a Jew, Herbert Samuel, to be the first High Commissioner of Palestine. In those early years, Zionism had the support of major personalities in the government who were still motivated by their Zionist religious commitments.

However, two problems appeared almost immediately. First, Arab resistance in Palestine challenged British authority, and second, decline in the influence of Christian Zionism in Britain gradually eroded British resolve. This decline in Christian support for Zionism was the primary reason for the eventual British departure from Palestine. Thereafter, the shift in British policy was, in great part, due to the decline in number and influence of similar personalities with such religious sentimentalities. In hindsight, it can be seen that the influence of Christian Zionism in Britain peaked in 1917, and experienced a long gradual decline thereafter.

Politicians sympathetic to the restoration of Israel such as Lloyd George, Smuts, and Balfour were not replaced by likeminded politicians of similar commitment. The growing indifference to Zionism was due largely to the fact that Evangelicals no longer influenced the key roles in London or Palestine to control government policy. Samuel and Plumer were supportive of Zionism is their roles as High Commissioner. Likewise, Churchill and Amery supported Zionism as best they could from the Colonial Office. This situation gradually changed after the Arab violence of 1928 and 1929.

When faced with Arab violence, Samuel replaced his Zionist ideals with a political pragmatism that he hoped would better serve all the communities of Palestine. Winston Churchill, despite a lifetime of commitment to Zionism, once appointed Colonial Secretary, opted for a broader, more regional approach. His 1922 White Paper was a shocking disappointment to Zionists, and in the end provided no appeasement to the Arabs. Yet, some Zionists still believed there was enough territory west of the Jordan River to establish a Jewish National Home. Martin Gilbert even asserted that Churchill's time at the Colonial Office was good for Zionism.[11]

Britain changed dramatically during the 1920's. The Great War had had a devastating effect on society. The social and political influence of the Bible and the Churches in Britain diminished. The Evangelicals of Britain, who had enjoyed power and influence during the late 19th century, were severely weakened. Not only were the Evangelicals in decline, but they were now more fractured in their voting patterns. The collapse of the Liberal Party after 1922 paralleled the decline in Evangelical Christian political influence. The resulting fragmentation of votes translated into a less focused political influence for Evangelicals and their ideals. A variety of religious factors played a part in the decline of the Evangelicals during the years following the Great War: the development of secular rationalism, Higher Criticism of the Scriptures, the growth of commercialism and the propagation of the scientific theory of the evolution of the species.

In Britain, with a falling trust in the authority of the Scriptures, there was no longer a fervent belief in the prophecies of the Bible. In hindsight, the bond that existed between British Evangelicals and Jewish Zionists lasted only for a brief moment in history. Both groups had agreed on a common goal; the restoration of the Jews to Palestine. Now that dream was being entrusted more and more to pragmatic, secularly minded politicians.

Despite numerical declines, the cause of Zionism still enjoyed the support of some influential Britons in the 1920's and 1930's. Philip Snowdon, Malcolm MacDonald and Arthur Henderson were some who still backed the ideals of Zionism. As encouraging as this was to the Zionists, these secondary personalities did not carry the political weight of earlier proponents. As well, certain elder statesmen such as Balfour, Lloyd George and Smuts still advocated the Zionist cause, but these men represented an influence from the past and not the current political power base.

The decline of British Evangelicals during the 1920's was correspondingly matched by the dramatic rise in the numbers and influence of Evangelicals in the United States during these years. With this rise in America came an increased interest in Zionism within the Churches and in politics. Although the American government still lacked the will and position to make its voice known, the day would come when American Christian Zionism would influence events in Palestine in a major way.

Violent Arab riots in Palestine in late 1928 and 1929 signaled a turning point in the Mandate. Increasing numbers of British troops and police were sent to Palestine in an attempt to quell the violence. After 1929, in the face of this opposition, the British attempted to show equal favour to the Jews and the Arabs. The government was unprepared for the sudden rise of Muslim opposition in Palestine and with a diminished commitment to Zionism at home. They were prepared to consider a new political course.

During the 1930's, most of the influential war leaders who backed the Balfour Declaration were out of power or had died. There was no clear political procedure of how to implement the intention of the Balfour Declaration. The High Commissioners of the 1930's each had their unique influence. Plumer and Wauchope favoured Zionism while Chancellor and MacMichael were opposed to it. During these years, British government policy in Palestine continued to change in light of the growing rift between the Jews and Arabs. Chancellor became the first High Commissioner to conclude that the Balfour Declaration was a blunder.[12] A series of government reports attempted to analyze the situation in Palestine and recommend solutions.[13] All three resulting reports were unacceptable to the Zionists. The Passfield White Paper of 1930 was overruled by Ramsay MacDonald's letter of 1931. His motives for intervening remain unclear. He may have acted on behalf of Labour Party politics, or he may have been compelled by his own personal sympathy to Zionism.

The Peel Commission Report of 1937 further distanced the government from the original intentions of the 1917 Cabinet. The Report illustrated changing British foreign policy in Palestine that no longer represented the spirit of the Balfour Declaration. During these years, new voices for Zionism participated in the debate. Men such as Wedgewood, Meinertzhagen, Wingate, Amery and Ormsby-Gore worked for the cause of Christian Zionism as they were able. Despite the fact that he was languishing in his self-described "Wilderness Years," Churchill continued to speak against government policies in Palestine and on behalf of Zionism.

During the 1930's, British society changed and with it the mindset of their political leaders and their foreign policy. Still, for much of the Mandate, some Zionists had widespread and high access to British political power. The Arabs never enjoyed this privilege in Britain. Blanche Dugdale (Balfour's niece) was a close friend of both Jewish leaders and important British politicians. Throughout the Mandate, Chaim Weizmann was a regular dinner companion with Winston Churchill, Clement Attlee, Archibald Sinclair (leader of the Liberal Party) and others.[14] The close nature of these relationships points out the real sympathy many British politicians maintained for Zionism. The Arabs of Palestine never enjoyed such favour and were frustrated with their lack of political success during the Mandate.

During this decade, the Evangelicals in the United States continued to expand in numbers and influence. President Hoover and diplomat James McDonald were especially supportive of Zionism. The establishment of the American Palestine Committee helped to move the cause of Christian Zionism from the Churches to the political arena.

In Britain, the governments of Baldwin and Chamberlain showed little interest in Zionism. By this time, the Evangelical influence in Britain offered less support to Zionism as many of the Churches of Britain adopted the doctrine of Replacement Theology, a belief system that no longer counted the Jewish people as the divinely Chosen People.

The 1939 White Paper was the government response to three years of Arab violence, bringing a new government policy to Palestine for the next five years. The outbreak of World War 2 in the autumn of

1939 delayed British consideration of departure from Palestine. The government was adamant about the five-year implementation of the White Paper, despite the hardships of the war.

In the late 1930's and 1940's, successive British governments tried to please both the Jews and the Arabs, but in the end, pleased no one. Zionists viewed High Commissioner MacMichael negatively as he abided by the White Paper and at times seemed extreme in the carrying out this policy. As the new Prime Minister, Churchill focused his attentions mainly on the war effort, but attempted to do some significant things for Zionism. Most noteworthy was his intervention with Roosevelt regarding delaying a majority vote in Palestine.

During World War 2, the declining influence of British Evangelicals corresponded with a similar decline in the voice of British Christian Zionism. By the 1940's, it was becoming evident to British politicians that the commitments implied by the Balfour Declaration were bringing unexpected hardship upon the Empire. Even though the British had entered the Middle East with good intentions, they were entangled in something beyond their control. The sentiments of the British government were now swinging to the Arabs. In 1943 Anthony Eden said, "If I must have preferences, let me murmur in your ear that I prefer Arabs to Jews."[15]

Near the end of the war, two eccentric, but significant, Christian Zionists, Josiah Wedgewood and Orde Wingate, died. They were among the last passionate British spokesmen for the cause of Christian Zionism. Meanwhile in America, Evangelical Christians were growing in numbers and were increasing their vocal support for Zionist aspirations. The public political work of the American Palestine Committee was important during the war, and set the stage for future American political involvement in Palestine.

As MacMichael left Palestine, the arrival of Lord Gort as the new High Commissioner was mildly effective in soothing tensions. At the death of Roosevelt, Vice President Harry Truman automatically became President. Regarding Palestine, President Truman's views, at first, were not clearly known. With the growing influence of the United States in the world, Zionists tried to anticipate how the new President might view their cause. In the beginning, he simply adhered to Roosevelt's policy of non-involvement.

With the end of the war in Europe, both the British and Americans anticipated a complicated situation in Palestine. Arab oil was now a major issue to the western developed nations. It was also understood in London and Washington that the Arabs in Palestine would react violently to any increase in Jewish immigration. Although Truman sympathized with Jewish suffering in Europe, he had still not yet actively supported the Zionist cause.

In Britain, Churchill's wartime coalition government was replaced with a new Labour government under Clement Attlee. At first, there seemed to be some hope for Zionists since the Labour Party had a tradition of supporting Zionism and had promised support at its 1944 Conference. However, Attlee and his new Foreign Minister, Ernest Bevin, displayed an attitude of antagonism to Zionism, partly based on a fearful desire to appease the Arabs, but mostly based on an indifference to Zionism. One of the main items on the agenda for the new Labour government was an exit strategy for Palestine. No longer did the government of Britain look with favour upon a Jewish National Home in Palestine.[16]

When the full scale of the Holocaust became known at the end of the war, many Jews concluded that the restrictive policies of the 1939 White Paper had contributed to the deaths of many Jews of Europe. One survivor of Auschwitz, Shalom Lindenbaum, believed of the White Paper, "It was an appeasement, a political appeasement and paid with the blood of the Jews."[17] In Palestine, the Jewish community responded to the British with anger and violence. Perhaps had the Conservatives formed a government in 1945, they may have assisted the Zionists. Churchill claimed as much in the House of Commons in August 1946, "Had I the opportunity of guiding the course of events after the war was won a year ago, I should have faithfully pursued the Zionist cause as I have defined it; and I have not abandoned it today, although this is not a very popular moment to espouse it."[18]

In Britain, the voice of Christian Zionism was muted during these post war years as Churchill took his place on the political sidelines. The role of Leader of the Opposition was not a mantle he took on easily, and he did not at first diligently engage himself in Zionist affairs. In October 1947, the editor of the *Jewish Telegraphic Agency* wrote, "With regard to Mr. Churchill, I would like to say that just at this moment he has more or less withdrew from Zionist work because he is disgusted by the terrorists and terrorism, and it is not easy to get him back into a proper frame of mind."[19]

In Jerusalem, Lord Gort and Cunningham were viewed as High Commissioners who were competent, fair-minded men, somewhat in favour of Zionism, who were attempting to hold control over a lost enterprise. In Palestine, during these last years of the Mandate, there was growing anti-Zionism and anti-Semitism among some of the British officers and bureaucrats of the Mandate.

The political influence of Evangelical Christian Zionism in Britain continued to diminish in the post war years. Their position in Britain was so weak that Bevin was able to declare in the House of Commons, "Balfour is dead." Tuchman attempted to articulate the gradual change of mind the British had about Zionism throughout the Mandate period. "The original pledge, which she soon found was awkward to keep, she attempted thereafter to whittle away, to invalidate, and at last, desperately weary of the entanglement, to cancel."[20]

In contrast to what was happening in Britain, the Evangelical Christians in America continued to grow in numbers and influence following World War 2. The United States emerged from the war as the most powerful nation in the world, willing and able to exert her influence. Contrary to Roosevelt's indifference to Zionism, Truman's evolving interest in the cause would come to represent America new foreign policy. The British decision to involve the Americans in deciding the future of Palestine resulted in the formation of the Anglo-American Committee who recommended partition. Truman risked a great deal supporting partition in 1947 as he acted to a large degree on his religious faith.

When the United Nations partition vote passed, the way was open for both the Jews and the Arabs of Palestine to each have political autonomy. Within six months, the British would be gone. The opportunity for independence waited for those who would seize it. However, it would now fall to the Americans, not the British, to assist the restoration of Israel.

The United States Facilitates the Zionist Dream

Christian Zionism was a significant factor behind American recognition of the new State of Israel in the spring of 1948. American recognition of Israel was not solely motivated by a policy of appealing to Jewish votes, nor was it simply part of a Cold War strategy. Rather, it resulted to a large degree from the growing influence of Christian Zionism in the nation and the personal religious beliefs of President Truman. In making his decision, Truman went against the advice of Secretary of State George Marshall and the State Department. The argument about Jewish voters turned out to be hollow. Truman lost Jewish votes in the 1948 campaign, but still won the election.

On May 14 1948, within minutes of Ben Gurion proclaiming the establishment of a Jewish State, Truman gave instructions to recognize the new State of Israel. News of the American recognition reached the provisional government gathered in Tel Aviv almost immediately. On that same day, Truman invited Weizmann to visit the White House. The American lead probably prompted the Soviet Union and several other countries to recognize Israel in the next few days.

During the 31 years from the Balfour Declaration to the American recognition of Israel, Evangelicalism and Christian Zionism had grown in size and force in the United States, while at the same time these beliefs had significantly declined in Britain. This is a significant factor in understanding both the British abandonment of Palestine and the American recognition of Israel in 1948.

Christian Zionism was long established in American Evangelical Christianity and contributed to a mindset of philosemitism and support for the restoration of Israel. Furthermore, Christian Zionism in America in 1948 was not a belief merely based on historical memory, but rather was a mindset that was alive and growing. Truman shared this religious belief, and after long reflection, made his decision to support partition, and then to unilaterally recognize the new state of Israel. The new Israeli nation was indebted to

Evangelical Christian Americans and to the personal intervention of Harry Truman.

Following Israeli independence, President Truman continued to assist the new Jewish nation. He asked James McDonald to be the first American ambassador to Israel. As Truman's personal choice, McDonald was an Evangelical Christian, and a committed Zionist. In circumventing the State Department to make this appointment, Truman was able to personally install a fellow Christian Zionist into this significant role. Michael Cohen recognized the uniqueness of the Gentile interest in Zionism. As he studied the phenomenon, he concluded that Christian Zionism was "motivated initially by Protestant Evangelical doctrine."[21]

The restoration of the State of Israel presented a profound theological question for any Christian. If the doctrine of Replacement Theology is accepted, then the restoration of Israel is a serious theological problem. However, if one believes the biblical prophets predicted a revived Israel, then the idea of a new Jewish State is welcomed with excitement. Paul Merkley wrote, "Thus, when Israel reappeared among the nations in a moment of time in the character of a State, the problem of the relationship between the destiny of the Jews and the destiny of the Church had to be restated. From one point of view, it became simpler, from another, more complicated."[22]

Merkley recognized the different doctrinal distinctions between various American Church denominations and concluded that it was within the Protestant dissenting camp that Zionism found a home.

> In 1947-48, that part of the Church in the West that is today called "fundamentalist" or "Evangelical" was overwhelmingly supportive of the Zionist solution to the Jewish problem. The rest of the Protestant Church was mostly well disposed, but with many dissenters. The Roman Catholic Church had powerful objections but did not feel able, in the light of the general humanitarian advantage that the Jewish cause briefly held in the immediate wake of the war, to compel nations with Roman Catholic populations to oppose.[23]

According to Peter Gardella, American sympathies for Zionism began early in her history. "American support for Israel began with Puritan hopes for the end of the world."[24] Even though America had a long history of neo-Puritan philosemitism, it was only in 1948 that she began her special support relationship with Israel. With Truman, the Evangelical pro-Zionist baton was passed to the Americans.

The British lost a great deal in their final handling of the Palestine Mandate. John Marlowe wrote, "The history of the Palestine Mandate is the history of a Jewish triumph, of an Arab tragedy and of a British failure."[25] Harris wrote in his biography of Attlee, "Britain left India with the good will and respect of the main communities in conflict; she left Palestine her name anathema to Jews and Arabs, her relationship with the United States embittered, and her reputation in the rest of the world embittered."[26]

For the British, the departure from Palestine was in some ways a relief, but was also a painful disappointment. The situation in Palestine had changed so much from 1917 to 1948. Various Jewish resistance groups claimed responsibility for pushing the British out, but from the British perspective, they left on their own. Despite their losses, had they been committed ideologically, they might have stayed longer. From the Balfour Declaration of 1917 to the final British departure from Palestine in 1948, the British nation largely changed its attitude toward the concept of the restoration of Israel. Frank Buxton, one of the members of the Anglo-American Committee, believed the changing British foreign policy damaged her reputation.

> There was a time...when England was so strong that muddling-through and stupidity were not especially harmful to her, she had so much reserve strength that she could retrieve her blunders. But now...stupidity and shortsightedness are unforgivable sins and may inflict wounds from which she cannot recover.[27]

In London, the British government initially decided not to recognize the new State of Israel. Bevin was angry and felt personally insulted by events in Palestine. He compared the new Israelis to

Nazis. In the House of Commons, Churchill expressed his delight at the new nation of Israel. Throughout 1948, the British government continued to refuse to recognize the new Jewish State.

Once the Israelis achieved independence, they were better able to objectively evaluate the motives of the British, but many still concluded that Britain betrayed them. According to Neomi Izhar, curator at the former British Detention Camp at Atlit, "If not the British, we may not have the State of Israel…on the other hand since Britain realized the power of the oil and the power of the Arabic countries who was around…they considered them much more than they considered the Jewish issue (sic)."[28]

Still, some British Gentiles maintained their commitment to Zionism all their lives. Richard Meinertzhagen was an example of an unselfishly committed Christian Zionist who held to his views even though there was no apparent personal benefit for himself. Peter Capstick saw Meinertzhagen as a "…staunch supporter of the Zionist cause and the Jews in the founding of the State of Israel in 1948. It was a burning loyalty to the end of his long life…"[29] Chapman wrote of Meinertzhagen, "The foundations Dick was laying now were to hold a lifetime of strong beliefs and take him into many a fray, often at the highest levels, as he fought for the Zionist cause and a home for the Jewish people. This cannot be done if the foundations of convictions are a mere veneer."[30]

Regardless of the pain and frustration of the Mandate period for the British, the intention of the Balfour Declaration became a reality. Cecil Roth credited the Balfour Declaration with playing a necessary part in Israeli independence. "It was the policy based on that Declaration, however hesitantly which made possible the laying of the foundations of the state of Israel."[31] By almost any measurement, compared to the other communities of the region, the Jews made the best use of the possibilities offered to them in 1948.

In due time, Christian Zionists witnessed not only the return of the Jews to their ancient land, but the restoration of the nation of Israel as a prosperous thriving democracy. It is an irony of history that Christianity, born in the land of Israel 2000 years before, would in turn help give birth again to the Jewish nation in the 20th century.

During the second decade of the 21st century, the Israeli-Arab conflict in the Middle East continues to be a source of many of the world's problems. On a rational level, it might seem prudent for the United States to withdraw her support for Israel and placate the Arab nations of the Middle East. There could conceivable be much to gain by winning the good opinion of over 20 Muslim nations. In contrast, having the favour of one small Jewish State does not seem so appealing. In the years ahead, the United States will undoubtedly reconsider her continued support for the ideal of biblical Zionism. The pages of history lay blank before us.

NOTES

❖ ❖ ❖

Overview
[1] Roger Finke and Rodney Stark, *The Churching of America, 1776-1990*, p. 16.
[2] Ibid.
[3] Ibid.
[4] Pew Research Center's Forum on Religion and Public Life, January 5, 2011.

Introduction
[1] Benson, Michael T., *Harry S. Truman and the Founding of Israel* (New York: McGraw Hill, 1997).
Cohen, Michael J., "Why Britain Left: The End of the Mandate," *The Weiner Library Bulletin*, Vol. 31, No. 44/46, 1978, pp. 74-86.
_____ *Churchill and the Jews* (London: Frank Cass, 1985).
_____ "Churchill and Zionism," Published Lecture Notes (London: Hillel House, March 13, 1974).
_____ and Kolinsky, Martin (eds.) *Demise of the British Empire in the Middle East* (London: Frank Cass, 1998).
Cohen, Michael J., *Palestine and the Great Powers 1945-1948* (New Jersey: Princeton University Press, 1982).
_____ *Palestine to Israel-From Mandate to Independence* (London: Frank Cass & Co. Ltd., 1988).
_____ *Retreat From the Mandate: The Making of British Policy 1936-1945* (London: Paul Elek, 1978).
_____*Truman and Israel* (Oxford: University of California Press, 1990).
Friedman, Isaiah, *The Question of Palestine, 1914-1918* (London: Routledge & Kegan, 1973).
Gardella, Peter, "Gentile Zionism," *Midstream* 37:4, May 1991, pp. 29-32.
Koestler, Arthur, *Promise and Fulfillment, Palestine 1917-1949* (London: Macmillian & Co. Ltd., 1949).
Kolinsky, Martin, *Britain's War in the Middle East, Strategy and Diplomacy, 1936-42* (London: MacMillian, 1999).
Levene, Mark, "Edge of Darkness," *Jewish Quarterly*, 3, 1991, pp. 31-36.

Louis, William Roger, *The British Empire in the Middle East 1945-1951* (Oxford: Clarendon Press, 1984).

_____ *The End of the Palestine Mandate* (London: I.B. Tauris & Co. Ltd., 1986).

Perko, F. Michael, "Contemporary American Christian Attitudes to Israel Based on Scriptures," *Israel Studies* Vol. 8, No. 2, Summer 2003, pp. 1-17.

Reinharz, Jehuda, "The Balfour Declaration and It's Maker: A Reassessment," *Journal of Modern History,* Vol. 3, 1992, pp. 455- 499.

Rose, Norman, *The Gentile Zionists* (London: Frank Cass, 1973).

Roth, Cecil, *Essays and Portraits in Anglo-Jewish History* (Philadelphia: The Jewish Society of America, 1962).

_____ *Remember the Days* (London: The Jewish Historical Society of England, 1966).

Sanders, Ronald, *The High Walls of Jerusalem* (New York: Holt, Rinehart and Winston, 1983).

Segev, Tom, *One Palestine, Complete* (New York: Metropolitan Books, 2000).

Shepherd, Naomi, *Alarms and Excursions* (London: Collins, 1990).

_____ *Plowing Sand-British Rule in Palestine 1917-1948* (London: Collins, 1999).

_____*The Zealous Intruders-The Western Rediscovery of Palestine*, (London: Collins, 1987).

Stein, Leonard, *The Balfour Declaration* (Jerusalem: The Magnes Press, Hebrew University, 1983).

_____ *Weizmann and England* (London: W. H. Allen, 1964).

_____ *Zionism* (London: Ernest Benn Ltd., 1925).

Tuchman, Barbara, *Bible and Sword: How the British Came to Palestine* (New York: New York University, 1956).

Verete, Mayir, *From Palmerston to Balfour: Selected Essays of Mayir Verete* (London: Frank Cass, 1992).

Verete, Mayir, "The Balfour Declaration and It's Makers," *Middle Eastern Studies*, January 1970, pp. 1-37.

Wasserstein, Bernard, *Britain and the Jews of Europe 1939-1945* (Oxford: Clarendon Press, 1979).

_____*The British in Palestine: The Mandatory Government and the Arab-Jewish Conflict 1917-1929* (London: Royal Historical Society, 1978).

[2] Christian Zionism overlaps with, but is distinct from, the 19th century movement for the Restoration of the Jews to the Holy Land which had both religiously and politically motivated supporters.

[3] Biblical passages used to support Christian Zionism are primarily the Old Testament Jewish prophets such as Isaiah and Ezekiel and the New Testament books of Romans and Revelation.

[4] Paul Charles Merkley, *Christian Attitudes toward the State of Israel*, p. 6.

[5] Based on such biblical prophecies as Ezekiel 37:22, "*And I will make them one nation in the land upon the mountain of Israel, and one king shall be king to them all.*"

6 Kelvin Crombie, *For the Love of Zion*, p. 11.
7 Herbert Samuel, *Memoirs*, p. 147.
8 Paul Charles Merkley, *Christian Attitudes toward the State of Israel*, p. 4.
9 Specifically Deuteronomy chapter 31, Ezekiel chapter 36, and the words of Jesus in Matthew 24.
10 Paul Charles Merkley, Christian Attitudes toward the State of Israel, p. 5.
11 This "more direct understanding" of Scripture is sometimes referred to as a "literal" interpretation of the Bible. Throughout this book, various academics and clergy members are quoted using the term "literal," even though it is not a term used by this author. The interpretation of any passage of Scripture has to take into account the historical and grammatical context of the text. It should be understood that the scope of the biblical subject matter of this book is limited to some aspects of eschatological prophecy.
12 Roger Finke and Rodney Stark, *The Churching of America, 1776-1990*, p. 16.
13 The land was promised to Abraham in Genesis 12:7, to Isaac in Genesis 26:3-4 and to Jacob in Genesis 28:13.
14 The term "Hebrew" seems to be derived from the Hebrew root "AVR" meaning to "cross over." This could be explained as a reference to Abraham crossing over the Euphrates River to arrive in Canaan.
15 It is from this name of Jerusalem that the term "Zion" or "Zionism" is derived.
16 The 6th century BCE Jewish return from Babylon is recorded in the TNK books of Ezra and Nehmiah. The one independent Jewish regime following the Babylon return was under the Maccabees during the intertestamental period in the 1st and 2nd centuries BCE.
17 The term "Jew" was taken from the name of one of Jacob's sons, "Yehudah" or "Judah."
18 Steven Runciman, *A History of the Crusades*, Vol. 1, p. 3.
19 It was also during the Crusades that hostility toward the Jews led to their expulsion from England in 1290.
20 Barbara Tuchman, *Bible and Sword: How the British Came to Palestine*, p. 53.
21 Steven Runciman, *A History of the Crusades*, Vol. 1, p. 3.
22 Ibid, p. 50.
23 Ibid, p. 107-108.
24 Barbara Tuchman, *Bible and Sword: How the British Came to Palestine*, p. ix.
25 Peter Capstick, *Warrior, The Legend of Colonel Richard Meinertzhagen* p. 249.
26 Silas Perry, *Britain Opens a Gateway* p. 9.
27 Barbara Tuchman, *Bible and Sword: How the British Came to Palestine*, p. 80.
28 Ibid, p. 1.
29 Ibid, p. 80.
30 Silas Perry, *Britain Opens a Gateway*, p. 22.
31 Barbara Tuchman, *Bible and Sword: How the British Came to Palestine*, p. 59, 81.
32 Arthur Balfour, *Speeches on Zionism*, p. 79.

33 Augustine, *The City of God*, Book 18:53, Book 18:28, in Ronald R. Stockton, "Christian Zionism: Prophecy and Public Opinion" p. 235.

34 Yaakov Ariel, *On Behalf of Israel, American Fundamentalist Attitudes Toward Jews, Judaism, and Zionism, 1865-1945*, p. 11.

35 Ibid.

36 The most common list of Christian Evangelical Pre-millennial Dispensations are: 1. The Dispensation of Innocence (Genesis 1:1–3:7), prior to Adam's fall. 2. The Dispensation of Conscience (Genesis 3:8–8:22), Adam to Noah. 3. The Dispensation of government (Genesis 9:1–11:32), Noah to Abraham. 4. The Dispensation of Patriarchal Rule (Genesis 12:1–Exod 19:25), Abraham to Moses. 5. The Dispensation of the Mosaic Law (Exodus 20:1–Acts 2:4), Moses to Christ. 6. The Dispensation of Grace (Acts 2:4–Revelation 20:3 the current Church age. 7. The Dispensation of the Messianic Millennial Kingdom, 1000 years, that has yet to come but soon will (Revelation 20:4–20:6). From the notes in the Scofield Bible, in C.I. Scofield, *The New Scofield Reference Bible*. (New York: Oxford University Press, 1976). A definition of the seven ages of Dispensationalism can be found in Sydney Ahlstrom, "A Religious History of the American People."

37 Yaakov Ariel, *American Premillennialism and its Attitudes Toward Jewish People, Judaism and Zionism, 1875-1925*, p. 2. Also see, Ernest R. Sandeen, *The Roots of Fundamentalism* (Grand Rapids: Baker Book House, 1978).

38 Yaakov Ariel, *On Behalf of Israel, American Fundamentalist Attitudes Toward Jews, Judaism, and Zionism, 1865-1945*, p. 11.

39 Michael Pragai, *Faith and Fulfillment-Christians and the Return to the Promised Land*, p. 147.

40 Herzl met Pope Pius X in the Vatican on January 25 1904, in Michael Pragai, *Faith and Fulfillment-Christians and the Return to the Promised Land*, p. 150.

41 Earle Cairns, *Christianity Through the Centuries*, p. 356.

42 Yaakov Ariel, *American Premillennialism and its Attitudes Toward Jewish People, Judaism and Zionism, 1875-1925*, p. 2.

43 The rapture is the Evangelical Christian belief that as part of the end of this Dispensation, true Christians will be taken up into heaven, see the New Testament letter from Paul to the Church of Thessalonica, 1 Thessalonians 4:13-18, in Yaakov Ariel, *On Behalf of Israel, American Fundamentalist Attitudes Toward Jews, Judaism, and Zionism, 1865-1945*, p. 94.

44 In 1905, Conservative Prime Minister Arthur Balfour's government passed the Aliens Act. The Bill was widely regarded as primarily intended to block the arrival of Jewish immigrants from eastern Europe. The final Bill was much revised due to pressure from the Liberals. Although this Bill could have suggested Balfour was anti-Semitic, his broader actions on behalf of the Jews would say otherwise.

45 From a memorandum Samuel wrote to the Cabinet in January 1915, Herbert Samuel, *Memoirs*, p. 3ff.

Chapter One: The Role of Christian Zionism behind the Balfour Declaration in 1917

[1] Arthur Balfour, *Speeches on Zionism*, p. 128.

[2] Since the outbreak of the Great War in 1914, the Cabinet of Prime Minister H. H. Asquith had gradually grown in size. After the Cabinet swelled to twenty-three men, it became too bulky to deal with the complex issues of the war and the whole Cabinet resigned. On December 4, Asquith offered his resignation to the King, and the King asked Andrew Bonar Law to form a government. However, Asquith refused to serve under Bonar Law. On December 7, Lloyd George became Prime Minister, in Christopher Lee, *This Sceptred Isle: Twentieth Century*, p. 102.

[3] Both Herbert Samuel and Lloyd George had been in the Asquith Cabinet.

[4] Probably Asquith found Lloyd Georges Zionism curious because Lloyd George was not Jewish, in Herbert Samuel, *Memoirs*, p. 143.

[5] Chaim Weizmann, *Trial and Error*, p. 151.

[6] A.J. Sylvester, *Life with Lloyd George, The Diary of A.J. Sylvester, 1931-1945*, p. 143.

[7] Frank Dilnot, *Lloyd George, The Man and His Story*, p. 37.

[8] Ibid, p. 21.

[9] The disestablishment of the Anglican Church in Wales occurred early in 1914.

[10] Herbert H. Asquith, *Memories and Reflections 1852-1937, Vol. I-II*, p. 219.

[11] Arthur Koestler, *Promise and Fulfillment*, p. 7.

[12] Successive editions of Encyclopaedia Judaica claiming this theory as fact convinced generations of Israelis, Jewish communities worldwide and many Arabs that this was the only motivation behind the Balfour Declaration.

[13] Palestine Royal Commission Report, (Peel Commission Report), July 1937, p. 17.

[14] Ibid.

[15] CAB, Cabinet Minutes, 24 143.

[16] Ibid, 23/4, no. 257 (12).

[17] David Lloyd George, *The Truth About the Peace Treaties II*, p. 1135ff.

[18] Leonard Stein, *The Balfour Declaration*, p. 516.

[19] David Lloyd George, *War Memoirs of David Lloyd George, II*, p. 586.

[20] Leonard Stein, *The Balfour Declaration*, p. 551.

[21] Encyclopaedia Judaica, 1972 ed., "Balfour Declaration," by Leonard Stein.

[22] Leonard Stein, *The Balfour Declaration*, p. 552.

[23] Isaiah Friedman, *The Question of Palestine: 1914-1918*, p. 290.

[24] The so-called Sykes Picot Agreement was the name given to the result of negotiations at the end of 1915 and beginning of 1916 between Mark Sykes of Britain and F. Georges Picot of France concerning the partition of the Ottoman Empire, including Palestine.

[25] The meeting supposedly took place on February 7 1917 in Rabbi Gaster's home, in Isaiah Friedman, *The Question of Palestine, 1914-1918*, p. 64.

[26] Mayir Verete, *From Palmerston to Balfour: Selected Essays of Mayir Verete*, p. 22.
[27] Ibid, p. 23.
[28] Leonard Stein, *The Balfour Declaration*, p. 122.
[29] Blanche Dugdale, *Arthur James Balfour*, p. 231.
[30] Encyclopaedia Judaica, 1972 ed., "Balfour, Arthur James." by Leonard Stein.
[31] Martin Gilbert, *Churchill: A Photographic Portrait*, p. 192.
[32] Perhaps John Buchan influenced Lloyd George at this time. Buchan was the Director of Information for the British government during the Lloyd George administration. Buchan was best known as the writer of the classic spy novel *Thirty Nine Steps*. The plot of the book is that a world conspiracy controlled governments, having the influence to initiate and terminate wars. This thinking was prevalent in the 1930's and perhaps Lloyd George made use of it.
[33] David Lloyd George, *The Truth About the Peace Treaties*, p. 721ff.
[34] David Lloyd George, *War Memoirs of David Lloyd George, II*, p. 586.
[35] David Fromkin, *A Peace to End all Peace*, p. 285.
[36] Richard Meinertzhagen, *Middle East Diary: 1917-1956*, p. 9.
[37] Meinertzhagen's credibility is validated by the influential positions he held, serving as Allenby's intelligence officer, liaison to the King V, Winston Churchill's personal secretary, and special envoy to Adolf Hitler.
[38] Mark Levene, "Edge of Darkness," p. 31.
[39] Jehuda Reinharz, "The Balfour Declaration and It's Maker," p. 493.
[40] Future Israeli Prime Minister Menachem Begin was an example of someone who contributed to the widespread acceptance of this theory. He was cynical of Britain's intentions toward Zionism. Begin believed Britain wanted Palestine for the sake of imperial power, but had to be "clever" about it. To Begin, the purpose behind the Balfour Declaration was, "to back a great ideal which would enable Britain to take control of Palestine without seeming to." Begin saw the Balfour Declaration as a way that Britain would promise the Jews a "home in Palestine," not "Palestine as a home." Britain would then have Palestine for herself and the Jews would have a home in it. In order to appreciate the opinions of Menachem Begin, it is necessary to contextualize the time of his writings. He was politically active in Palestine late in the Mandate when relations with Britain had soured. By the 1930's and 1940's, Begin saw the British as an enemy, in Menachem Begin, *The Revolt*, p. 31.
[41] Mayir Verete, "Kitchener, Grey and the Question of Palestine in 1915-16," p. 43.
[42] John Marlowe, *Arab Nationalism and British Imperialism, A Study in Power Politics*, p. 31.
[43] Isaiah Friedman, *The Question of Palestine: 1914-1918*, p. 291.
[44] Balfour's statement to the Cabinet was made on October 31 1917, in CAB, Cabinet Minutes, 23/4, no. 261 (12).
[45] Mayir Verete, *From Palmerston to Balfour: Selected Essays of Mayir Verete*, p. 25.
[46] Mayir Verete, "The Balfour Declaration and It's Makers," p. 51.

[47] Mayir Verete, *The Balfour Declaration and It's Makers*, p. 51.
[48] In a way, the Sykes Picot agreement represented one of the last vestiges of the 19th century "Great Game," where France and Britain conspired to keep Russian influence out of Central Asia and the Middle East.
[49] Mayir Verete, "The Balfour Declaration and It's Makers," p. 61.
[50] Ibid, p. 50.
[51] Ibid.
[52] Ibid, p. 52-53.
[53] Mayir Verete, "The Balfour Declaration and It's Makers," p. 53.
[54] Ibid, p. 52.
[55] Ibid, p. 63-64.
[56] Ibid, p. 67.
[57] From an article written in 1943 by Blanche Dugdale, in Paul Goodman, *The Jewish National Home*, p. 10.
[58] Eitan Bar Yosef, "Christian Zionism and Victorian Culture," p. 37.
[59] Ibid, p. 39.
[60] From a memorandum from Samuel to the Cabinet in January 1915, "The Future of Palestine," Oxford, MECA, Samuel Papers, Box 1, Breakup of the Ottoman Empire (Palestine).
[61] *Balfour Declaration*, Encyclopaedia Judaica, (Jerusalem: Keter Publishing, 1972 ed.) and Avraham Sela, *Political Encyclopedia of the Middle East* (Jerusalem: The Jerusalem Publishing House Limited, 1999).
[62] Leonard Stein, *The Balfour Declaration*, p. 135.
[63] Herbert Samuel, *Memoirs*, p. 147.
[64] Franz Kobler, *The Vision Was There*, p. 120.
[65] Leonard Stein, *The Balfour Declaration*, p. 474.
[66] Ibid
[67] Vladimir Halperin, *Lord Milner and the Empire*, p. 170.
[68] Ibid.
[69] Isaiah Friedman, *The Question of Palestine 1914-1918*, p. 257-258.
[70] Vladimir Halperin, *Lord Milner and the Empire*, p. 45-46.
[71] CAB, Cabinet Papers, 24/30 G.T. 2406.
[72] Curzon's statement in Cabinet was on October 4 1917, in Isaiah Friedman, *The Question of Palestine, 1914-1918*, p. 25.
[73] David Gilmour, *Curzon, Imperial Statesman*, p. 483.
[74] Barbara Tuchman, *Bible and Sword: How the British Came to Palestine*, p. 333.
[75] From a memorandum from Curzon to the Cabinet, October 26 1917, in David Lloyd George, *The Truth About the Peace Treaties II*, p. 1123.
[76] David Gilmour, *Curzon, Imperial Statesman*, p. 482.
[77] Leonard Stein, *The Balfour Declaration*, p. 474.
[78] Ibid.
[79] Isaiah Friedman, *The Question of Palestine*, p. 268.
[80] Leonard Mosley, *Curzon*, p. 165.

[81] In 1904, Curzon was Governor General of India. When a difference of opinion occurred between Curzon and Lord Kitchener, Curzon failed to obtain the support of Balfour's government.
[82] Leonard Stein, *The Balfour Declaration*, p. 475.
[83] Leonard Mosley, *Curzon*, p. 165.
[84] Sarah Millin, *General Smuts*, p. 166.
[85] It is doubtful that the majority of Jews at this time held "Zionist opinions." Curzon knew this. It is likely that Curzon was building the case against himself in order that his concession would be more dignified.
[86] CAB, Cabinet Papers, 23/4, no. 261 (12).
[87] Barbara Tuchman, *Bible and Sword, How the British Came to Palestine*, p. 347.
[88] Leonard Stein, *The Balfour Declaration*, p. 480-481.
[89] Gideon Shimoni, *Jews and Zionism: The South African Experience*.
[90] Jan Christian Smuts was Prime Minister of South Africa from 1939-1948.
[91] Leonard Stein, *The Balfour Declaration*, p. 483.
[92] Encyclopaedia Judaica, 1972 ed., "Smuts, Jan Christian."
[93] Jan C. Smuts, *A Great Historic Vow*, p. 1.
[94] The article appeared in the *Zionist Record*, February 1917, in Leonard Stein, *The Balfour Declaration*, p. 478.
[95] From a diary entry September 21 1917, Chaim Weizmann, *Trial and Error*, p. 258.
[96] Speech at Johannesburg, November 3 1919, in Leonard Stein, *The Balfour Declaration*, p. 59.
[97] CAB, Cabinet Papers, 24/24 G.T. 1868.
[98] Isaiah Friedman, *The Question of Palestine: 1914-1918*, p. 259.
[99] Ibid, p. 25.
[100] In the *Jewish Chronicle*, April 9, 1909.
[101] In the London *Times*. May 24, 1917, in Paul Mendes-Flohr, and Jehuda Reinharz, *The Jew in the Modern World*, p. 580.
[102] Stuart Cohen, *English Zionists and British Jews*, 1982, p. 155.
[103] Ibid, p 130.
[104] By Nathan Sokolow, Yehiel Tschlenow and Chaim Weizmann, in the *Jewish Chronicle*, December 21, 1917, p.16, in Paul Mendes-Flohr, and Jehuda Reinharz, *The Jew in the Modern World*, p. 580.
[105] *Jewish Chronicle*, November 19 1920, The National Archives, London, Zionism, FO 141 742/3.
[106] Cabinet discussion, October 4 1917, David Lloyd George, *The Truth About the Peace Treaties II*, p. 1134.
[107] Isaiah Friedman, *The Question of Palestine: 1914-1918*, p. 259.
[108] CAB, Cabinet Papers, 21/28 G.T. 2263.
[109] Chaim Weizmann, *Trial and Error*, p. 259-260.
[110] Palestine Royal Commission Report, (Peel Commission Report), July 1937, p. 18.
[111] Chaim Weizmann, *Trial and Error*, p. 194.

Partners Together in this Great Enterprise

[112] Letter from Amery to Carson, September 4 1917, Leo S. Amery, *The Leo Amery Diaries, Vol. I, 1896-1929,* p. 170.
[113] Balfour's mother wrote this prayer in 1851 at the age of 26. Barbara Tuchman, *Bible and Sword, How the British Came to Palestine,* p. 337.
[114] Blanche Dugdale, *The Balfour Declaration: Origins and Background,* p. 5.
[115] Barbara Tuchman, *Bible and Sword, How the British Came to Palestine,* p. 311.
[116] Leonard Stein, *The Balfour Declaration,* p. 428.
[117] Ibid, p. 159.
[118] Max Egremont, *Balfour,* p. 296.
[119] Speech on July 12 1920 in Arthur Balfour, *Speeches on Zionism,* p. 21.
[120] Leonard Stein, *The Balfour Declaration,* p. 59.
[121] Naomi Shepherd, *The Zealous Intruders-The Western Rediscovery of Palestine,* p. 14.
[122] Blanche Dugdale, *The Balfour Declaration: Origins and Background,* p.5.
[123] Blanche Dugdale, *The Balfour Declaration: It's Origins,* p. 4, in, Paul Goodman, *The Jewish National Home,* p. 4.
[124] Isaiah Friedman, *The Question of Palestine 1914-1918,* p. 138.
[125] Doreen Ingrams, *Palestine Papers 1917-1922: Seeds of Conflict,* p. 9.
[126] Barbara Tuchman, *Bible and Sword, How the British Came to Palestine,* p. 311.
[127] Ian Malcolm, *Lord Balfour, a Memory,* p. 93, (New Testament quote is 2 Timothy 4:7).
[128] "Alia" is the Hebrew term for Jewish immigration to Eretz Israel.
[129] Encyclopaedia Judaica, 1972 ed., "Balfour, Arthur James."
[130] From an article written in 1943 by Blanche Dugdale, in Paul Goodman, *The Jewish National Home,* p. 9.
[131] Barbara Tuchman, *Bible and Sword, How the British Came to Palestine,* p. 312.
[132] Henderson's conversion took place in 1879, in Colin Ford, *A Hundred Years Ago: Britain in the 1800's,* p. 200.
[133] Stephen Koss, *Nonconformity in Modern British Politics,* p. 149.
[134] John Grigg, *Lloyd George: From War to Peace,* p. 483.
[135] Colin Ford, *A Hundred Years Ago: Britain in the 1800's,* p. 200.
[136] Henry Pelling, *A Short History of the Labour Party,* p. 189.
[137] Colin Ford, *A Hundred Years Ago: Britain in the 1800's,* p. 200.
[138] War Aims Memorandum, Labour Party August 1917 from Joseph Gorny, *The British Labour Movement and Palestine 1917-1948,* p. 7.
[139] Jehuda Reinharz, *The Balfour Declaration and It's Maker,* p. 466.
[140] War Aims Memorandum, Labour Party August 1917, in Leonard Stein, *The Balfour Declaration,* p. 475.
[141] The other advocates mentioned are Milner, Smuts, Lloyd George and Balfour, in Leonard Stein, *The Balfour Declaration,* p. 476.
[142] George Barnes, *From the Workshop to the War Cabinet,* p. 63.

[143] Edward Marjoribanks, *The Life of Lord Carson*.
[144] Interview with Harold Arkell, Brantford Ontario, September 1995. Edward Carson died October 22 1935.
[145] David Lloyd George, *War Memoirs*, p. 1020.
[146] Leonard Stein, *The Balfour Declaration*, p. 474.
[147] Jonathan Bardon, *A History of Ulster*, p. 433.
[148] Encyclopaedia Britannica, 1974 ed., "Law, Andrew Bonar."
[149] Ibid.
[150] Leonard Stein, *The Balfour Declaration*, p. 473.
[151] Ibid.
[152] Robert Blake, *The Unknown Prime Minister*, p. 368.
[153] From an interview on October 19 1917, in Leonard Stein, *The Balfour Declaration*, p. 473.
[154] Robert Blake, *The Unknown Prime Minister*, p. 343.
[155] Leonard Stein, *The Balfour Declaration*, p. 474.
[156] Robert Blake, *The Unknown Prime Minister*, p. 533.
[157] Martin Gilbert, Lecture: *"Churchill and the Jews: A Lifelong Friendship,"* Kehilat Moreshet Avraham, East Talpiot, Jerusalem, February 24 2008.
[158] Robert Lloyd George, *David & Winston, How a Friendship Changed History*, p. 10.
[159] Chaim Weizmann, *Trial and Error*, p. 152.
[160] Ibid.
[161] Robert Lloyd George, *David & Winston, How a Friendship Changed History*, p. 176.
[162] Leonard Stein, *The Balfour Declaration*, p. 142.
[163] Mayir Verete, *From Palmerston to Balfour: Selected Essays of Mayir Verete*, p. 1.
[164] Isaiah Friedman, *The Question of Palestine 1914-1918*, p. 284.
[165] David Fromkin, *A Peace to End All Peace*, p. 267.
[166] Graham Davies, *The Chosen People, Wales and Jews*, p. 92.
[167] Encyclopaedia Judaica, 1972 ed., "Lloyd George, David."
[168] Graham Davies, *The Chosen People, Wales and Jews*, p. 93.
[169] Encyclopaedia Britannica, 1974 ed., "Lloyd George, David."
[170] Ibid.
[171] A. J. Sylvester, *Life with Lloyd George, The Diary of A.J. Sylvester, 1931-1945*, p. 142.
[172] Arthur Koestler, *Promise and Fulfillment*, p. 6.
[173] Barbara Tuchman, *Bible and Sword, How the British Came to Palestine*, p. 337.
[174] Ibid.
[175] CAB, Cabinet Papers, 23/4 G.T., no 245 (18).
[176] Ibid, 24 143.
[177] Ibid, 24/4 G.164.
[178] Ibid, 23/4, no. 257 (12), October 25 1917 minutes.

[179] Blanche Dugdale, *The Balfour Declaration: Origins and Background*, in Jehuda Reinharz, *The Balfour Declaration and It's Maker*, p. 487.

[180] CAB, Cabinet Papers, 23/4, no. 261 (12).

[181] On this day of decision, none of the Cabinet Ministers objected to the term "National Home," which had been an issue for two months.

[182] The London *Times*, December 20 1929.

[183] Winston Churchill was strangely silent at this time regarding his opinion about the Balfour Declaration. In his work, "Churchill's Promised Land, Zionism and Statecraft," Michael Makovsky who studied the topic extensively, claimed, "Through all of this, Churchill was utterly silent about Zionism. There is no record that Churchill commented at all on the Balfour Declaration while he was Minister of Munitions." His only related reference to Palestine at the time had to do with Allenby's conquest when Churchill announced to a crowd in Bedford in late 1917, "What Richard Coeur de Lion was not able to achieve, British troops have accomplished," in Michael Makovsky, *Churchill's Promised Land, Zionism and Statecraft*, p. 78, and in Rhode James, *Speeches*, 3:2584, in Michael Makovsky, *Churchill's Promised Land, Zionism and Statecraft*, p. 78.

[184] The Balfour Declaration was composed on October 31 1917 and dated by the Cabinet on November 2 1917.

[185] Mayir Verete, "The Balfour Declaration and It's Makers," p. 63.

[186] Ibid.

[187] Barbara Tuchman, *Bible and Sword, How the British Came to Palestine*, p. 312.

[188] Charles Townshend, "Going to the Wall: The Failure of British Rule in Palestine, 1928-31," p. 25.

[189] Blanche Dugdale, *The Balfour Declaration: Origins and Background*, p. 2.

[190] Arthur Balfour, *Speeches on Zionism*, p. 127.

[191] Ibid, p. 31.

[192] Lloyd George, Balfour, Smuts, Bonar Law, Carson, Curzon and Henderson.

[193] Lloyd George was raised in the home of his uncle, a Baptist Minister, Bonar Law's father was a Presbyterian Minister in New Brunswick and George Curzon's father was a Low Anglican Minister.

[194] Arthur Henderson was an ordained Methodist Evangelist and Minister.

Chapter Two: The Place of Christian Zionism in the Establishment of the Mandate, 1918-1928

[1] Most German families who first arrived in the 1870's left or were deported shortly after the end of the Great War. The British deported those who remained during World War 2.

[2] Letter from Emery to mother, on September 4 1919, Oxford, MECA, Emery Papers, Box 1, File 1.

[3] The Colonial Secretary was also known as the Colonial Minister.

[4] By the end of the Mandate, particularly under the government of Clement Attlee from 1945-1951, the Foreign Office took more responsibility for Palestine.

[5] See Appendix V for complete list of Secretaries of State for the Colonies, 1916-1950.
[6] Bevin served as Foreign Minister for a total of 6 years, but only 3 years during the Mandate. See Appendix for complete list of Foreign Secretaries, 1916-1950.
[7] Leo Amery was Colonial Secretary from 1924-1929. William Ormsby-Gore held the post from 1936-1939.
[8] The Armenian community was offered a National Home at the Versailles Peace Talks with the agreement of the fallen Ottoman regime, but the new Turkish government of Ataturk later rejected the agreement. Three Armenian regions were identified: Western Armenia, Wilsonian Armenia and the French-Armenian region. A series of treaties beginning with the Treaty of Batum in 1918 attempted to establish Armenian autonomy. The Treaty of Alexandropol followed in 1920 (not ratified) and the Treaty of Kars in 1921, ratified in 1923, by which time the Soviet Union was involved. Despite all this diplomatic activity, true political independence eluded the Armenian people.
[9] House of Lords Record Office, London, Lloyd George Papers F/12/3/25.
[10] An exception to this was the interest the British gave to the Garden Tomb in East Jerusalem, which quickly became established as the Protestant rival to the Church of the Holy Sepulchre site, even though there was no traditional or archaeological evidence to support the claims of the site.
[11] In 1852, the Ottoman Sultan Abdul Mejid introduced the religious status quo, freezing rights of worship and possession for the religious communities in the Holy Land. In the 1878 Treaty of Berlin, the nations of Europe reaffirmed the status quo of the Holy Places. Throughout the Mandate years to follow, the religious status quo was maintained in Palestine, as it was during the Jordanian and Israeli regimes.
[12] The National Archives, London, Zionism, FO 141 742/3.
[13] Ibid, CAB 24/136.
[14] The National Archives, London, FO 141 742/5.
[15] Ibid, FO 141 742.
[16] Bishop Rennie MacInnes was the Anglican Bishop of Jerusalem from 1915 to 1931, in Inger Marie Okkenhaug, *The Qualities of Heroic Living, of High Adventure and Endeavour, Anglican Missionaries and Education in Palestine 1888-1948*, p. 143.
[17] 260   The low Anglican "Christ Church" at Jaffa Gate called their society the "Church Mission to the Jews," in Inger Marie Okkenhaug, *The Qualities of Heroic Living, of High Adventure and Endeavour, Anglican Missionaries and Education in Palestine 1888-1948*, p. 144.
[18] Inger Marie Okkenhaug, *The Qualities of Heroic Living, of High Adventure and Endeavour, Anglican Missionaries and Education in Palestine 1888-1948*, p. 144.
[19] Bernard Wasserstein in Inger Marie Okkenhaug, *The Qualities of Heroic Living, of High Adventure and Endeavour, Anglican Missionaries and Education in Palestine 1888-1948*, p. 143.

[20] Letter from Meinertzhagen to Lloyd George on March 25 1919, Oxford, MECA, Meinertzhagen Papers, File 1.
[21] Eitan Bar Yosef, "Christian Zionism and Victorian Culture," p. 39.
[22] Israel State Archives, Bols Papers, April 21 1920, Government Secretariat, M/1/38.
[23] Naomi Shepherd, *The Zealous Intruders-The Western Rediscovery of Palestine*, p. 14.
[24] Letter from the Zionist Commission, May 30 1919, House of Lords Record Office, London, Lloyd George Papers LG/F/47/8/19.
[25] The Paris Peace Talks became known as the Versailles Conference. In reality, the Versailles Conference was a series of Conferences conducted between 1919 and 1922 in various locations. The main Conferences were the Versailles Conference in 1919 and the Conference of London in February 1920. Following these sessions were the San Remo Conference in Italy in April 1920, and the Sevres Conference in France in August 1920. The final negotiations did not conclude until 1922.
[26] Lawrence Davidson, *America's Palestine*, p. 16.
[27] Melvin I. Urofsky, *American Zionism from Herzl to the Holocaust*, p.184.
[28] Ibid, p. 228.
[29] Ibid.
[30] Dreyfus was a Jewish French Army Captain accused of spying in 1894. After conviction and years of imprisonment, Dreyfus was eventually found to be innocent. Clemenceau's role in the reversal of the Dreyfus case is discussed in David R. Watson, *Georges Clemenceau: A Political Biography* (London, 1974).
[31] Peter Capstick, Warrior, *The Legend of Colonel Richard Meinertzhagen*, p. 254.
[32] The British proposed three levels of Mandates, A, B and C. Level A was for regions holding the potential of self-determination such as Palestine. Even though Palestine was "A" level as a Mandate, it mostly looked like a Crown Colony for the entire Mandate period.
[33] Margaret MacMillan, *Paris 1919*, p. 98.
[34] Iraq was mandated to Great Britain in 1920, while Lebanon and Syria were mandated to France in 1920.
[35] John J. McTague, "Zionist-British Negotiations over the Draft Mandate for Palestine, 1920," p. 283.
[36] Chaim Weizmann, *Trail and Error*, p. 280.
[37] Curzon Foreign Office minutes, March 20 1920, FO 371/860/1447.
[38] John J. McTague, "Zionist-British Negotiations over the Draft Mandate for Palestine, 1920," p. 291.
[39] The agreement was signed on January 3 1919, in Margaret MacMillan, *Paris 1919*, p. 422.
[40] Letter from Feisal to Samuel, December 10 1919, Oxford, MECA, Samuel Papers, Box 1. Translated from the original French by Benjamin D. Schmidt.
[41] Abdullah of Jordan, *Memoirs of King Abdullah of Transjordan*, p. 139.
[42] Ibid.
[43] The main Armenian appeal was presented on February 26 1919.

[44] The main Zionist presentation was on February 23 1919, Margaret MacMillan, *Paris 1919*, p. 419.
[45] Chaim Weizmann, *Trial and Error*, p. 305.
[46] Peter Capstick, *Warrior, The Legend of Colonel Richard Meinertzhagen*, p. 258.
[47] Mark Cocker, *Richard Meinertzhagen, Soldier, Scientist and Spy*, p. 126.
[48] Christopher Lee, *This Sceptred Isle: Twentieth Century*, p.108-123.
[49] Jeremy Black, *A New History of Wales*, p. 191.
[50] Earle E. Cairns, *Christianity through the Centuries*, p. 452.
[51] Steven Koss, *Nonconformity in Modern British Politics*, p. 125.
[52] See appendix 11, from Steven Koss, *Nonconformity in Modern British Politics*, p. 11.
[53] Steven Koss, *Nonconformity in Modern British Politics*, p. 10.
[54] Ibid, p. 151.
[55] Ibid, p. 144.
[56] Herbert Samuel, *Memoirs*, p. 139.
[57] Samuel arrived in Paris in January 1919, in Bernard Wasserstein, *Herbert Samuel, A Political Life*, p. 239.
[58] Herbert Samuel, *Memoirs*, p. 148.
[59] Oxford, MECA, Samuel Papers, Box 1, File 3.
[60] Bernard Wasserstein, *Herbert Samuel, A Political Life*, p. 239-240.
[61] Letter from Samuel to Curzon on February 20 1920, House of Lords Record Office, London, Herbert Samuel Papers SAM/H/20.
[62] House of Lords Record Office, London, Herbert Samuel Papers SAM/H/20.
[63] Dinner took place in Jerusalem on November 8 1919, Jenifer Glynn, *Tidings from Zion, Helen Bentwich's Letters from Jerusalem, 1919-1931*, p. 37.
[64] The skirmish took place on March 1 1920.
[65] Tom Segev, *One Palestine, Complete*, p. 138.
[66] Peter Capstick, *Warrior, The Legend of Colonel Richard Meinertzhagen*, p. 269.
[67] The meeting took place on November 9 1914, Herbert Samuel, *Memoirs*, p. 142.
[68] Letter from Samuel to Lloyd George, April 25 1920, Herbert Samuel, *Memoirs*, p. 151.
[69] Herbert Samuel, *Memoirs*, p. 151.
[70] Oxford, MECA, Samuel Papers, Box 1, File 5.
[71] Herbert Samuel, *Memoirs*, p. 150.
[72] The meeting took place on May 12 1920, Herbert Samuel, *Memoirs*, p. 152.
[73] House of Lords Record Office, London, Lloyd George Papers F/12/3/32d.
[74] Letter from Lloyd George to Allenby, April 29 1920, House of Lords Record Office, London, Lloyd George Papers F/12/3/32(a).
[75] Letter from Allenby to Lloyd George, May 6 1920, House of Lords Record Office, London, Lloyd George Papers F/12/3/32(a).
[76] Hebrew University Archive, Givat Ram Campus, Jerusalem, Storrs Papers.
[77] Herbert Samuel, *Memoirs*, p. 149.

[78] Samuel speech delivered in Palestine on July 7 1920, in Bernard Wasserstein, *Herbert Samuel, A Political Life,* p. 249.
[79] From a speech on July 20 1920, Arthur Balfour, *Speeches on Zionism*, p. 31.
[80] Letter from Meir to Curzon, October 16 1920, The National Archives, London, Zionism, FO 141 742/3.
[81] Steven Koss, *Nonconformity in Modern British Politics*, p. 40.
[82] Tom Segev, *One Palestine, Complete,* p. 396.
[83] Steven Koss, *Nonconformity in Modern British Politics*, p. 37.
[84] Ibid, p. 101.
[85] Ibid, p. 76.
[86] Ibid, p. 11.
[87] Oxford, MECA, Samuel Papers, Box 1, File 2.
[88] Israel State Archives, Jerusalem, Zionist Organizations to all Zionist Federations, April 18 1919, I L3/31.
[89] Samuel is writing with the benefit of hindsight, in Herbert Samuel, *Memoirs*, p. 153.
[90] Ruth Jordan, *Daughter of the Waves, Memories of Growing up in Pre-War Palestine*, p. 96.
[91] Ibid.
[92] Letter, February 5 1921, Oxford, MECA, Samuel Papers, Box 1, File 2.
[93] Oxford, MECA, Samuel Papers, Box 1, File 2.
[94] The House of Lords contains a large amount of data pertaining to these issues, House of Lords Record Office, London, Lloyd George Papers F/12/3 and F/13/1.
[95] Letter Churchill to Samuel on February 16 1921, Oxford, MECA, Samuel Papers, Box 1, File 2.
[96] Martin Gilbert, Lecture: *"Churchill and the Jews: A Lifelong Friendship,"* Kehilat Moreshet Avraham, East Talpiot, Jerusalem, February 24 2008.
[97] In a letter from Churchill to his mother, September 8 1898, in Martin Gilbert, *Churchill and the Jews: A Lifelong Friendship,* p. 3.
[98] Martin Gilbert, Lecture: *"Churchill and the Jews: A Lifelong Friendship,"* Kehilat Moreshet Avraham, East Talpiot, Jerusalem, February 24 2008.
[99] Ibid.
[100] Michael J. Cohen, *Churchill and the Jews,* p. 79-80.
[101] In the generations to come, the entire Hussein family eventually lost their thrones except for Abdullah who was ceded the Transjordan, later to be recreated as the Kingdom of Jordan.
[102] Gilbert Lecture at Hillel House, London, March 13 1974, in Martin Gilbert, *Churchill and Zionism,* p. 10.
[103] Reports of the Commission of Inquiry with Correspondence Relating Thereto, 1921, p. 60, in Tom Segev, *One Palestine, Complete,* p. 183.
[104] Oxford, MECA, Bentwich Papers, Box 1, File 1.
[105] Letter from Police Captain Reginald Moncton, May 3 1921, Oxford, MECA, Moncton Papers, Box 1, File 1.
[106] Bernard Wasserstein, *Herbert Samuel, A Political Life,* p. 257.

[107] Bernard Wasserstein, *Herbert Samuel, A Political Life*, p. 257.
[108] Telegram from Samuel to Churchill, December 12 1921, Oxford, MECA, Samuel Papers, Box 1, File 2.
[109] The so-called "Churchill White Paper" of 1922 was sometimes referred to as "British Policy in Palestine." The official name of the document was "Palestine Correspondence with the Palestine Arab Delegation and the Zionist Organization." It was made up of nine documents and Churchill's memorandum was an enclosure to document #5.
[110] Margaret MacMillan, *Paris 1919*, p. 424.
[111] Michael Makovsky, *Churchill's Promised Land, Zionism and Statecraft*, p. x.
[112] Steven Hayward, *Churchill on Leadership*, p. 53.
[113] The National Archives, CO 733 14.
[114] Steven Hayward, *Churchill on Leadership*, p. 54.
[115] Michael Makovsky, *Churchill's Promised Land, Zionism and Statecraft*, p. 1.
[116] Ibid, p. 3.
[117] Haifa Congress of Palestinian Arabs, Memorandum, March 14 1921, Central Zionist Archives.
[118] Winston Churchill, *The River War*, p. 248-250.
[119] Churchill papers, Churchill Archives, Churchill College, Cambridge, 17/20.
[120] Martin Gilbert, *Churchill and the Jews, a Lifelong Friendship*, p. 84.
[121] Ibid, p. 85.
[122] At the 1937 Peel Commission, Sir Horace Rumbold asked Churchill over 100 questions. His answers were kept secret at the time by the Commission, in Martin Gilbert, *Churchill and the Jews: A Lifelong Friendship*, p. 111.
[123] Martin Gilbert, *Churchill and the Jews: A Lifelong Friendship*, p. 114.
[124] Letter from Rothschild to Churchill, February 1 1955, Churchill Archives, Cambridge, 2/197.
[125] Margaret MacMillan, *Paris 1919*, p. 424.
[126] Peter Capstick, *Warrior, The Legend of Colonel Richard Meinertzhagen*, p. 259.
[127] The article was in the November 3 edition of *Ha Aretz*. on the 50th anniversary of the Balfour Declaration, in Oxford, MECA, Meinertzhagen Papers, File 1.
[128] Writing 70 years later, Benjamin Netanyahu, Prime Minister of Israel, considered the effect of the 1922 separation of Transjordan from Palestine. "With one stroke of the pen, it (the Colonial Office) lopped off nearly eighty percent of the land promised the Jewish people." Even though the Churchill administration at the Colonial Office made this decision favouring the Arabs, they were unimpressed. In 1922, the Arab Congress rejected the British Mandate over Palestine, in Benjamin Netanyahu, *A Durable Peace*, p. 55.
[129] Margaret MacMillan, *Paris 1919*, p. 425.
[130] The riots began on May 1 1921 during a Jewish May Day march.
[131] Evyator Friesel in "British Policy in Palestine: The Churchill Memorandum of 1922," in Richard I. Cohen, editor, *Vision and Conflict in the Holy Land*, p. 195.
[132] Ibid.

[133] House of Lords Record Office, London, Herbert Samuel Papers SAM/H/20.
[134] Letter from Herbert Samuel to Lucy Franklin, May 3, 1920, Herbert Samuel Papers, Library of the House of Lords, London, B/12.
[135] Evyator Friesel in "British Policy in Palestine: The Churchill Memorandum of 1922," in Richard I. Cohen, editor, *Vision and Conflict in the Holy Land*, p. 195.
[136] Evyatar Friesel, "Herbert Samuel's Reassessment of Palestine in 1921," p. 221.
[137] Ibid, p. 221.
[138] Ibid, p. 215.
[139] Ibid, p. 230-231.
[140] Ibid, p. 216.
[141] Ibid, p. 236.
[142] Ibid.
[143] Herbert Samuel to Colonial Office, May 3, 1921, in Evyator Friesel in "British Policy in Palestine: The Churchill Memorandum of 1922" in Richard I. Cohen, editor, *Vision and Conflict in the Holy Land*, p. 196.
[144] Letter from Samuel to Churchill, March 24 1922, Colonial Office papers, 733/34, in Martin Gilbert, *Churchill and the Jews*, a *Lifelong Friendship*, p. 68.
[145] Historical Statistics of the United States, the Bureau of the Census, U.S. Department of the Census, p. 228-229.
[146] Ibid, p. 226.
[147] Sydney Ahlstrom, *A Religious History of the American People*, p. 914.
[148] Ibid, p. 898.
[149] Historical Statistics of the United States, the Bureau of the Census, U.S. Department of the Census, p. 228-229.
[150] Ibid.
[151] Harry Tees, *United Christian Council in Israel Year Book 2006*, p. 88.
[152] Ibid, p. 48.
[153] Ibid, p. 56.
[154] Jack Padwa, "You don't have to be Jewish to be a Zionist," p. 80.
[155] Speech made on January 13 1922, The National Archives, London, Zionism, FO 141 742/3.
[156] Lawrence Davidson, *America's Palestine*, p. 51.
[157] Ibid, p. 86.
[158] Jill Hamilton, *Gods, Guns and Israel, Britain, the First World War and the Jews in the Holy Land*, p. 216.
[159] Jack Padwa, "You don't have to be Jewish to be a Zionist," p. 80.
[160] Margaret MacMillan, *Paris 1919*, p. 424.
[161] Ibid, p. 425.
[162] Encyclopedia Britannica, Twelfth Edition, Vol. 32, "Zionism" (New York, 1922), p. 1131.
[163] Bonar Law became Prime Minister on October 23 1922.
[164] Jill Hamilton, Gods, *Guns and Israel, Britain, the First World War and the Jews in the Holy Land*, p. 215.

[165] House of Lords Speech on March 27 1923, in Sahar Huneidi, *A Broken Trust, Herbert Samuel, Zionism and the Palestinians 1920-1925*, p. 61.
[166] Lawrence Davidson, *America's Palestine*, p. 34.
[167] Letter from Clarke to Churchill, September 4 1922, Churchill Archives, Cambridge, CHAR 2/124B/109-111.
[168] Leon Simon and Leonard Stein, *Awakening Palestine*, p. 265.
[169] When Israel conquered and held the Golan Heights in June 1967, Syria claimed that the Golan Heights had always been a part of Syria. It remained an unsolved political problem between Israel and Syria into the 21st Century as United Nations military personnel continue to patrol the Golan Heights border.
[170] Arthur Balfour, Presbyterian; Henry Campbell-Bannerman, Presbyterian; H.H. Asquith, Congregationalist; David Lloyd George, Baptist; Andrew Bonar Law, Free Church of Scotland; Stanley Baldwin, Methodist/Anglican (Although Stanley Baldwin was an Anglican during his political career, his family were originally Methodists. Baldwin's parents left the Methodist Church to join the Anglican Church); James Ramsay MacDonald, Presbyterian; Neville Chamberlain, Unitarian; Winston Churchill, Anglican; Clement Attlee Anglican, see Appendix 4.
[171] In the *Morning Post*, August 28 1923, in Steven Koss, *Nonconformity in Modern British Politics*, p. 167.
[172] Steven Koss, *Nonconformity in Modern British Politics*, p. 178.
[173] Letter from the Zionist Organization to Deedes, April 17 1923, Oxford, MECA, Deedes Papers, Box 1, File 2.
[174] Letter from Keren Hayesod Fund to Deedes, December 30 1923, Oxford, MECA, Deedes Papers, Box 1, File 5.
[175] Wyndham Deedes Street is in the German Colony neighbourhood of Jerusalem.
[176] Jill Hamilton, *Gods, Guns and Israel, Britain, the First World War and the Jews in the Holy Land*, p. 214.
[177] Ibid, p. 215.
[178] Leo S. Amery, *My Political Life, Vol. II*, p. 22.
[179] Ibid, p. 28.
[180] The Zionist community of Palestine discouraged the use of German, Russian or Yiddish in favour of Hebrew. Hebrew usage was growing, but problems persisted. Telegrams could not be sent in Hebrew, because international servers worked with Latin letters. In Palestine, most Telegraph workers understood Arabic or English, but not all understood Hebrew.
[181] Central Zionist Archive, Frederick Kisch diary, April 5 1925, S 25/3272. Kisch was a long serving officer during the Mandate. After Kisch was killed in action during World War 2, Norman Bentwich wrote his biography, *Brigadier Frederick Kisch: Soldier and Zionist*.
[182] Bertha Spafford Vester, *Our Jerusalem*, p. 318.
[183] Norma Bentwich wrote of the day in 1950, in Oxford, MECA, Bentwich Papers, Box 1, File 9.
[184] Oxford, MECA, Bentwich Papers, Box 1, File 9.

[185] Telegram from Weizmann to Deedes, April 3, Oxford, MECA, Deedes Papers, Box 1, File 5.
[186] Oxford, MECA, Emery Papers, Box 2, File 4, Compilation of letters to family, p.119.
[187] Letter from Weizmann to Samuel, June 4 1925, Oxford, MECA, Samuel Papers, Box 1, File 4.
[188] Letter from ZO regarding Samuel, July 10 1925, Oxford, MECA, Samuel Papers, Box 1, File 4.
[189] Letter from ZO regarding Samuel, September 17 1925, Oxford, MECA, Samuel Papers, Box 1, File 4.
[190] Charles Harington, *Plumer of Messines*, p. 240.
[191] Bernard Wasserstein, *Herbert Samuel, A Political Life*, p. 405.
[192] Charles Harington, *Plumer of Messines*, p. 250.
[193] Ibid, p. 240.
[194] Ibid, p. 241.
[195] Bertha Spafford Vester, *Our Jerusalem*, p. 319.
[196] Norman Bentwich, *My Seventy-Seven Years, An Account of My Life and Times, 1883-1960*, p. 84.
[197] Ibid, p. 83.
[198] Norman Bentwich, *My Seventy-Seven Years, An Account of My Life and Times, 1883-1960*, p. 83.
[199] Gradually, as the Arab Christian population became smaller in comparison to the Muslims, the Muslims realized they did not need Arab Christian support. Besides, the Christian Arabs did not share the same level of fear of Zionism as the Muslims. The leaders of the Christian community knew they would be in a politically subservient role in the future whether the Jews or the Muslims ruled. Perhaps they believed a Jewish government would not be any harder to live under than a Muslim regime.
[200] In the 21st century, the building is one of the main municipal buildings of the Jerusalem City Hall complex in Kikar Safra, Jerusalem. Part of the inscription reads, "To the Glory of God and in the faith of Jesus Christ, Thy Word is Truth."
[201] Charles Harington, *Plumer of Messines*, p. 241.
[202] Joshua B. Stein, *Our Great Solicitor, Josiah C. Wedgwood and the Jews*, p. 11.
[203] Wedgwood's report was dated December 23 1926, Joshua B. Stein, "Josiah Wedgwood and the Seventh Dominion Scheme," p. 144.
[204] Joshua B. Stein, "Josiah Wedgwood and the Seventh Dominion Scheme," p. 144.
[205] Ibid, p. 145.
[206] Letter from ZO to Wedgwood, December 30 1926, Oxford, MECA, Deedes Papers, Box 1, File 5.
[207] In January 1927, for example, a civil war in China greatly occupied the attention of the Cabinet, in Christopher Lee, *This Sceptred Isle: Twentieth Century*, p. 153.
[208] H.H. Asquith, *Fifty Years of British Parliament*.

[209] The earthquake struck on July 11 1927. It was the only large earthquake of the Mandate years.
[210] The term "Hill of Evil Council" may have even older origins. Local tradition identifies this hill as the place where King Solomon built pagan altars for his foreign wives, hence the name.
[211] From Ariel L Avineri, *Jewish Settlement and the Change of Dispossession, 1878-1948*, p. 112ff, in Tom Segev, *One Palestine, Complete*, p. 275.
[212] Peter Capstick, *Warrior, The Legend of Colonel Richard Meinertzhagen*, p. 264.
[213] Oxford, MECA, Deedes Papers, Box 1, File 5.
[214] Ibid.
[215] Joshua B. Stein, *Our Great Solicitor, Josiah C. Wedgwood and the Jews*, p. 11.
[216] In 1928, the six British Dominions were Canada, Australia, New Zealand, South Africa, Newfoundland and Ireland.
[217] Joshua B. Stein, *Josiah Wedgwood and the Seventh Dominion Scheme*, pp. 141-155.
[218] Joshua B. Stein, *Our Great Solicitor, Josiah C. Wedgwood and the Jews*, p. 18.
[219] Ibid, p. 21.
[220] Ibid, p. 15.
[221] Letter from Sokolow to Wedgwood, July 5 1928, Keele University Library Archives.
[222] On May 16 1929, the Palestine Branch of the Seventh Dominion League was formed in Jerusalem. On this occasion, the Branch Committee wrote this letter to Josiah C. Wedgwood. Keele University Library Archives.
[223] Letter from Balfour to Samuel, May 14 1929, Hebrew University Archive, Givat Ram Campus, Jerusalem, Balfour Papers.
[224] Joshua B. Stein, *Our Great Solicitor, Josiah C. Wedgwood and the Jews*, p. 35.
[225] Letter from Storrs, March 20 1928, Hebrew University Archive, Givat Ram Campus, Jerusalem, Storrs Papers.
[226] Ronald Storrs, *The Memoirs of Sir Ronald Storrs*, p. 357.
[227] Storrs father was an Evangelical Minister, in Ronald Storrs, *The Memoirs of Sir Ronald Storrs*, p. 357.
[228] Writing in 1937, Ronald Storrs, *The Memoirs of Sir Ronald Storrs*, p. 360.
[229] Ronald Storrs, *The Memoirs of Sir Ronald Storrs*, p. 361.
[230] Norman Bentwich, *Wanderer Between Two Worlds*, p. 139.
[231] David Ben-Gurion, *Ben Gurion Looks Back*, p. 69.
[232] This is a quote from the Old Testament Book of Judges, chapter 3, verse 11 and other similar texts. The concept is that the Israel was well governed and blessed with peace. Hence the expression, "and the land had rest," in Charles Harington, *Plumer of Messines*, p. 260.
[233] Charles Harington, *Plumer of Messines*, p. 264.
[234] Martin Gilbert, Lecture: *"Churchill and the Jews: A Lifelong Friendship,"* Kehilat Moreshet Avraham, East Talpiot, Jerusalem, February 24 2008.
[235] Steven Koss, *Nonconformity in Modern British Politics*, p. 178.

[236] Steven Koss, *Nonconformity in Modern British Politics*, p. 181.
[237] In The London *Times*, December 20 1929.

Chapter Three: The Challenges of the Mandate and the Decline of British Christian Zionism, 1929-1939

[1] Memorandum, January 17 1929, The National Archives, London, Zionism, FO 141 742/3.
[2] The phrase is a quote from the New Testament passage of 2 Timothy 4:7. It is a favorite passage for Evangelicals denoting personal spiritual dedication, from Ian Malcolm, *Lord Balfour, A Memory*, p. 93.
[3] Blanche Dugdale, *The Balfour Declaration: Origins and Background*, p.5.
[4] Norman Rose, *The Gentile Zionists*, p. ix.
[5] In late 1929, events in American would soon have repercussions around the world. On October 29, the New York Stock Market crashed. Following a week of Stock Market instability, prices fell to record lows. The Stock Market fell 12 percent on this one day alone. The DOW eventually fell 89 percent. The Stock Market crash and the beginning of the Depression were to become indirect political factors in Palestine.
[6] In late 1928, John Chancellor arrived in Palestine to assume the role of High Commissioner. There had been a gap of five months from the time of Plumer's departure in July and Chancellor's arrival.
[7] The Gregorian calendar date was Sunday September 23 1928.
[8] The Muslims used this tactic themselves. By declaring a prayer site to be a Mosque, Muslims could then insist it must forever be a Mosque.
[9] Perhaps Duff could have handled the screen incident quietly, but instead he gathered a group of armed police officers who stormed the Wall.
[10] Norman Bentwich, *Wanderer Between Two Worlds*, p 149.
[11] Rhodes House Library, Oxford, Chancellor papers, farewell speech, Chancellor Papers, 15:5,ff. 17-18.
[12] Bernard Wasserstein, *The British in Palestine: The Mandatory Government and the Arab-Jewish Conflict 1917-1929*, p. 156.
[13] Leo S. Amery, *My Political Life, Vol. II*, p. 42.
[14] This day, the ninth day of the month of Av on the Jewish calendar marks the day of the destruction of the Temple by the Babylonians in 586 BCE and by the Romans in 70 CE.
[15] The one fatality was a Jewish man, Abraham Mizrahi.
[16] Letter from Kisch to Zionist Executive, London, October 19 1928, Central Zionist Archives S25/3090.
[17] H. C. Luke, *Cities and Men*, Vol. 2, p. 15.
[18] Colonial Office minutes recorded by G. M. Clauson, October 9 1923, The National Archives, CO733/60/117.
[19] Records of the United Sates Consulate in Jerusalem, Palestine, Confidential Correspondence, 1920-1935, in Tom Segev, *One Palestine, Complete*, p. 315ff.
[20] The Jewish community had existed in Hebron since biblical times.

[21] Cafferata was an experienced Army officer who had served in the Great War and in Ireland.
[22] Cafferata's is documented in testimony in Bernard Wasserstein, *The British in Palestine: The Mandatory Government and the Arab-Jewish Conflict 1917-1929*.
[23] Central Zionist Archives, Testimony Summaries, S25/4601.
[24] Richard Crossman, *A Nation Reborn, The Israel of Weizmann, Bevin and Ben Gurion*, p. 64.
[25] Shmuel Yosef Agnon, *From Myself to Myself*, p. 406. Agnon (1888-1970) received the Nobel Prize in literature in 1966.
[26] Oxford, MECA, Chancellor Papers, File 1.
[27] Charles Townshend, "Going to the Wall: The Failure of British Rule in Palestine, 1928-1931," p. 27.
[28] Tom Segev, *One Palestine, Complete*, p. 331.
[29] Charles Townshend, "Going to the Wall: The Failure of British Rule in Palestine, 1928-1931," p. 35.
[30] Rivka Burg, survivor of the 1929 Hebron massacre, interview in Israel 2005 by Hugh Kitson, *The Forsaken Promise*.
[31] Oxford, MECA, Luke Papers, Box 1, File 1.
[32] Bernard Wasserstein, *The British in Palestine: The Mandatory Government and the Arab-Jewish Conflict 1917-1929*.
[33] Charles Townshend, "Going to the Wall: The Failure of British Rule in Palestine, 1928-31," p. 38.
[34] Wedgwood volunteered his services in August 1929, in a letter from Wedgwood to Weizmann, August 26 1929, Chaim Weizmann Archives, Rehovot.
[35] Joshua B. Stein, "Josiah Wedgwood and the Seventh Dominion Scheme," p. 147.
[36] Jabotinsky's letter was sent to Wedgwood in December 1929, in Joshua B. Stein, "Josiah Wedgwood and the Seventh Dominion Scheme," p. 147.
[37] Leopold Amery (1873-1955), in Leo Amery, *My Political Life, Vol. I-III*.
[38] Amery served as Under-Secretary of State for the Colonies in Lloyd George's government from 1919 to 1921. This was followed by the post of First Lord of the Admiralty from 1922 to 1924 and then Colonial Secretary from 1924 to 1929. Amery lost office when Ramsay MacDonald and the Labour Party formed the government in 1929. He remained out of office throughout the 1930s and emerged as one of the Party's leading critics of the government's appeasement policy, in Leo Amery, *My Political Life, Vol. I-III*.
[39] Leo S. Amery, *My Political Life, Vol. II*, p. 22.
[40] Ibid, p. 28.
[41] Ibid, p. 41.
[42] Ibid, p. 42.
[43] After World War 2, the Foreign Office gradually assumed more control over Palestine than the Colonial Office.
[44] Rubinstein, William D., "The Secret of Leopold Amery," pp. 175-196.
[45] According to Rabbinic teaching, Jewishness is determined through the mother.

[46] Amery's younger son, Julian, (1919-1996), a prominent Conservative Minister under Prime Ministers Macmillan and Heath, also supported Zionism, in Davis Douglas, "Balfour Declaration's author was a secret Jew," *The Jerusalem Post*, January 12, 1999.
[47] Oxford, MECA, Chancellor Papers, Chancellor report dated May 27 1930.
[48] Ibid, File 2, May 27 1930, Chancellor Report p. 2.
[49] Ibid, p. 4.
[50] Martin Kolinsky, *Law, Order and Riots in Mandatory Palestine, 1928-35*, p. 11.
[51] Oxford, MECA, Chancellor Papers, File 2, May 27 1930, Chancellor Report p. 10.
[52] Ibid, p. 13.
[53] Ibid, p. 14.
[54] Rhodes House Library, Oxford, Chancellor papers, farewell speech, Chancellor Papers, 15:5,ff. 17-18.
[55] The Committee was formed on November 12 1929.
[56] Invitations were sent to 31 MP's, Central Zionist Archives, F13/56.
[57] Norman Rose, *The Gentile Zionists*, p. 5.
[58] Katharine Higgons, *Persistence of Antiquity, Biography of Martin Conway*, Research Forum 2005.
[59] Weizmann Diaries, November 25, 1929, Chaim Weizmann Archives, Rehovot.
[60] Notes from meeting between Smuts and Weizmann, December 3 1929, Chaim Weizmann Archives, Rehovot.
[61] Ibid.
[62] Bernard Wasserstein, *The British in Palestine: The Mandatory Government and the Arab-Jewish Conflict 1917-1929*, p. 156.
[63] Guests included Wedgwood, J. Buchan, A. Eden, and Blanche Dugdale, Weizmann archives, in Norman Rose, *The Gentile Zionists*, p. 5.
[64] The London *Times*, December 20, 1929.
[65] Norman Rose, *The Gentile Zionists*, p. 6.
[66] Ibid, p. 7.
[67] Ibid.
[68] Gabi Sheffer, "Intentions and Results of British Policy in Palestine: Passfield's White Paper," p. 46.
[69] Ibid, p. 47.
[70] Ibid.
[71] Ibid, p. 48.
[72] Ibid.
[73] The Hope Simpson Report, Palestine, Report on Immigration, Land Settlement and Development, by Sir John Hope Simpson, C.I.E., Presented by the Secretary of State for the Colonies to Parliament by Command of His Majesty, October 1930, London: His Majesty's Stationary Office, 1930.
[74] Norman Rose, *The Gentile Zionists*, p. 17.
[75] The Fabian Society believed that capitalism had created an unjust and inefficient society and eventually merged into the Labour Party.

[76] Ben-Gurion, David, *Ben Gurion Looks Back,* p. 71.
[77] Norman Rose, *The Gentile Zionists,* p. 17.
[78] Ibid, p. 10.
[79] From a letter written by Amery on October 20 1930, Leo S. Amery, *My Political Life, Vol. II,* p. 42.
[80] Open letter from Prime Minister MacDonald to Chaim Weizmann, February 13 1931.
[81] Alan Bullock, *The Life and Times of Ernest Bevin,* Vol. I, Trade Union Leader, 1881-1940, p. 456.
[82] Colin Ford, *A Hundred Years Ago: Britain in the 1800's,* p. 200.
[83] Henderson's conversion took place in 1879, in Colin Ford, *A Hundred Years Ago: Britain in the 1800's,* p. 200.
[84] Stephen Koss, *Nonconformity in Modern British Politics,* p. 149.
[85] Joseph Gorny, *The British Labour Movement and Zionism 1917-1948,* p. 53.
[86] Alan Bullock, *The Life and Times of Ernest Bevin,* Vol. I, Trade Union Leader, 1881-1940, p. 456.
[87] The London *Times,* October 25, 1930, in Norman Rose, *The Gentile Zionists,* p. 17.
[88] Richard Crossman was a Labour MP continuously from 1945-1974. As an ardent Zionist, he made a study of the Labour Party's support of Zionism.
[89] Richard Crossman, *A Nation Reborn, The Israel of Weizmann, Bevin and Ben Gurion,* p. 70.
[90] Norman Rose, *The Gentile Zionists,* p. 28.
[91] Gabi Sheffer, "Intentions and Results of British Policy in Palestine: Passfield's White Paper," p. 55.
[92] Ben-Gurion, David, *Ben Gurion Looks Back,* p. 71.
[93] Joseph Gorny, *The British Labour Movement and Zionism 1917-1948,* p. 91.
[94] Lord Elton, *The Life of James Ramsay MacDonald 1866-1919,* p. 39.
[95] Joseph Gorny, *The British Labour Movement and Zionism 1917-1948,* p. 84.
[96] Ibid, p. xii.
[97] Richard Crossman, *A Nation Reborn, The Israel of Weizmann, Bevin and Ben Gurion,* p. 66.
[98] Rhodes House Library, Oxford, Chancellor letter to his son, October 26 1930, Chancellor Papers, 16:3 f.123.
[99] Richard Crossman, *A Nation Reborn, The Israel of Weizmann, Bevin and Ben Gurion,* p. 64.
[100] David Ben-Gurion, *Ben Gurion Looks Back,* p. 96.
[101] F. Michael Perko, "Contemporary American Christian Attitudes to Israel Based on Scriptures," *Israel Studies,* Vol. 8, No. 2, Summer 2003, p. 3.
[102] Article by Churchill, *Sunday Chronicle,* November 8 1931.
[103] Martin Gilbert, Lecture: *"Churchill and the Jews: A Lifelong Friendship,"* Kehilat Moreshet Avraham, East Talpiot, Jerusalem, February 24 2008.
[104] The shipboard service took place on Sunday August 10, 1941, in Winston Churchill, *The Second World War,* Vol. III, p. 431.

[105] Churchill's private secretary at the time was Jock Colville. The Duke of Windsor who was left waiting was the former King Edward VIII, in Billy Graham, *Just As I Am*, p. 235-237. Billy Graham, in his autobiography, "Just as I am," also claimed the British royal family consistently encouraged his evangelistic meetings. This was especially true of Queen Elizabeth II who gathered her family on numerous occasions in order to have Graham preach to them. Graham claimed he would disclose few details of these meetings "out of respect for her privacy and that of her family, in Billy Graham, *Just As I Am*, p. 697.

[106] David Ben Gurion, *Memoirs*, Vol.1, p. 483.

[107] Rhodes House Library, Oxford, Chancellor letter to his son, November 15 1930, Chancellor Papers, 16:3 ff.157-161.

[108] Ibid, Chancellor letter to his son, October 23 1930, Chancellor Papers, 16:3 ff.26-31.

[109] Bernard Wasserstein, *The British in Palestine: The Mandatory Government and the Arab-Jewish Conflict 1917-1929*, p. 156.

[110] Historical Statistics of the United States, the Bureau of the Census, U.S. Department of the Census, p. 228-229.

[111] Kevin Phillips, *American Theocracy* (New York: Viking, 2006) p. 48.

[112] Sydney Ahlstrom, *A Religious History of the American People*, p. 914.

[113] Historical Statistics of the United States, the Bureau of the Census, U.S. Department of the Census, p. 228-229.

[114] Harry Tees, *United Christian Council in Israel Year Book 2006*, p. 80.

[115] Now known as "Jerusalem Cornerstone," the organization was still active in Israel in the 21st century, in Harry Tees, *United Christian Council in Israel Year Book 2006*, p. 100.

[116] Message of support from President Herbert Hoover for Jewish Organizations meeting in Madison Square Gardens to protest the events in Palestine, August 29 1929.

[117] Melvin I. Urofsky, *American Zionism from Herzl to the Holocaust*, p. 395.

[118] Message from President Herbert Hoover to the Zionist Organization of America on the anniversary of the Balfour Declaration, October 29 1932.

[119] Emanuel Neumann, *In the Arena*, p. 114, in David Arnow, "The Holocaust and the Birth of Israel: Reassessing the Causal Relationship," p. 258.

[120] Melvin I. Urofsky, *American Zionism from Herzl to the Holocaust*, p. 396.

[121] Allis Radosh, City University of New York, Lecture: "Truman, Jews and Zionism," Hebrew University, Jerusalem, The Harry S. Truman Research Institute, May 29 2008.

[122] See Appendix 12, 13, 14 for a listing of all U.S. Presidents and their religious affiliation.

[123] Letter from President Herbert Hoover to the American Palestine Committee, January 11 1932.

[124] David Ben-Gurion, *Ben Gurion Looks Back*, p. 71.

[125] The National Archives, Letter from Wauchope to Ormsby-Gore, June 24 1936, CO, 733/297 75156.

[126] David Ben Gurion, Memoirs, Vol. III, p. 64.
[127] Report from Frederick Kisch, October 14, 1931, Central Zionist Archive, Jerusalem, S25/30.
[128] Letter from Arthur Wauchope to Moshe Shertok, December 29 1937, Central Zionist Archive, Jerusalem, S25/31.1.
[129] Letter from Arthur Wauchope to Josiah C. Wedgwood, January 22 1934, Keele University Library Archives.
[130] Letter from Josiah C. Wedgwood to Arthur Wauchope, January 29 1934, Keele University Library Archives.
[131] Allenby dismounted and made this statement when he entered the Old City through Jaffa Gate in December 1917. Even though Allenby bitterly opposed the appointment of a Jew, Herbert Samuel, as the first High Commissioner of Palestine in 1922, Allenby's ceremonial dismounting and related statement endeared him to Christian Zionists.
[132] These words were preserved in ceramic on the front of the West Jerusalem YMCA, across from the King David Hotel. The West Jerusalem YMCA is still functioning with a mix of Jewish, Arab and expatriate membership.
[133] Peter Capstick, *Warrior, The Legend of Colonel Richard Meinertzhagen* p. 265.
[134] Interview with Valentine Vester, Jerusalem, December 9 2004.
[135] Letter from Ben Gurion to Wauchope, July 30 1934, Central Zionist Archive, Jerusalem, S25/16/1.
[136] Oxford, MECA, Bentwich Papers, Box 1, File 1.
[137] Martin Kolinsky, *Britain's War in the Middle East, Strategy and Diplomacy, 1936-42*, p. 53.
[138] Ibid, p. 49.
[139] Statement from Eden on June 20 1936, Martin Kolinsky, *Britain's War in the Middle East, Strategy and Diplomacy,* 1936-42, p. 54.
[140] Charles Townshend, "The Defense of Palestine: Insurrection and Public Security 1936-1939," p. 918.
[141] This would be Baldwin's third term as Prime Minister. He served as PM from 1923-1924, 1924-1929 and 1935-1937.
[142] H. Montgomery Hyde, *Baldwin, The Unexpected Prime Minister*).
[143] Keith Middlemas and John Barnes, *Baldwin, A Biography* (London: Weidenfeld and Nicholson, 1969), p. 548.
[144] The National Archives, London, Stanley Baldwin Papers, FO 800/423.
[145] The National Archives, London, Samuel Hoare Papers 1935 Foreign Minister, CO 852/21/2.
[146] Malcolm MacDonald was the son of the former Prime Minister Ramsay MacDonald. Although he was known in 1935 as a supporter of Zionism, in later years he would leave Zionists bitterly disappointed.
[147] Norman Rose, *The Gentile Zionists*, p. 57.
[148] David Ben-Gurion, *Ben Gurion Looks Back,* p. 84.
[149] House of Commons, March 24, 1936, Parliamentary Debates.
[150] Norman Rose, *The Gentile Zionists*, p. 62.

[151] Wedgewood, letter to his daughter Cynthia, in Norman Rose, *The Gentile Zionists*, p. 62.
[152] Steven Koss, *Nonconformity in Modern British Politics*, p. 185.
[153] Ibid, p. 11.
[154] See appendix 11, from Steven Koss, *Nonconformity in Modern British Politics*, p. 11.
[155] Cosmo Lang, Archbishop of Canterbury quote, in the *Jerusalem Post*, from Rafael Medoff, February 21 2006.
[156] There is no record of decisive action taken by Lloyd George, in a letter from Smuts to Lloyd George, July 23 1936, House of Lords Record Office, London, Lloyd George Papers LG/G/18/b/10.
[157] Ronald W. Zweig, *Britain and Palestine during the Second World War*, p. 1.
[158] The Peel Commission worked from November 11 1936 until January 17 1937.
[159] Lord Peel's was William Wellesley Peel, the 1st Earl of Peel (1867-1937).
[160] Palestine Royal Commission Report, (Peel Commission Report), p. 394.
[161] Ibid.
[162] Israel State Archives, Jerusalem, Herbert Samuel Letter, RG 100, Box 649, File 18.
[163] Palestine Royal Commission Report, (Peel Commission Report), p. 396.
[164] Ibid, p. 380.
[165] Ibid, p. 394.
[166] Ibid, p. 381.
[167] Ibid.
[168] Notes on dinner, June 8 1937, Weizmann Archives, in Norman Rose, *The Gentile Zionists*, p. 62.
[169] Letter from Emery to family, November 22 1936, Oxford, MECA, Emery Papers, Box 1, File 2.
[170] Leo S. Amery, *My Political Life, Vol. II*, p. 251.
[171] Ibid.
[172] Letter from Wedgwood to Churchill, March 23 1937, Churchill Archives, Cambridge, CHAR 2/315/3.
[173] Letter from Samuel to Churchill, April 13 1937, Churchill Archives, Cambridge, CHAR 2/315/9.
[174] Letter from Samuel to CO, June 15 1937, Israel State Archives, Jerusalem, Herbert Samuel Letter, RG 100, Box 649, File 19.
[175] Dugdale Diaries, Rehovot, in Norman Rose, *The Gentile Zionists*, p. 133.
[176] Trevor Royle, *Orde Wingate, Irregular Soldier*, p. 5.
[177] Ibid, p. 7.
[178] Ibid, p. 10.
[179] Ibid, p. 16.
[180] Leonard Mosley, *Gideon Goes to War*, p. 10.
[181] Ibid, p. 11.
[182] Ibid, p. 34.
[183] Ibid.

[184] Leonard Mosley, *Gideon Goes to War*, p. 43.
[185] Ibid, p. 37.
[186] Trevor Royle, *Orde Wingate, Irregular Soldier*, p. 103.
[187] Ibid, p. 98.
[188] Ibid, p. 99.
[189] Leonard Mosley, *Gideon Goes to War*, p. 39.
[190] Ibid, p. 40.
[191] Ibid, p. 47.
[192] Mordecai Naor, *Lexicon of the Haganah Defense Force* (Hebrew), Israel Ministry of Defense, in Tom Segev, *One Palestine, Complete, p.* 429ff.
[193] Ben-Gurion, David, *Ben Gurion Looks Back*, p. 89.
[194] Leonard Mosley, *Gideon Goes to War,* p. 43. The Israelis did in fact bring Herzl's bones to Israel, but chose to rebury them in Jerusalem, not in Haifa as Wingate recommended.
[195] Leonard Mosley, *Gideon Goes to War*, p. 55.
[196] Ibid, p. 53.
[197] Ibid, p. 61. The quotation is from the book of Judges 6:14, King James 1611 Bible. The context is the Lord speaking to Gideon to not be afraid to fight the Midianites and thus save Israel.
[198] Robert Slater, *Warrior Statesman-The Life of Moshe Dayan*, p. 45
[199] Ibid, p. 45.
[200] Ibid, p. 46.
[201] Interview with the London *Observer,* January 16 1972, in Robert Slater, *Warrior Statesman-The Life of Moshe Dayan*, p. 45.
[202] Robert Slater, *Warrior Statesman-The Life of Moshe Dayan*, p. 45-46.
[203] Ibid, p. 48.
[204] Ibid, p. 48.
[205] Ibid, p. 47.
[206] Yossi Harel, interview in Israel 2005 by Hugh Kitson, *The Forsaken Promise*.
[207] Leonard Mosley, *Gideon Goes to War*, p. 75.
[208] Charles Townshend, "The Defense of Palestine: Insurrection and Public Security 1936-1939," p. 937.
[209] Leonard Mosley, *Gideon Goes to War*, p. 78.
[210] Trevor Royle, *Orde Wingate, Irregular Soldier*, p. 3.
[211] Yossi Harel, interview in Israel 2005 by Hugh Kitson, *The Forsaken Promise*.
[212] Robert Slater, *Warrior Statesman-The Life of Moshe Dayan*, p. 48.
[213] Central Zionist Archives, S25/9783, "Sellers of Land to Jews," January 5 1937.,
[214] Letter from Wauchope to the CO, July 14 1937, The National Archives, London, Correspondence with Permanent Under Secretaries and High Commissioners. CO 967/93.
[215] Ibid.
[216] The National Archives, London, Correspondence with Permanent Under Secretaries and High Commissioners. CO 967/93.

[217] Wauchope dissolved the Arab Higher Committee on October 1 1937, in Joel S. Migdal, *Palestinian Society and Politics*, p. 24.
[218] The National Archives, London, Correspondence with Permanent Under Secretaries and High Commissioners. CO 967/93.
[219] Tom Segev, *One Palestine, Complete*, p. 415.
[220] Ben-Gurion, David, *Ben Gurion Looks Back*, p. 70.
[221] The National Archives, Letter from Wauchope to Ormsby-Gore, June 24 1936, CO, 733/297 75156.
[222] Harold MacMichael was a nephew of Lord Curzon.
[223] Letter from MacMichael to Tegart, June 4 1939, Oxford, MECA, Charles Tegart Papers, 4:4.
[224] Letter from Ormsby-Gore to MacMichael, December 15 1937, Oxford, MECA, MacMichael Papers, Box 1, File 1.
[225] Decades later, the Municipality of Jerusalem named streets after the Jewish men hung by the British. "Shlomo Ben Yosef Street" is in the Jerusalem neighbourhood of Armon HaNaziv (Palace of the Governor) which is named after Government House, the High Commissioner's residence.
[226] In late 1937, the Colonial Office, determined to establish order in Palestine, sent Sir Charles Tegart to Palestine to advise on dealing with Arab guerrillas. Tegart arrived with 25,000 new soldiers and police. This was the largest military force to leave Britain since the Great War. Some of Tegart's ideas were to build a security fence along the northern border, use imported Doberman security dogs from South Africa and establish a training school to train police interrogators. He also advised that a number of militarized police "fortress" be constructed throughout Palestine. Tens of the reinforced concrete block structures were built to the same basic plan at key intersections across Palestine. Despite his best efforts, the violence grew, in Oxford, MECA, Tegart Papers, Box1, File 3.
[227] Bernard Montgomery, *The Memoirs of Field Marshal the Viscount Montgomery*, p. 46.
[228] Letter from Ormsby-Gore to Chamberlain, January 9 1938, The National Archive, London, FO 371/21836.
[229] The four Presidents to precede Roosevelt were from lower Nonconformist denominations: Hoover (Quaker), Coolidge (Congregational), Harding (Baptist) and Wilson (Presbyterian).
[230] John W. Mulhall, *America and the founding of Israel*, p. 98-99.
[231] Jack Padwa, "You don't have to be Jewish to be a Zionist," p. 81.
[232] Presidential greetings to the United Palestine Appeal, February 6 1937.
[233] Lawrence Davidson, *America's Palestine*, p. 137.
[234] The organization and magazine continued into the 21st century as the Friends of Israel Gospel Ministry, Bellmawr, New Jersey.
[235] J. Addison Bell, "Christendom Needs Zionism," p. 2.
[236] J. Addison Bell, "The Government is With Us," p. 1.
[237] James McDonald, *My Mission in Israel 1948-1951*, p. xiii.
[238] Ibid.

[239] Lawrence Davidson, *America's Palestine*, p. 141.
[240] The National Archives, London, CO 967/94.
[241] Lawrence Davidson, *America's Palestine*, p. 171.
[242] The 11th chapter of Paul's letter to the Romans was used as a key scriptural text to prove this doctrine.
[243] The London *Times*, October 22 1938.
[244] Letter from Langston to the *Palestine Post*, January 24 1939 Oxford, MECA, Samuel Papers, Box 1.
[245] Oxford, MECA, Samuel Papers, Box 1.
[246] Letter from Samuel to Ormsby-Gore, April 7 1938, Israel State Archives, Jerusalem, Herbert Samuel Letter, RG 100, Box 649, File 20.
[247] Joseph Gorny, *The British Labour Movement and Zionism 1917-1948*, p. 5.
[248] Ibid, p 120.
[249] Ibid, p. 121.
[250] The London *Times*, May 5 1938.
[251] Michael J. Cohen, *Retreat from the Mandate*, p. 49.
[252] Joshua B. Stein, *Our Great Solicitor, Josiah C. Wedgwood and the Jews*, p. 11.
[253] Ibid.
[254] David Lloyd George, *The Truth About the Peace Treaties*, p. 721ff.
[255] A. J. Sylvester, *Life with Lloyd George, The Diary of A.J. Sylvester, 1931-1945*, p. 142.
[256] Oxford, MECA, Cunningham Papers, Box 4, File 4.
[257] CAB, Cabinet minutes, 24/285, Committee on Palestine, April 20, 1939.
[258] CAB, Cabinet Papers, 23/4, no. 261 (12).
[259] CAB, Cabinet Papers, December 21 1938, 23/96.
[260] Ronald W. Zweig, *Britain and Palestine during the Second World War*, p. 1.
[261] Norman Rose, *The Gentile Zionists*, p. 206.
[262] Dugdale's reference to MacDonald helping his father probably refers to how Malcolm carried messages from his father the PM to Weizmann in 1931, Dugdale Diaries, Rehovot, in Norman Rose, *The Gentile Zionists*, p. 62.
[263] Norman Rose, *The Gentile Zionists*, p. 208.
[264] Andrea Bosco and Cornelia Navari, *Chatham House and British Foreign Policy 1919-1945*, (London: Lothian Foundation Press, 1994), p. 187. Essays from Conferences at Mansfield College, Oxford University, March 1992.
[265] William Roger Louis, *The British Empire in the Middle East 1945-1951*, p. 385.
[266] David Ben-Gurion, *Ben Gurion Looks Back*, p. 84.
[267] Ronald W. Zweig, *Britain and Palestine during the Second World War*, p. 179.
[268] Martin Kolinsky, *Britain's War in the Middle East, Strategy and Diplomacy, 1936-42*, p. 78.
[269] Michael J. Cohen, *Retreat From the Mandate: The Making of British Policy 1936-1945*, p. 87.
[270] David Ben-Gurion, *Ben Gurion Looks Back*, p. 84.
[271] Ibid, p. 85.

[272] White Paper 1939, Palestine: A Statement of Policy, (May 1939), The May White Papers, Cmd. 6019.
[273] ESCO Foundation for Palestine, *Palestine, A Study of Jewish, Arab, and British Policies*, p. 895.
[274] House of Commons, May 23 1939, Parliamentary Debates.
[275] Ibid.
[276] Martin Gilbert, Lecture: *"Churchill and the Jews: A Lifelong Friendship,"* Kehilat Moreshet Avraham, East Talpiot, Jerusalem, February 24 2008.
[277] Ben-Gurion, David, *Ben Gurion Looks Back*, p. 101.
[278] Michael J. Cohen, *Churchill and the Jews*, p. 183.
[279] House of Commons, May 23, 1939, Parliamentary Debates.
[280] Lawrence Davidson, *America's Palestine*, p. 141.
[281] Henry Feingold, *Zion in America*, p. 291.
[282] Montgomery letter to General Alan Brooke, July 21 1939, The National Archives, WO, 216/49.
[283] Naomi Izhar, resident historian, former British Detention Camp at Atlit, Israel, interview in Israel 2005 by Hugh Kitson, *The Forsaken Promise*.
[284] *Jerusalem Post* Archives, Jerusalem.
[285] Richard Meinertzhagen diary, from Hugh Kitson, *The Forsaken Promise*.
[286] Peter Capstick, *Warrior, The Legend of Colonel Richard Meinertzhagen*, p. 269.
[287] Richard Meinertzhagen, *Middle East Diary, 1917-1956*, p. 171.
[288] The meeting took place on December 17 1939, when Churchill was First Lord of the Admiralty, in Michael J. Cohen, *Churchill and the Jews*, p. 194.
[289] David Ben Gurion, Memoirs, Vol. VI, p. 511ff.
[290] Ben-Gurion, David, *Ben Gurion Looks Back*, p. 101.
[291] Ronald W. Zweig, *Britain and Palestine during the Second World War*, p. 27.
[292] Martin Kolinsky, *Law, Order and Riots in Mandatory Palestine, 1928-35*, p. 2.
[293] Charles Townshend, "Going to the Wall: The Failure of British Rule in Palestine, 1928-31," p. 38.
[294] Michael J. Cohen, *Retreat from the Mandate*, p. ix
[295] Evyatar Friesel, "The Holocaust and the Birth of Israel," p. 51.

Chapter Four: Christian Zionism Waits through the War Years, 1940-1945

[1] Michael J. Cohen, *Retreat from the Mandate*, p. 87.
[2] Norman Rose, *The Gentile Zionists*, p. 62.
[3] Ibid, p. 71.
[4] In September 1940, the Italian Air Force bombed Tel Aviv, killing over 100 people. The bombing was an extraordinary event. Nine months later, in June 1941, the Italian bombers returned. These were exceptional events temporarily placing Jews, Arabs and British in the same plight.
[5] Oxford, MECA, Jerusalem and East Mission Archive, Box 67, File 3.

[6] Letter from Chancellor to MacMichael, March 9 1940, Oxford, MECA, MacMichael Papers, Box 1, File 4.
[7] The protest started on March 2 1940, *Jerusalem Post* Archive, Jerusalem, March 3 1940.
[8] Oxford, MECA, MacGillivray Papers, Box 1, File 2.
[9] *Jerusalem Post* Archive, Jerusalem, March 6 1940.
[10] Letter from Weizmann to MacMichael, March 20 1940, Chaim Weizmann Archives, Rehovot, File # 2213, III, 20-25.
[11] Martin Gilbert, Lecture: *"Churchill and the Jews: A Lifelong Friendship,"* Kehilat Moreshet Avraham, East Talpiot, Jerusalem, February 24 2008.
[12] Three days later, he addressed the House of Commons, promising "blood, toil, tears and sweat." Churchill also declared the aim of his government was victory.
[13] David Ben Gurion, *Memoirs*, Vol. VI, pp. 292, 327.
[14] Michael J. Cohen, *Churchill and the Jews*, p. 229.
[15] Churchill told the Cabinet this in April 1943, in Winston Churchill, *The Second World War: The Hinge of Fate*, Vol. IV, p. 758.
[16] The meeting took place on July 25 1940, in Chaim Weizmann Archives, Rehovot, File # 2235, VII, 23-26.
[17] David Ben-Gurion, *Ben Gurion Looks Back*, p. 85.
[18] Meeting on January 28 1941, Chaim Weizmann Archives, Rehovot, File # 2271, I, 27-31.
[19] Vera Weizmann, *The Impossible Takes Longer, Memoirs of Vera Weizmann*, p. 192.
[20] At this time, Chaim Weizmann and his wife paid the ultimate sacrifice for the war effort. Their 25-year-old son Michael was killed in action on February 11 1942 during World War 2 as a fighter pilot in the Royal Air Force. Churchill personally intervened to try to find out if Michael had survived but to no avail, Chaim Weizmann Archives, Rehovot, File # 2271, I, 27-31.
[21] Letter from Weizmann to Bevin, December 21 1943, Chaim Weizmann Archives, Rehovot, File # 2480.
[22] Ibid, March 3, at Chaim Weizmann Archives, Rehovot, File # 2491, III, 6.
[23] Martin Kolinsky, *Britain's War in the Middle East, Strategy and Diplomacy, 1936-42*, p. 196.
[24] Ibid, p. 198.
[25] The Mufti arrived in Berlin on November 30 1941, Martin Kolinsky, *Britain's War in the Middle East, Strategy and Diplomacy, 1936-42*, p. 198.
[26] Tom Segev, *One Palestine, Complete*, p. 464.
[27] The Mufti later emerged in Egypt where he lived out the rest of his life, dying in 1974.
[28] Michael J. Cohen, *Churchill and the Jews*, p. 243.
[29] Ibid, p. 244.
[30] Joshua B. Stein, *Our Great Solicitor, Josiah C. Wedgwood and the Jews*, p. 11.
[31] Letter from Arthur Creech-Jones to Josiah C. Wedgwood, February 4 1942, Keele University Library Archives.

[32] Joshua B. Stein, *Our Great Solicitor, Josiah C. Wedgwood and the Jews*, p. 11.
[33] Wedgwood served in the Cabinet of the first Labour government of Ramsay MacDonald from January to November 1924. In the Cabinet, Wedgwood held the post of Chancellor of the Duchy of Lancaster.
[34] Joshua B. Stein, *Our Great Solicitor, Josiah C. Wedgwood and the Jews*, p. 15.
[35] Ibid, p 15.
[36] Joshua B. Stein, "Josiah Wedgwood and the Seventh Dominion Scheme," p. 155. The State of Israel named a street in Jerusalem after Josiah Wedgwood.
[37] Norman Rose, *The Gentile Zionists*, p. 92.
[38] Benjamin Dunkelman, *Dual Allegiance*, p. 152.
[39] Canadian Prime Minister Mackenzie King took little interest in Zionism. Although he paid lip service to religion, he personally sought spiritual advice through séances and crystal balls, believing he was communicating with the dead. His eccentric tastes in spiritual matters were unknown to most Canadians during his lifetime.
[40] Letter from Weizmann to widow of Orde Wingate, October 27 1944, in 1957, the State of Israel founded the "Wingate Institute" in Netanya, north of Tel Aviv. The Wingate Institute is now the National Center for Physical Education and Sport in Israel, Chaim Weizmann Archives, Rehovot, File # 2527, X, 26-31.
[41] Martin Gilbert, *Churchill and the Jews: A Lifelong Friendship*, p. 184.
[42] Ibid, p. 209.
[43] Ibid.
[44] Letter from Churchill to Temple, October 29 1942, Churchill Archives, Cambridge, CHAR 2/124B/109-111.
[45] The London *Times*, December 5 1942.
[46] Ibid.
[47] The "bar" is the place where the accused stand to hear the charges against them in a British court of law. Hugh Kitson, *The Forsaken Promise*.
[48] John Kent, *William Temple: Church, State and Society in Britain 1880-1950*.
[49] Martin Gilbert, Lecture: *"Churchill and the Jews: A Lifelong Friendship,"* Kehilat Moreshet Avraham, East Talpiot, Jerusalem, February 24 2008.
[50] Ibid.
[51] Ibid.
[52] Prime Minister's Personal Minute, September 10 1942: Premier papers 4/52/5, in Martin Gilbert, *Churchill and the Jews: A Lifelong Friendship*, p. 265.
[53] Apparently Spears did not know Gilbert was Jewish, in Martin Gilbert, Lecture: *"Churchill and the Jews: A Lifelong Friendship,"* Kehilat Moreshet Avraham, East Talpiot, Jerusalem, February 24 2008.
[54] Martin Gilbert, Lecture: *"Churchill and the Jews: A Lifelong Friendship,"* Kehilat Moreshet Avraham, East Talpiot, Jerusalem, February 24 2008.
[55] Churchill War Papers archive, in Martin Gilbert, *"Churchill and the Jews: A Lifelong Friendship,"* p. 215.
[56] Historical Statistics of the United States, the Bureau of the Census, U.S. Department of the Census, p. 228-229.

[57] Melvin I. Urofsky, *American Zionism from Herzl to the Holocaust*, p. 396.
[58] Howard M. Sachar, *A History of Jews in America*, p. 581.
[59] Emanuel Neumann, *In the Arena,* p. 114, in David Arnow, "The Holocaust and the Birth of Israel: Reassessing the Causal Relationship," *The Journal of Israeli History*, p. 258.
[60] Weizmann, Ben Gurion, and Nahum Goldmann were there, in Evyatar Friesel, "The Holocaust and the Birth of Israel," *The Weiner Library Bulletin*, p. 52.
[61] Evyatar Friesel, "The Holocaust and the Birth of Israel," *The Weiner Library Bulletin*, p. 53.
[62] Michael J. Cohen, *Truman and Israel*, p. 40.
[63] Thomas Kolsky, *Jews Against Zionism*, p. 35, in David Arnow, "The Holocaust and the Birth of Israel: Reassessing the Causal Relationship," p. 258.
[64] Truman speech was delivered in April 1943, in Chicago, in Michael J. Cohen, *Truman and Israel*, p. 37.
[65] The Jewish National Home in Palestine, Sol Bloom, Chairman, Committee of Foreign Affairs House of Representatives, Seventy-Eighth Congress, Second Session, House Resolutions 418 and 419, January 27 1944.
[66] ESCO Foundation for Palestine, Palestine: A Study of Jewish, Arab, and British Policies, p. 1077.
[67] Bernard Wasserstein, *Britain and the Jews of Europe 1939-1945,* p. 35.
[68] David Ben-Gurion, *Ben Gurion Looks Back,* p. 76.
[69] Bernard Wasserstein, *Britain and the Jews of Europe 1939-1945,* p. 35.
[70] Ibid, p 35.
[71] Letter from Churchill to Weizmann, October 30 1942, Churchill Archives, Cambridge, CHAR 20/81/128.
[72] Ronald W. Zweig, *Britain and Palestine during the Second World War*, p. 40.
[73] Tom Segev, *One Palestine, Complete*, p. 460.
[74] David Ben-Gurion, *Ben Gurion Looks Back,* p. 95.
[75] Michael J. Cohen, *Churchill and the Jews*, p. 255.
[76] The National Archives, London, CO 967/94.
[77] Members of Lehi (Stern Gang) carried out the assassination attempt.
[78] Letter from Ben Gurion to MacMichael, August 9 1944, Central Zionist Archives, Jerusalem, S25/6828, File 45, p. 6.
[79] Ben Gurion on MacMichael, April 1944, Central Zionist Archives, Jerusalem, S25/197.
[80] David Ben-Gurion, *Ben Gurion Looks Back,* p. 76.
[81] Menachem Begin Archive, Jerusalem, File 143.
[82] David Ben-Gurion, *Ben Gurion Looks Back,* p. 75.
[83] Norman and Helen Bentwich, *Mandate Memories, 1918-1948,* p. 170.
[84] Letter from Oliver Stanley to Chaim Weizmann, in The National Archives, London, CO 967/98.
[85] The National Archives, London, CO 967/98.
[86] He had been the Commander in Chief of the British Expeditionary Force in France in 1939-1940.

[87] J. R. Colville, *Man of Valour, Field Marshal Lord Gort, V.C.*, p. 260.
[88] Ibid.
[89] Ibid.
[90] Ibid.
[91] Letter from Lord Gort to MacMichael, December 5 1944, Oxford, MECA, MacMichael Papers, Box 1, File 4.
[92] Menachem Begin Archive, Jerusalem, File 143.
[93] Norman and Helen Bentwich, *Mandate Memories, 1918-1948*, p. 170.
[94] Ibid, p.171.
[95] From a conversation between David Ben-Gurion and Lord Gort in 1944, in David Ben Gurion, *Ben Gurion Looks Back*, p. 75.
[96] Christopher Sykes in *Crossroads to Israel*, quoted in J. R. Colville, *Man of Valour, Field Marshal Lord Gort, V.C.*, p. 261.
[97] J. R. Colville, *Man of Valour, Field Marshal Lord Gort, V.C.*, p. 261.
[98] Michael J. Cohen, *Churchill and the Jews*, p. 307.
[99] Richard Crossman, A *Nation Reborn, The Israel of Weizmann, Bevin and Ben Gurion*, p. 66.
[100] Michael J. Cohen, *Churchill and the Jews*, p. 307.
[101] Ibid, p. 259.
[102] The National Archives, London, CO 967/94.
[103] Ibid.
[104] Menachem Begin Archive, Jerusalem, File 425.
[105] Letter from Cunningham to MacMichael, December 19 1944, Oxford, MECA, MacMichael Papers, Box 1, File 4.
[106] Article in the *Washington Post*, May 18 1939, in Michael J. Cohen, *Truman and Israel*, p. 45.
[107] Michael J. Cohen, *Truman and Israel*, p. 31.

Chapter Five: The British Abandon and America Assumes the Mantle of Christian Zionism, 1945-1947

[1] Martin Gilbert, *Churchill and the Jews: A Lifelong Friendship*, p. 265.
[2] The National Archives, London, CO 967/94.
[3] See Appendix 12 for a list of the Religious Affiliations of the Presidents of the United States.
[4] The Yalta Conference ended on February 11, 1945. Roosevelt's main meeting with Ibn Saud was on February 14. Churchill's main meeting with Ibn Saud took place on February 17, 1945.
[5] Nicholas Bethell, *The Palestine Triangle, The Struggle between the British, the Jews and the Arabs 1935-1948*, p. 196.
[6] Martin Gilbert, Lecture: *"Churchill and the Jews: A Lifelong Friendship,"* Kehilat Moreshet Avraham, East Talpiot, Jerusalem, February 24 2008.
[7] Gilbert claimed the archives of Churchill's talks with the Ibn Saud were sealed for 100 years, until 2045, but Gilbert gained access to them, Martin Gilbert,

Lecture: *"Churchill and the Jews: A Lifelong Friendship,"* Kehilat Moreshet Avraham, East Talpiot, Jerusalem, February 24 2008.

[8] Martin Gilbert, *Churchill and the Jews: A Lifelong Friendship,* p. 230.

[9] Truman assumed the office of the Presidency on April 12 1945.

[10] "Manhattan Project" was the secret American code name for the project for the development of the Atom Bomb, in Barton J. Bernstein, and Allen J. Matuson, *The Truman Administration,* p. 3.

[11] Harry S. Truman Library and Museum, Independence, Missouri, in Ami Isseroff, MidEastWeb, 2003.

[12] Letter from Churchill to Weizmann, June 9 1945, Churchill Archives, Cambridge, CHAR 20/234/30.

[13] Churchill Archives, Cambridge, CHAR 20/234/40.

[14] Letter from Churchill to Weizmann, June 29 1945, Churchill Archives, Cambridge, 20/234.

[15] Letter from Lord Stanley to Lord Gort, June 11 1945, The National Archives, London, CO 967/94.

[16] Kenneth Harris, *Attlee,* p. 390.

[17] The Arabs knew oil was their chief weapon. The original countries of the League of Arab States were Saudi Arabia, Syria, Lebanon, Iraq, Transjordan and Egypt.

[18] Although the Arabs of Palestine sent observers to the 1945 meetings of the Arab League.

[19] When the war began, most Arabs backed Germany. Throughout the war, the Mufti was a friend and guest of Hitler.

[20] Richard Crossman, *A Nation Reborn, The Israel of Weizmann, Bevin and Ben Gurion,* p. 66.

[21] This concept was written into a Labour Party Resolution in May 1945.

[22] William Louis, *The British Empire in the Middle East 1945-1951,* p. 388.

[23] Martin Jones, *Failure in Palestine-British and United States Policy after the Second World War,* p. 41.

[24] The Labour Party was gradually changing in this regard. Richard Crossman also had such a background.

[25] During the war, Attlee was Lord Privy Seal, Dominions Secretary and Lord President of the Council.

[26] Cyril Clemens, *A Man from Limehouse, Clement Richard Attlee,* p. 1.

[27] Ibid, p. 4.

[28] Morrison joined Ramsay MacDonald's government as Minister of Transport in 1929.

[29] House of Commons, May 23 1939, Parliamentary Debates.

[30] Ibid.

[31] Martin Jones, *Failure in Palestine-British and United States Policy after the Second World War,* p. 42.

[32] Trevor Evans, *Bevin,* p. 28.

[33] Alan Bullock, *The Life and Times of Ernest Bevin,* Vol. I, p. 8.

[34] Ibid, p. 9.

[35] Alan Bullock, *The Life and Times of Ernest Bevin*, Vol.1, p. 9.
[36] Ibid.
[37] Ibid.
[38] George Wallis in Alan Bullock, *The Life and Times of Ernest Bevin*, Vol. I, p. 10.
[39] Alan Bullock, *The Life and Times of Ernest Bevin*, Vol. I, p. 13.
[40] Ibid.
[41] Trevor Evans, *Bevin*, p. 46.
[42] Alan Bullock, *The Life and Times of Ernest Bevin*, Vol. I, p. 15.
[43] Ibid, p. 15.
[44] Ibid, p. 9.
[45] Trevor Evans, *Bevin*, p. 169.
[46] Norman Bentwich, *My Seventy-Seven Years, An Account of My Life and Times, 1883-1960*, p. 150.
[47] David Ben-Gurion, *Ben Gurion Looks Back*, p. 96.
[48] Ibid, p. 96.
[49] Ibid, p. 97.
[50] Ibid, p. 96.
[51] Peter Weiler, *Ernest Bevin*, p. 170.
[52] Martin Jones, *Failure in Palestine-British and United States Policy after the Second World War*, p 49.
[53] Ibid, p. 49.
[54] Ibid, p. 39.
[55] David A. Charters, *The British Army and Jewish Insurgency in Palestine, 1945-47*, p. 18.
[56] David Ben-Gurion, *Ben Gurion Looks Back*, p. 83.
[57] Ibid.
[58] Martin Jones, *Failure in Palestine-British and United States Policy after the Second World War*, p. 50.
[59] Golda Meir, *A Land of Our Own, An Oral Autobiography*, p. 54.
[60] Ibid, p. 61.
[61] Chaim Weizmann, *Trial and Error*, p. 539.
[62] Andrea Bosco and Cornelia Navari, *Chatham House and British Foreign Policy 1919-1945*, p.187. Essays from Conferences at Mansfield College, Oxford University, March 1992.
[63] Blanche Dugdale, *The Diaries of Blanche Dugdale 1936-1947*, pp. 154-155.
[64] Historical Statistics of the United States, the Bureau of the Census, U.S. Department of the Census, pp. 228-229.
[65] Billy Graham, *Just As I Am*, pp. 286-296.
[66] James Byrnes was raised as a Catholic who sometimes attended Episcopalian Churches as an adult.
[67] Abba Eban, *Abba Eban*, p. 59.
[68] David A. Charters, *The British Army and Jewish Insurgency in Palestine, 1945-47*, p. 30.

[69] Abba Eban, *Abba Eban*, p. 59.
[70] The most significant impact was that only 1500 Jewish refugees a month would be allowed into Palestine.
[71] Letter from Gort to MacMichael, March 4 1945, Oxford, MECA, MacMichael Papers, Box 1, File 4.
[72] Ibid, June 18 1945, Oxford, MECA, MacMichael Papers, Box 1, File 4.
[73] Oxford, MECA, MacMichael Papers, Box 1, File 4.
[74] Julias P. Kleeberg, *Recollections of a Medical Doctor in Jerusalem, 1930-1988*, pp. 105-106.
[75] Ibid, p. 106.
[76] The meeting with President Truman took place on September 29 1945.
[77] *Jerusalem Post* Archive, Jerusalem, October 19 1945.
[78] By December 1945, approximately 550 Jews a day were transferring from Poland into Germany, from Ronald Zweig, New York University, Lecture: "The U.S. Army, the Displaced Persons and American Palestine Policy," Hebrew University, Jerusalem, The Harry S. Truman Research Institute, May 29 2008.
[79] Bevin's remarks were made on November 13 1945, Abba Eban, *Abba Eban*, p. 59.
[80] The next federal election was scheduled for November 1948, 37 months away, in Abba Eban, *Abba Eban*, p. 59.
[81] Lawrence Davidson, *America's Palestine*, p. 197.
[82] House of Commons, November 13 1945, Parliamentary Debates.
[83] House of Commons, January 29 1949, Parliamentary Debates.
[84] J. R. Colville, *Man of Valour, Field Marshal Lord Gort, V.C.*, p. 264.
[85] Ibid, p. 265.
[86] Ibid, p. 165.
[87] Letter from Gort to the Jewish Agency, November 4 1945, Central Zionist Archives, Jerusalem, S25/6830, File 82, p. 13.
[88] J. R. Colville, *Man of Valour, Field Marshal Lord Gort, V.C.*, p. 266.
[89] Cunningham arrived on November 8 1945, in Oxford, MECA, MacGillivray Papers, Box 1, File 1.
[90] Norman Bentwich, *My Seventy-Seven Years, An Account of My Life and Times, 1883-1960*, p. 212.
[91] Alan Cunningham was born in 1887 and lived until 1983.
[92] Interview with Penny Tancred, daughter in law of Field Marshal Sir Alan Cunningham, London, April 2006.
[93] Norman & Helen Bentwich, *Mandate Memories, 1918-1948*, p. 171.
[94] The first such meeting took place on November 23 1945, Oxford, MECA, Cunningham Papers, Box 5, File 1.
[95] Zeev Sharef, *Three Days*, p. 263.
[96] Norman Bentwich, *My Seventy-Seven Years, An Account of My Life and Times, 1883-1960*, p. 212.
[97] David Ben-Gurion, *Ben Gurion Looks Back,* p. 81-82.
[98] Oxford, MECA, Cunningham Papers, Box 4, File 3.

[99] Cunningham received his orders on November 11 1945, Oxford, MECA, Cunningham Papers, Box 1, File 1.
[100] Bevin's statement was made on November 13 1945, in Chaim Weizmann, *Trial and Error*, p. 541.
[101] Chaim Weizmann, *Trial and Error*, p. 541.
[102] Abba Eban, *Abba Eban*, p. 45.
[103] Oxford, MECA, Cunningham Papers, Box 1, File 1.
[104] Michael J. Cohen, *Truman and Israel*, p. 55.
[105] Ibid, p. 51.
[106] The Taft-Wagner Resolution was S. R. 247 and the Wright-Compton Resolution was H.R. 418.
[107] Michael J. Cohen, *Truman and Israel*, p. 85.
[108] Ibid, p. 87.
[109] Allen Weinstein and Moshe Ma'oz, *Truman and the American Commitment to Israel*, p. 114.
[110] Ibid, p. 65.
[111] Peter Weiler, *Ernest Bevin*, p. 169.
[112] Kenneth Harris, *Attlee*, p. 388.
[113] Ibid, p. 390.
[114] Ibid, p. 390.
[115] Ibid, p. 391.
[116] Ibid, p. 390.
[117] The Anglo-American Committee Report was officially released on April 20 1946.
[118] Menachem Begin, *The Revolt, The Story of the Irgun*, p. 202.
[119] Oxford, MECA, MacMichael Papers, Box 1, File 4.
[120] Bevin's request was made on April 18 1946, in David A. Charters, *The British Army and Jewish Insurgency in Palestine, 1945-47*, p. 32.
[121] A few days later, on May 1 1946, the Anglo-American Committee of Inquiry published its report.
[122] House of Commons, May 1 1946, Parliamentary Debates.
[123] Bevin statement on June 12 1946, Ze'ev Venia Hadari, *Second Exodus, The Full Story of Jewish Illegal Immigration to Palestine, 1945-1948*, p. 287.
[124] The new Morrison-Grady Committee began and finished their work in July 1946.
[125] McDonald' reference to Hitler's quote "telling a big lie" may seem at first to be a mistake, since it is well known that Joseph Goebbels used this phrase in his 1941 article "From Churchill's Lie Factory." However, Hitler did in fact first use the phrase "the big lie," in *Mein Kampf* in 1925, criticizing the Jews for their use of "the big lie."
[126] James McDonald, *My Mission in Israel 1948-1951*, p. 24.
[127] Ibid, p. 25.
[128] Ibid.
[129] Ibid, p. 26.

[130] Richard Crossman, *Palestine Mission, A Personal Record*, p. 240.
[131] Article by Crossman in the *New Statesman and Nation*, May 11 1946, Richard Crossman, *Palestine Mission, A Personal Record*, p. 241.
[132] House of Commons, July 1 1946, Parliamentary Debates, also in Richard Crossman, *Palestine Mission, A Personal Record*, p. 249ff.
[133] Telegram from Truman to Attlee, July 2 1946, Israel State Archive, Jerusalem, Microfilm Box 1171, FO 800/485, p. 9.
[134] Israel State Archive, Jerusalem, Microfilm Box 1171, FO 800/485, p. 10.
[135] Harry S. Truman Library and Museum, Independence, Missouri, in Ami Isseroff, MidEastWeb, 2003.
[136] Ronald Zweig, New York University, Lecture: "The U.S. Army, the Displaced Persons and American Palestine Policy," Hebrew University, Jerusalem, The Harry S. Truman Research Institute, May 29 2008.
[137] Harry S. Truman Library and Museum, Independence, Missouri, in Ami Isseroff, MidEastWeb, 2003.
[138] Michael J. Cohen, *Truman and Israel*, p. 144.
[139] Allis Radosh, City University of New York, Lecture: "Truman, Jews and Zionism," Hebrew University, Jerusalem, The Harry S. Truman Research Institute, May 29 2008.
[140] Oxford, MECA, Cunningham Papers, Box 1, File 1.
[141] Their meeting took place on March 9 1946, in Oxford, MECA, Cunningham Papers, Box 5, File 2.
[142] Oxford, MECA, Cunningham Papers, Box 5, File 2.
[143] Telegram from Cunningham to Bevin, April 2 1946, Oxford, MECA, Cunningham Papers, Box 1, File 1.
[144] Ernest Bevin signed the Treaty of Alliance, in Abdullah of Jordan, *Memoirs of King Abdullah of Transjordan*, p. 249.
[145] Abdullah of Jordan, *Memoirs of King Abdullah of Transjordan*, p. 249.
[146] Letter from Weizmann to Churchill and Smuts, April 14 1946, Chaim Weizmann Archives, Rehovot, File # 2651, IV, 14-17.
[147] Letter from Weizmann to Attlee, April 16 1946, Chaim Weizmann Archives, Rehovot, File # 2651, IV, 14-17.
[148] Letter from Weizmann to Bevin, April 16 1946, Chaim Weizmann Archives, Rehovot, File # 2651, IV, 14-17.
[149] Letter from McDonald to Weizmann, April 17 1946, Chaim Weizmann Archives, Rehovot, File # 2651, IV, 14-17.
[150] Ze'ev Venia Hadari, *Second Exodus, The Full Story of Jewish Illegal Immigration to Palestine, 1945-1948*, p. 286.
[151] The transition took place on May 9, 1946, Menachem Begin, *The Revolt*, p. 53.
[152] Menachem Begin, *The Revolt*, p. 200.
[153] Interview with Shalom Lindenbaum, Auschwitz survivor, Cyprus detainee, Camp Atlit detainee, Jerusalem, April, 2006.
[154] Interview with Rita Mouchabeck, Jerusalem, March 17 2006.
[155] Israel State Archive, Jerusalem, Microfilm Box 1171, FO 800/485, p. 75.

[156] Operation "Markolet" (known as the Night of the Bridges) was a Haganah operation on the night of June 16-17 1946. Its aim was to destroy 11 bridges linking Palestine to the neighboring countries of Lebanon, Syria, Jordan and Egypt. The operation achieved its goal and transportation was suspended. To disguise and protect the real operations and to confuse the British, approximately 50 diversional operations and ambushes were carried out throughout the country on the same night.
[157] *Jerusalem Post* Archive, Jerusalem, June 30 1946.
[158] Golda Meir, *A Land of Our Own, An Oral Autobiography*, p. 64.
[159] Ibid, p. 64-65.
[160] Ibid, p. 65.
[161] Ibid.
[162] Oxford, MECA, Cunningham Papers, Box 1, File 1.
[163] The explosives were hidden in milk cans as part of the kitchen food deliveries. Despite an alleged telephone warning, the British did not evacuate the building.
[164] Julias P. Kleeberg, *Recollections of a Medical Doctor in Jerusalem, 1930-1988*, p. 108.
[165] Oxford, MECA, Cunningham Papers, Box 1, File 1.
[166] David Ben-Gurion, *Ben Gurion Looks Back*, p. 67.
[167] William Roger Louis, *The End of the Palestine Mandate*, p. 10.
[168] Thurston Clarke, *By Blood and Fire-July 22 1946-The Attack on the King David Hotel*. p. 257.
[169] Julias P. Kleeberg, *Recollections of a Medical Doctor in Jerusalem, 1930-1988*, p. 110.
[170] Ibid, p. 110.
[171] Ibid, p. 111.
[172] *Dafka* is a Hebrew word meaning "just because." The understanding of the word is that there is no rational reason for what is happening.
[173] Julias P. Kleeberg, *Recollections of a Medical Doctor in Jerusalem, 1930-1988*, p. 111.
[174] Ibid, p. 112.
[175] Ibid, p. 110-111.
[176] John Kimche was editor of the London weekly, *The Jewish Observer*.
[177] Vera Weizmann, *The Impossible Takes Longer, Memoirs of Vera Weizmann*, p. 210.
[178] Letter from Attlee to Truman, July 25 1946, Israel State Archive, Jerusalem, Microfilm Box 1171, FO 800/485, p. 79.
[179] Israel State Archive, Jerusalem, Microfilm Box 1171, FO 800/485, p. 95.
[180] Allen Weinstein and Moshe Ma'oz, *Truman and the American Commitment to Israel*, p. 117.
[181] Michael J. Cohen, *Truman and Israel*, p. 91.
[182] Oxford, MECA, Cunningham Papers, Box 1, File 2.
[183] *Time and Tide* was a left-wing political magazine, founded in 1920 by Lady Margaret Rhondda. The magazine was edited initially by Helen Archdale, then

Lady Rhondda took over in 1926. At first the magazine supported left-wing causes but over the years the magazine moved to the right. *Time and Tide* hired a wide variety of writers, never made a profit and ceased production in the 1970's.

[184] Article in *Time and Tide*, August 31 1946, Chaim Weizmann Archives, Rehovot, File # 2684, VIII, 26-31.

[185] Norman and Helen Bentwich, *Mandate Memories, 1918-1948,* pp. 176-177.

[186] The meeting was held on September 11 1946, Oxford, MECA, Cunningham Papers, Box 1, File 2.

[187] Letter from Bevin to American Ambassador in London, October 4 1946, Israel State Archive, Jerusalem, Microfilm Box 1171, FO 800/485, p. 31.

[188] Telegram, October 11 1946, Israel State Archive, Jerusalem, Microfilm Box 1171, FO 800/485, p. 39.

[189] It seems Truman's use of the number 100,000 was somewhat symbolic. It represented the kind of gesture Truman wanted to see, and it happened to be the number of British troops in Palestine, in Israel State Archive, Jerusalem, Microfilm Box 1171, FO 800/485, p. 40.

[190] Israel State Archive, Jerusalem, Microfilm Box 1171, FO 800/485, p. 46.

[191] Peter Weiler, *Ernest Bevin,* p. 170.

[192] Ibid, p. 170.

[193] Mikardo was a Jewish Zionist leader, in Peter Weiler, *Ernest Bevin,* p. 170.

[194] Ritchie Ovendale, "The Palestine Policy of the British Labour Government 1945-1947," p. 73.

[195] *Jerusalem Post* Archive, Jerusalem, December 10 1946.

[196] Vera Weizmann, *The Impossible Takes Longer, Memoirs of Vera Weizmann,* p. 199.

[197] Richard Crossman, *A Nation Reborn, The Israel of Weizmann, Bevin and Ben Gurion,* p. 73.

[198] Peter Weiler, *Ernest Bevin,* p. 172.

[199] Letter from Weizmann to Crossman, March 12 1947, The National Archives, London, Weizmann Papers, CO 733/495/1.

[200] Richard Crossman, *Palestine Mission.*

[201] Ibid, p. 14.

[202] Ibid, p. 60.

[203] Weizmann report, March 2 1947, The National Archives, London, Weizmann Papers, CO 733/495/1.

[204] William Roger Louis, *The End of the Palestine Mandate,* p. 1.

[205] Cabinet memorandum, January 3 1947, in Ritchie Ovendale, "The Palestine Policy of the British Labour Government 1945-1946," p. 76.

[206] Norman and Helen Bentwich, *Mandate Memories, 1918-1948,* p. 171.

[207] William Roger Louis, *The British Empire in the Middle East 1945-1951,* p. 383.

[208] This means Bevin was an Imperialist from a low class of society, from William Roger Louis, *The End of the Palestine Mandate,* p. 3.

[209] William Roger Louis, *The End of the Palestine Mandate,* p. 3.

[210] House of Commons, January 31 1947, Parliamentary Debates.
[211] Martin Gilbert, Lecture: *"Churchill and the Jews: A Lifelong Friendship,"* Kehilat Moreshet Avraham, East Talpiot, Jerusalem, February 24 2008.
[212] Elizabeth Monroe, *Britain's Moment in the Middle East, 1914-1956*, p. 166.
[213] The National Archives, London, Ernest Bevin Papers TNA FO 800/987, No.47/135.
[214] Meeting between Bevin and US Ambassador, April 2 1948, The National Archives, London, Ernest Bevin Papers TNA FO 800/987, Pa/48/11.
[215] Norman Bentwich, *My Seventy-Seven Years, An Account of My Life and Times, 1883-1960*, p. 213.
[216] Menachem Begin Archive, Jerusalem, File 425.
[217] Michael Lang, *One Man In His Time, The Diary of a Palestine Policeman 1946-48*, p. 6.
[218] Ibid, p. 94.
[219] Ibid, p. 59.
[220] The meeting took place in London on February 18 1947.
[221] House of Commons, February 25 1947, Parliamentary Debates.
[222] William Roger Louis, *The British Empire in the Middle East 1945-1951*, p. 383.
[223] Abba Eban, *Abba Eban*, p. 71.
[224] Richard Crossman, *A Nation Reborn, The Israel of Weizmann, Bevin and Ben Gurion*, p. 70.
[225] Abba Eban, *Abba Eban*, p. 85.
[226] Ibid.
[227] House of Commons, March 3 1947, Parliamentary Debates.
[228] Michael Makovsky, *Churchill's Promised Land, Zionism and Statecraft*, p. 7.
[229] Oxford, MECA, Cunningham Papers, Box 4, File 4.
[230] The Special Committee was called UNSCOP (The United Nations Special Committee on Palestine) and completed its report on August 31 1947 in Geneva, in the *Palestine Post*, May 19 1947.
[231] Chaim Weizmann's testimony before the United Nations Committee on Palestine, October 18 1947, in Mordecai S. Chertoff, *Zionism*, p. 11.
[232] The 1947 UNSCOP was composed of representatives from 11 nations, but not the UK or the US.
[233] Abba Eban, *Abba Eban*, p. 85.
[234] Oxford, MECA, Cunningham Papers, Box 1, File 4.
[235] Ibid, Box 2, File 1.
[236] *Jerusalem Post* Archive, Jerusalem, March 3 1947.
[237] In early May, an event in the north of Palestine illustrated the difficulties Cunningham was experiencing in controlling the situation. Jews disguised as British soldiers had driven up to the Akko prison and blown a hole in the outside wall. One hundred and ninety one Arab and 60 Jewish prisoners escaped through the breach. The British authorities only managed to recapture some, in Oxford, MECA, Cunningham Papers, Box 2, File 1.

[238] Christopher Sykes, *Cross Roads to Israel*, p. 384.
[239] Yossi Harel, Commander of the *Exodus*, 1947, interview in Israel 2005 by Hugh Kitson, *The Forsaken Promise*.
[240] David Parsons, "The Christian Role in Israel's Rebirth," *Word from Jerusalem ICEJ*, May 2008, p. 8.
[241] Ibid.
[242] Cunningham reports dated July 16 1947, Oxford, MECA, Cunningham Papers, Box 5, File 2.
[243] Oxford, MECA, Cunningham Papers, Box 5, File 2.
[244] Arthur Creech Jones informed the General Assembly on September 26 1947, in David A. Charters, *The British Army and Jewish Insurgency in Palestine, 1945-47*, p. 12.
[245] House of Commons, September 27 1947, Parliamentary Debates.
[246] The Christian Council on Palestine was a broadly based American Protestant Christian group and was active during the 1940's to show support for Zionism. Even liberal Protestantism, which has historically opposed Zionism, contributed clergymen to the Council of Palestine during World War 2.
[247] Harry S. Truman Library and Museum, Independence, Missouri, in Ami Isseroff, MidEastWeb, 2003.
[248] Ibid.
[249] Notification to Truman took place on September 29 1947.
[250] Michael J. Cohen, *Truman and Israel*, p. 82.
[251] Ibid, p. 157.
[252] *Forrest C. Pogue, George C. Marshall: Statesman 1945-1959, p. 346.*
[253] Loy Henderson was director of the State Department's Office of Near Eastern and African Affairs.
[254] *Forrest C. Pogue, George C. Marshall: Statesman 1945-1959, p. 346.*
[255] Ibid.
[256] Evyatar Friesel, "The Holocaust and the Birth of Israel," p. 56.
[257] Michael J. Cohen, *Truman and Israel*, p. 165.
[258] Evyatar Friesel, "The Holocaust and the Birth of Israel," p. 56.
[259] Ibid, p. 57.
[260] The men were staying at the Waldorf Astoria, in Abba Eban, *Abba Eban, An Autobiography*, p. 93.
[261] Abba Eban, *Abba Eban, An Autobiography*, p. 93.
[262] Oxford, MECA, Cunningham Papers, Box 2, File 2.
[263] Telegram from Cunningham to FO, November 1 1947, Oxford, MECA, Cunningham Papers, Box 2, File 3.
[264] See the Appendix 5 for details of how each member country of the UN voted.
[265] *Forrest C. Pogue, George C. Marshall: Statesman 1945-1959, p. 353.*
[266] Peter Weiler, *Ernest Bevin*, p. 173.
[267] Richard Crossman, *A Nation Reborn, The Israel of Weizmann, Bevin and Ben Gurion*, p. 69.
[268] Benjamin Netanyahu, *A Durable Peace*, p. 80.

[269] Truman even lost the State of New York, in Michael J. Cohen, Bar Ilan University, Lecture: "The Domestic Factor," Hebrew University, Jerusalem, The Harry S. Truman Research Institute, May 29 2008.
[270] Zeev Sharef, *Three Days,* p. 298.
[271] Dr. Stanley Taylor, Brigham Young University, Utah, in Michael T. Benson, *Harry S. Truman and the Founding of Israel,* p. vii.
[272] Dr. Stanley Taylor, in Michael T. Benson, *Harry S. Truman and the Founding of Israel,* p. xi.
[273] Michael J. Cohen, *Truman and Israel,* p. 3.
[274] Ibid, p. 5.
[275] Ibid, p. 4.
[276] Ibid, p. 6.
[277] Told to Merle Miller, in Michael J. Cohen, *Truman and Israel,* p. 6.
[278] Robert Phillips, "Another Look-Give 'Em Heaven Harry!" in *Kansas City Star,* 21 December 1976, in Michael T. Benson, *Harry S. Truman and the Founding of Israel,* p. 32.
[279] Michael J. Cohen, *Truman and Israel,* p. 18.
[280] Michael T. Benson, *Harry S. Truman and the Founding of Israel,* p. 196.
[281] Michael J. Cohen, *Truman and Israel,* p. 97.
[282] Letter from Cunningham to CO, December 6 1947, Oxford, MECA, Cunningham Papers, Box 2, File 3.
[283] Michael J. Cohen, *Palestine to Israel, From Mandate to Independence,* p. 220.
[284] Ronald W. Zweig, *Britain and Palestine during the Second World War,* p. 182.

Chapter Six: The End of the Mandate and the Significance of Christian Zionism in the American Recognition of Israel in 1948

[1] *Jerusalem Post,* May 23 2008.
[2] 1948 was a pivotal year in world history. The Soviet Union tested its first atom bomb and the North Atlantic Treaty Organization was formed. In religious developments, The World Council of Churches was founded. China and India were struggling for independence, both large countries with populations of hundreds of millions. Yet the story of the new State of Israel was the largest international story of the year in the United States, in Lorraine Glennon, *Our Times,* p. 356.
[3] The National Archives, London, Anthony Eden Papers FO 371/68405.
[4] Ibid.
[5] Letter, January 24 1948, The National Archives, London, Anthony Eden Papers FO 371/68405.
[6] Yaakov Ariel, *On Behalf of Israel, American Fundamentalist Attitudes Toward Jews, Judaism, and Zionism, 1865-1945,* p. 94.
[7] Christopher Lee, *This Sceptred Isle: Twentieth Century,* p. 273.
[8] Ibid.
[9] Ibid, p. 335.
[10] David Butler et al, *Twentieth Century British Political Facts 1900-2000,* p. 559.

[11] David Butler, et al, *Twentieth Century British Political Facts, 1900-2000*, p. 560.
[12] Ibid.
[13] Ibid, p. 561.
[14] Steven Koss, *Nonconformity in Modern British Politics*, p. 178.
[15] Ibid, p. 223.
[16] Ibid, p. 226.
[17] Ibid, p. 7.
[18] The Puritans in America were optimistic, spiritual people. They valued Old Testament principles, some of which became incorporated into American culture. When American Presidents Jimmy Carter, Ronald Reagan, Bill Clinton and George W. Bush used statements like "Christian Nation," "A City Set on a Hill," "Destiny," "Providence," "Equality" and "Freedom," they were using value terms from the Puritan roots of early American culture.
[19] Robert T. Handy, *The Holy Land in American Protestant Life 1800-1948*, p. 36.
[20] Yaakov Ariel, *On Behalf of Israel, American Fundamentalist Attitudes Toward Jews, Judaism, and Zionism, 1865-1945, p.* 9-13, also see footnote 75 in Eitan Bar Yosef, "Christian Zionism and Victorian Culture" p. 44.
[21] Yaakov Ariel, *On Behalf of Israel, American Fundamentalist Attitudes Toward Jews, Judaism, and Zionism, 1865-1945, p.* 94.
[22] Historical Statistics of the United States, the Bureau of the Census, U.S. Department of the Census, p. 228-229.
[23] Sydney Ahlstrom, *A Religious History of the American People*, p. 913.
[24] If the Holocaust is defined from 1933 to the immediate post-war period, in David Arnow, "The Holocaust and the Birth of Israel: Reassessing the Causal Relationship," p. 258.
[25] Billy Graham, *Just As I Am*, p. 157.
[26] The New Your City Crusade was held in the spring and summer of 1957, in Billy Graham, *Just As I Am*, p. 321.
[27] Graham and his team continued to conduct gospel Crusades in America and throughout the world for the next 50 years.
[28] Billy Graham, *Just As I Am*, pp. xix, 157.
[29] The White House meeting took place in 1950, in Billy Graham, *Just As I Am*, p. xx.
[30] Ian J. Bickerton, *A Concise History of the Arab-Israeli Conflict*, p. 90.
[31] Rabbi Silver was a Reform Rabbi from Cleveland, Ohio.
[32] Harry S. Truman Library and Museum, Independence, Missouri, in Ami Isseroff, MidEastWeb, 2003.
[33] Harry S. Truman Library and Museum, Independence, Missouri, from Michael J. Cohen, Bar Ilan University, Lecture: "The Domestic Factor," Hebrew University, Jerusalem, The Harry S. Truman Research Institute, May 29 2008.
[34] Ibid.
[35] Michael J. Cohen, Bar Ilan University, Lecture: "The Domestic Factor," Hebrew University, Jerusalem, The Harry S. Truman Research Institute, May 29 2008.
[36] Ian J. Bickerton, *A Concise History of the Arab-Israeli Conflict*, pp. 90-91.

[37] Ian J. Bickerton, *A Concise History of the Arab-Israeli Conflict*, p. 91.
[38] Canada, New Zealand, Australia and South Africa were considered for the role. The United States did not trust the Soviets to serve in Palestine, in Oxford, MECA, Cunningham Papers, Box 3, File 4.
[39] Michael J. Cohen, *Truman and Israel*, p. 209.
[40] *Forrest C. Pogue, George C. Marshall: Statesman 1945-1959, p. xiv.*
[41] Ibid, p. *370.*
[42] Ibid, p. *371.*
[43] Harry S. Truman Library and Museum, Independence, Missouri, from Michael J. Cohen, Bar Ilan University, Lecture: "The Domestic Factor," Hebrew University, Jerusalem, The Harry S. Truman Research Institute, May 29 2008.
[44] *Forrest C. Pogue, George C. Marshall: Statesman 1945-1959, p. xiv.*
[45] Michael J. Cohen, Bar Ilan University, Lecture: "The Domestic Factor," Hebrew University, Jerusalem, The Harry S. Truman Research Institute, May 29 2008.
[46] *Forrest C. Pogue, George C. Marshall: Statesman 1945-1959, p. 371.*
[47] Ibid, p. *370.*
[48] Ronald Radosh, City University of New York, Lecture: "Truman, Jews and Zionism," Hebrew University, Jerusalem, The Harry S. Truman Research Institute, May 29 2008.
[49] *Time*, March 31 2003, Canadian Edition p. 29.
[50] Although the Israel Declaration of Independence did not contain any overt reference to God, it did acknowledge the concept "Rock of Israel" (Zur Yisrael) which may be a reference to God.
[51] Part of the difference was in their attitude toward the British. Ben Gurion had opposed the British while Weizmann was dedicated to cooperation.
[52] Chaim Weizmann, *Trial and Error,* pp. 584-585.
[53] Lawrence Davidson, *America's Palestine*, p. 196.
[54] Chaim Weizmann, *Trial and Error,* p. 585.
[55] Ibid., pp. 480ff.
[56] Michael Pragai, *Faith and Fulfillment-Christians and the Return to the Promised Land*, p. 147.
[57] Chaim Weizmann, *Trial and Error,* p. 587.
[58] *Forrest C. Pogue, George C. Marshall: Statesman 1945-1959, p. 373.*
[59] Ibid.
[60] Ibid.
[61] Michael J. Cohen, *Truman and Israel*, p. xi.
[62] Allen Weinstein and Moshe Ma'oz, *Truman and the American Commitment to Israel,* p. 111.
[63] Truman was referring to the Persian King Cyrus who permitted the Jewish exiles to return to the land of Israel to restore their country. The Bible references for this event are; 2 Chronicles chapter 36 and Ezra chapter 1.
[64] Michael J. Cohen, Bar Ilan University, Lecture: "The Domestic Factor," Hebrew University, Jerusalem, The Harry S. Truman Research Institute, May 29 2008.
[65] Ibid.

[66] Richard Kirkendall, University of Washington, Lecture: "The Truman Period as a Research Field," Hebrew University, Jerusalem, The Harry S. Truman Research Institute, May 29 2008.

[67] Truman's Executive Order to end segregation was made in January 1948. He did not carry this out through legislation, but rather through presidential administrative action.

[68] Interview with Melvin Leffler, University of Virginia, Hebrew University, Jerusalem, May 29 2008.

[69] Melvin Leffler, University of Virginia, Lecture: "Summary: Why did President Truman Support the Establishment of the State of Israel?" Hebrew University, Jerusalem, The Harry S. Truman Research Institute, May 29 2008.

[70] Lawrence Davidson, *America's Palestine*, p. 174.

[71] David Ben-Gurion, *Ben Gurion Looks Back*, p. 116.

[72] Truman wrote this on May 26 1952, in Jack Padwa, "You don't have to be Jewish to be a Zionist," p. 81.

[73] Michael J. Cohen, *Truman and Israel*, p. 7.

[74] Yehuda Avner, *Jerusalem Post* Archive, Jerusalem, August 3 2004.

[75] Ibid.

[76] Ibid.

[77] Ronald Radosh, City University of New York, Lecture: "Truman, Jews and Zionism," Hebrew University, Jerusalem, The Harry S. Truman Research Institute, May 29 2008.

[78] Michael J. Cohen, Bar Ilan University, Lecture: "The Domestic Factor," Hebrew University, Jerusalem, The Harry S. Truman Research Institute, May 29 2008.

[79] Ronald Radosh, City University of New York, Lecture: "Truman, Jews and Zionism," Hebrew University, Jerusalem, The Harry S. Truman Research Institute, May 29 2008.

[80] Melvin Leffler, University of Virginia, Lecture: "Summary: Why did President Truman Support the Establishment of the State of Israel?" Hebrew University, Jerusalem, The Harry S. Truman Research Institute, May 29 2008.

[81] When Martin Gilbert lectured in Jerusalem about Churchill, (see Lecture: *"Churchill and the Jews: A Lifelong Friendship,"* Kehilat Moreshet Avraham, East Talpiot, Jerusalem, February 24 2008), his only reference to Truman was this one quote. If heard out of context, it portrays Truman as an anti-Semite, in Harry S. Truman Library and Museum, Independence, Missouri, from Michael J. Cohen, Bar Ilan University, Lecture: "The Domestic Factor," Hebrew University, Jerusalem, The Harry S. Truman Research Institute, May 29 2008.

[82] Melvin Leffler, University of Virginia, Lecture: "Summary: Why did President Truman Support the Establishment of the State of Israel?" Hebrew University, Jerusalem, The Harry S. Truman Research Institute, May 29 2008.

[83] Harry S. Truman Library and Museum, Independence, Missouri, in Ami Isseroff, MidEastWeb, 2003.

[84] Michael T. Benson, *Harry S. Truman and the Founding of Israel*, p. 2.

[85] Ronald R. Stockton, "Christian Zionism: Prophecy and Public Opinion," p. 234.

[86] Golda Meir, *My Life, The Autobiography of Golda Meir*, p. 188.
[87] David Ben-Gurion, *Ben Gurion Looks Back*, p. 116.
[88] Michael J. Cohen, *Truman and Israel*, p. xiii.
[89] Chaim Weizmann, *Trial and Error*, p. 585.
[90] Ibid, p. 585.
[91] Chaim Weizmann, *Trial and Error*, p 588.
[92] Oxford, MECA, D'Arcy Papers, Box 1, File 1.
[93] Ibid, Cunningham Papers, Box 3, File 4.
[94] Letter from Abdullah to Cunningham, April 10 1948, Oxford, MECA, Cunningham Papers, Box 6, File 2.
[95] Letter from Glubb to D'Arcy, June 21 1948, Oxford, MECA, D'Arcy Papers, Box 1, File 1.
[96] Winston Churchill, in The London *Times*, May 5 1938.
[97] House of Commons, June 9 1948, Parliamentary Debates.
[98] James McDonald, *My Mission in Israel 1948-1951*, p. 26.
[99] Tom Segev, *One Palestine, Complete*, p. 4-5.
[100] The National Archives, London, CO 967/104.
[101] Tom Segev, *One Palestine, Complete*, p. 514.
[102] Oxford, MECA, Cunningham Papers, Box 3, File 1.
[103] Letter, January 7 1948, Oxford, MECA, Cunningham Papers, Box 3, File 3.
[104] Oxford, MECA, Cunningham Papers, Box 5, File 4.
[105] *Jerusalem Post* Archive, Jerusalem, February 23 1948.
[106] Interview with Ben Zion Borohov, December 2 2004, Jerusalem.
[107] R. M. Graves, *Experiment in Anarchy*, p. 147.
[108] Ibid.
[109] Schlomo Hillel, interview in Israel 2005 by Hugh Kitson, *The Forsaken Promise*.
[110] Dov Chaikin, interview in Israel 2005 by Hugh Kitson, *The Forsaken Promise*.
[111] Interview with Zvi Kalisher, Jerusalem, March 2006.
[112] House of Lords Record Office, London, Herbert Samuel Papers SAM/H/11.
[113] Ibid.
[114] Ibid.
[115] Letter from Rachel Yanait to Cunningham, April 2 1948, Israel State Archive, Jerusalem, Cunningham, RG 169, Box 2077, File 11.
[116] Israel State Archive, Jerusalem, RG 160, Box 2319, File 25.
[117] Oxford, MECA, Emery Papers, Box 2, File 4.
[118] Letter from Norman to family, March 28 1948, Oxford, MECA, Dorothy Norman Papers, Box 1, File 1.
[119] Oxford, MECA, Dorothy Norman Papers, Box 1, File 1.
[120] House of Commons, April 28 1948, Parliamentary Debates.
[121] Ibid.
[122] Mr. Shinwell was a Jewish MP, in Christopher Mayhew's diary, May 1948, in Peter Weiler, *Ernest Bevin*, p. 171.

[123] William Roger Louis, The British Empire in the Middle East 1945-1951, p. 384.
[124] Meeting, April 22 1948, Bernard Montgomery, *The Memoirs of Field Marshal the Viscount Montgomery*, p. 473.
[125] Tom Segev, *One Palestine, Complete*, p. 513.
[126] Shlomo Hillel, interview in Israel 2005 by Hugh Kitson, *The Forsaken Promise*.
[127] John Glubb was sometimes known in the Arab community as Glubb Pasha.
[128] Clement Attlee, *As it Happened*,
[129] Cyril Clemens, *A Man from Limehouse, Clement Richard Attlee*, p. 1
[130] Ibid, p. 174.
[131] Ibid, p. 175.
[132] Richard Crossman, *A Nation Reborn, The Israel of Weizmann, Bevin and Ben Gurion*, p. 68.
[133] Ibid, p. 69.
[134] Joseph Gorny, *The British Labour Movement and Zionism, 1917-1948*, p. 216.
[135] James McDonald, *My Mission in Israel 1948-1951*, p. 6.
[136] Ibid, p. 114.
[137] Ibid, p. 166.
[138] Ibid, p. 258.
[139] Ibid, p. 273.
[140] Ibid.
[141] Menachem Begin, *The Revolt, The Story of the Irgun*, p. 200.
[142] Letter from Weizmann to Churchill, August 6 1948, Leonard Stein, *Weizmann and England*, p. 31-32.
[143] Undated letter from Winston Churchill to Josiah C. Wedgwood, Keele University Library Archives.
[144] House of Commons, March 28 1945, Parliamentary Debates.
[145] Benjamin Dunkelman, *Dual Allegiance*, p. 153.
[146] Ibid, p. 158.
[147] Miles Constable, "George Beurling," article for the Royal Canadian Air Force, Ottawa: 1998, p. 2.
[148] The new Israeli government respected the work Beurling had done by reinterring his remains in Israel on Mount Carmel with full military honours in 1950, in Benjamin Dunkelman, *Dual Allegiance*, p. 151.
[149] Peter Capstick, *Warrior, The Legend of Colonel Richard Meinertzhagen*, p. 272.
[150] Speech on January 26 1949, Peter Weiler, *Ernest Bevin*, p. 173.
[151] James McDonald, *My Mission in Israel 1948-1951*, p. 22.
[152] Ibid.
[153] Peter Weiler, *Ernest Bevin*, p. 173.
[154] Speech on January 26 1949, in Jill Hamilton, *Gods, Guns and Israel, Britain, the First World War and the Jews in the Holy Land*, p. 241.
[155] James McDonald, *My Mission in Israel 1948-1951*, p. 6.
[156] Michael J. Cohen, *Churchill and the Jews*, p. 322.

[157] In 1955, when Churchill resigned as Prime Minister, the *Jerusalem Post* reported the event, declaring that Israel joined the world in a warm tribute to Churchill who at a number of times declared he was "a warm Zionist." The *Post* published the 1944 exchange of letters between Chaim Weizmann and Churchill. The letters had led to the creation of the Jewish Brigade Group in the British Army, in The *Jerusalem Post* Archive, Jerusalem, April 6 1955.

[158] *Time*, March 31 2003, Canadian Version, p. 29.

Chapter Seven: Various Christian Denominations and their Views on Zionism

[1] The doctrine of eschatology is the study of the end times. The doctrine of hermeneutics is the study of the interpretation of Scripture.

[2] Roger Finke and Rodney Stark, *The Churching of America, 1776-1990*, p. 248.

[3] Interview with Rev. Lindell Browning, Director of the Church of the Nazarene in the Middle East, Jerusalem, 2006.

[4] Roger Finke and Rodney Stark, *The Churching of America, 1776-1990*, p. 248-249.

[5] Ibid.

[6] Paul Charles Merkley, *Christian Attitudes toward the State of Israel*, p. 4.

[7] Ibid.

[8] Ibid.

[9] Ibid.

[10] Ibid, p. 5.

[11] Biblical passages used to support Christian Zionism are primarily the Old Testament Jewish prophets such as Isaiah and Ezekiel and the New Testament books of Romans and Revelation.

[12] St. George's Cathedral is an Anglican Cathedral in Jerusalem, established in 1899. It is the seat of the Bishop of Jerusalem of the Episcopal Church in Jerusalem and the Middle East.

[13] Interview with Rev. William Broughton, Episcopalian Priest, St. George's Cathedral, Jerusalem April 2009.

[14] Ibid.

[15] Ibid.

[16] Ibid.

[17] Paul Charles Merkley, *Christian Attitudes toward the State of Israel*, p. 25.

[18] Interview with Rev. Charles Musgrave, Minister of St. Andrews Presbyterian Church, Jerusalem, 2006.

[19] St. Andrew's Presbyterian Church in Jerusalem was built as a memorial to the Scottish soldiers who died in the region during World War I. Opened in 1930, it is a congregation of the Church of Scotland.

[20] Interview with Rev. John Cubie, Minister of St, Andrews Presbyterian Church, Jerusalem, April 2009.

[21] Paul Charles Merkley, *Christian Attitudes toward the State of Israel*, p. 37.

[22] Paul Charles Merkley, *Christian Attitudes toward the State of Israel*, p. 38.
[23] Ibid, p. 43.
[24] Ibid, p. 24.
[25] Interview with Rev. William Broughton, Episcopalian Priest, St. George's Cathedral, Jerusalem April 2009.
[26] Ibid.
[27] Ibid.
[28] Ibid.
[29] *Lutz, Charles and Smith, Robert O.,* Christians and a Land Called Holy: How We Can Foster Justice, Peace, and Hope *(Minneapolis: Fortress, 2005),*
[30] Reinhold Niebuhr died in 1971, in Paul Charles Merkley, *Christian Attitudes toward the State of Israel*, p. 25.
[31] Interview with Halvor Ronen, Director of "Home for Bible Translators and Scholars," Jerusalem, April, 2009.
[32] Rev. Robert O. Smith, "Toward a Lutheran Response to Christian Zionism," p. 3. Smith was the Continental Desk Director for Europe and the Middle East for the Evangelical Lutheran Church of America. This article was originally presented before the Evangelical Lutheran Church of America Conference of Bishops gathering in San Mateo, California in March 2008.
[33] Rev. Robert O. Smith, "Toward a Lutheran Response to Christian Zionism," p. 14.
[34] *Lutz, Charles and Smith, Robert O.,* Christians and a Land Called Holy: How We Can Foster Justice, Peace, and Hope *(Minneapolis: Fortress, 2005), and Meyer, Carl S.,* Moving Frontiers: Readings in the History of the Lutheran Church, Missouri Synod (St. Louis: Concordia Publishing House, 1964).
[35] See Bruce R. McConkie, *Mormon Doctrine*, Kurt Van Gorden, *Mormonism* and Philip L. Marlow, *Mormons and the Bible, The Place of the Latter Day Saints in American Religion.*
[36] See Bruce R. McConkie, *Mormon Doctrine*, and Kurt Van Gorden, *Mormonism.*
[37] Rafael Medoff, "Pelosi's Father Defied FDR on Holocaust and Zionism," *Jerusalem Post*, April 12 2007.
[38] Ibid.
[39] By the beginning of the 21st century, the WCC had 349 member denominations in 120 countries for a total membership of approximately 560 million people.
[40] The first assembly of the World Council of Churches was on August 22 1948 in Nieuwe Kerk, Amsterdam. In 1948, membership was 144 denominations. By 1996, the WCC had expanded to 320 denominations. The major Churches outside the WCC are the Catholic Church and most Evangelical and Fundamental denominations, see Paul Charles Merkley, *Christian Attitudes toward the State of Israel*, p. 29.
[41] Paul Charles Merkley, *Christian Attitudes toward the State of Israel*, p. 45.
[42] Shlomo Aronson, *Hitler, the Allies and the Jews*, p. 352.
[43] James Byrnes was raised as a Catholic who sometimes attended Episcopalian Churches as an adult.

[44] Abba Eban, *Abba Eban*, p. 59.
[45] David A. Charters, *The British Army and Jewish Insurgency in Palestine, 1945-47*, p. 30.
[46] Abba Eban, *Abba Eban*, p. 59.
[47] Since 1971, Tantur Ecumenical Institute in Jerusalem has worked under the guidance of both Protestant and Roman Catholic rectors. Tantur has involved over 4,500 Orthodox, Protestant, Anglican and Roman Catholic participants to its ecumenical programs.
[48] Michael B. McGarry, *Christology After Auschwitz*, (New York: Paulist Press, 1977). Another example of the writings of Father McGarry is, *Christmas letter to Bethlehem*, Common Ground News Service, 18 December 2008, www.commongroundnews.org.
[49] Interview with Father Michael McGarry, Rector of Tantur Ecumenical Institute in Jerusalem, April 2009.
[50] Ibid.
[51] Ibid.
[52] Since its foundation in 1890 by Father Lagrange, the Ecole Biblique in Jerusalem has been administered by Dominican Priests. The Ecole Biblique has taught generations of scholars in biblical exegesis, archeology and in ancient near-eastern history.
[53] Interview with Dr. Christophe Rico of the Dominican Ecole Biblique, Jerusalem, April 2009.
[54] Ibid.
[55] Ibid.
[56] Rafael Medoff, "Pelosi's Father Defied FDR on Holocaust and Zionism," *Jerusalem Post,* April 12 2007.
[57] Ibid.
[58] Ibid.
[59] Ibid.
[60] Ibid.
[61] Ibid.
[62] Ibid.
[63] Ibid.
[64] Ibid.
[65] Ibid.
[66] Ibid.
[67] Ibid.
[68] Israel National News Press Release, New York, August 15 2007.
[69] Ibid.
[70] Catechism of the Catholic Church, Second Edition English translation, Libreria Editrice, Vaticana, Intratext editorial staff, with corrections by Pope John Paul II, 1997, Paragraph 63.
[71] Ibid.
[72] Ibid, Paragraph 439.

[73] The Ratisbonne Institute in Jerusalem is part of the Catholic Order of the Congregation of the Religious of Our Lady of Sion, founded by Theodore and Alphonse Ratisbonne who were born into a Jewish family in Strasbourg but converted to Catholicism in France the 1820's. The Order is active in France, Brazil and Jerusalem, from the statement of the "Congregation of the Religious of the Our Lady of Sion," Jerusalem, 2009.
[74] From the Statement of the "Congregation of the Religious of the Our Lady of Sion," Jerusalem, 2009.
[75] Ibid.
[76] Ibid.
[77] Interview with Father Stephen Kuncherakatt of the Ratisbonne Institute, Jerusalem, April 2009. The Ratisbonne Institute has been known as the Salesian Monastery Ratisbonne since 2004. The facility on Rehov Shmuel was turned over to the Vatican in 1984.
[78] Interview with Father Stephen Kuncherakatt of the Ratisbonne Institute, Jerusalem, April 2009.
[79] Ibid.
[80] Interview with Dr. Christophe Rico of the Dominican Ecole Biblique, Jerusalem, April 2009
[81] Interview with Father Michael McGarry, Rector of Tantur Ecumenical Institute in Jerusalem, April 2009.
[82] Ibid.
[83] Ibid.
[84] Interview with Dr. Christophe Rico of the Dominican Ecole Biblique, Jerusalem, April 2009
[85] Ibid.
[86] Interview with Father Michael McGarry, Rector of Tantur Ecumenical Institute in Jerusalem, April 2009.
[87] Ibid.
[88] Ibid.
[89] Ibid.
[90] Ibid.
[91] Ibid.
[92] Interview with Dr. Christophe Rico of the Dominican Ecole Biblique, Jerusalem, April 2009.
[93] Ibid.
[94] Ibid.
[95] Ibid.
[96] Ibid.

Chapter Eight: British Closure and American Christian Zionism Following Israeli Independence, 1949-21st Century

[1] Michael J. Cohen, *Churchill and the Jews*, p. 314.

[2] Letter from Churchill to Weizmann, November 19 1951, Martin Gilbert, *Churchill and Zionism,* lecture at Hillel House, London, March 13 1974, p. 27.
[3] On occasion of hearing of the death of Chaim Weizmann, House of Commons, November 10 1952.
[4] Peter Capstick, *Warrior, The Legend of Colonel Richard Meinertzhagen,* p. 275.
[5] Observed at the Weizmann mansion in Rehovot, Israel. Parked outside the home is the 1950 Lincoln Cosmopolitan limousine that President Truman gave as a gift to Chaim Weizmann, 2006.
[6] Ernest Bevin's obituary was published in the London *Times* on April 14 1951.
[7] Abba Eban, *Abba Eban,* p. 59.
[8] Peter Weiler, *Ernest Bevin,* p. 1.
[9] Truman wrote this on May 26 1952, in Jack Padwa, "You don't have to be Jewish to be a Zionist," p. 81.
[10] Vera Weizmann, *The Impossible Takes Longer, Memoirs of Vera Weizmann,* p. 255.
[11] Ibid.
[12] Letter from Ben Gurion to Truman, May 7 1964, David Ben Gurion House, Tel Aviv, Personal Letters.
[13] Historical Statistics of the United States, the Bureau of the Census, U.S. Department of the Census, p. 228-229.
[14] Billy Graham, *Just As I Am,* pp. 192, 199.
[15] Ibid. p 199.
[16] Even though Eisenhower was raised Brethren, in Billy Graham, *Just As I Am,* p. 199.
[17] Stephen E. Ambrose, *Eisenhower: Soldier and President,* p. 16.
[18] Ralph, C. Reynolds, "Preserving the Wall," p. 15.
[19] Bill H.R. 619, H.R. Res. 396 and 36 U.S.C. Section 186, in Ralph, C. Reynolds, "Preserving the Wall," p. 15.
[20] The regular use of "In God We Trust" on US coins began in 1908, in Ralph, C. Reynolds, "Preserving the Wall," p. 15.
[21] Paul Charles Merkley, *Christian Attitudes toward the State of Israel,* p. 39.
[22] *Moody Monthly,* Chicago, October 1967.
[23] Paul Charles Merkley, *Christian Attitudes toward the State of Israel,* p. 41.
[24] Dr. Douglas Young, Jerusalem University College, Mount Zion, Israel, 1971.
[25] Jerry Falwell, *The Fundamental Phenomenon,* p. 215.
[26] Observed at David Ben Gurion home, personal library, Sde Boker, Negev, Israel.
[27] Billy Graham's address to the National Executive Council of the American Jewish Committee on October 30 1977.
[28] Jerry Falwell, *The Fundamental Phenomenon,* p. 215.
[29] According to a number of press accounts, Falwell's influence meant so much to the Israeli government that immediately after Israel bombed Iraq's nuclear reactor in 1981, Israeli Prime Minister Menachem Begin telephoned Jerry Falwell before calling President Ronald Reagan to ask Falwell to explain to the Christian public

the reasons for the bombing, in Bill Berkowitz, "Politics US: Father of Christian Zionism Leaves the Building," Conservative Watch, June 1 2008.

[30] Gallop Poll Report #259, Princeton, New Jersey, April 1987, p. 28.

[31] Peter Gardella, "Gentile Zionism" p. 29.

[32] *Historical Statistics 2005* (Cambridge: Cambridge University Press, 2005), in *Newsweek*, January 23 2006.

[33] 1453 Ronald R. Stockton, "Christian Zionism: Prophecy and Public Opinion," p. 234.

[34] Ibid, p. 235.

[35] Ibid, p. 246.

[36] Ibid, p. 253.

[37] *Jerusalem Post*, June 17 2005.

[38] Michael T. Benson, *Harry S. Truman and the Founding of Israel*, p. 2.

[39] Ibid, p. 1.

[40] From his Jewish perspective, perhaps Kissinger meant something more like "religious importance" rather that "sentimental importance," in Michael T. Benson, *Harry S. Truman and the Founding of Israel*, p. 2.

[41] *Jerusalem Post*, December 29 2005.

[42] Survey conducted in March 2008 by Joshua Fund, Washington D.C., in Jerusalem Post, April 10 2008.

[43] Pew Research Center's Forum on Religion and Public Life, January 5, 2011.

[44] http://pewforum.org/government/faith-on-the-hill—the-religious-composition-of-the-112th-congress.aspx.

[45] Pew Research Center's Forum on Religion and Public Life, January 5, 2011.

[46] The next President, John F. Kennedy (1961-63) was a Catholic, but seemed to be personally supportive of Israel even though he had little opportunity to act on any views he might have had. Graham described one occasion in January 1961 when Kennedy asked Graham about biblical prophecy, complaining that his Church "did not tell us much about it." Graham told the President what the Bible taught, and Kennedy expressed a desire to speak about it again someday, but they never had the opportunity, in Billy Graham, *Just As I Am*, p. 395.

[47] "Disciples of Christ" were a group that broke from the Baptists in the late 19th century. They still held to the same evangelical doctrines as Baptists, but advocated simpler forms of worship.

[48] Billy Graham, *Just As I Am*, p. 405.

[49] Ibid, p. 404.

[50] President Johnson, speech before American B'nai B'rith on September 10 1968, in Bernard Reich, *Quest For Peace*.

[51] Billy Graham, *Just As I Am*, p. 440.

[52] President Gerald Ford, White House Press Conference with PM Rabin, September 10 1974.

[53] In calling himself "Born Again," Carter was referring to the words of Jesus in the New Testament gospel of John, Chapter 3, where Jesus stated that a person needs to be "born again" in order to enter the Kingdom of Heaven.

[54] Jack Padwa, "You don't have to be Jewish to be a Zionist," p. 81.
[55] Allen Weinstein and Moshe Ma'oz, *Truman and the American Commitment to Israel*, p. 14.
[56] White House press release, Washington D.C., March 21 1978.
[57] Jimmy Carter at the United Jewish Appeal National Youth Leadership Conference, February 25 1980.
[58] Reagan was baptized and joined the Church on June 21 1922, Mary Beth Brown, *Hand of Providence, The Strong and Quiet Faith of Ronald Reagan*, p. 34.
[59] Mary Beth Brown, *Hand of Providence, The Strong and Quiet Faith of Ronald Reagan*, p. 45.
[60] Billy Graham, *Just As I Am*, p. 534.
[61] Steven Hayward, *Greatness, Reagan, Churchill, and the making of Extraordinary Leaders*, p. 54.
[62] Ibid.
[63] Speech to the Annual Convention of the National Religious Broadcasters Association, January 30 1984.
[64] Steven Hayward, *Greatness, Reagan, Churchill, and the making of Extraordinary Leaders*, p. 81.
[65] Mary Beth Brown, *Hand of Providence, The Strong and Quiet Faith of Ronald Reagan*, p. 167.
[66] Ibid.
[67] Presidential letter to the Zionist Organization of America, October 29 1984.
[68] Remarks in New York City on Receiving the Charles Evans Hughes Gold Medal of the National Conference of Christians and Jews, March 23 1982.
[69] Reagan remarks at a White House meeting with Jewish leaders, February 2 1983.
[70] Reagan remarks at the welcoming ceremony for President Chaim Herzog of Israel, November 10 1987.
[71] On January 16 1991, the first day of the Gulf War, George Bush asked Billy Graham to spend the evening with him at the White House. Bush later wrote Graham, "Billy, Thank you for being with us at this critical moment in world history, George Bush," in Billy Graham, *Just As I Am*, p. 584.
[72] White House letter to AIPAC Conference attendees, May 17 1989.
[73] President George Bush address to the United Nations, September 23 1991.
[74] Letter from President Bill Clinton to Prime Minister Benjamin Netanyahu on occasion of Israel's 50 years of independence.
[75] President Clinton's reply when Israeli ambassador Shoval presented his credentials at the White House, September 10 1998.
[76] Speech to the American Jewish Committee, May 3 2001.
[77] Address to the "National Commemoration of the Days" Remembrance, April 19 2001.
[78] President's remarks at the "National Dinner Celebrating Jewish Life in America," September 14 2005.

[79] The most probable reasons for the embargo were that weapons were available from Europe and that the United States did not want to antagonize the neighbouring Arab States.
[80] Stephen E. Ambrose, *Eisenhower: Soldier and President*, p. 429-433.
[81] Jerusalem Newswire, www.jnewswire.com, Bridges for Peace, May 19 2006.
[82] Jerusalem Newswire, www.jnewswire.com Bridges for Peace, January 5 2004.
[83] Ibid.
[84] The ceremony took place at the Knesset on May 18 2005, *Jerusalem Post*, May 19 2005.
[85] Al-Sharq Al-Awsat on August 18 2005,
[86] Palestinian Supreme Islamic Judicial Council, 2006 website, from Jerusalem Newswire, www.jnewswire.com, Bridges for Peace, Jerusalem, Israel.
[87] *Jerusalem Post*, George Conger, February 8, 2006.
[88] Canon Andrew White, interview in Israel 2005 by Hugh Kitson, *The Forsaken Promise*.
[89] Filmed in Atlit, Israel 2006 by Hugh Kitson, *The Forsaken Promise*.
[90] Canon Andrew White, interview in Israel 2005 by Hugh Kitson, *The Forsaken Promise*.

Conclusion

[1] Lloyd George, Balfour, Smuts, Bonar Law, Carson, Curzon and Henderson.
[2] Lloyd George was raised in the home of his uncle, a Baptist Minister, Bonar Law's father was a Presbyterian Minister in New Brunswick and George Curzon's father was a Low Anglican Minister.
[3] Arthur Henderson was an ordained Methodist Evangelist and Minister.
[4] Blanche Dugdale, *The Balfour Declaration: Origins and Background*, p. 2.
[5] Arthur Balfour, *Speeches on Zionism*, p. 127.
[6] Ibid, p. 31.
[7] John Marlowe, *The Seat of Pilate: An Account of the Palestine Mandate*, p. 2.
[8] Elizabeth Monroe, *Britain's Moment in the Middle East, 1914-1956*, p. 43.
[9] This is an instructive example of how the emotions raised by the issue can cloud objectivity. in "Arnold Toynbee on the Arab-Israeli Conflict," *Journal of Palestine Studies*, 2/3, Spring 1973, p. 3, in William Roger Louis, *The End of the Palestine Mandate*, p. 28.
[10] Barnet Litvinoff, *Weizmann, Last of the Patriarchs*, p. 111.
[11] Martin Gilbert, Lecture: *"Churchill and the Jews: A Lifelong Friendship,"* Kehilat Moreshet Avraham, East Talpiot, Jerusalem, February 24 2008.
[12] Charles Townshend, "Going to the Wall: The Failure of British Rule in Palestine, 1928-31," p. 38.
[13] The Shaw Commission led to the Hope Simpson Commission, which led to the Passfield White Paper.
[14] David Ben Gurion, *Memoirs* Vol. II, p. 304; Vol. I, pp. 180, 366.

[15] Eden to Harvey, 7 September 1943, in Bernard Wasserstein, *Britain and the Jews of Europe 1939-1945*, p. 34.
[16] Alan Clark, *The Tories, Conservatives and the Nation State 1922-1997*, p. 266.
[17] Shalom Lindenbaum, Auschwitz survivor, former Cyprus Detention Camp internee and former Atlit Detention Camp internee, interview in Israel 2005 by Hugh Kitson, *The Forsaken Promise*.
[18] Michael J. Cohen, *Churchill and the Jews*, p. 314.
[19] Ibid, p. 313.
[20] Barbara Tuchman, *Bible and Sword: How the British Came to Palestine*, p. 349.
[21] Michael J. Cohen, *Churchill and the Jews*, p. 11.
[22] Paul Charles Merkley, *Christian Attitudes toward the State of Israel*, p. 5.
[23] Ibid, p. 6.
[24] Peter Gardella, "Gentile Zionism," p. 29.
[25] John Marlowe, *The Seat of Pilate: An Account of the Palestine Mandate*, p. 1.
[26] Kenneth Harris, *Attlee*, p. 388.
[27] William Roger Louis, *The End of the Palestine Mandate*, p. 10.
[28] Neomi Izhar, Resident historian, former British Detention Camp at Atlit, Israel, interview in Israel 2005 by Hugh Kitson, *The Forsaken Promise*.
[29] Peter Capstick, *Warrior, The Legend of Colonel Richard Meinertzhagen*, p. 166-167.
[30] Ibid, p. 244.
[31] Cecil Roth, *Essays and Portraits in Anglo-Jewish History*, p. 21.

APPENDIXES

❖ ❖ ❖

APPENDIX 1
Members of the British Cabinet at the Time of the Debate and Publishing of the Balfour Declaration in 1917 and their Countries of Origin.

David Lloyd George, 1863-1945, Wales
Arthur Balfour, 1848-1930, Scotland
Andrew Bonar Law, 1858-1923, Canada
Edward Carson, 1854-1935, Northern Ireland
George Nathanael Curzon, 1859-1925, England
Alfred Milner, 1854-1925, Germany
George Barnes, 1859-1940, Scotland
Arthur Henderson, 1863-1935, Scotland
Jan Christian Smuts, 1870-1950, South Africa
Edwin Montagu, 1879-1924, England

APPENDIX 2
Members of the British Cabinet at the Time of the Publishing of the Balfour Declaration in 1917, their Personal Religious Affiliation and their Support for the Declaration

Lloyd George, Baptist, yes
Arthur Balfour, Presbyterian, yes
Andrew Bonar Law, Presbyterian, yes
Edward Carson, Presbyterian, yes
George Nathanael Curzon, Anglican, yes with reservations
Alfred Milner, not affiliated, yes
George Barnes, not affiliated, yes

Arthur Henderson, Methodist, yes
Jan Christian Smuts, Christian Reform, yes
Edwin Montagu, Jewish, no

APPENDIX 3
High Commissioners of Palestine during the British Mandate

1. 1920-1925 Herbert Samuel
2. 1925-1928 Herbert Plumer (departed in July 1928)
3. 1928-1931 Sir John Chancellor (arrived in November 1928)
4. 1931-1937 Arthur Wauchope (arrived in November 1931)
5. 1937-1944 Harold MacMichael
6. 1944-1945 Lord Gort. (died after serving about a year)
7. 1945-1948 Alan Cunningham (arrived in November 1945, departed in May 1948)

APPENDIX 4
Church and Party Affiliation of the Prime Ministers of Great Britain during the first half of the 20th Century

-1902-1905, Arthur Balfour, (Conservative) Presbyterian
-1905-1908, Henry Campbell-Bannerman (Liberal) Presbyterian
-1908-1915, H.H. Asquith, (Liberal) Congregationalist
-December 1916-October 1922, David Lloyd George, (Liberal) Baptist
-October 1922-May 1923, Andrew Bonar Law, (Conservative) Free Church of Scotland
-May 1923-January 1924, November 1924-June 1929, June 1935-May 1937, Stanley Baldwin, (Conservative) Congregational to Anglican
-January 1924-November 1924, June 1929-June 1935, Ramsay MacDonald (Labour) Presbyterian
-May 1937-May 1940, Neville Chamberlain (Conservative) Unitarian
-1940-1945, Winston Churchill, (Conservative) Anglican
-1945-1951, Clement Attlee (Labour) Anglican

APPENDIX 5
Secretary of State for the Colonies during the British Mandate of Palestine

1916-1919, Walter Hume Long (December 10 1916 - January 10 1919)
1919-1921, Alfred Milner (January 19 1919 - February 13 1921)
1921-1922, Winston Churchill (February 13 1921 – October 19 1922)
1922-1924, Victor Cavendish (October 24 1922 – January 22 1924)
1924, James Henry Thomas (January 22 1924 – November 3 1924)
1924-1929, Leo Amery (November 6 1924 – June 4 1929)
1929-1931, Sydney James Webb, Lord Passfield (June 7 1929 – August 24 1931)
1931, James Henry Thomas (August 25 1931 – November 5 1931)
1931-1935, Philip Cunliffe-Lister (November 5 1931 – June 7 1935)
1935, Malcolm MacDonald (June 7 1935 – November 22 1935)
1935-1936, James Henry Thomas (November 22 1935 – May 22 1936)
1936-1938, William Ormsby-Gore (May 28 1936 – May 16 1938)
1938-1940, Malcolm MacDonald (May 16 1938 – May 12 1940)
1940-1941, George Ambrose Lloyd (May 12 1940 – February 8 1941)
1941-1942, Walter Edward Guinness, 1st Baron Moyne February 8 1941 – February 22 1942)
1942, Robert Arthur James Gascoyne-Cecil (February 22 1942 – November 22 1942)
1942-1945, Oliver Frederick Stanley (November 22 1942 – July 26 1945)
1945-1946, George Hall (August 3 1945 – October 4 1946)
1946-1950, Arthur Creech-Jones (October 4 1946 – February 28 1950)

APPENDIX 6
Secretary of State for Foreign Affairs during the British Mandate of Palestine

1916-1919, Arthur Balfour
1919-1924, George Curzon
1924, Ramsay MacDonald
1924-1929, Austen Chamberlain
1929-1931, Arthur Henderson
1931-Rufas Isaacs
1931-1935, John Allsebrook Simon
1935, Samuel Hoare
1935-1938, Anthony Eden
1938-1940, Edward Wood, Viscount Halifax
1940-1945, Anthony Eden
1945-1951, Ernest Bevin

APPENDIX 7
The UN Vote for Partition, 1947

Afghanistan-no, Argentina-abstain, Australia-yes, Belgium-yes, Bolivia-yes, Brazil-yes, Byelorussian-yes, Canada-yes, Chile-abstain, China-abstain, Colombia-abstain, Costa Rica-yes, Cuba-no, Czechoslovakia-yes, Denmark-yes, Dominican Republic-yes, Ecuador-yes, Egypt-no, El Salvador-abstain, Ethiopia-abstain, France-yes, Greece-no, Guatemala-yes, Haiti-yes, Honduras-abstain, Iceland-yes, India-no, Iran-no, Iraq-no, Lebanon-no, Liberia-yes, Luxembourg-yes, Mexico-abstain, Netherlands-yes, New Zealand-yes, Nicaragua-yes, Norway-yes, Pakistan-no, Panama-yes, Paraguay-yes, Peru-yes, Philippines-yes, Poland-yes, Saudi Arabia-no, Siam-abstain, Sweden-yes, Syria-no, Turkey-no, Ukraine-yes, South Africa-yes, USSR-yes, United Kingdom-abstain, USA-yes, Uruguay-yes, Venezuela-yes, Yemen-no, Yugoslavia-abstain

APPENDIX 8
Population of Palestine 1919-1936 (source: Peel Report, 1937)

Year	Moslems	Christians	Jews	Total
1919	515,000	62,500	65,300	647,850
1922	589,000	71,000	83,000	745,000
1936	859,000	77,000	400,000 (est.)	1,336,518

APPENDIX 9
Number of Jews in Palestine (source: Peel Report, 1937)

Before the Great War	90,000
At British conquest 1917	55,000
January 1921	64,000
1925	121,000
1926	140,000
1936	370,483

APPENDIX 10
Jewish Immigration into Palestine (Source: Peel Report, 1937)

Year	Jews	Others
1920	5,514	202
1921	9,149	190
1922	7,844	284

1923	7,421	570
1924	12,856	697
1925	33,801	840
1926	13,081	829
1927	2,713	882
1928	2,178	908
1929	5,249	1,317
1930	4,944	1,489
1931	4,075	1,458
1932	9,553	1,736
1933	30,327	1,650
1934	42,359	1,784
1935	61,854	2,293
1936	29,727	1,944

APPENDIX 11
Number of Nonconformist Candidates in the British General Elections

Year	Candidates from all Parties	Elected
1900	171	109
1906	223	185
1910 (Jan)	195	131
1910 (Dec)	186	136
1918	182	88
1922	222	78
1923	207	119
1924	222	80
1929	262	103
1935	146	65

APPENDIX 12
Religious Affiliation of United States Presidents

George Washington, 1789-1797, Episcopalian
John Adams, 1797-1801, Congregationalist
Thomas Jefferson, 1801-1809, Episcopalian, Unitarian
James Madison, 1809-1817, Episcopalian
James Monroe, 1817-1825, Episcopalian
John Quincy Adams, 1825-1829, Unitarian

Andrew Jackson, 1829-1837, Presbyterian
Martin Van Buren, 1837-1841, Dutch Reformed
William Henry Harrison, 1841, Episcopalian Presbyterian
John Tyler, 1841-1845, Episcopalian
James Knox Polk, 1845-1849, Presbyterian, Methodist
Zachary Taylor, 1849-1850, Episcopalian
Millard Fillmore, 1850-1853, Unitarian
Franklin Pierce, 1853-1857, Episcopalian
James Buchanan, 1857-1861, Presbyterian
Abraham Lincoln, 1861-1865, Baptist, Deist
Andrew Johnson, 1865-1869, Protestant, no specific denomination
Ulysses S. Grant, 1869-1877, Presbyterian, Methodist
Rutherford B. Hayes, 1877-1881, Presbyterian, Methodist
James Garfield, 1881, Disciples of Christ
Chester A. Arthur, 1881-1885, Episcopalian
Grover Cleveland, 1885-1889, 1893-1897, Presbyterian
Benjamin Harrison, 1889-1893, Presbyterian
William McKinley, 1897-1901, Methodist
Theodore Roosevelt, 1901-1909, Dutch Reformed, Episcopalian
William Howard Taft, 1909-1913, Unitarian
Woodrow Wilson, 1913-1921, Presbyterian
Warren G. Harding, 1921-1923, Baptist
Calvin Coolidge, 1923-1929, Congregationalist
Herbert Hoover, 1929-1933, Quaker
Franklin Roosevelt, 1933-1945, Episcopalian
Harry Truman, 1945-1953, Baptist
Dwight Eisenhower, 1953-1961, Brethren
John F. Kennedy, 1961-1963, Roman Catholic
Lynden B. Johnson, 1963-1969, Disciples of Christ
Richard Nixon, 1969-1974, Quaker
Gerald Ford, 1974-1977, Episcopalian
Jimmy Carter, 1977-1981, Baptist
Ronald Reagan, 1981-1989, Disciples of Christ
George H. W. Bush, 1989-1993, Episcopalian
William Clinton, 1993-2001, Baptist
George W. Bush, 2001-2009, Methodist
Barack Obama, 2009-, United Church of Christ

APPENDIX 13
Summary of Religious Affiliation of United States Presidents (Until and including the Presidency of Barack Obama)

Episcopalian, 11
Presbyterian, 10
Methodist, 5
Baptist, 4
Unitarian, 4
Disciples of Christ, 3
Dutch Reformed, 2
Quaker, 2
Congregationalist, 2
Brethren, 1
United Church of Christ, 1
Roman Catholic, 1 (John F. Kennedy)

APPENDIX 14
Summary of Religious Affiliation of United States Vice Presidents (Until and including the Presidency of Barack Obama)

Presbyterian, 12
Episcopalian, 10
Dutch Reformed, 4
Congregationalist, 4
Methodist, 4
Baptist, 4
Unitarian, 3
Lutheran, 1
Disciples of Christ, 1
Quaker, 1
Brethren, 1
Roman Catholic, 1 (Joseph Biden 2009-)
Protestant, 8 (denomination unknown)

BIBLIOGRAPHY

❖ ❖ ❖

ABBREVIATIONS

AMF: American Messianic Fellowship
CA: Churchill Archives, Cambridge
CAB: Cabinet Minutes of the government of Great Britain
CO: Colonial Office (Great Britain)
CZA: Central Zionist Archive
FO: Foreign Office (Great Britain)
HMSO: His Majesty's Stationary Office
ICEJ: International Christian Embassy of Jerusalem
ISA: Israel State Archives
MECA: Middle East Centre Archives, St. Anthony's College, Oxford
RHL: Rhodes House Library, Oxford
NA: National Archives, formerly PRO (Public Records Office), Kew Gardens, London
UCCI: United Christian Council of Israel
YMCA: Young Men's Christian Association

UNPUBLISHED SOURCES AND DIRECTORIES

ARCHIVES IN BRITAIN

Cambridge, Churchill Archives, Churchill College, Cambridge
-Personal papers and correspondence of Winston Churchill

Keele, Special Collections and Archives, Keele University Library, Keele University, England
-Personal papers and correspondence of Josiah C. Wedgwood

London, House of Lords Public Records Office, London
-Herbert Samuel papers
-Lloyd George papers

London, The National Archives, Kew Gardens, London (formerly The Public Records Office)
-Stanley Baldwin papers, FO
-Ernest Bevin papers, FO
-British Cabinet Minutes, various years
-John Chancellor files, CO
-British Colonial Office files
-Anthony Eden papers, FO
-British Foreign Office files
-Herbert Samuel papers, FO
-Montgomery papers
-Samuel Hoare papers, CO
-Peace Conference 1919 British Delegation notes, FO
-Correspondence between Permanent Under Secretaries and Palestine High Commissioners, CO
-Chaim Weizmann papers, CO
-Zionism files, FO

Oxford, Middle East Center Archives, St. Anthony's College, Oxford University, Oxford, England
-Edmund Allenby papers
-Gertrude Bell papers
-Norman Bentwich papers
-John Chancellor papers
-Gilbert Clayton papers
-Alan Cunningham papers
-John D'Arcy papers
-Wyndham Deedes papers
-Susanna Emery papers
-Harry Luke papers
-Charles MacGillivray papers
-Harold MacMichael papers
-Richard Meinertzhagen papers
-Henry McMahon papers
-Reginald Moncton papers
-Dorothy Norman papers
-Herbert Samuel papers
-Charles Tegart papers
-Woodrow Wilson papers

Oxford, Rhodes House Library, Oxford
-Chancellor Papers

British Libraries Providing Secondary Sources Relating to the Mandate Period
-Cambridge, Churchill Archives, Churchill College, Cambridge
-Keele University Library, Keele
-The National Library, London
-Oxford, The Jerusalem and East Mission Archive

ARCHIVES IN ISRAEL

Central Archives for the History of the Jewish People, Hebrew University of Jerusalem,
Givat Ram Campus, Jerusalem
-Arthur Balfour papers
-Lord Shaftsbury papers
-Ronald Storrs papers

Central Zionist Archives, Zalmon Shazar Blv., Jerusalem
-David Ben Gurion papers
-Lord Gort papers
-Frederick Kisch papers
-Harold MacMichael papers
-Jewish Agency papers
-Moshe Shertok papers
-Arthur Wauchope papers
-Zionist Executive papers
-Survey of the Arab Press

Chaim Weizmann Archives, Weizmann Institute of Science, Rehovot, Israel
-Personal papers and correspondence of Chaim Weizmann.

Christ Church Heritage Centre, Jaffa Gate, Old City, Jerusalem
-Archive of the Anglican Church in Eretz Israel

David Ben Gurion Archives, Sde Boker, Negev, Israel
-Personal library and partial collection of Ben Gurion's papers and correspondence

David Ben Gurion House, Ben Gurion Boulevard, Tel-Aviv
-Personal library and partial collection of Ben Gurion's papers and correspondence

Institute of Contemporary Jewry, Oral History Division Archives, Hebrew University of Jerusalem, Givat Ram Campus, Sprinzak Building, Jerusalem
-Collection of 20th century oral Jewish history

Israel State Archives, Mikor Haim, Talpiot, Jerusalem
-Antonius collection
-Bols papers
-Library of the Mandate period and early Israel independence period
-Herbert Samuel papers
-Various contemporary newspapers

Jerusalem Archives, Jerusalem Post, Ohaliav, Romema, Jerusalem
-Palestine Post/Jerusalem Post archives throughout the Mandate to the present

Jerusalem Municipality City Archives, Kikar Safra, Building #1, Jerusalem
-Library of the history of the City of Jerusalem from the late Ottoman period to the present

Menachem Begin Archive, Yemen Moshe, Jerusalem
-Personal papers and correspondence of Menachem Begin

Yad VaShem Archives
-Various general information relating to the last years of the Mandate and the Holocaust

Israeli Libraries Providing Secondary Sources Relating to the Mandate Period
-Ben Zvi Memorial Archive, Abrabanal St., Jerusalem
-Jewish National and University Library, Hebrew University Library, Givat Ram Campus, Jerusalem
-Tantur Ecumenical Centre Library, Gilo, Jerusalem
-West Jerusalem YMCA British Officer's Library, King David Street, Jerusalem
-Jerusalem University College Library, Mount Zion, Jerusalem

ADDITIONAL SITES IN ISRAEL

Other sites in Israel which proved helpful in understanding the British Palestine Mandate period were,
-Government House in Armon HaNaziv, Jerusalem, now the UN headquarters for the region
-St. Andrews Church in West Jerusalem, library
-St. Georges Church in East Jerusalem
-Christ Church, Jaffa Gate, Old City, Jerusalem

-King David Hotel, West Jerusalem
-The American Colony Hotel, and Spafford Children's Hospital, East Jerusalem
-British Central Prison, Jerusalem, now a museum
-British Mandate Courthouses, Jerusalem, now Israeli Courthouses
-Mount Herzl, Jerusalem
-Various British and Anzac battle sites and War Cemeteries, Gaza, Negev, Judean Hills and Jerusalem
-Various British police stations and fortresses, Jerusalem, Acre and Latrun
-Various sites of the 1937 Peel Commission, Jerusalem
-Augusta Victoria Hospital, Mount of Olives, East Jerusalem, first home of the High Commissioner

ARCHIVAL SOURCES

Foreign Office, Index to the Correspondence of the Foreign Office (later Public Record Office, now The National Archives).

Foster, Janet, et al, British Archives: A Guide to Archive Resources in the United Kingdom (Surrey, England: MacMillian Publishers, 1982).

Jones, Philip, Britain and Palestine 1914-1948 Archival Sources for the History of the British Mandate (Oxford: Oxford University Press, 1979).

Matthews, Neil and Doreen Wainwright, A Guide to Manuscripts and Documents in the British Isles Relating to the Middle East and North Africa (Oxford: Oxford University Press, 1980).

Stenton, M., et al, Who's Who of British Members of Parliament, Vol. II 1886-1919, Vol. III 1919-1945 (Sussex: Harvester Press, 1979).

Weaver, J.R.H., Dictionary of National Biography. Second Supplement 1901-1911, (Oxford, Oxford University Press, 1920).

_____ Dictionary of National Biography, Third Supplement 1912-1921 (Oxford: Oxford University Press, 1927).

_____ Dictionary of National Biography. Fourth Supplement 1922-1930 (Oxford: Oxford University Press, 1930).

Wigoder, Geoffrey, Dictionary of Jewish Biography (Jerusalem: Jerusalem Press, 1991).

Woodward, E.L. et al, Documents on British Foreign Policy 1919-1939 (London: Her Majesty's Stationary Office, 1952).

INTERVIEWS

CONTEMPORARY INTERVIEW SOURCES

Isaiah Adler, Jewish, born in Jerusalem 1926, officer in the Jewish Brigade in Palestine during World War 2, Jerusalem, September 26 2007.

Harold Arkell, born in 1927 in Ulster, attendee of the funeral of Edward Carson in Northern Ireland in 1935, Ontario, Canada, September 1995.

Joseph Bar David, Jewish, born in Tiberius in 1944, witnessed departure of British in May 1948, Yad HaShmonah, Israel, February 2008.

Subhi Ballan, Christian Arab born and raised in Cana, Galilee in 1932, witnessed the British departure in 1948, Jerusalem, March 2006.

Ben Zion Barohov, Jewish, born in Jerusalem in 1925, raised in Jerusalem during the Mandate, witnessed the departure of the British in 1948, Jerusalem, November 2004.

Shalom Lindenbaum, born in Poland in 1926, Jewish Auschwitz survivor, Cyprus camp detainee, Camp Atlit detainee, Jerusalem, April 2006.

Zvi Kalisher, born in Poland in 1930, Jewish Warsaw Ghetto survivor, Cyprus detainee, Jewish resistance fighter, East Talpiot, Jerusalem, March 2006.

Rita Mouchabeck, Christian Arab born in Jerusalem in 1925, graduate of the British High School in Jerusalem, worked for the British at the Russian Compound police station until the end of the Mandate in 1948, Jerusalem, March 2006.

Valentine Vester, born in 1907, British Christian, wife of Horatio Vester, daughter in law of Bertha Spafford Vester, long time resident of Jerusalem, owner of American Colony Hotel, Jerusalem, December 2004.

LATER INTERVIEW SOURCES

Rev. William Broughton, Episcopalian Priest, St. George's Cathedral, Jerusalem, April 2009.

Rev. Lindell Browning, Director of the Church of the Nazarene in the Middle East, Jerusalem, 2006.

Kelvin Crombie, Historian at Christ Church, Jerusalem, various occasions 1994-2007.

Rev. John Cubie, Minister, St, Andrews Presbyterian Church, Jerusalem, April 2009.

Rev. Thomas Jamison, Director of American Messianic Fellowship, Tel Aviv, 2007

Jonathan Kaplan, Middle East History Professor, Jerusalem University College, Hebrew University, Jerusalem, various occasions, 1993-2007.

Father Stephen Kuncherakatt of the Ratisbonne Institute, Jerusalem, April 2009.

Rev. Greg Kingry, Director of Southern Baptists in Israel, Baptist House, Jerusalem, 2005.

Melvin Leffler, Professor, University of Virginia, Hebrew University, Jerusalem, May 29 2008.

Father Michael McGarry, Rector of Tantur Ecumenical Center in Jerusalem, April 2009.

Rev. Charles Musgrave, Minister of St. Andrews Presbyterian Church, Jerusalem, 2006.

Rev. David Pileggi, Historian at Christ Church, Jerusalem, various occasions, 1993-2007.

Halvor Ronen, Director, "Home for Bible Translators and Scholars," Jerusalem, April, 2009.

Dr. Christophe Rico of the Dominican Ecole Biblique, Jerusalem, April 2009.

Tom Segev, Journalist and Middle East historian, Jerusalem, various telephone interviews, 2003-2007.

Penny Tancred, daughter in law of Field Marshal Alan Cunningham, last High Commissioner of Palestine, London, April 2006.

Various interviews in Israel and England through Hugh Kitson and Rosie Ross for the documentary film The Forsaken Promise, Hatikvah Film Trust, West Sussex, UK, 2005-2007.

Various interviews with representatives of the International Christian Embassy, German Colony, Jerusalem, 2002-2007.

CONTEMPORARY PUBLISHED GOVERNMENT SOURCES

The Churchill White Paper, Statement of British Policy on Palestine, June 1922, Correspondence with the Palestine Arab Delegation and the Zionist Organization. Cmd. 1700.

The Haycroft Report into the Disturbances of May 1921, with Correspondence, October 1921, Cmd. 1540.

The Hogarth Message, Statements made on behalf of His Majesty's Government during the year 1918 by Commander D.G. Hogarth of the Arab Bureau of Cairo, in regard to the future status of certain parts of the Ottoman Empire (London: His Majesty's Stationary Office, 1939).

The Hope Simpson Report, Palestine, Report on Immigration, Land Settlement and Development, by Sir John Hope Simpson, C.I.E., Presented by the Secretary of State for the Colonies to Parliament by Command of His Majesty, October 1930, (London: His Majesty's Stationary Office, 1930) Cmd. 3686.

Historical Statistics of the United States, the Bureau of the Census with the Cooperation of the Social Science Research Council, U.S. Department of Commerce, Frederick H. Mueller, U.S. Department of the Census, Robert W. Burgess, Director, United States Government, Washington D.C., 1960.

House of Commons, Parliamentary Debates, Official Report, London, His Majesty's Stationary Office, various debates from the 1917 through to the 1950's.

House of Lords, Parliamentary Debates, Official Report, London, His Majesty's Stationary Office, various debates from 1920-1939.

House of Representatives, United States of America, Sol Bloom, Chairman, Committee of Foreign Affairs House of Representatives, The Jewish National Home in Palestine, Hearings before the Committee on Foreign Affairs House of Representatives, 78th Congress, Second Session on H. Res. 418 and H. Res. 419. Resolutions Relative to the Jewish National Home in Palestine, Feb 8, 9, 15, 16, 1944.

Jewish Agency Documents related to Palestine. Memoranda on the Development of the Jewish National Home, 1930-1938; Palestine, The Disturbances of 1936; The Jewish Case Against the White Paper, 1939.

Joint Anglo-American Committee of Inquiry, US Department of State, Hearings, Washington D.C., 1946.

Prime Minister Ramsey MacDonald letter to Chaim Weizmann, February 13 1931.

McMahon Letters, Correspondence between Sir. Henry McMahon, His Majesty's High Commissioner at Cairo and The Sherif Hussein of Mecca, July 1915 to March 1916 (ten letters) (London: His Majesty's Stationary Office, 1939) Cmd. 5957.

The Passfield White Paper, A Statement of Policy (October 1930). Cmd. 3692.

Peel Commission Report, Palestine Royal Commission Report (His Majesty's Stationary Office, London, July 1937, Cmd. 5479.

The Realities of American-Palestine Relations, (Washington: Public Affairs Press, 1949).

Herbert Samuel Report, An Interim Report on the Civil Administration of Palestine, 1 July 1920-30 June 1921. Cmd. 1499.

The Shaw Report on the Disturbances of August 1929 (March 1930), Cmd. 3530.

United Nations, Report to the General Assembly by the United Nations Special Committee on Palestine, Geneva, Switzerland, August 31 1947 (London: His Majesties Stationary Office, 1947).

Woodhead Report, The Palestine Partition Plan, October 1938, Cmd. 5854.

White Paper 1939, Palestine: A Statement of Policy, (May 1939), The May White Papers, Cmd. 6019.

CONTEMPORARY PUBLISHED PRIMARY SOURCES

Abdullah of Jordan, Memoirs of King Abdullah of Transjordan (London: Jonathan Cape, 1950).

Agnon, Shmuel Yosef, From Myself to Myself (Jerusalem: Keter Press, 1976).

Amery, Leo S., My Political Life, Vol. I-III, (London: Hutchenson, 1953).

Ashbee, C., A Palestine Notebook, 1918-1923 (London: 1938).

Asquith, Herbert H., Letters to Venetia (Oxford: Oxford University Press, 1982).

_____ Fifty Years of British Parliament (Boston: Little, Brown and Co., 1926).

_____ Memories and Reflections 1852-1937, Vol. I-II (London: Cassell and Co. Ltd., 1928).

_____ Moments of Memory, Recollections and Impressions (London: Hutchenson & Co., 1937).

Asquith, Margot, Margot Asquith, An Autobiography, Four Volumes (New York: George H. Doran Co., 1920).

Attlee, Clement R., As It Happened, (Kingswood, Surry: The Windmill Press, 1954).

Balfour, Arthur James, Chapters of Autobiography. (London: Cassell and Company, 1930).

_____Criticism and Beauty: Lectures for 1909 (Oxford: Clarendon Press, 1910).

_____ A Defense of Philosophic Doubt (London: Hodder and Stoughton, 1920).

_____ Essays and Addresses (Edinburgh: David Douglas, 1893).

_____ The Foundations of Belief (London: Longmans, Green, & Co., 1895).

_____ Retrospect: An Unfinished Autobiography, 1848-1886 (Cambridge: Riverside Press, 1930).

_____ Speeches on Zionism (London: Arrowsmith, 1928).

_____ Theism and Humanism (London: Hodder and Stoughton, 1915).

Barnes, George N., History of the International Labour Office (London: Williams and Norgate Ltd., 1926).

_____ From the Workshop to the War Cabinet (London: Jenkins, 1923).

Begin, Menachem, The Revolt, translated from Hebrew by Shmuel Katz, (London: W. H. Allen, 1951).

Ben-Gurion, David, Ben Gurion Looks Back (London: Weidenfeld and Nicholson, 1965).

_____ The Jews in their Land (London: Aldus Books, 1966).

_____ Memoirs (London: Aldus Books, 1973).

_____ The Peel Report and the Jewish State (London: 1938).

Bentwich, Norman, My Seventy-Seven Years, An Account of My Life and Times, 1883-1960 (London: Routledge & Kegan Paul Ltd., 1962).

_____ Wanderer Between Two Worlds (London: Kegan, Paul, Trench, Trubner & Co. Ltd., 1941).

_____ and Helen Bentwich, Mandate Memories, 1918-1948 (New York: Schocken Books, 1965).

Bernadotte, Count Folke, To Jerusalem, (London: Hodder and Stoughter, 1951).

Brandeis, Louis D., Brandeis on Zionism (Washington: Zionist Organization of America, 1942).

Churchill, Winston S., The Aftermath (London: Macmillian & Co. Ltd., 1940).

_____ A Churchill Reader (Cambridge: Houghton Mifflin Co., Riverside, 1954).

_____ Great Contemporaries (London: Macmillian & Co., 1942).

_____ The Great War (London: George Newness Ltd, 1933).

_____ The River War, Two Volumes (London: Longmans, 1899).

_____ The Second World War, Vol. I-VI, (London: Houghton Mifflin Co., 1949-1953).

_____ Thoughts and Adventures (London: Macmillian & Co., 1942).

_____ The World Crisis 1911-1918 (London: Macmillian & Co., 1923).

Crossman, Richard, Palestine Mission (New York: Harper, 1947).

Duff, D. V., Sword for Hire (London: 1937).

Dugdale, Blanche, ed. by Norman Rose, The Diaries of Blanche Dugdale 1936-1947 (London: Vallentine Mitchell, 1973).

Dunkelman, Benjamin, Dual Allegiance (Halifax: Formac Publishing, 1976).

Eban, Abba, Abba Eban (London: Futura Publications Ltd., 1979).

Eden, Anthony, Memoirs, 2 vols. (London and New York: 1962, 1964).

Falls, Cyril, Military Operations: Egypt and Palestine: June 1917-1919 (London: His Majesty's Stationary Office, 1930).

Glubb, John Bagot, The Story of the Arab Legion (London: Hodder & Stoughter, 1948).

Glynn, Jenifer, Tidings from Zion, Helen Bentwich's Letters from Jerusalem, 1919-1931 (London: I.B. Tauris Publishers, 2000).

Goldmann, Nahum, Sixty Years of Jewish Life, The Autobiography of Nahum Goldmann (New York: Holt, Rinehart and Winston, 1969).

Graves, R.M., Experiment in Anarchy (London: V. Gollencz, 1949).

Hadawi, Sami, The Palestine Diary (New York: New World Press, 1972).

Jordan, Ruth, Daughter of the Waves, Memories of Growing up in Pre-War Palestine (New York: Taplinger Publishing Company, 1983).

Keith-Roach, Edward, Pasha of Jerusalem, Memoirs of a District Commissioner under the British Mandate (London: The Radcliffe Press, 1994).

Kisch, Frederick H., Palestine Diary (London: Victor Gollancz Ltd., 1938).

Kleeberg, Julius P., Recollections of a Medical Doctor in Jerusalem 1930-1988 (Basel: Karger, 1992).

Lang, Michael, One Man In His Time, The Diary of a Palestine Policeman 1946-48 (Sussex: The Book Guild Ltd., 1997).

Lawrence, T.E., Revolt in the Desert (New York: George Doran Co., 1927).

Lloyd George, David, The Truth About the Peace Treaties (London: Victor Gollancz Ltd., 1939).

_____ War Memoirs of David Lloyd George, 2 Vols. (London: Odhams Press Limited, 1936).

Lord Moran, Winston Churchill: The Struggle for Survival, 1940-1965, Taken from the Diaries of Lord Moran (London: Sphere Books Limited, 1966).

Luke, H. C., Cities and Men, Three Volumes (London: 1953-1956).

MacDonald, Malcolm, Titans and Others (London: Collins, 1972).

Marlowe, John, The Seat of Pilate-An Account of the Palestine Mandate (London: The Cresset Press, 1959).

McDonald, James, My Mission in Israel 1948-1951 (New York: Simon & Schuster, 1951).

Meinertzhagen, Richard, Middle East Diary: 1917-1956 (London: Cresset Press, 1959).

Meir, Golda, A Land of Our Own, An Oral Autobiography (New York: G.P. Putnam's Sons, 1973).

_____ My Life, The Autobiography of Golda Meir (London: Futura Publications Limited, 1975).

Montgomery, Bernard, The Memoirs of Field Marshal the Viscount Montgomery (London: Collins, 1958).

Patterson, J. H., With the Judaeans in the Palestine Campaign (London: Hutchinson and Co., 1922).

Philby, H. St. J. B., Arabian Days, An Autobiography by H. St. J. B. Philby (London: Robert Hale Ltd., 1948).

Ruppin, Arthur, Memoirs, Diaries, Letters (London: Weidenfeld and Nicolson, 1971).

Samuel, Edwin. A Life Time in Jerusalem: The Memoirs of the Second Viscount Samuel (Jerusalem: Israel Universities Press, 1970).

Samuel, Herbert, Memoirs (London: The Cresset Press, 1945).

Stone, I.F., Underground to Palestine (New York: Pantheon Books, 1978).

Smuts, Jan C., A Great Historic Vow, (London: The Jewish Agency for Palestine, 1930).

Storrs, Ronald, The Memoirs of Sir Ronald Storrs (New York: G.P. Putnam's Sons, 1937).

Sylvester, A.J., Life with Lloyd George, The Diary of A.J. Sylvester, 1931-1945 (London: Cross, MacMillian, 1975).

Truman, Harry, Memoirs, Years of Trial and Hope (London and New York: 1956).

_____ Plain Speaking, An oral record based on interviews with Merle Miller conducted in the early 1960's (New York: Tess Press, 2004).

Vester, Bertha Spafford, Our Jerusalem (Jerusalem: American Colony, 1950).

Weizmann, Chaim, Trial and Error (London: East and West Library, 1950).

Weizmann, Vera, The Impossible Takes Longer, Memoirs of Vera Weizmann (London: Hamish Hamilton, 1967).

PUBLISHED JOURNAL SOURCES

Ariel, Yaakov, "Postville: A Clash of Cultures in Heartland America," American Jewish History, Vol. 89, No. 3, September 2001, pp. 313-315.

Arnow, David, "The Holocaust and the Birth of Israel: Reassessing the Causal Relationship," The Journal of Israeli History, Vol. 15, No. 3, August 1994, pp. 257-281.

Bell, J. Addison, "Christendom Needs Zionism," The Christian Zionist, Vol. 1, No. 1, December 15 1937, pp. 1-2.

_____ "The Government is With Us," The Christian Zionist, Vol. 1, No. 2, January 1 1938, pp. 1-2.

Bar Yosef, Eitan, "Christian Zionism and Victorian Culture," Israel Studies, Vol. 8, No. 2, Summer 2003, pp. 18-44.

Blackstone, William E., "William E. Blackstone, Zionist," The New Palestine, March 7 1941, pp. 2-4.

Buhler, Jurgen, "The History of Christian Zionism," Word from Jerusalem ICEJ, May 2008, p. 6.

Cohen, Michael C., "Why Britain Left: The End of the Mandate," The Weiner Library Bulletin, Vol. 31, No. 44/46, 1978, pp. 74-86.

Constable, Miles, "George Beurling," article for the Royal Canadian Air Force, Ottawa: 1998, pp.1-4.

Crombie, Kelvin, "Allenby, Anzacs, and the View From Our Roof," Shalom 3, 1992, pp. 7-11.

Friedman, Isaiah, "British Plans for the Restoration of Jews to Palestine, 1840-1850," Cathedra 56, 1990, pp. 42-69.

Friesel, Evyatar, "Herbert Samuel's Reassessment of Palestine in 1921," Studies in Zionism Vol. 5, No. 2. 1984, pp. 213-237.

_____ "The Holocaust and the Birth of Israel," The Weiner Library Bulletin, Vol. 32, No. 49/50, 1979, pp. 51-59.

Gardella, Peter, "Gentile Zionism," Midstream 37:4, May 1991, pp. 29-32.

Gillon, D.Z., "The Antecedents of the Balfour Declaration," Middle Eastern Studies, 5, 1969, pp. 131-150.

Levene, Mark, "Edge of Darkness," Jewish Quarterly, 3, 1991, pp. 31-36.

McTague, John J., "Zionist-British Negotiations over the Draft Mandate for Palestine, 1920," Jewish Social Studies, 42/3-4, 1980, pp. 281-292.

Ovendale, Ritchie, "The Palestine Policy of the British Labour Government 1945-1946," Royal Institute of International Affairs, Vol. 55, No. 3, July 1979, pp. 409-431.

Padwa, Jack, "You don't have to be Jewish to be a Zionist," International Forum for a United Jerusalem, 2000, pp. 80-81.

Parsons, David, "The Christian Role in Israel's Rebirth," Word from Jerusalem ICEJ, May 2008, p. 8.

Perko, F. Michael, "Contemporary American Christian Attitudes to Israel Based on Scriptures," Israel Studies Vol. 8, No. 2, Summer 2003, pp. 1-17.

Reinharz, Jehuda, "The Balfour Declaration and It's Maker: A Reassessment," Journal of Modern History, Vol. 3, 1992, pp. 455- 499.

Reynolds, Ralph C., "Preserving the Wall," The Newsletter of The Americans United for Separation of Church and State, Vol. 3, No. 3, pp. 10-15.

Rose, Norman, "The Arab Rulers in Palestine, 1936: The British Reaction," Journal of Modern History, Vol. 44, No. 2, June 1972, pp. 213-231.

Rosenthal, Marvin, "Can These Bones Live?" Zion's Fire Vol. 4, No. 5, Sept/Oct 1993, pp. 11-18.

Rubinstein, William D., "The Secret of Leopold Amery," Historical Research, Vol. 73, Issue 181, January 2003, pp. 175-196.

Sheffer, Gabi, "Intentions and Results of British Policy in Palestine: Passfield's White Paper," Middle Eastern Studies, 1973, Vol. 9, No. 1, pp. 46-55.

Stein, Joshua B, "Josiah Wedgwood and the Seventh Dominion Scheme," Studies on Zionism 2, 1990, pp. 141-155.

Stockton, Ronald R., "Christian Zionism: Prophecy and Public Opinion," The Middle East Journal, Vol. 41, No. 2, Spring 1987, pp. 234-253.

Townshend, Charles, "The Defense of Palestine: Insurrection and Public Security 1936-1939," The English Historical Review, Harlow, Essex: Longman, October 1988, pp. 917-949.

_____ "Going to the Wall: The Failure of British Rule in Palestine, 1928-31," The Journal of Imperial and Commonwealth History Vol. 30, No. 2, London: Frank Cass, May 2002, pp. 25-52.

Tsimhoni, Daphne, "The British Mandate and the Status of the Religious Communities in Palestine," (in Hebrew), Cathedra for the History of Eretz Israel and its Yishuv, No.80, June 1996, pp. 150-174.

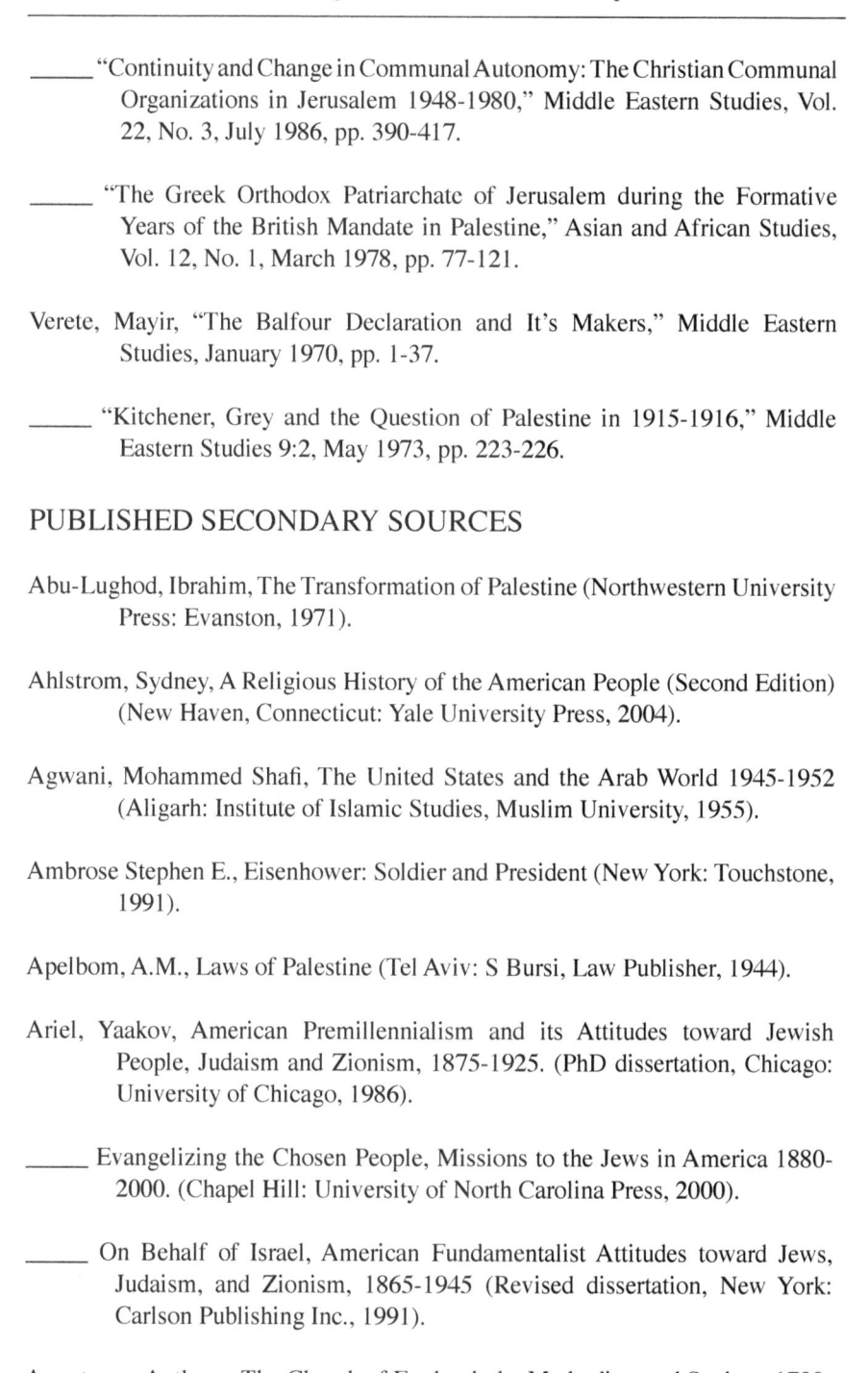

____ "Continuity and Change in Communal Autonomy: The Christian Communal Organizations in Jerusalem 1948-1980," Middle Eastern Studies, Vol. 22, No. 3, July 1986, pp. 390-417.

____ "The Greek Orthodox Patriarchate of Jerusalem during the Formative Years of the British Mandate in Palestine," Asian and African Studies, Vol. 12, No. 1, March 1978, pp. 77-121.

Verete, Mayir, "The Balfour Declaration and It's Makers," Middle Eastern Studies, January 1970, pp. 1-37.

____ "Kitchener, Grey and the Question of Palestine in 1915-1916," Middle Eastern Studies 9:2, May 1973, pp. 223-226.

PUBLISHED SECONDARY SOURCES

Abu-Lughod, Ibrahim, The Transformation of Palestine (Northwestern University Press: Evanston, 1971).

Ahlstrom, Sydney, A Religious History of the American People (Second Edition) (New Haven, Connecticut: Yale University Press, 2004).

Agwani, Mohammed Shafi, The United States and the Arab World 1945-1952 (Aligarh: Institute of Islamic Studies, Muslim University, 1955).

Ambrose Stephen E., Eisenhower: Soldier and President (New York: Touchstone, 1991).

Apelbom, A.M., Laws of Palestine (Tel Aviv: S Bursi, Law Publisher, 1944).

Ariel, Yaakov, American Premillennialism and its Attitudes toward Jewish People, Judaism and Zionism, 1875-1925. (PhD dissertation, Chicago: University of Chicago, 1986).

____ Evangelizing the Chosen People, Missions to the Jews in America 1880-2000. (Chapel Hill: University of North Carolina Press, 2000).

____ On Behalf of Israel, American Fundamentalist Attitudes toward Jews, Judaism, and Zionism, 1865-1945 (Revised dissertation, New York: Carlson Publishing Inc., 1991).

Armstrong, Anthony, The Church of England, the Methodists and Society: 1700-1850 (London: University of London Press, 1973).

Aronson, Shlomo, Hitler, the Allies and the Jews (Cambridge: Cambridge Press, 2004).

Ashley, Maurice, The Greatness of Oliver Cromwell (London: Collier-Macmillan, 1969).

Augustine, The City of God (Translated by Marcus Dods) (New York: Modern Library).

Avineri, Ariel L., Jewish Settlement and the Change of Dispossession, 1878-1948 (Hebrew) (Tel Aviv: Ha Kibbutz Ha Me'uhad, 1980).

Balshone, Benjamin, Determined, (New York: Bloch Publishing Co., 1984).

Barlow, Philip L., Mormons and the Bible: The Place of Latter Day Saints in American Religion (Oxford: Oxford University Press, 1997).

Ben Arieh, Yehoshua, Jerusalem and the British Mandate (Jerusalem: Yad Izhak Ben-Zvi, 2003).

Ben-Dor, Gabriel, The Palestinians and the Middle East Conflict (Haifa: Institute of Middle East Studies, University of Haifa, 1979).

Bence-Jones, Mark, The Viceroys of India (London: Constable, 1982).

Benson, Michael T., Harry S. Truman and the Founding of Israel (New York: McGraw Hill, 1997).

Bentwich, Norman, et al, Brigadier Frederick Kisch, Soldier and Zionist (London: Valentine, Mitchell & Co., 1966).

_____ Fulfillment in the Promised Land, 1917-1937 (London: The Soncino Press, 1938).

_____ Wandering Between Two Worlds (London: Kegan Paul, Trench, Trubner & Co., Ltd., 1941).

Berkowitz, Michael, Zionist Culture and West European Jewry Before the First World War (Cambridge: Cambridge University Press, 1993).

Bernstein, Barton J., and Matuson, Allen J., The Truman Administration (New York: Harper & Row, 1968).

Bethell, Nicholas, The Palestine Triangle, The Struggle between the British, the Jews and the Arabs 1935-1948 (London: Andre Deutsch, 1979).

Bickerton, Ian J., A Concise History of the Arab-Israeli Conflict, (New York: Prentice Hall, 2002).

Birrell, Francis, Gladstone (New York: Collier, 1962).

Black, Jeremy, A New History of Wales (Phoenix Mill: Sutton Publishing, 2000).

Blackstone, William E., Jesus is Coming, 3rd Edition (Chicago: Fleming H. Revell, 1908). (Note: This book was translated into Hebrew in 1925 for Jewish readers in Palestine).

Blake, Robert, Disraeli (London: Eyre & Spottiswoode, 1966).

_____ The Unknown Prime Minister (London: Eyre and Spottiswoode, 1955).

Bosco, Andrea, et al, Chatham House and British Foreign Policy 1919-1945 (London: Lothian Foundation Press, 1994).

Bowle, John, Viscount Samuel (London: Victor Gollancz Ltd., 1957).

Brands, H. W., Into the Labyrinth, The United States and the Middle East 1945-1993 (New York: McGraw Hill, 1994).

Brecher, Frank W., Reluctant Ally, United States Foreign Policy toward the Jews from Wilson to Roosevelt (Westport, CT: Greenwood Press, 1991).

Brenchley, Frank, Britain and the Middle East, An Economic History 1945-1987 (London: Lester Crook Academic Publishing, 1989).

Brown, Mary Beth, Hand of Providence, The Strong and Quiet Faith of Ronald Reagan (Nashville: Nelson Current, 2004).

Bruce, Anthony, The Last Crusade, The Palestine Campaign in the First World War (London: John Murray, 2002).

Bullock, Alan, The Life and Times of Ernest Bevin, Vol. I, Trade Union Leader, 1881-1940 (London: Heinemann, 1960).

_____ The Life and Times of Ernest Bevin, Vol. 2, Minister of Labour 1940-1945 (London: Heinemann, 1967).

_____ The Life and Times of Ernest Bevin, Vol. 3, Foreign Secretary, 1945-1951 (London: Heinemann, 1983).

Butler, David, et al, Twentieth Century British Political Facts 1900-2000 (London: MacMillian, 2000).

Cailingold, Asher, An Unlikely Heroine, Esther Cailingold's Fight for Jerusalem (London: Vallentine Mitchell, 2000).

Cairns, Earle E., Christianity through the Centuries (Grand Rapids, Michigan: Zondervan, 1979).

Capstick, Peter Hathaway, Warrior, The Legend of Colonel Richard Meinertzhagen (New York: St. Martin's Press, 1998).

Charters, David A., The British Army and Jewish Insurgency in Palestine, 1945-47 (London: MacMillian Press, 1989).

Chertoff, Mordecai S., Zionism (New York: Herzl Press, 1975).

Clark, Alan, The Tories, Conservatives and the Nation State 1922-1997 (London: Weidenfeld & Nicolson, 1998).

Clarke, Thurston, By Blood and Fire-July 22, 1946-The Attack on the King David Hotel. (New York: G.P. Putnam's Sons, 1981).

Clemens, Cyril, A Man from Limehouse, Clement Richard Attlee (St. Louis, Missouri: C.B. Nicholson Printing Co., 1946).

Cocker, Mark, Richard Meinertzhagen, Soldier, Scientist and Spy (London: Mandarin, 1990).

Cohen, Michael J., Churchill and the Jews (London: Frank Cass, 1985).

_____ "Churchill and Zionism," Published Lecture Notes (London: Hillel House, March 13, 1974).

_____ and Kolinsky, Martin (eds.) Demise of the British Empire in the Middle East (London: Frank Cass, 1998).

_____ The Origins of the Arab Zionist Conflict (Los Angeles: University of California, 1987).

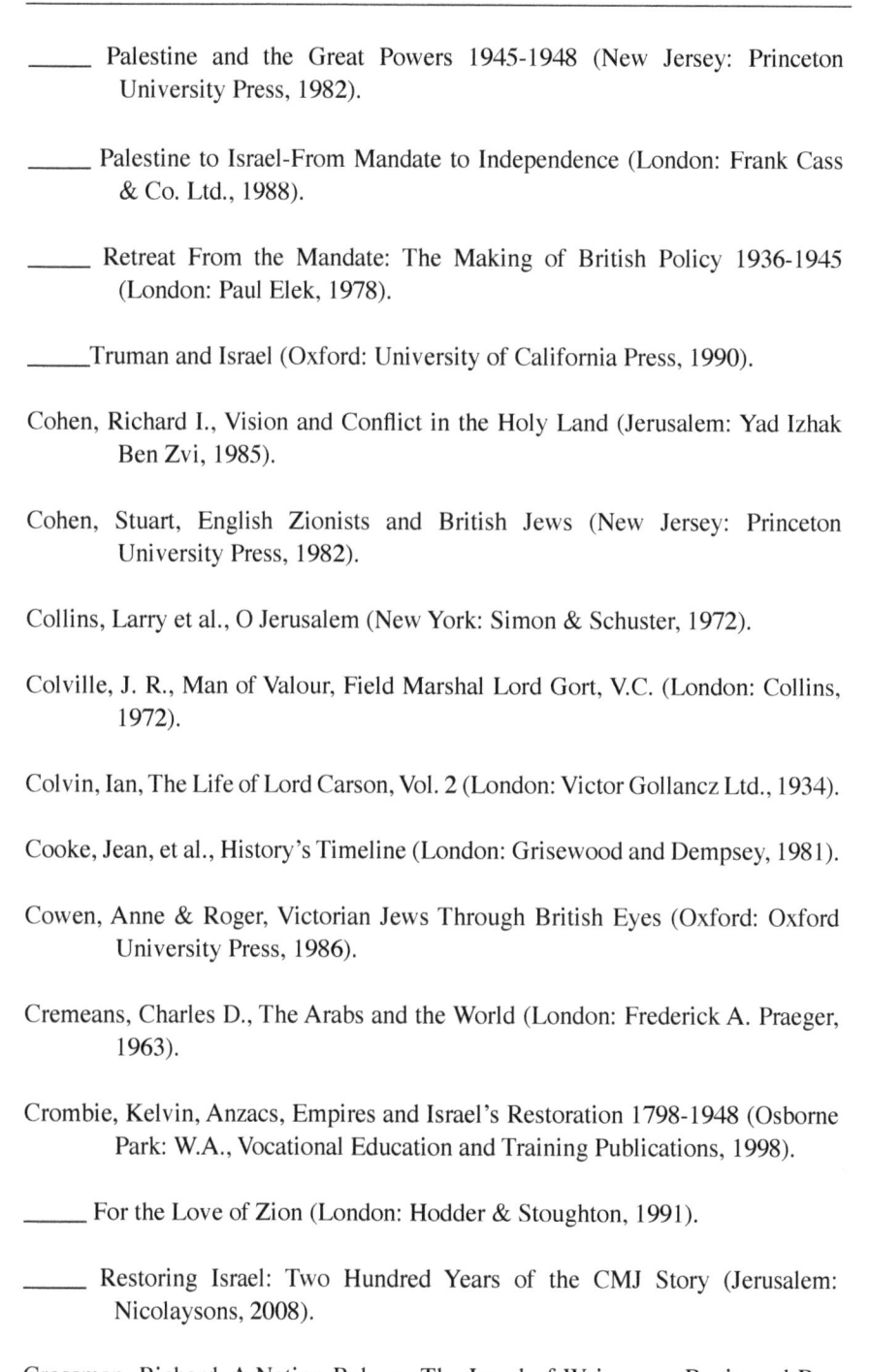

_____ Palestine and the Great Powers 1945-1948 (New Jersey: Princeton University Press, 1982).

_____ Palestine to Israel-From Mandate to Independence (London: Frank Cass & Co. Ltd., 1988).

_____ Retreat From the Mandate: The Making of British Policy 1936-1945 (London: Paul Elek, 1978).

_____ Truman and Israel (Oxford: University of California Press, 1990).

Cohen, Richard I., Vision and Conflict in the Holy Land (Jerusalem: Yad Izhak Ben Zvi, 1985).

Cohen, Stuart, English Zionists and British Jews (New Jersey: Princeton University Press, 1982).

Collins, Larry et al., O Jerusalem (New York: Simon & Schuster, 1972).

Colville, J. R., Man of Valour, Field Marshal Lord Gort, V.C. (London: Collins, 1972).

Colvin, Ian, The Life of Lord Carson, Vol. 2 (London: Victor Gollancz Ltd., 1934).

Cooke, Jean, et al., History's Timeline (London: Grisewood and Dempsey, 1981).

Cowen, Anne & Roger, Victorian Jews Through British Eyes (Oxford: Oxford University Press, 1986).

Cremeans, Charles D., The Arabs and the World (London: Frederick A. Praeger, 1963).

Crombie, Kelvin, Anzacs, Empires and Israel's Restoration 1798-1948 (Osborne Park: W.A., Vocational Education and Training Publications, 1998).

_____ For the Love of Zion (London: Hodder & Stoughton, 1991).

_____ Restoring Israel: Two Hundred Years of the CMJ Story (Jerusalem: Nicolaysons, 2008).

Crossman, Richard, A Nation Reborn, The Israel of Weizmann, Bevin and Ben Gurion (London: Hamish Hamilton, 1960).

Crowe, J.H.V., General Smut's Campaign in East Africa (London: John Murray, 1918).

Currie, William E., God's Little Errand Boy, William Blackstone (Chicago: American Messianic Fellowship, 1987).

Curzon, George, Travels with a Superior Person (London: Sigwick & Jackson, 1985).

Dann, Uriel et al., The Great Powers in the Middle East 1919-1939 (New York: Holmes & Meier, 1988).

Davidson, Lawrence, America's Palestine (Gainsville: University Press of Florida, 2001).

Davies, Graham, The Chosen People, Wales and Jews (Bridgend, Wales: Poetry Wales Press Limited, 2002).

Deedes, Sir Wyndham et al., Palestine 1917-1944 (London: The British Association for the Jewish National Home in Palestine, 1944).

Dennis, Barbara, Reform and Intellectual Debate in Victorian England (New York: Croom Helm, 1987).

Dilnot, Frank, Lloyd George, The Man and His Story (New York: Harper, 1917).

Dudman, Helga and Ruth Kark, The American Colony (Jerusalem: Carta, 1998).

Dugdale, Blanche, Arthur James Balfour (London: Hutchenson, 1936).

_____ The Balfour Declaration, Origins and Background (London: Jewish Agency for Palestine, 1940).

Eban, Abba, Abba Eban, An Autobiography (New York: Random House, 1977).

Edelman, M., Ben Gurion: A Political Biography (London: 1964).

Edwardes, O.J., Palestine: Land of Broken Promises (London: Dorothy Crisp & Co., 1946).

Egremont, Max, Balfour (London: Collins, 1980).

Elath, E., Memoirs of Sir Wyndam Deeds (London: 1958).

Eliav, Mordechai, Britain and the Holy Land 1838-1914, (Jerusalem: Yad Izhak Ben Zvi and Magnes Press, Hebrew University, 1997).

Ellisen, Stanley A., Who Owns the Land? (Portland, Oregon: Multnomah, 1991).

Elton, Godfrey (Lord Elton), The Life of James Ramsay MacDonald 1866-1919 (London: Collins, 1939).

Encyclopaedia Britannica, (Cambridge: University Press, 11th Edition, 1910).

Encyclopaedia Britannica, (Cambridge: University Press, 12th Edition, 1922).

Encyclopaedia Britannica, (Chicago: University of Chicago, 1974 Edition).

Encyclopaedia Judaica, (Jerusalem: Keter Publishing, 1970 Edition).

ESCO Foundation for Palestine, Palestine: A Study of Jewish, Arab and British Policies (New Haven: Yale University Press, 1947).

Evans, Trevor, Bevin (London: George Allen & Unwin Ltd., 1946).

Farago, Ladislas, Palestine at the Crossroads (New York: G.P. Putnam's Sons, 1937).

Feingold, Henry L., Zion in America (New York: Twayne Publishers Inc., 1974).

Feldman, David, Englishmen and Jews, Social Relations and Political Culture 1840-1914 (New Haven: Yale University Press, 1994).

Finke, Roger and Stark, Rodney, The Churching of America, 1776-1990 (New Brunswick, New Jersey: Rutgers University Press, 2000).

Fisher, Carol A., and Krinsky, Fred, Middle East in Crisis (Syracuse: Syracuse University Press, 1959).

Fishman, Hertzel, American Protestantism and a Jewish State (Detroit: Wayne State University Press, 1973).

Fletcher-Jones, Pamela, The Jews of Britain: A Thousand Years of History (Gloucestershire: The Windrush Press, 1990).

Ford, Colin et al, A Hundred Years Ago: Britain in the 1880's (Middlesex: Allen Lane, 1983).

Foster, R.F., Modern Ireland, 1600-1972 (London: Penguin, 1988).

Friedman, Isaiah, The Question of Palestine, 1914-1918 (London: Routledge & Kegan, 1973).

Friesel, Evyatar, Zionist Policy After the Balfour Declaration 1917-22 (Tel Aviv: Hakibbutz Hameuchad Publishing, 1972).

Fromkin, David, A Peace to End all Peace (New York: Henry Holt & Co., 1989).

Ganin, Zvi, Truman, American Jewry, and Israel, 1945-1948 (New York: Holmes & Meier Publishers Inc., 1979).

Gaustad, Edwin Scott, A Documentary History of Religion in America to the Civil War (Grand Rapids: Eerdmans, 1983).

_____ A Documentary History of Religion in America Since 1865 (Grand Rapids: Eerdmans, 1983).

Gerner, Deborah J., One Land, Two Peoples (Boulder, Colorado: Westview Press, 1994).

Gilbert, Martin, The Arab-Israeli Conflict-It's History in Maps (London: Weidenfield and Nicolson, 1974).

_____ Churchill: A Life (London: Minerva, 1991).

_____ Churchill: A Photographic Portrait (William Heinemann: London, 1974).

_____ Churchill and the Jews, a Lifelong Friendship (New York: Henry Holt and Company, 2007).

Gilmour, David, Curzon, Imperial Statesman, (New York: Rarrar, Straus and Giroux, 2003).

Gitlin, Jan, The Conquest of Acre Fortress (Tel Aviv: Hadar Publishing House, Tel Aviv, 1982).

Glennon, Lorraine, Our Times (Atlanta: Time Warner, 1994)

Goldschmidt, Arthur, Jr., A Concise History of the Middle East (Boulder, Colorado: Westview Press, 1979).

Goodman, Paul, Chaim Weizmann (London: J. M. Dent, 1945).

_____ The Jewish National Home (London: J.M. Dent, 1943).

Gorny, Joseph, The British Labour Movement and Zionism 1917-1948 (London: Frank Cass, 1983).

Graham, Billy, Just As I Am (New York: Harper, 2007).

Grant, George, The Blood of the Moon: The Roots of the Middle East Crisis (Brentwood, Tennessee: Wolgemuth & Hyatt, 1991).

Grant, Neil, The Partition of Palestine (New York: Franklin Watts Inc., 1973).

Greaves, Richard L., Saints and Rebels: Seven Nonconformists in Stuart England (London: Mercer University Press, 1985).

Grigg, John, Lloyd George: From Peace to War (Bungay, Suffolk: Methuen, 1985).

Guedalla, Philip, The Queen and Mr. Gladstone (London: Hodder & Stoughton, 1958).

Gurock, Jeffrey S., American Jewish History: The Colonial and Early National Periods 1654-1800 (New York: Routledge, 1998).

Hadari, Ze'ev Venia, Second Exodus, The Full Story of Jewish Illegal Immigration to Palestine, 1945-1948 (London: Vallentine Mitchell, 1991).

Hagy, James W., This Happy Land: The Jews of Colonial and Antebellum Charleston (Tuscaloosa: University of Alabama Press, 1993).

Halamish, Aviva, The Exodus Affair. Holocaust Survivors and the Struggle for Palestine (London: Valentine, 1998).

Hall, Walter Phelps, Empire to Commonwealth (New York: Henry Holt and Company, 1928).

Halliday, F.E., A Concise History of England (London: Thames and Hudson, 1974).

Halperin, Samuel, The Political World of American Zionism (Silver Springs: 1985).

Halperin, Vladimir, Lord Milner and the Empire (London: Odhams Press, 1952).

Hamilton, Jill, Gods, Guns and Israel, Britain, the First World War and the Jews in the Holy Land (Sparkford, England: Sutton Publishing, 2004).

Handy, Robert T., The Holy Land in American Protestant Life 1800-1948 (New York: Arno Press, 1981).

_____ Britain and Zionism, The Fateful Entanglement (Belfast: Blackstaff Press, 1980).

Hanna, P., British Policy in Palestine (Washington: 1942).

Harington, Charles, Plumer of Messines (London: John Murray, 1938).

Harris, Kenneth, Attlee (London: Weidenfeld and Nicolson, 1995).

Harris, R.W. A Short History of 18th Century England (New York: Mentor, 1963).

Hayward, Steven, Churchill on Leadership (New York: Gramercy Books, 2004).

_____ Greatness, Reagan, Churchill, and the making of Extraordinary Leaders (New York: Crown Forum, 2005).

Heller, Joseph, The Stern Gang, Ideology, Politics and Terror 1940-1949 (London: Frank Cass, 1995).

_____ Zionism and Arabism (London: Frank Cass, 1987).

Heyck, T.W., The Transformation of Intellectual Life in Victorian England, (London: Croom Helm, 1982).

Heyd, Michael and Katz, Shaul and Lavsky, Hagit, The History of the Hebrew University of Jerusalem: A Period of Consolidation and Growth (Jerusalem: The Hebrew University Magnes Press, 2005) (In Hebrew).

Higgons, Katharine, Persistence of Antiquity, A Biography of Martin Conway (Conway Library Project/Research Forum 2005).

Hiro, Dilip. Holy Wars-The Rise of Islamic Fundamentalism (New York: Routledge, 1989).

Hirst, Francis W. The Consequences of the War to Great Britain (London: Victor Gollancz Ltd., 1938).

Hodder, Edwin, The Life and Work of the Seventh Earl of Shaftesbury (London: Cassell, 1887).

Hooper, C.A., The Civil Law of Palestine and Trans-Jordan (London: Street & Maxwell Ltd., 1934).

Huneidi, Sahar, A Broken Trust-Herbert Samuel and the Palestinians (London: I.B. Tauris & Co. Ltd., 2001).

Hurewitz, J. C., Middle East Politics: The Military Dimension (New York: Praeger Publishers, 1970).

_____ The Struggle for Palestine (New York: 1950).

Hyamson, Albert M., Palestine Under the Mandate, 1920-1948 (Westport Conn: Greenwood Press, 1976).

Hyde, H. Montgomery, Baldwin, The Unexpected Prime Minister (London: Hart-Davis, MacGibbon, 1973).

Ingrams, Doreen, Palestine Papers 1917-1922 Seeds of Conflict (New York: George Braziller, 1973).

James, Robert Rhodes, Anthony Eden (London: Papermac, 1987).

Jones, Martin, Failure in Palestine-British and United States Policy after the Second World War (London: Mansell Publishing, 1986).

Jones, Philip, Britain and Palestine 1914-1948 (Oxford: Oxford University Press, 1979).

Kark, Ruth, American Consuls in the Holy Land 1832–1914 (Detroit: Wayne State University Press; Jerusalem: Magnes Press, 1994).

Katz, Samuel, Battleground-Fact and Fancy in Palestine (New York: Bantam Books, 1973).

_____ Lone Wolf, A Biography of Vladimir (Ze'ev) Jabotinsky (New York: Barricade Books, 1996).

Kay, Zachariah, Canada and Palestine (Jerusalem: Israel University Press, 1978).

Kayyali, A.W., Palestine: A Modern History (London: Croom Helm, 1978).

Kedourie, Elie, England and the Middle East (London: Mansell Publishing, 1987).

_____ et al, Palestine and Israel in the 19th and 20th Centuries (London: Frank Cass, 1982).

_____ Politics in the Middle East (Oxford: Oxford University Press, 1992).

_____ Zionism and Arabism in Palestine and Israel (London: Frank Cass, 1982).

Kent, John, William Temple: Church, State and Society in Britain 1880-1950 (Cambridge: Cambridge University Press, 1992).

Kershaw, Ian, Making Friends with Hitler, Lord Londonderry, the Nazis and the Road to War (New York: The Penguin Press, 2004).

Kimche, Jon, Seven Fallen Pillars-The Middle East, 1915-1950 (London: Secker and Warburg, 1950).

_____ The Unromantics (London: Weidenfeld and Nicolson, 1968).

Kobler, Franz, Napoleon and the Jews (New York: Schocken, 1976).

_____ The Vision Was There (London: Lincolns-Prager, 1956).

Koestler, Arthur, Promise and Fulfillment, Palestine 1917-1949 (London: Macmillian & Co. Ltd., 1949).

Kolinsky, Martin, Britain's War in the Middle East, Strategy and Diplomacy, 1936-42 (London: MacMillian, 1999).

_____ Law, Order and Riots in Mandatory Palestine, 1928-35 (London: St. Martin's Press, 1993).

Kolsky, Thomas, A., Jews Against Zionism (Philadelphia: 1990).

Koss, Stephen, Nonconformity in Modern British Politics (Hamden, Connecticut: Archon Books, 1975).

Kurzman, Dan, Ben Gurion: Prophet of Fire (New York: Simon and Shuster, 1983).

Kushner, Tony, The Jewish Heritage in British History (London: Frank Cass, 1992).

Laqueur, Walter, The History of Zionism (New York: Schocken Books, 1989).

Lasdun, Susan, Making Victorians (London: Victor Gollancz Ltd., 1983).

Lawrence, A.W., T.E. Lawrence (London: Jonathan Cape, 1937).

Lee, Christopher, This Sceptred Isle: Twentieth Century (London: BBC Worldwide Limited, 1999).

Lenczowski, George, The Middle East in World Affairs (London: Cornell University Press, 1980).

Leslie, Shane, Mark Sykes, His Life and Letters (London: Cassell and Co., 1923).

Levenberg, Haim, Military Preparations of the Arab Community in Palestine 1945-1948 (London: Frank Cass, 1993).

Levitt, Ruth, George Eliot: The Jewish Connection (Jerusalem: Masada Ltd., 1975).

Lipman, V.D., A History of the Jews in Britain Since 1858 (London: Leicester Press, 1990).

_____ Three Centuries of Anglo-Jewish History (Cambridge: The Jewish Historical Society of England, Heffer & Sons, 1961).

Litvinoff, Barnet, Weizmann, Last of the Patriarchs (New York: Putnam's, 1976).

Lloyd George, Robert, David & Winston, How a Friendship Changed History (London: John Murray, 2005).

Lloyd, T.O., Empire to Welfare State (Oxford: Oxford Press, 1986).

Lorch, Netanel, The Edge of the Sword. Israel's War of Independence 1947-49 (Jerusalem: Masada Press, 1961).

_____ One Long War-Arab Verses Jew Since 1920 (Jerusalem: Keter Publishing, 1976).

Lossin, Yigal, Pillar of Fire (Jerusalem: Shikmona Publishing Company, 1992).

Louis, William Roger, The British Empire in the Middle East 1945-1951 (Oxford: Clarendon Press, 1984).

_____ The End of the Palestine Mandate (London: I.B. Tauris & Co. Ltd., 1986).

Lustick, Ian, Arabs in the Jewish State (Austin: University of Texas Press 1980).

Lutz, Charles and Smith, Robert O., Christians and a Land Called Holy: How We Can Foster Justice, Peace, and Hope (Minneapolis: Fortress, 2005).

MacMillan, Margaret, Peacemakers, The Paris Conference of 1919 and Its Attempt to End War (London: John Murray, 2001).

MacMillan, Margaret, Paris 1919 (New York: Random House, 2001).

Makovsky. Michael, Churchill's Promised Land, Zionism and Statecraft (New Haven: Yale University Press, 2007).

Malcolm, Ian, Lord Balfour: A Memory (London: Macmillan, 1930).

Manchester, William, The Last Lion, Winston Spencer Churchill, Visions of Glory 1874-1932 (London: Abacus, 1993).

Mangan, J.A., The Games Ethic and Imperialism (Middlesex: Viking, 1986).

Manuel, Frank E. The Realities of American-Palestine Relations (Westport, Connecticut: Greenwood Press, 1949).

Marjoribanks, Edward, The Life of Lord Carson, Vol. 1 (London: Victor Gollancz Ltd., 1932).

Marlowe, John, Arab Nationalism and British Imperialism, A Study in Power Politics (London: The Cresset Press, 1961).

_____, Rebellion in Palestine (London: The Cressent Press, 1946).

_____, The Seat of Pilate: An Account of the Palestine Mandate (London: The Cresset Press, 1959).

Maugham, Robin, Approach to Palestine (London: Falcon Press, 1947).

Mendes-Flohr, Paul and Reinharz, Jehuda, The Jew in the Modern World (New York: Oxford University Press, 1995).

Merkley, Paul Charles, Christian Attitudes toward the State of Israel (Montreal: McGill-Queens University Press, 2001).

_____, The Politics of Christian Zionism 1891-1948 (London: Frank Cass, 1998).

Meyer, Carl S., Moving Frontiers: Readings in the History of the Lutheran Church, Missouri Synod (St. Louis: Concordia Publishing House, 1964).

McConkie, Bruce R., Mormon Doctrine (Salt Lake City, Utah: Bookcraft Publications, 1958).

McCullough, David, Truman (New York: Simon & Schuster, 1992).

Middlemas, Keith and Barnes, John, Baldwin, A Biography (London: Weidenfeld and Nicholson, 1969).

Migdal, Joel S., Palestinian Society and Politics (Princeton, New Jersey: Princeton University Press, 1980).

Miller, Rory, Divided Against Zionism 1945-1948 (London: Frank Cass, 2000).

Millin, Sarah Gertrude, General Smuts (London: Faber and Faber, 1936).

Mitchell, Sally, Victorian Britain (New York: Garland Publishing, 1988).

Moody, Dwight L., To All People (New York: E. B. Treat, 1877).

Monroe, Elizabeth, Britain's Moment in the Middle East 1914-1971 (London: Chatto & Windus, 1981).

_____ Philby of Arabia (Reading, UK: Ithaca Press, Garnet Publishing, 1973).

Morris, Benny, Righteous Victims, A History of the Zionist-Arab Conflict 1881-1999 (London: John Murray, 1999).

Mosley, Leonard, Curzon (London: Longmans, Green, & Co., 1961).

_____ Gideon Goes to War, (New York: Charles Scribner's Sons, 1955).

Mulhall, John W., America and the founding of Israel (Los Angeles: Deshon Press, 1995).

Naor, Mordecai, The Twentieth Century in Eretz Israel (Tel Avi: Am Oved Publishers, 1996).

Nachmani, Amikam, Great Power Discord in Palestine. The Anglo-American Committee of Inquiry into the Problems of Jewry and Palestine, 1945-1946 (London: Frank Cass, 1987).

Netanyahu, Benjamin, A Durable Peace, (New York: Warner Books, 2000).

Nevakivi, Jukka, Britain, France and the Arab Middle East: 1914-1920 (London: University of London, 1969).

Newton, Frances E., Fifty Years in Palestine (London, Coldharbour Press 1948).

Nicolson, Harold, Curzon: The Last Phase (London: Constable & Co., 1934).

Nutting, Anthony, Lawrence of Arabia (London: Louvain Landsborough Ltd., 1961).

Ofer, Dalia, Escaping the Holocaust, Illegal Immigration to the Land of Israel, 1939-1944 (Oxford: Oxford University Press, 1990).

Okkenhaug, Inger Marie, The Qualities of Heroic Living, of High Adventure and Endeavour, Anglican Missionaries and Education in Palestine 1888-1948 (Leiden: Brill, 2002).

Pappé, Ilan, Britain and the Arab-Israeli Conflict 1948-51 (Basingstoke, Hampshire: Macmillian Press in association with St. Anthony's College, Oxford, 1988).

Parsons, David, Swords into Ploughshares, Christian Zionism and the Battle of Armageddon (Jerusalem: International Christian Embassy, 2005).

Pelling, Henry, A Short History of the Labour Party (London: MacMillan Press, 1985).

Perkin, Harold, The Origins of Modern English Society 1780-1880 (London: Routledge & Kegan Paul, 1969).

Perry, Silas S., Britain Opens a Gateway (London: Museum Press, 1944).

Peters, Joan, From Time Immemorial-The Origins of the Arab-Jewish Conflict over Palestine (New York: Harper & Row, 1984).

Peters, Rudolph, Islam and Colonialism-The Doctrine of Jihad in Modern History (The Netherlands: Moulton Publishers, 1979).

Pew Research Center's Forum on Religion and Public Life, January 5, 2011.

Phillips, Kevin, American Theocracy (New York: Viking, 2006).

Pogue, Forrest C., George C. Marshall: Statesman 1945-1959 (New York: Penguin, 1989).

Polk, William R., The United States and the Arab World (Cambridge, Massachusetts: Harvard University Press, 1969).

Pollock, John, Shaftesbury: The Poor Man's Earl (London: Hodder and Stoughton, 1985).

Pragai, Michael J., Faith and Fulfillment-Christians and the Return to the Promised Land (London: Vallentine, Mitchell & Co., 1985).

Pugh, Martin, Lloyd George (New York: Longman Inc., 1988).

Raymond, E.T., Mr. Balfour, A Biography (London: Collins, 1920).

Reader, W.J., Victorian England (London: B.T. Batsford Ltd., 1974).

Reich, Bernard Reich, Quest For Peace (New Jersey: Transaction Books, Inc., 1977)

Reid Banks, Lynne, Torn Country, An Oral History of the Israeli War of Independence (New York: Franklin Watts, 1982).

Reinharz, Jehuda and Anita Shapira (editors), Essential Papers on Zionism (New York: New York University Press, 1976).

_____ The Making of a Statesman (Oxford: Oxford Press, 1993).

Robert, Rhodes James, Anthony Eden (London: MacMillian, 1986).

Robbins, Keith, The Blackwell Biographical Dictionary of British Political Life (London: Basil Blackwell Ltd., 1990).

Rodinson, Maxime, Israel and the Arabs (Second Edition, New York: Penguin Books, 1982).

Rogan, Eugene L. and Shlaim E., (eds.) The War for Palestine. Rewriting the History of 1948 (Cambridge: Cambridge University Press, 2001).

Rose, Norman, The Gentile Zionists (London: Frank Cass, 1973).

_____ Chaim Weizmann (New York: Viking, 1986).

Roth, Cecil, Anglo-Jewish Letters 1158-1917 (London: Soncino Press, 1938).

_____ Essays and Portraits in Anglo-Jewish History (Philadelphia: The Jewish Society of America, 1962).

_____ A History of the Jews in England (Oxford: Clarendon Press, 1941).

_____ Remember the Days (London: The Jewish Historical Society of England, 1966).

Royle, Trevor, Orde Wingate, Irregular Soldier, (London: Weidenfeld & Nicolson, 1995).

Rubinstein, William D., The History of the Jews in the English Speaking World: Great Britain (New York: St. Martins Press, 1996).

_____ and Rubinstein, Hilary L., Philosemitism, Admiration and Support in the English-Speaking World for Jews, 1840-1939 (London: MacMillan Press, 1999).

Runciman, Steven, A History of the Crusades, Three Volumes (Cambridge: University Press, 1957).

Sachar, Howard M., The Emergence of the Middle East: 1914-1924 (New York: Garland Publishing, 1987).

_____ Israel, The Establishment of a State (London: 1959).

_____ A History of Jews in America (New York: 1992).

_____ The Rise of Israel, Section III: 1940-1948 (New York: Garland Publishing, 1987).

_____ The Rise of Israel, Section III: Jewish Resistance to British Rule in Palestine, 1944-1947 (New York: Garland Publishing, 1987).

Samuel, Rinna, A History of Israel (London: Butler and Tanner, 1989).

Sandeen, Ernest R., The Roots of Fundamentalism (Grand Rapids: Baker Book House, 1978).

Sanders, Ronald, The High Walls of Jerusalem (New York: Holt, Rinehart and Winston, 1983).

Savage, Raymond, Allenby of Armageddon (London: Hodder and Stoughton, 1925).

Sayigh, Rosemary, Palestinians: From Peasants to Revolutionaries, (London: Zed Press, 1979).

Sela, Avraham, Political Encyclopedia of the Middle East (Jerusalem: The Jerusalem Publishing House Limited, 1999).

Schmidt, David W., The Contribution of British Evangelical Thought to the Making of the Balfour Declaration, unpublished thesis for M.A. in Middle Eastern History (Jerusalem: Jerusalem University College, 1995).

Schulze, Kirsten E., The Arab-Israeli Conflict (New York: Longman, 1999).

Scofield, C. I., The New Scofield Reference Bible (useful for dispensational reference notes) (New York: Oxford University Press, 1976).

Scult, Mel, Millennial Expectations and Jewish Liberties (Leiden: E. J. Brill, 1978).

Segev, Tom, One Palestine, Complete (New York: Metropolitan Books, 2000).

Shaftesly, John M., Remember the Days (London: The Jewish Historical Society of England, 1966).

Shamir, Ronen, The Colonies of Law, Colonialism, Zionism and Law in Early Mandate Palestine (Cambridge: Cambridge Press, 2000).

Shepherd, Naomi, Alarms and Excursions (London: Collins, 1990).

_____ Plowing Sand-British Rule in Palestine 1917-1948 (London: Collins, 1999).

_____The Zealous Intruders-The Western Rediscovery of Palestine, (London: Collins, 1987).

Sherman, A.J., Mandate Days. British Lives in Palestine 1918-1948 (Slovenia: Thames & Hudson, 1997).

Shimoni, Gideon, Jews and Zionism: The South African Experience (Oxford: Oxford University Press, 1980).

Sidebotham, Herbert, Great Britain and Palestine (London: 1937).

_____ England and Palestine-Essays Toward the Restoration of the Jewish State (London: Constable and Company Ltd., 1918).

Silverfarb, Daniel, The Twilight of British Ascendancy in the Middle East-A Case Study of Iraq, 1941-1950 (New York: St. Martin's Press, 1994).

Simon, Leon and Leonard Stein, Awakening Palestine (London: John Murray, 1923).

Slater, Robert, Warrior Statesman-The Life of Moshe Dayan (New York: St. Martin's Press. 1991).

Smith, Charles D., Palestine and the Arab-Israeli Conflict (New York: St. Martin's Press, 1996).

Sokolow, Nahum, History of Zionism 1600-1918 (London: Longman's, Green & Co., 1919).

Standard Jewish Encyclopedia (Jerusalem: Massadah Publishing, 1966).

Stein, Joshua B., Our Great Solicitor, Josiah C. Wedgwood and the Jews (Selinsgrove: Susquehanna University Press, 1992).

Stein, Leonard, The Balfour Declaration (Jerusalem: The Magnes Press, Hebrew University, 1983).

_____ Weizmann and England (London: W. H. Allen, 1964).

_____ Zionism (London: Ernest Benn Ltd., 1925).

Stevenson, John, British Society 1914-45 (London: Penguin Books, 1984).

Sykes, Christopher, Cross Roads to Israel, (London: Collins, 1965).

_____ Orde Wingate (New York: Word Publishing, 1959).

_____ Two Studies in Virtue (London: 1953).

Taylor, A.J.P., English History 1914-1945 (Oxford: Clarendon Press, 1965).

Taylor, Alan R., Prelude to Israel (New York: Philosophical Library, 1959).

Tees, Harry, United Christian Council in Israel Year Book 2006 (Jerusalem: UCCI, 2006).

Thomas, Gordon & Witts, Max Morgan, Voyage of the Damned (New York: Stein and Day, 1974).

Thurston, Clarke, By Blood and Fire-July 22, 1946-The Attack on the King David Hotel (New York: G.P. Putnam's Sons, 1981).

Torossian, Sarkis, From Dardanelles to Palestine (Boston: The Meader Press, 1947).

Tsimhoni, Daphne, The Christian Communities in Jerusalem and the West Bank Since 1948, An Historical, Social and Political Study (New York: Praeger, 1993).

Tuchman, Barbara, Bible and Sword: How the British Came to Palestine (New York: New York University, 1956).

_____ The Proud Tower (New York: Ballantine Books, 1994).

Twain, Mark, The Innocents Abroad (New York: Harper & Brothers, 1911).

Tyerman, Christopher, England and the Crusaders (Chicago: University of Chicago Press, 1988).

Udin, Sophie A., Palestine and Zionism, January 1946-December 1948 (New York: Zionist Archives and Library, 1949).

Urofsky, Melvin I., American Zionism from Herzl to the Holocaust (New York: Anchor Books, 1976).

Van Gorden, Kurt, Mormonism (Grand Rapids: Zondervan, 1995).

Verete, Mayir, From Palmerston to Balfour: Selected Essays of Mayir Verete (London: Frank Cass, 1992).

Vital, David, Zionism, the Crucial Phase (Oxford: Clarendon Press, 1987).

Ward, A.W., et al, The Cambridge History of English Literature, 15 Vols. (Cambridge: Cambridge University Press, 1907-1927).

Wasserstein, Bernard, Britain and the Jews of Europe 1939-1945 (Oxford: Clarendon Press, 1979).

_____The British in Palestine: The Mandatory Government and the Arab-Jewish Conflict 1917-1929 (London: Royal Historical Society, 1978).

_____Herbert Samuel, A Political Life (Oxford: Clarendon Press, 1992).

Watson, David R., Georges Clemenceau: A Political Biography (London, 1974).

Wavell, Archibald, Allenby: A Study in Greatness (London: George Harrap, 1941).

Weiler, Peter, Ernest Bevin (Manchester: Manchester University Press, 1993).

Wells, H.G., A Short History of the World (London: Labour Publishing, 1926).

Weinstein, Allen and Ma'oz, Moshe, Truman and the American Commitment to Israel (Jerusalem: The Magnes Press, 1981).

Wilson, Evan M., Jerusalem, Key to Peace, (Washington D.C: The Middle East Institute, 1970).

Winter, J.M., The Great War and the British People, (London: Macmillan, 1985).

Wolff, Richard, Israel Act 3 (Wheaton: Tyndale, 1967).

Wrench, John Evelyn, Alfred Lord Milner, The Man of No Illusions 1854-1925 (London: Eyre & Spottiswoode Ltd., 1958).

Young, Kenneth, Arthur James Balfour, (London: G. Bell and sons Ltd., 1963).

Zadka, Saul, Blood in Zion, How the Jewish Guerrillas drove the British out of Palestine (London: Brassey's, 1995).

Zweig, Ronald W., Britain and Palestine during the Second World War (London: The Boydell Press, 1986).

LECTURES

Cohen, Michael J., Bar Ilan University, Lecture: "The Domestic Factor," Hebrew University, Jerusalem, The Harry S. Truman Research Institute, May 29 2008.

Gilbert, Martin, Lecture: "Churchill and the Jews: A Lifelong Friendship," Kehilat Moreshet Avraham, East Talpiot, Jerusalem, February 24 2008.

Kirkendall, Richard, University of Washington, Lecture: "The Truman Period as a Research Field," Hebrew University, Jerusalem, The Harry S. Truman Research Institute, May 29 2008.

Leffler, Melvin, University of Virginia, Lecture: "Summary: Why did President Truman Support the Establishment of the State of Israel?" Hebrew University, Jerusalem, The Harry S. Truman Research Institute, May 29 2008.

Radosh, Ronald, City University of New York, Lecture: "Truman, Jews and Zionism," Hebrew University, Jerusalem, The Harry S. Truman Research Institute, May 29 2008.

Radosh, Allis, City University of New York, Lecture: "Truman, Jews and Zionism," Hebrew University, Jerusalem, The Harry S. Truman Research Institute, May 29 2008.

Zweig, Ronald, New York University, Lecture: "The U.S. Army, the Displaced Persons and American Palestine Policy," Hebrew University, Jerusalem, The Harry S. Truman Research Institute, May 29 2008.

INTERNET PUBLICATIONS

Ami Isseroff, MidEast Web

Common Ground News Service, 18 December 2008, www.commongroundnews.org.

Jerusalem Newswire, www.jnewswire.com, Bridges for Peace.

Nerel, Gershon. "Anti-Zionism in the 'Electronic Church' of Palestinian Christianity,"

http://pewforum.org/government/faith-on-the-hill-the-religious-composition-of-the-112th-congress.aspx

http://sicsa.huji.ac.il/nerelprinter.pdf.

INDEX

❖ ❖ ❖

Abdullah I, King, Transjordan, 91, 104, 110, 125, 188, 242, 301

Allenby, Edmund, 77, 85, 91, 98, 99, 119, 126, 161, 270, 360

Amery, Leo, 61, 82, 118, 125, 132, 135, 138, 143, 144, 146, 149. 151, 164, 168, 169, 174, 186, 191, 360, 363

Asquith, H. H., 37, 38, 39, 70, 126

Attlee, Clement, 152, 153, 168, 218, 219, 222, 224, 225, 229, 237, 238, 239, 240, 243, 244, 247, 249, 253, 263, 267, 286, 306, 309, 358, 363, 365, 369

Baldwin, Stanley, 118, 151, 163, 164, 191, 363

Balfour, Arthur, Balfour Declaration, 35, 36, 37, 39, 40, 41, 42, 43, 44, 45, 46, 47, 48, 50, 51, 52, 53, 54, 55, 56, 57, 58, 59, 60, 61, 62, 63, 64, 65, 66, 67, 68, 69, 70, 71, 72, 73, 74, 75, 76, 77, 78, 79, 80, 81, 83, 84, 85, 86,87, 89, 90, 91, 94, 96, 98, 99, 100, 102, 103, 104, 106, 107, 108, 109, 110, 113, 114, 115, 116, 119, 120, 121, 122, 125, 126, 127, 129, 131, 133, 133, 135, 136, 138, 142, 143, 145, 146, 147, 148, 149, 150, 151, 152, 153, 158, 160, 163, 164, 165, 166, 167, 168, 174, 178, 182, 183, 184, 186, 187, 188, 190, 191, 192, 193, 194, 204, 206, 219, 224, 226, 233, 236, 243, 251, 254, 255, 268, 269, 270, 273, 274, 289, 299, 301, 302, 303, 304, 305, 306, 309, 311, 314, 315, 316, 323, 329, 339, 340, 340, 345, 354,

356, 357, 358, 359, 360, 362, 363, 364, 366, 367, 369, 370

Barnes, George, 39, 53, 65, 66, 67, 74, 76, 151, 163, 345

Bentwich, Norman, 95, 105, 119, 120, 123, 131, 137, 140, 141, 162, 208, 209, 210, 222, 231, 232, 248, 252, 254

Bevin, Ernest, 82, 151, 152, 153, 154, 197, 198, 219, 220, 221, 222, 223, 224, 225, 226, 228, 229, 230, 232, 233, 234, 236, 237, 238, 239, 243, 244, 247, 248, 249, 250, 251, 252, 253, 254, 255, 257, 263, 267, 268, 301, 302, 307, 308, 309, 310, 314, 315, 316, 340, 358, 365, 366, 369

Bols, Jan, 86

Bonar Law, Andrew, 39, 53, 68, 69, 74, 76, 115, 118, 270

Bush, George, 343, 350, 351

Bush, George W., 332, 351, 352, 353

Canada, 68, 74, 115, 128, 200, 312, 313

Carson, Edward, 53, 61, 67, 68, 74, 76

Carter, Jimmy, 348, 349, 353

Chamberlain, Austin, 151

Chamberlain, Neville, 135, 151, 164, 183, 186, 188, 191, 196, 363

Chancellor, John, 39, 108, 131, 132, 137, 138, 140, 141, 142, 143, 144, 145, 146, 148. 153, 156, 160, 190, 195, 218, 362

Churchill, Winston, 44, 69, 73, 82, 83, 103, 104, 106, 107, 108, 109, 110, 112, 115, 116, 132, 135, 151, 154, 155, 164, 166, 168, 169, 180, 182, 183, 186, 187, 188, 189, 191, 194, 196, 197, 201, 202, 213, 206, 207, 210, 211, 212, 215, 216, 217, 228, 230, 237,

242, 252, 253, 255, 256, 268, 271, 301, 302, 311, 312, 315, 316, 339, 360, 361, 363, 364, 365, 366, 370

Churchill White Paper, 1922, 107, 108, 109, 110, 112

Clinton, William, 351, 353

Coolidge, Calvin, 114, 215

Creech-Jones, Arthur, 197, 199, 224, 250, 252, 253, 255, 258, 268

Crossman, Richard, 139, 151, 153, 210, 217, 239, 250, 251, 255, 263, 268, 309

Curzon, George Nathanael, 39, 46, 52, 53, 54, 55, 56, 57, 74, 76, 89, 94, 96, 98, 100, 114

Cunningham, Alan, 211, 231, 232, 233, 234, 242, 245, 254, 256, 257, 258, 262, 266, 301, 302, 303, 305, 306, 308, 316, 366

D'Arcy, John, 231

Deedes, Wyndham, 81, 117, 118, 120, 127, 128

Dugdale, Blanche, 42, 50, 62, 63, 64, 65, 75, 78, 136, 169, 184, 226, 358, 363

Eban, Abba, 171, 226, 234, 246, 255, 261, 340

Eden, Anthony, 163, 164, 286, 364

Eisenhower, Dwight, 341, 342, 346, 352

Emery, Susanna, 81, 121, 131, 307

Feisal, Emir, 90, 91, 104, 125, 256, 256

Ford, Gerald, 348, 353

Gort, Lord, 194, 208, 209, 210, 212, 217, 228, 231, 232, 232, 364, 366

Graham, Billy, 155, 181, 289, 290, 341, 342, 343, 347

Harding, Warren, 113, 114, 215

Harrison, Earl, 227, 327, 328

Henderson, Arthur, 39, 52, 65, 66, 67, 74, 132, 146, 150, 151, 153, 361

Henderson, Loy, 227, 260, 327

Hoare, Samuel, 164, 196

Hoover, Herbert, 158, 159, 191, 215, 363

Hope-Simpson Commission, 147, 148, 190

Hussein, Sherif of Mecca, 90, 242

Hussein family, 104, 125, 242, 387

Johnson, Lynden, 346, 347

Kennedy, John F., 332, 352, 353

Kisch, Frederick, 119, 138, 160

Lawrence, T. E., 104, 110, 114, 156, 157, 179, 296

Lloyd George, David, 37, 38, 39, 40, 41, 42, 43, 45, 46, 47, 48, 49, 50, 52, 53, 55, 60, 63, 64, 65, 68, 69, 70, 71, 72, 73, 74, 76, 78, 85, 86, 87, 92, 96, 97, 98, 99, 101, 103, 110, 115, 131, 133, 136, 147, 151, 152, 153, 165, 166, 168, 183, 221, 226, 269, 273, 304, 311, 312, 314, 358, 360, 362

Luke, Harry, 138, 139, 141

MacDonald, Malcolm, 185, 186

MacDonald, Ramsey, 82, 118, 132, 147, 149, 150, 151, 152, 156, 160, 163, 164, 182, 183, 184, 185, 185, 218, 361

MacGillivary, 256

MacMichael, Harold, 177, 190, 195, 206, 207, 208, 209, 210, 211, 212, 228, 238, 362, 364

Mair, Golda, 225, 244, 244, 245, 246, 294, 300, 387

McDonald, James, 179, 191, 194, 237, 238, 239, 243, 244, 302, 310, 311, 314, 317, 363, 368

McMahon, Henry, Letters, 91, 104

Meinertzhagen, Richard, 45, 46, 85, 88, 91, 92, 96, 98, 110, 127, 161, 161, 189, 191, 313, 339, 363, 370, 370

Milner, Alfred, 39, 50, 52, 53, 74, 75, 76, 102, 103

Moncton, Reginald, 106

Montagu, Edwin, 39, 52, 59, 60, 61, 62, 74, 75, 101

Mufti, Grand of Jerusalem, 104, 105, 123, 124, 137, 138, 139, 162, 163, 166, 175, 183, 186, 198, 199, 284

Nixon, Richard, 347

Obama, Barak, xiii

Olmert, Ehud, 332

Ormsby-Gore, William, 82, 164, 168, 176, 177, 178, 182, 191, 363

Passfield, Lord, White Paper, 118, 143, 146, 147, 148, 149, 150, 151, 152, 153, 154, 156, 160, 190, 191, 362

Plumer, Herbert, 122, 123, 124, 125, 126, 131, 135, 137, 146, 190, 209, 360, 362

Rabin, Yitzhak, 348

Reagan, Ronald, 349, 350, 353

Roosevelt, Franklin, 178, 180, 187, 191, 201, 202, 204, 205, 212, 213, 215, 216, 230, 259, 267, 326, 327, 330, 331, 337, 364

Samuel, Herbert, 37, 52, 59, 78, 82, 90, 93, 94, 96, 97, 98, 99, 101, 102, 103, 104, 105, 106, 111, 112, 115, 120, 121, 122, 129, 131, 132, 135, 146, 151, 164, 166, 169, 182, 196, 109, 245, 271, 306, 348, 360, 361

Sharett, Moshe, 171

Smuts, Jan Christian, 39, 42, 43, 50, 52, 55, 56, 57, 58, 58, 59, 74, 76, 131, 133, 146, 147, 148, 165, 165, 242, 274, 301, 316, 339, 360, 362

Spafford, family, 119, 277

Storrs, Ronald, 86, 95, 96, 99, 103, 105, 130, 136

Truman, Harry, 194, 203, 204, 205, 212, 213, 216, 226, 227, 229, 230, 234, 235, 236, 237, 238, 239, 240, 241, 247, 249, 250, 258, 260, 261, 263, 264, 265, 266, 268, 272, 285, 286, 289, 290, 291, 292, 293, 294, 295, 296, 297, 298, 299, 300, 302, 310, 311, 316, 317, 327, 328, 331, 337, 340, 343, 345, 352, 364, 365, 366, 367, 368, 369

Vester, Valentine, 161

Wauchope, Arthur, 160, 161, 162, 175, 176, 190, 209, 362

Weizmann, Chaim, 37, 40, 41, 43, 44, 45, 48, 49, 50, 52, 58, 60, 61, 63, 66, 69, 70, 71, 72, 78, 88, 89, 90, 91, 93, 95, 97, 101, 102, 107, 109, 110, 111, 115, 119, 120, 120, 121, 142, 143, 146, 147, 149, 150, 151, 152, 153, 164, 166, 168, 169, 171, 172, 175, 176, 180, 183, 186, 189, 195, 197, 198, 199, 200, 206, 208, 209, 210, 211, 215, 216, 217, 225, 226, 228, 234, 242, 243, 244, 245, 247, 248, 250, 251, 255, 256, 261, 262, 281, 290, 291, 293, 294, 295, 297, 300, 301, 305, 306, 309, 310, 311, 315, 316, 339, 340, 363, 367

White Paper, 1939, 72, 82, 132, 134, 148, 149, 150, 151, 152, 154, 160, 173, 183, 184, 185, 186, 187, 188, 189, 190, 191, 192, 193, 195, 196, 199, 201, 205, 206, 212, 219, 223, 224, 227, 233, 237, 239, 361, 364, 365

Wilson, Woodrow, 75, 86, 87, 88

Wingate, Orde, 95, 136, 170, 171, 172, 173, 174, 191, 200, 212, 275, 312, 363, 364